# Strategic Management and Innovative Applications of E-Government

Andreea Molnar
*Lancaster University, UK*

A volume in the Advances in
Electronic Government, Digital
Divide, and Regional Development
(AEGDDRD) Book Series

Published in the United States of America by
   IGI Global
   Information Science Reference (an imprint of IGI Global)
   701 E. Chocolate Avenue
   Hershey PA, USA 17033
   Tel: 717-533-8845
   Fax: 717-533-8661
   E-mail: cust@igi-global.com
   Web site: http://www.igi-global.com

Library of Congress Cataloging-in-Publication Data

Names: Molnar, Andreea, 1984- editor.
Title: Strategic management and innovative applications of e-government /
  Andreea Molnar, editor.
Description: Hershey, PA : Information Science Reference, 2019. | Includes
  bibliographical references.
Identifiers: LCCN 2018003922| ISBN 9781522562047 (hardcover) | ISBN
  9781522562054 (ebook)
Subjects: LCSH: Internet in public administration. | Strategic planning.
Classification: LCC JF1525.A8 S886 2019 | DDC 352.3/802854678--dc23 LC record available at
https://lccn.loc.gov/2018003922

This book is published in the IGI Global book series Advances in Electronic Government, Digital Divide, and Regional Development (AEGDDRD) (ISSN: 2326-9103; eISSN: 2326-9111)

British Cataloguing in Publication Data
A Cataloguing in Publication record for this book is available from the British Library.

All work contributed to this book is new, previously-unpublished material.
The views expressed in this book are those of the authors, but not necessarily of the publisher.

For electronic access to this publication, please contact: eresources@igi-global.com.

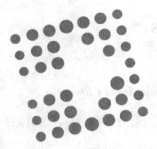

# Advances in Electronic Government, Digital Divide, and Regional Development (AEGDDRD) Book Series

ISSN:2326-9103
EISSN:2326-9111

Editor-in-Chief: Zaigham Mahmood, University of Derby, UK & North West University, South Africa

## MISSION

The successful use of digital technologies (including social media and mobile technologies) to provide public services and foster economic development has become an objective for governments around the world. The development towards electronic government (or e-government) not only affects the efficiency and effectiveness of public services, but also has the potential to transform the nature of government interactions with its citizens. Current research and practice on the adoption of electronic/digital government and the implementation in organizations around the world aims to emphasize the extensiveness of this growing field.

**The Advances in Electronic Government, Digital Divide & Regional Development (AEGDDRD)** book series aims to publish authored, edited and case books encompassing the current and innovative research and practice discussing all aspects of electronic government development, implementation and adoption as well the effective use of the emerging technologies (including social media and mobile technologies) for a more effective electronic governance (or e-governance).

## COVERAGE

- Online Government, E-Government, M-Government
- Frameworks and Methodologies for E-Government Development
- Social Media, Web 2.0, and Mobile Technologies in E-Government
- Urban Development, Urban Economy
- ICT Infrastructure and Adoption for E-Government Provision
- Public Information Management, Regional Planning, Rural Development
- Case Studies and Practical Approaches to E-Government and E-Governance
- Current Research and Emerging Trends in E-Government Development
- Issues and Challenges in E-Government Adoption
- Knowledge Divide, Digital Divide

IGI Global is currently accepting manuscripts for publication within this series. To submit a proposal for a volume in this series, please contact our Acquisition Editors at Acquisitions@igi-global.com or visit: http://www.igi-global.com/publish/.

# Titles in this Series

*For a list of additional titles in this series, please visit:*
*https://www.igi-global.com/book-series/advances-electronic-government-digital-divide/37153*

***Media Diplomacy and Its Evolving Role in the Current Geopolitical Climate***
Swati Jaywant Rao Bute (Jagran Lakecity University, India)
Information Science Reference • ©2018 • 211pp • H/C (ISBN: 9781522538592) • US $195.00

***Global Leadership Initiatives for Conflict Resolution and Peacebuilding***
Andrew H. Campbell (International Peace and Leadership Institute, USA)
Information Science Reference • ©2018 • 331pp • H/C (ISBN: 9781522549932) • US $225.00

***Financial Sustainability and Intergenerational Equity in Local Governments***
Manuel Pedro Rodríguez Bolívar (University of Granada, Spain) and María Deseada López
Subires (University of Granada, Spain)
Information Science Reference • ©2018 • 343pp • H/C (ISBN: 9781522537137) • US $205.00

***Handbook of Research on Modernization and Accountability in Public Sector Management***
Graça Maria do Carmo Azevedo (University of Aveiro, Portugal) Jonas da Silva Oliveira
(ISCTE – Instituto Universitário de Lisboa, Portugal) Rui Pedro Figueiredo Marques
(University of Aveiro, Portugal) and Augusta da Conceição Santos Ferreira (University of
Aveiro, Portugal)
Information Science Reference • ©2018 • 539pp • H/C (ISBN: 9781522537311) • US $285.00

***Knowledge-Based Urban Development in the Middle East***
Ali A. Alraouf (Qatar Urban Planning, Qatar)
Information Science Reference • ©2018 • 310pp • H/C (ISBN: 9781522537342) • US $185.00

***Nationalism, Social Movements, and Activism in Contemporary Society Emerging Research...***
Emily Stacey (Swansea University, UK)
Information Science Reference • ©2018 • 135pp • H/C (ISBN: 9781522554332) • US $155.00

*For an entire list of titles in this series, please visit:*
*https://www.igi-global.com/book-series/advances-electronic-government-digital-divide/37153*

701 East Chocolate Avenue, Hershey, PA 17033, USA
Tel: 717-533-8845 x100 • Fax: 717-533-8661
E-Mail: cust@igi-global.com • www.igi-global.com

# Table of Contents

# Detailed Table of Contents

**Chapter 1**

Toward the Improvement of Emergency Response Utilizing a Multi-Tiered
Systems Integration Approach: A Research Framework ......................................1

*Michael A. Erskine, Middle Tennessee State University, USA*
*Will Pepper, Better Than Free LLC, USA*

This chapter presents an extension of the Emergency Description Information
Technology (EDIT) project to facilitate the effective collection and communication of
information during an emergency. New academic findings and industry technologies
inform a modified research framework. The research framework contains four primary
research areas that are described in detail. Extending the design-science approach
used for the EDIT project could improve emergency communications during large-
scale international gatherings, as well as for community emergency response.

**Chapter 2**

Live Video Communication in Prehospital Emergency Medicine ......................26

*Camilla Metelmann, Greifswald University, Germany*
*Bibiana Metelmann, Greifswald University, Germany*

Prehospital emergency medicine treats time-critical diseases and conditions and
aims to reduce morbidity and mortality. The progression of emergency medicine is
an important topic for governments worldwide. A problem occurs when paramedics
need assistance at the emergency site by emergency doctors, who cannot be present.
Video-communication in real-time from the emergency site to an emergency doctor
offers an opportunity to enhance the quality of emergency medicine. The core piece
of this study is a video camera system called "LiveCity camera," enabling real-time
high quality video connection of paramedics and emergency doctors. The impact
of video communication on emergency medicine is clearly appreciated among
providers, based upon the extent of agreement that has been stated in this study's
questionnaire by doctors and paramedics. This study was part of the FP7-European
Union funded research project "LiveCity" (Grant Agreement No. 297291).

The purpose of this chapter is to explore the emerging social media practices of governments and citizens. The study takes on the status of an exploratory case study and draws on a grounded research approach. The case study shows an emerging social media practice that is embedded in and driven by a diversity of contradictions. The study identifies the following three contradictions as the most significant: communicative contradictions between service administration and community feeling, organizational contradictions between central control and local engagement, digital platform contradictions between municipal website and social media. The chapter presents a single-case study, which is a small contribution to the initial understanding of the social media practices of governments and citizens. The analysis indicates how a local municipality in its social media practices on Facebook is embedded in and driven by contradictions, and hence offers insights into a new way of understanding the challenges and opportunities of government social media.

# Chapter 4

Field operations in municipal governments have undergone fundamental adjustments. This empirical study investigated the ramifications of the strategic shift in government field operations when mobile information and communication technologies (ICTs) were introduced for field crews in a multiyear process. The implementation had to overcome several serious socio-technical challenges. The data were collected using cognitive work analysis (CWA) and interpreted from a structurationist perspective. The study filled an important methodological gap: While structuration theory (ST) has been criticized for its paucity of guidance for empirical research, CWA has been denounced for its deterministic engineering approach to social systems. However, the subordination of the micro-meso-level CWA framework into the grand theory of ST resulted in an approach referred to as situated action analysis, which was found particularly useful for elucidating the observed feedbacks between human agency, the shaping of the information (technology) artifact, and the organizational structure.

The continuing erosion of citizen trust and confidence in government has been attributed to a number of factors. This chapter examines the potential role of digital transformation of government in reversing this decline. Based on a systematic literature review, key factors that influence citizen trust and confidence in government as an institution are identified, including citizen satisfaction and expectations, government transparency and accountability, transformation of government, and government performance. The review of the literature also reveals a lack of knowledge and understanding of how transformation of government can influence the growing decline in citizen engagement with government. To address this gap, a conceptual model capturing the key constructs is proposed to support a better understanding of strategies for rebuilding trust and confidence in government administrations through transformation of government.

**Chapter 6**

  *Amizan Omar, Brunel University London, UK*
  *Craig Johnson, University of Bradford, UK*
  *Vishanth Weerakkody, University of Bradford, UK*

Digitally-enabled service transformation (DEST) in the public sector (PS) offers a unique opportunity for public administration (PA) and information systems (IS) disciplines to interlace. Such uniqueness has enabled a deviance in the theoretical selection from the adoption of native PA/IS theories to imported social sciences theories including institutional and structuration. Institutional theory provides a way of viewing and explaining why and how institutions emerge in a certain way within a given context, but it falls under the criticism of structural bias as it avoids explanations situated at individual or same level of analysis. Such a gap is filled with structuration theory adoption, focusing on how institutional structures arise, or are maintained through the interplay process. The fusion of such concepts would potentially enrich the debates on DEST in PS by provoking new insights to keep the "research talking."

**Chapter 7**

  *Bruna Diirr, Federal University of the State of Rio de Janeiro*
   *(UNIRIO), Brazil*
  *Renata Araujo, Federal University of the State of Rio de Janeiro*
   *(UNIRIO), Brazil*
  *Claudia Cappelli, Federal University of the State of Rio de Janeiro*
   *(UNIRIO), Brazil*

Several discussions enforce the need for a greater engagement of society in public issues and show how ICTs can enhance it. This chapter presents the idea of conversations about public services. It is argued that by making society aware of how a service is provided—its process—citizens may develop a better attitude for interacting with government and other service users. Both society and governmental service providers can discuss problems, correct available information, and increase their knowledge about the processes, thus providing closer ties between them. This chapter also presents a tool designed to support these conversations and the results obtained with a case study of its use. The results suggest that conversations have stimulated interaction among citizens and services providers as well as allowed service improvement opportunities.

## Chapter 8

Smart Government and the Maturity Levels of Sociopolitical Digital Interactions: Analysing Temporal Changes in Brazilian E-Government Portals176

*Herman Resende Santos, Independent Researcher, Brazil*
*Dany Flávio Tonelli, Universidade Federal de Lavras, Brazil*

The emerging concept of smart government has a deep connection with the capacity to equalize high levels of performance and responsiveness in order to promote and enable development and prosperity. The expansion of public space towards the digital environment and increasing contextual complexity push governments to new perspectives concerning political and administrative dimensions. The capacity to interact virtually with citizens leads to the concept of sociopolitical digital interactions and the exploration of a conceptual framework called sociopolitical digital interactions' maturity (SDIM) directed the conducting of this study through a qualitative methodological approach. A comparative content analysis of the 27 Brazilian states' government websites was structured on 2013 and 2018 verifications. In this lapse time, the poor adoption of crowdsourcing digital tools denoted low governmental capacity to explore collective intelligence as well as an unwillingness concerning the adoption of citizen-centric models and a lack of openness to co-creative interaction processes.

## Chapter 9

A Quantitative Evaluation of Costs, Opportunities, Benefits, and Risks Accompanying the Use of E-Government Services in Qatar ............................200

*Karim Al-Yafi, Qatar University, Qatar*

Providers of e-government systems and policymakers recognize that usability and adoption are key success indicators of e-government services. Borrowed from the field of e-commerce, several models were proposed and tested in the literature to evaluate users' adoption of e-government services in different contexts. This chapter examines users' satisfaction with e-government services in Qatar reflected by the cost, opportunity, benefit, and risk of using these e-services. After a quick review on research works done on evaluating e-government services in the Middle East region, quantitative data collected from three e-government services in Qatar is presented and analyzed using structural equation modelling techniques. Results revealed that while the hypotheses linking cost and opportunity to satisfaction were rejected, benefits and risk were significantly able to explain the level of users' satisfaction with e-government services.

# Preface

Usage of technology to support the government services, electronic government (e-government), has been introduced with the aim of increasing the efficiency of e-government, improving transparency, citizens involvement and quality of citizens lives and reducing costs. E-Government projects have been undertaken across the world both in developed and developing countries, however, not all of them have been successfully adopted.

This book aims to provide an overview of the existing work in the area with the aim of better understand: the current state of the art, novel application of technology and government services, identify the factors that lead to the successful adoption of the existing services and provide workable solutions for strategic management for e-government projects.

These topics have received a lot of interests both from the governments globally but also from the research community. As a research field, e-government is well known to be widely multidisciplinary (Das et al., 2017; Molnar et al., 2015; Scholl et al., 2014), drawing from several fields, and the chapters from this book highlight this multidisciplinary nature.

## TARGET AUDIENCE

This book is of relevance to the following readers:

- Students and researchers in the field of e-government and strategic management
- Practitioners and professionals in e-government
- Project managers of e-government services
- Decisions makers in the government and public services
- General public interested in innovation in e-government.

# ORGANIZATION OF THE BOOK

The book has nine chapters. Each of them is briefly described below:

Chapter 1 focuses on facilitating and improving community emergency response and communication during large international gatherings. Drawing from research and industry a research framework is proposed. The authors discuss the future research opportunities in the area and the practical implications.

Chapter 2 as the previous chapter focuses on emergency medicine. The focus of the chapter is on the prehospital emergency of time-critical diseases and conditions. A solution to improve the communication between paramedics and emergency doctors by using high-quality video communication. The focus on the chapter is on the video camera which has been adapted to the needs of the paramedics and the results of an evaluation of the communication between doctors and paramedics.

Chapter 3 explores the usage of social media practices among government and citizens. An exploratory case study focusing on using Facebook in a local municipality is presented. The results found that social media usage is entrenched in and driven by three most significant contractions. The contradictions are referring to communication, organisation and the digital platform.

Chapter 4 looks into field operations in municipal governments. Using an empirical case study, the chapter identifies the ramifications of the strategic field operations shift when mobile information and communication technologies were used for field crews. The study has determined that information artefacts and information are important allocative and authoritative resources.

Chapter 5 reviews the literature on e-government focusing on factors that influence citizens trust and confidence in government. The review identifies several key factors, including citizen satisfaction and expectations, government transparency and accountability, the transformation of government, and government performance. One of the outcomes of the review is the lack of knowledge of how government transformation could improve citizens engagement. The study proposes a solution to this issue, by providing a conceptual model.

Chapter 6 also addresses the digital services transformation in public services, but it focuses on different theories. It poses that in this context public administration and information systems should work together and enrich the debate on digitally enabled service transformation and providing new insights.

Chapter 7 proposes the usage of conversation about public services as a mean to create citizens engagement with them. It argues that by discussing problems, correct the available information and enhance existing knowledge, the ties between society and governmental services provider will improve. The chapter introduces a tool to support these conversations and its evaluation. The study has shown that the tool proposed to encourage interaction among service providers and citizens and provided an opportunity to improve services.

Chapter 8 introduces an emerging concept, Smart Government. It also provides a comparative analysis of the content of 27 Brazilian states' government websites. The study concludes that there is a poor adoption of crowdsourcing digital tools. It poses that this denotes low governmental capacity to use collective intelligence, an unwillingness to adopt citizen-centric models and lack of openness for co-creation processes.

Chapter 9 starts with a review of the research done on e-valuating e-Government services in the Middle East region. Afterwards, evaluates user satisfaction with e-Government services in Qatar focusing on cost, opportunity, benefit and risk. The results have shown that benefits and risk were able to explain user satisfaction with e-Government services.

*Andreea Molnar*
*Lancaster University, UK*

## REFERENCES

Das, A., Singh, H., & Joseph, D. (2017). A longitudinal study of e-government maturity. *Information & Management*, *54*(4), 415–426. doi:10.1016/j.im.2016.09.006

Molnar, A., Janssen, M., & Weerakkody, V. (2015, May). E-government theories and challenges: findings from a plenary expert panel. In *Proceedings of the 16th Annual International Conference on Digital Government Research* (pp. 160-166). ACM. 10.1145/2757401.2757419

Scholl, H. J. J., & Dwivedi, Y. K. (2014). Forums for electronic government scholars: Insights from a 2012/2013 study. *Government Information Quarterly*, *31*(2), 229–242. doi:10.1016/j.giq.2013.10.008

# Chapter 1

# Toward the Improvement of Emergency Response Utilizing a Multi-Tiered Systems Integration Approach:
## A Research Framework

**Michael A. Erskine**
*Middle Tennessee State University, USA*

**Will Pepper**
*Better Than Free LLC, USA*

## ABSTRACT

*This chapter presents an extension of the Emergency Description Information Technology (EDIT) project to facilitate the effective collection and communication of information during an emergency. New academic findings and industry technologies inform a modified research framework. The research framework contains four primary research areas that are described in detail. Extending the design-science approach used for the EDIT project could improve emergency communications during large-scale international gatherings, as well as for community emergency response.*

DOI: 10.4018/978-1-5225-6204-7.ch001

## INTRODUCTION

According to the National Emergency Number Association (NENA), there are over 6,000 public-safety answering points (PSAPs) in the United States alone (NENA, 2014). Yet, public safety representatives suggest that a large number of emergency calls cannot be completed, as the current generation of wireless communication technology cannot adequately determine the position of a caller (Fung, 2014a). Additionally, of one thousand PSAPs, only 187 report a 'great deal' of confidence when receiving data from wireless carriers (Fung 2014a). Furthermore, it has been stated that only a fraction of all PSAPs can receive and interpret short messaging service (SMS) data. Yet, over 70 percent of the 400 thousand individuals in the United States that call PSAPs each day connect via mobile devices. Most of these mobile devices likely had the capability to transmit SMS data. While the United States Federal Communications Commission (FCC) recently voted to mandate that all cellular service providers must support the capability of mobile devices to connect to PSAPs using SMS, it is still unclear how incident location information will be provided to dispatchers (Fung 2014b).

While there are initiatives to support the transmission of emergency information using short message service (SMS) communications, organizations such as the FCC, CTIA and NENA continue to emphasize the importance of voice communication in emergencies unless there are significant reasons that prohibit someone from doing so (CTIA, 2014; FCC, 2014; NENA, 2014). Thus, it will be essential for such a system to demonstrate viability and positive improvements before gaining acceptance and endorsements from organizations that represent emergency response services. While there have been advances in the development of improved PSAP technology, it has been slow to be implemented. For example, many PSAPs do not yet have the capability to respond to SMS, a technology that has existed for over 25 years and is already experiencing declines as it is replaced with instant messaging services. For instance, recent data suggests that 22% of U.S. adults use the WhatsApp messenger service (Pew, 2018).

While PSAPs are challenged by technical constraints, they must also deal with human communication barriers, including excess background noise, language barriers, caller hysteria, or the inability to precisely describe the incident location. As these challenges exist during normal PSAP operation (Osher, 2013), large-scale public events further highlight the need for an improved process and technology. For instance, public events, such as the Olympics, the Munich Oktoberfest and the Vienna Donauinselfest attract 680 thousand international visitors, 6.4 million total visitors and over 1 million international visits, respectively (Office for National Statistics, 2012; Oktoberfest, 2013; Die Presse, 2014). Perhaps, of a greater concern are the large pilgrimages, such as those including the 120 million pilgrims of the Kumbh Mela, the 17 million pilgrims of the Arba'een to Karbala, or the 2 million pilgrims of the Hajj to Mecca (Hills, 2014; Cockburn, 2017; Smith, 2017). International visitors to such large-scale public gatherings may not be familiar with local emergency telephone numbers, may not know the local language sufficiently to explain details of an emergency, and may not be familiar enough with an area to adequately describe the emergency location. Surprisingly, the information systems literature barely addresses such issues. One exception is Yang, Su, and Yuan (2012) who researched fire disasters at major public events, including the 2008 Beijing Olympics.

Globally, there are numerous emergency telephone number standards and various levels of awareness. In addition, regional or international visitors may not be familiar with such numbers outside their home regions. In the United States the designated universal emergency number is 911, while in the European Union this number is 112, or 000 in Australia. Providing an expert system that can accurately determine the correct emergency number could be extremely useful in a natural disaster situation. For instance, at a global tourist destination such as Paris, where the local emergency number is 112, a visitor from Mexico may incorrectly dial 066, which is the emergency number that would be more familiar. Travelers may also encounter language barriers when contacting emergency services. Mobile expert systems could gather pertinent information in the native language and share such information with the closest emergency dispatcher in the language of the PSAPs geographic area. Prototyping an application that can connect individuals with the proper emergency response infrastructure, based on need and location, could overcome several barriers, such as a lack of awareness regarding local emergency numbers, language or other communications barriers and automatically transmitting key information such as location coordinates.

While the benefits of existing emergency response systems are substantial, an alternative to traditional voice-only calls could provide additional benefits. Recent advances in mobile technology present a unique opportunity to address current drawbacks. Modern smartphones with large displays and various sensors could provide additional benefits not previously available. While the global trend of consumers moving from fixed telephone systems to mobile devices presents communication challenges (Sayed, Tarighat and Khajehnouri, 2005; FCC, 2014), there could also be significant benefits. The impact of mobile devices on emergency call centers is already evident, as for example, of the approximately 240 million emergency calls made in the United States each year, nearly one third are placed from mobile devices (NENA, 2014; CTIA, 2014). This is not surprising considering that as of December 2012, 38.2% of U.S. households were wireless only and that the U.S. penetration of wireless devices had reached 102.2% (CTIA, 2014).

In the United States, 77 percent of all mobile subscribers utilize a smartphone (Pew, 2018). This continued trend toward global adoption of smartphone technology presents a unique opportunity to enhance emergency services data collection by leveraging the capabilities of such devices instead of relying solely on voice and limited SMS capabilities. The benefits of similar systems, such as vehicle telematics that can place calls based on environmental conditions, such as an airbag deployment or collision detection, have already reduced the amount of time between an incident and a call (911.gov, 2014).

The purpose of this research framework is to conceptualize, design and develop a mobile expert system to optimize emergency reporting, assessment, and response. The development of such systems aligns with the global initiative of modernizing government services to support contemporary technologies. Surprisingly, the information systems scholarship, and more specifically the e-government research area, has largely avoided addressing the reporting, collecting and disseminating emergency information. For example, between 2003 and 2013, the 'basket of eight' top information systems journals address this issue in only six relevant studies (Venkatesh, 2013).

By utilizing a process-based design science approach this research aims to leverage information technology research to reduce errors in the collection of emergency incident information and to optimize the reporting of an emergency incident. Design science research has been defined as an attempt to develop tools that serve humans and human purposes in order to try to understand the environment around us. The two axes of design science research include research activities (theorizing, building, evaluating, and justifying) and research outputs (constructs, frameworks, methodologies, and concrete supporting evidence) as suggested by March and Smith (1995). Furthermore, while traditional design projects focus on the contribution of utility, a design science approach contributes to the knowledge base as well as the utility (Hevner, Park, and Ram 2014).

## A DESIGN SCIENCE APPROACH

The benefits of using empirical research with a design science approach include (1) progress in the information systems scholarship, (2) an investigation into commonalities between current or past situations and theory, (3) solutions for known or unknown problems, (4) results that influence and build potentially new solutions to problems, (5) and the use of empirical research in new environments to test results in a method involving solutions for future problems (Hevner, March, Park, and Ram 2004; Neuman 2006; Anderson, Donnellan, and Hevner 2011; Gregor and Baskerville 2012; Bider, Johannesson, and Perjons 2013). Furthermore, it is suggested that design science research address a conceptual, research and developmental dimension (Gregg, Kulkarni, and Vinzé 2001).

Design science theory addresses problems that are either "unsolved" and must be addressed in innovative ways, or "solved" problems that can be improved through more efficient techniques (Hevner and Chatterjee 2010). Following with the well-established principles of design science research, the first component of this research project was an empirical investigation into the primary information required by emergency dispatchers. This data was gathered through an open-ended questionnaire asking emergency services dispatchers to state the four to five information items that are required to successfully dispatch appropriate personnel. Considering this, a prototype application was developed to demonstrate the proposed effectiveness of an expert system to reduce communications errors in emergency situations (Erskine & Pepper, 2016).

## A RESEARCH FRAMEWORK

The research framework highlights four research focus areas: incident reporting, volunteer citizen, emergency responder, and integration. Each of these areas, and specific research topics, are addressed next.

*Figure 1. Research framework*

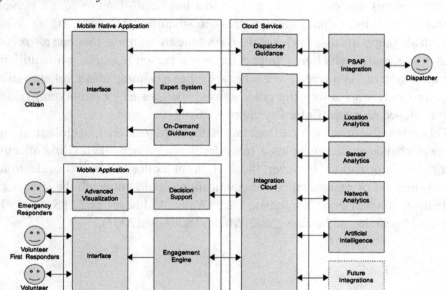

# INCIDENT REPORTING RESEARCH FOCUS AREAS

## Reporting Interface

While many communities have invested heavily into emergency call centers and supporting infrastructure, evidence suggests that more can be done to ensure efficiencies of such systems. For example, language or cultural barriers may prevent voice calls, operators may have difficulty identifying key information due to noise and other distractions, tense situations may cause communication challenges, and sometimes information is incorrectly interpreted resulting in inefficient responses. When a traumatic event, such as an accident occurs individuals encounter various emotions that can potentially be exasperated through adrenaline that clouds communication and judgment (Howie, 2008). Such states of emotion could lead to information that is unusable, convoluted, or time delayed, thus affecting the dispatcher's ability to effectively assign first responders. Studies have also addressed the misinterpretation between callers and dispatchers caused by hysteria, emotion and anger (Tracy and Tracy, 1998; Whalen and Zimmerman, 1998; Garcia and Parmer, 2011).

An important consideration during the visual design of an interface to a next-generation emergency response system is the development of a concise and calming layout. Highly stressful situations often cause individuals to easily loose concentration. Thus, simple questions were developed to allow witnesses and victims to concisely provide key information. Additionally, the color scheme of the application interface includes various shades of green, a color that has been found to ease a nervous individual or an individual in a high-pressure situation (Rousseau, 2008). While research also supports that shades of the color blue are calming, they can also evoke feelings of sadness, which may impact the way a person responds while utilizing the expert system. As a green color scheme evokes a calming effect, relieves stress and improves reading ability, this color scheme is suggested for prototyping related design-science research (Color Psychology, 2014).

This research considers that there are many organizational, sociological, and technical challenges that may arise from developing a new method in collecting emergency information, however the benefit of collecting specific electronic data to augment or replace voice communications could outweigh the significant implementation barriers (Churchman, 1979; Walls, Widmeyer, and El Sawy, 1992; Markus, Majchrzak, and Gasser 2002; Manoj and Baker 2007).

## Reporting Expert System

Early identification and response to life-threatening medical emergencies, such as pediatric out-of-hospital cardiac arrests, have been shown to increase survival outcomes (Kwan & Ng, 2017). An additional concern is that non-emergency calls can place a burden on responders (Snooks, Williams, Crouch, Foster, Hartley-Sharpe, and Dale, 2002). Palumbo, Kubincanek, Emerman, Jouriles, Cydulka, and Shard (1996) found that in 74 percent of emergency call cases dispatchers and physicians disagreed on whether emergency medical services with basic or advanced life support should be dispatched. Through the use of an expert system to ascertain whether a perceived emergency incident necessitates emergency responders, the burden placed on emergency responders for non-emergency calls could be reduced.

When former and current emergency dispatchers were asked the five most important pieces of information a caller needs to relay in a crisis, the response was unanimous with the key piece of information being the location of the incident (Erskine & Pepper, 2016). The second most important piece of information was "what", "what's wrong", or "what's the problem/situation" (fourteen times). The third most requested information item was "who", "name(s)", and "parties involved" (ten times), with fourth being a phone number in case of the call is dropped or background noise interference (five times). Interestingly, the fifth most popular answer may be asked more for the benefit of the first responders: are there any weapons at the scene (six times)?

To better understand the key information necessary to successfully dispatch the appropriate resources in an emergency, key patterns in such situations were analyzed. While this ongoing research area will benefit from the gathering of data from actual emergencies, this initial research project uses qualitative research methods that rely on an inductive, discovery methodology to utilize determine vital information, allowing latent knowledge gaps to be addressed (Heredero, Berzosa, and Santos, 2010; Myers, 1997). This type of approach has already informed the development of information systems, such as those systems that rely on communal assistance (Dedrick and West 2005). To develop emergency response workflows, Erskine & Pepper (2016) identified fifty-five emergency agencies that provided public information to assist callers. Data was collected, transcribed, summarized into descriptive codes to organize the observations and then categorized as patterns emerged. Then the codes were refined based on the patterns and interactions among the concepts. Linkages were reported that further support the need to formulate a theory that will support the development of a model assisted with observed facts (Myers, 2009).

The required information for first responders begins with an inquiry of the location and a description of the emergency incident. This basic information can already determine which type of emergency response may be necessary. Examples of situations meriting different responders would be that the information of "intersection of 4th and Main streets" and "shooting" would result in the allocation of the nearest police cruiser, whereas "127 Jerome Street" and "choking" would result in the allocation of an ambulance and paramedics. While this early information would allow emergency services to be instantly deployed, as additional information is acquired, additional units, specialized equipment or auxiliary personnel could be added. For instance, for the "shooting" example an ambulance could be added as more information is gathered. As community emergency response resources vary, such workflows must be designed and evaluated for various municipalities and regions independently.

## Reporting On-Demand Guidance

During the stress of an emergency, sometimes a trained first responder may have difficulty recalling first responder knowledge and skills. Additionally, when response times are inadequate, an expert system that diagnosed a particular response could provide on-demand guidance or coaching. For instance, smartphone applications and even digital watch applications that provide CPR coaching during emergencies have been developed (Thygerson et al., 2012; Bachmann et al., 2015; Gruenerbl et al., 2015). Similarly, several devices exist that can provide real-time feedback to emergency responder and first responders using accelerometers already exist (Yeongtak et al., 2015) although their efficacy is questionable (Zapletal et al., 2014).

## VOLUNTEER CITIZEN RESEARCH FOCUS AREAS

### Citizen Engagement Engine

Several researchers have investigated ways to motivate citizens to become active participants in the emergency response workflow. While motivating citizens remains challenging, Kasper et al. (2017) identified organizational structures, regular gatherings, and a meaningful purpose provided a foundation for citizen engagement as first responders.

A version of a first responder software application, FirstAED, was tested in a rural setting in Denmark over a 24-month period. The results of 718 cases report that 89% of the time, the first responders arrived before an ambulance and that the software reduced the response time from fifteen minutes to four minutes and nine seconds (Henriksen et al 2016). Furthermore, photographs sent over smartphone devices are currently assisting first responders assess damage and need of emergency personnel (Wang et al 2014). Crowdsourced information, or information collected from various individuals, was pilot tested during the 2014 FIFA World Cup in Brazil, but resulted in "severe usability issues" (Holl et al. 2017). Therefore, the need for better and more user-friendly emergency situational software exists.

In addition to medical information, details regarding psychiatric conditions could be transmitted as well. This could be especially helpful, as previous studies have discovered significant benefits of responding with a specialized crisis team to deal with psychiatric emergency services. For instance, such a response can provide a positive intervention and can reduce the need for hospitalization (Scott, 2000; Sabnis and Glick, 2012).

## Citizen Responder Interface

The development of smartphone applications that may be utilized during times of stress or danger is key to assisting first responders (Schleicher et al. 2014). Smartphone tools to assist first responders and those requiring emergency services include GDACSmobile, a combination of smartphone software and the social media system, and SmartRescue, a smartphone sensor application. Both applications were studied for human-computer interactions and usability. Among the items tested for usability include layout (menus, browsing, navigation, and icon), hardware (battery life, touch screen, mobility, screen size), and even the "fat finger problem" in which a finger is unable to interact with the application with precision. Even though both programs have some ease of use benefits, as well as they utilize context-aware software that uses smartphone sensors to report and record details of a physical environment, a recent report states that they both would benefit from improvements (Sarshar et al 2015).

## EMERGENCY RESPONDER RESEARCH FOCUS AREAS

## Emergency Responder Decision Support

Depending on the incident type, a decision-support system designed for emergency responders could be enhanced using data captured and analyses conducted through the conceptual research framework. For instance, real-time information captured by flood sensors and heart-rate monitors could allow an emergency responder to continually assess and re-prioritize response efforts. Furthermore, the collected data attributes from existing emergency dispatch transcripts could be analyzed in real-time and analyzed for patterns using decision-support systems. The use of such technology has been demonstrated to allow decision-makers to predict large-scale disasters. Furthermore, the use of crowd-sourced information has been suggested to aid decision makers with determining appropriate responses to natural disasters (Erskine and Gregg, 2012; Horita and Albuquerque, 2013; Horita et al. 2013). Finally, such systems could have a greater capability of detecting disasters by analyzing real-time digital emergency communications.

## Emergency Responder Advanced Visualization

Technical advances and large quantities of collected and examined data allow for new visualization approaches. For instance, Horita et al. (2015) developed a dashboard that combined remote sensing data and citizen observations to compose effective visualizations. Moreover, Tashakkori et al. (2015) developed a three-dimensional visualization model that could prove effective for emergencies in complex structures. Furthermore, while Sebillo et al. (2016) explored the use of augmented reality for the training of emergency responders, the capability of augmented reality to support emergency responders outside of training scenarios is evident. As new data streams and subsequent analyses are developed, new visualization techniques for emergency responders will provide numerous opportunities for exploration.

## INTEGRATION CLOUD RESEARCH FOCUS AREAS

An understanding of how individuals can benefit from an intelligent system to ensure accurate collection and communication of emergency data provides a unique exploration opportunity for the information systems scholarship. For instance, while numerous systems designed to collect public safety-data exist, such systems can only provide a benefit if the collected information is accurate (Shah, Bao, Lu, & Chen, 2011). Such a system could be integrated with other e-government initiatives that address improved emergency resource dispatching and citizen communications. In addition to sharing public safety information, other examples such systems include safety-reporting technology in the construction, manufacturing, logistics and aviation sectors.

## PSAP Dispatcher Guidance

An important research stream includes simulations of emergency events using traditional telephone dispatch and the prototyped expert system. The authors expect that using a laboratory setting to record the information acquisition times of the prototyped software verses a simulated emergency phone will result in software acquiring crucial information more rapidly than the traditional verbal communication. Previous research supports that data communications can provide the same information as verbal communications, but more efficiently (Pepper, Aiken, & Garner, 2011). Another research component would be to utilize actual emergency dispatch information and call transcripts and compare these to use of the mobile expert system in order to quantify efficiencies. Additionally, benefits and drawbacks based on environmental and user characteristics could be explored to determine how versatile such a system would be in actual use. Furthermore, exploration will need to be performed in determining how to most effectively integrate such a system into an actual dispatch facility or how such a system should behave outside a compatible region. Specifically, the effectiveness of integrating with or simply augmenting an existing computer aided call handling (CACH) systems will need to be examined.

## Location Analytics and Geolocation Services

Large quantities of geospatially references data provide additional opportunities for exploration (e.g., Jern et al., 2010). For instance, location analytics can establish information relationships that may not be obvious through traditional analytic approaches. Furthermore, one of the core requirements to dispatch emergency services to the site of an emergency, is to identify the exact location of the emergency. Specifically, the Federal Communications Commission (FCC) in the U.S. and the Directive for Mobile Communication in the E.U. require the capability to determine a caller's location (Junglas and Watson, 2008).

## Sensor Analytics

Decreasing technology sensor costs and increased connectivity capabilities have introduced or expanded field sensing capabilities (Akyildiz et al., 2002; Lorincz et al., 2004; Prusty & Mohanty, 2018). Such sensors include weather stations, seismographs, flood sensors, traffic cameras, acoustic gunshot detectors, and smoke sensors. Through the acquisition and analysis of data streams from such devices emergency response systems could present targeted information to victims, first responders, and emergency responders. Furthermore, such technologies could augment decision support systems to present areas of impact that may have been impacted by specific disasters (Erskine and Gregg, 2012; Horita et al. 2015).

## Network Analytics

Through an examination of social media systems and other networked systems such as regional PSAPs, real-time data could be examined to determine if a potential disaster has struck, or to even predict a disaster. Analyses of social media have already revealed the opportunities for such capabilities (e.g., Cheong & Cheong, 2011; Gao et al., 2011; Kryvasheyeu et al., 2015; Anson et al., 2017).

## Artificial Intelligence

Continued investment and growth of artificial intelligence development have provided another area of investigation. Several research streams have already explored the efficacy of artificial intelligence applications to support emergency response (e.g., Imran et al. 2014; Bui et al. 2016; Armstrong et al. 2016; Aziz et al., 2017; McGovern et al., 2017).

## Future Integrations

As new technologies are developed or proposed, it will be imperative that the research framework explores the incorporation of additional and new data streams and capabilities. For instance, as simulation training has been found to improve intervention performance (Meischke et al., 2017), it is suggested that a simulation component be available in the future. During appropriate times, such a component could provide simulations to test existing algorithms, to train machine learning algorithms, and to train human participants. In addition to virtual simulations, it has been suggested that universities can provide proxies for testing of systems during large public events (Tapia et al. 2016).

Moreover, vehicle-based monitoring systems continue to decrease the number of fatalities involved in automobile accidents and are now being aided through the use of smartphone technology, such as reporting an accident to first responders (Engelbrecht et al 2015). As a new generation of semi-autonomous and perhaps fully autonomous vehicles reach consumers, it is very likely that their sophisticated sensors will detect emergencies, including crimes. Such vehicles could be provided the capability to report such emergencies without human intervention.

In addition to the automatic communication of location information, critical medical information could also be transmitted. For instance, medial allergies or pre-existing medical conditions could be transmitted automatically along with the dispatch communication. This would be the equivalent of a digital medical bracelet. It has been documented that emergency medical services (EMS) providers often do not have sufficient access to pre-existing medical information when responding to incidents (Finnell and Overhage, 2010). While there has been an effort to link such data to EMS services, these may only be available locally or regionally. When travelling internationally it would become increasingly difficult to notify a dispatcher of specific pre- existing medical conditions.

Perhaps the capture, analysis, and response of instant messaging input could be examined in the near future. The use of instant messaging applications during the response phase of emergency has already been documented (Baytiyeh, 2018). Similarly, the use of social media to communicate has demonstrated resilience during disasters that could be augmented to facilite effective responses (Reuter et al., 2017). In addition to capture social media streams, a user-centered approach could be developed to tailor warning messages for large populations (Schoeder et al., 2016).

Additionally, such a system could be deployed specifically to deal with emergency communications during a large-scale disaster. The benefits of mobile decision support systems to aid disaster response have been demonstrated and explored in several studies (Thompson, Altay, Green & Lapetina, 2006; Erskine & Gregg, 2012; Erskine, Sibona & Kalantar, 2013). In addition to facilitating post-disaster emergency information sharing, such systems can also be used to predict natural-disaster emergency situations (Brovelli & Cannata, 2004; Cannata, Marzochhi, & Molinari, 2012; Suri & Hofierka, 2004).

## CONCLUSION

This chapter utilizes a design-science approach to address a global problem: the efficient collection and effective communication of data that is essential to those in and responding to an emergency. This capability would closely align with other e-government initiatives that leverage contemporary technologies to enhance government processes. By focusing on retrieval of pertinent information about emergency incidents in an extremely efficient manner (e.g., including mobile device decision-trees that gather user information while automatically sending location variables), such optimization processes may decrease response time, diminish lost or undecipherable verbal incident descriptions, and address the many other communication issues that arise from traditional voice-based emergency response systems.

This chapter presents several implications on the information systems and e-government scholarships. Specifically, researchers can benefit from the specific process-based design science approach applied to the examination of emergency communications that incorporates existing knowledge from literature and empirical studies as well as the collection of new evidence. This approach can be used to identify problems in other information systems and e-government research domains. By choosing to use a design science approach, future research can benefit from the application of theory and empirical evaluations (Hevner, March, Park, and Ram 2004; Venable, Pries-Heje, and Baskerville 2014).

Each of these implications provides significant future research opportunities. Benefits to scholarly research include an examination of information systems literature in the context of emergency services. Specifically, important studies that inform the design science process of emergency information communications were presented. Additionally, a significant research gap demonstrates the need for e-government and information systems scholars to further examine how emergency management workflows can be improved.

Furthermore, this chapter suggests several practical implications. First, an extensive body of global emergency dispatch communications problems is presented. Second, developers of emergency response systems are presented with an enhanced communications method over traditional voice-only communications. Such technology could be used to aid in communicating when language barriers are present or when information is better presented visually. Such technology could provide significant benefits to emergency managers at large-scale events. Third, the benefits of developing workflows for specific emergency incidents are described. For instance, such workflows can be leveraged to automate responses without the need for dispatcher intervention. Fourth, mobile application designers and developers may benefit through the utilization of concise and calming interfaces when developing tools to be used by individuals in highly stressful situations. Finally, an integration is suggested for incorporating EDIT into existing PSAP workflows. Organizations and individuals who create technologies related to emergency response management may benefit from these findings.

While the global implementation of a next-generation emergency response system would take substantial resources and planning, implementations for large-scale, international events such as the FIFA World Cup or the Olympic games could provide immediate value. Such events would be ideal test environments for such a system as a) a heavy emphasis is placed on safety, b) visitors may not be familiar with local emergency response numbers and c) because visitors may represent a variety of cultures and languages that such a tool must accommodate.

## ACKNOWLEDGMENT

This research received no specific grant from any funding agency in the public, commercial, or not-for-profit sectors.

# REFERENCES

Akyildiz, I. F., Su, W., Sankarasubramaniam, Y., & Cayirci, E. (2002). A survey on sensor networks. *IEEE Communications Magazine*, *40*(8), 102–114. doi:10.1109/MCOM.2002.1024422

Allen, D. K., Karanasios, S., & Norman, A. (2013). Information sharing and interoperability: The case of major incident management. *European Journal of Information Systems*.

Ammenwerth, E., Buchauer, A., Bludau, B., & Haux, R. (2000). Mobile information and communication tools in the hospital. *International Journal of Medical Informatics*, *57*(1), 21–40. doi:10.1016/S1386-5056(99)00056-8 PMID:10708253

Anderson, J., Donnellan, B., & Hevner, A. (2011). Exploring the relationship between design science research and innovation: A case study of innovation at Chevron. *Communications in Computer and Information Science*, (286): 116–131.

Anson, S., Watson, H., Wadhwa, K., & Metz, K. (2017). Analysing social media data for disaster preparedness: Understanding the opportunities and barriers faced by humanitarian actors. *International Journal of Disaster Risk Reduction*, *21*, 131–139. doi:10.1016/j.ijdrr.2016.11.014

Armstrong, S., Bostrom, N., & Shulman, C. (2016). Racing to the precipice: A model of artificial intelligence development. *AI & Society*, *31*(2), 201–206. doi:10.100700146-015-0590-y

Aziz, K., Haque, M. M., Rahman, A., Shamseldin, A. Y., & Shoaib, M. (2017). Flood estimation in ungauged catchments: Application of artificial intelligence based methods for Eastern Australia. *Stochastic Environmental Research and Risk Assessment*, *31*(6), 1499–1514. doi:10.100700477-016-1272-0

Bachmann, D. J., Jamison, N. K., Martin, A., Delgado, J., & Kman, N. E. (2015). Emergency preparedness and disaster response: There's an app for that. *Prehospital and Disaster Medicine*, *30*(5), 486–490. doi:10.1017/S1049023X15005099 PMID:26369629

Baytiyeh, H. The use of mobile technologies in the aftermath of terrorist attacks among low socioeconomic populations. *International Journal of Disaster Risk Reduction*. doi:10.1016/j.ijdrr.2018.02.001

Bider, I., Johannesson, P., & Perjons, E. (2013). Using empirical knowledge and studies in the frame of design science research. *Proceedings of the 8th International Conference on Design Science at the Intersection of Physical and Virtual Design*, 463-470. 10.1007/978-3-642-38827-9_38

Boonstra, A., Broekhuis, M., Offenbeek, M. V., & Wortmann, H. (2011). Strategic alternatives in telecare design: Developing a value-configuration-based alignment framework. *The Journal of Strategic Information Systems*, *20*(2), 198–214. doi:10.1016/j.jsis.2010.12.001

Brovelli, M. A., & Cannata, M. (2004). Digital Terrain model reconstruction in urban areas from airborne laser scanning data: The method and an example for Pavia (Northern Italy). *Computers & Geosciences*, *30*(4), 325–331. doi:10.1016/j.cageo.2003.07.004

Bui, D. T., Pradhan, B., Nampak, H., Bui, Q. T., Tran, Q. A., & Nguyen, Q. P. (2016). Hybrid artificial intelligence approach based on neural fuzzy inference model and metaheuristic optimization for flood susceptibilitgy modeling in a high-frequency tropical cyclone area using GIS. *Journal of Hydrology (Amsterdam)*, *540*, 317–330. doi:10.1016/j.jhydrol.2016.06.027

Cannata, M., Marzochhi, R., & Molinari, M. (2012). Modeling of landslide-generated tsunamis with GRASS. *Transactions in GIS*, *16*(2), 191–214. doi:10.1111/j.1467-9671.2012.01315.x

CCA. (2014). *About CCA*. Retrieved September 27, 2014, from https://competitivecarriers.org/about/about-rca-2/914473

Chen, R., Sharman, R., Rao, H. R., & Upadhyaya, S. J. (2013). Data model development for fire related extreme events: An activity theory approach. *Management Information Systems Quarterly*, *37*(1), 125–147. doi:10.25300/MISQ/2013/37.1.06

Cheong, F., & Cheong, C. (2011). Social Media Data Mining: A Social Network Analysis of Tweets During The 2010-2011 Australian Floods. *PACIS*, *11*, 46–46.

Churchman, C. W. (1979). *The Systems Approach*. Dell.

Cockburn, P. (2017). Arbaeen: Millions of Shia Muslims take part in world's greatest pilgrimage as Isis is finally defeated. *The Independent*. Retrieved March 13, 2018 from: http://www.independent.co.uk/news/world/middle-east/arbaeen-pilgrimage-kerbala-shia-isis-defeat-muslims-thousands-killed-middle-east-iraq-najaf-a8046621.html

Color Psychology. (2014). Retrieved September 27, 2014, from http://psychology. about.com/od/sensationandperception/a/colorpsych.htm

CTIA. (2014). *Wireless quick facts*. Retrieved September 27, 2014, from http://www. ctia.org/your-wireless-life/how-wireless-works/wireless-quick-facts

Dedrick, J., & West, J. (2003). Why firms adopt open source platforms: a grounded theory of innovation and standards adoption. *Proceedings of the workshop on standard making: A critical research frontier for information systems*, 236-257.

911. Dispatch. (2014). *Required emergency information*. Retrieved September 27, 2014, from http://www.911dispatch.com/info/calltaking/calltaker.html

eMarketer. (2013). *Smartphone adoption tips past 50%*. Retrieved from http:// www.emarketer.com/Article/Smartphone-Adoption-Tips-Past-50-Major-Markets-Worldwide/1009923

Engelbrecht, J., & Booysen, M. J., Van Rooyen, G-J., & Bruwer, F. J. (2015). Survey of smartphone-based sensing in vehicles for intelligent transportation system applications. *IET Intelligent Transport Systems*. doi:10.1049/iet-its.2014.0248

Erskine, M. A., & Gregg, D. G. (2012). Utilizing volunteered geographic information to develop a real-time disaster mapping tool: a prototype and research framework. *Proceedings of the Conference on Information Resource Management*.

Erskine, M. A., & Pepper, W. (2016). Enhancing Emergency Response Management using Emergency Description Information Technology (EDIT): A Design Science Approach. In E-Health and Telemedicine: Concepts, Methodologies, Tools, and Applications (pp. 1264-1278). IGI Global.

Erskine, M. A., Sibona, C., & Kalantar, H. (2013). Aggregating, analyzing and diffusing natural disaster information: a research framework. *Proceedings of the Nineteenth Americas Conference on Information Systems*.

FCC. (2014a). Retrieved March 13, 2018, from https://www.fcc.gov/files/text-911-master-psap-registryxlsx

FCC. (2014b). Retrieved September 27, 2014, from http://www.fcc.gov/guides/wireless-911-Services

Ferneley, E., & Light, B. (2006). Secondary user relations in emerging mobile computing environments. *European Journal of Information Systems*, *15*(3), 301–306.

Finnell, J. T., & Overhage, J. M. (2010). Emergency medical services: the frontier in health information exchange. *American Medical Informatics Association Annual Symposium Proceedings*, 222.

Fitzgerald, G., & Russo, N. L. (2005). The turnaround of the London ambulance service computer-aided dispatch system (LASCAD). *European Journal of Information Systems*, *14*(3), 244–257.

Fruhling, A., & Vreede, G. J. D. (2006). Field experiences with eXtreme programming: Developing an emergency response system. *Journal of Management Information Systems*, *22*(4), 39–68. doi:10.2753/MIS0742-1222220403

Fung, B. (2014a, April 27). Cellphone calls to 911 prove hard to trace. *Washington Post*.

Fung, B. (2014b, August 9). FCC is requiring broad support of text-to-911. *Washington Post*.

Gao, H., Barbier, G., & Goolsby, R. (2011). Harnessing the crowdsourcing power of social media for disaster relief. *IEEE Intelligent Systems*, *26*(3), 10–14. doi:10.1109/MIS.2011.52

Garcia, A. C., & Parmer, P. A. (1999). Misplaced mistrust: The collaborative construction of doubt in 911 emergency calls. *Symbolic Interaction*, *22*(4), 297–324. doi:10.1525i.1999.22.4.297

Gill, A., Alam, S., & Eustace, J. (2014). *Using Social Architecture to Analyzing Online Social Network Use in Emergency Management*. Academic Press.

911. gov. (2014). *Current 911 data collection*. Retrieved September 27, 2014, from http://www.911.gov/pdf/Current911DataCollection-072613.pdf

Gregg, D. G., Kulkarni, U. R., & Vinzé, A. S. (2001). Understanding the philosophical underpinnings of software engineering research in information systems. *Information Systems Frontiers*, *3*(2), 169–183. doi:10.1023/A:1011491322406

Gregor, S., & Baskerville, R. (2012). The fusion of design science and social science research. *Information Systems Foundation Workshop*, Canberra, Australia.

Gruenerbl, A., Pirkl, G., Monger, E., Gobbi, M., & Lukowicz, P. (2015, September). Smart-watch life saver: smart-watch interactive-feedback system for improving bystander CPR. In *Proceedings of the 2015 ACM International Symposium on Wearable Computers* (pp. 19-26). ACM. 10.1145/2802083.2802086

Henriksen, F. L., Schorling, P., Hansen, B., Schakow, H., & Larsen, M. L. (2016). FirstAED emergency dispatch, global positioning of community first responders with distinct roles - a solution to reduce the response times and ensuring an AED to early defibrillation in the rural area Langeland. *International Journal of Networking and Virtual Organisations*, *16*(1), 86. doi:10.1504/IJNVO.2016.075131

Heredero, C., Berzosa, D., & Santos, R. (2010). The implementation of free software in firms: An empirical analysis. *The International Journal of Digital Accounting Research*, *10*, 113–130.

Hevner, A. R., & Chaterjee, S. (2010). *Design Research in Information Systems*. New York: Springer. doi:10.1007/978-1-4419-5653-8

Hevner, A. R., March, S. T., Park, J., & Ram, S. (2004). Design science in information systems research. *Management Information Systems Quarterly*, *28*(1), 75–105. doi:10.2307/25148625

Hills, S. (2013). World's biggest religious festival comes to an end after 120 million pilgrims cleansed their sins during two month celebration. *The Daily Mail*. Retrieved March 13, 2018 from: http://www.dailymail.co.uk/news/article-2291379/Kumbh-Mela-Worlds-biggest-religious-festival-comes-end-120-million-pilgrims-cleansed-sins-month-celebration.html

Holl, K., Nass, C., Villela, K., & Vieira, V. (2016). Towards a lightweight approach for on-site interaction evaluation of safety-critical mobile systems. *Procedia Computer Science*, *94*, 41–48. 10.1016/j.procs.2016.08.010

Horita, F. E., & de Albuquerque, J. P. (2013). An approach to support decision-making in disaster management based on volunteer geographic information (VGI) and spatial decision support systems (SDSS). *Proceedings of the 10th International Conference on Information Systems for Crisis Response and Management*, 12-15.

Horita, F. E., de Albuquerque, J. P., Degrossi, L. C., Mendiondo, E. M., & Ueyama, J. (2015). Development of a spatial decision support system for flood risk management in Brazil that combines volunteered geographic information with wireless sensor networks. *Computers & Geosciences*, *80*, 84–94. doi:10.1016/j.cageo.2015.04.001

Horita, F. E. A., Degrossi, L. C., de Assis, L. F. G., Zipf, A., & de Albuquerque, J. P. (2013). The use of volunteered geographic information (VGI) and crowdsourcing in disaster management: a systematic literature review. *Proceedings of the Nineteenth Americas Conference on Information Systems*.

Howie, C. (2008). What to do after a car accident. *CNN*. Retrieved September 27, 2014, from http://www.cnn.com/2008/LIVING/wayoflife/05/09/car.accident/

Imran, M., Castillo, C., Lucas, J., Meier, P., & Vieweg, S. (2014, April). AIDR: Artificial intelligence for disaster response. In *Proceedings of the 23rd International Conference on World Wide Web* (pp. 159-162). ACM.

Jern, M., Brezzi, M., & Lundblad, P. (2010). Geovisual analytics tools for communicating emergency and early warning. In *Geographic Information and Cartography for Risk and Crisis Management* (pp. 379–394). Berlin: Springer. doi:10.1007/978-3-642-03442-8_26

Junglas, I. A., & Watson, R. T. (2008). Location-based services. *Communications of the ACM, 51*(3), 65–69. doi:10.1145/1325555.1325568

Kasper, N., Nabecker, S., Twerenbold, G. A., Gurtner, S., & Greif, R. (2017). Keeping laypersons as first responders engaged: A qualitative, focus group interview study. *Resuscitation, 118*, e10. doi:10.1016/j.resuscitation.2017.08.037

Kryvasheyeu, Y., Chen, H., Moro, E., Van Hentenryck, P., & Cebrian, M. (2015). Performance of social network sensors during Hurricane Sandy. *PLoS One, 10*(2), e0117288. doi:10.1371/journal.pone.0117288 PMID:25692690

Kwan, J., & Ng, Y. Y. (2017). Asking the right questions. *Resuscitation, 116*, A9–A10. doi:10.1016/j.resuscitation.2017.05.013 PMID:28506864

Leidner, D. E., Pan, G., & Pan, S. L. (2009). The role of IT in crisis response: Lessons from the SARS and Asian Tsunami disasters. *The Journal of Strategic Information Systems, 18*(2), 80–99. doi:10.1016/j.jsis.2009.05.001

Lindsey, B. (2011). Social media and disasters: Current uses, future options, and policy considerations. *Congressional Research Service, 7*(5700), 1–10.

Lorincz, K., Malan, D. J., Fulford-Jones, T. R., Nawoj, A., Clavel, A., Shnayder, V., ... Moulton, S. (2004). Sensor networks for emergency response: Challenges and opportunities. *IEEE Pervasive Computing, 3*(4), 16–23. doi:10.1109/MPRV.2004.18

Manoj, B. S., & Baker, A. H. (2007). Communication challenges in emergency response. *Communications of the ACM, 50*(3), 51–53. doi:10.1145/1226736.1226765

March, S. T., & Smith, G. F. (1995). Design and natural science research on information technology. *Decision Support Systems, 15*(4), 251–266. doi:10.1016/0167-9236(94)00041-2

Markus, M. L., Majchrzak, A., & Gasser, L. (2002). A design theory for systems that support emergent knowledge processes. *Management Information Systems Quarterly, 26*(3), 179–212.

McGovern, A., Elmore, K. L., Gagne, D. J. II, Haupt, S. E., Karstens, C. D., Lagerquist, R., ... Williams, J. K. (2017). Using Artificial Intelligence to Improve Real-Time Decision-Making for High-Impact Weather. *Bulletin of the American Meteorological Society*, *98*(10), 2073–2090. doi:10.1175/BAMS-D-16-0123.1

Moreno, A., Garrison, P., & Bhat, K. (2017). WhatsApp for monitoring and response during critical events: Aggie in the Ghana 2016 election. *Proceedings of the 14th ISCRAM Conference*.

Myers, M. (1997). *Qualitative research in information systems*. MIS Quarterly Discovery.

Myers, M. (2009). Qualitative Research in Business and Management. *Sage (Atlanta, Ga.)*.

NENA. (2014). *911 Statistics*. Retrieved September 27, 2014, from https://www.nena.org/?page=911Statistics

Neuman, W. L. (2006). *Social Research Methods. Qualitative and Quantitative Approaches*. Pearson.

Office for National Statistics. (2012). *London 2012 Olympic & Paralympic Games attracted 680,000 overseas visitors*. Retrieved September 27, 2014, from http://www.ons.gov.uk/ons/dcp29904_287477.pdf

Oktoberfest. (2013). *The Oktoberfest 2013 roundup*. Retrieved September 27, 2014, from http://www.oktoberfest.de/en/article/About+the+Oktoberfest/About+the+Oktoberfest/The+O ktoberfest+2013+roundup/3734/

Osher, C. N. (2013). Operator error: how emergency calls are managed by dispatchers can be problematic. *The Denver Post*. Retrieved September 27, 2014, from http://www.denverpost.com/ci_22500950/denvers-911-call-performance-audits-reveal-problems

Palumbo, L., Kubincanek, J., Emerman, C., Jouriles, N., Cydulka, R., & Shade, B. (1996). Performance of a system to determine EMS dispatch priorities. *The American Journal of Emergency Medicine*, *14*(4), 388–390. doi:10.1016/S0735-6757(96)90056-X PMID:8768162

Pepper, W., Aiken, M., & Garner, B. (2011). Usefulness and usability of a multilingual electronic meeting system. *Global Journal of Computer Science and Technology*, *11*(5), 34–40.

Pew Research Center. (2018). *Mobile Fact Sheet*. Retrieved March 13, 2018 from: http://www.pewinternet.org/fact-sheet/mobile/

Prusty, A. R., & Mohanty, A. (2018). Prospect of Low Power Sensor Network Technology in Disaster Management for Sustainable Future. In *Handbook of Research on Environmental Policies for Emergency Management and Public Safety* (pp. 123–145). IGI Global. doi:10.4018/978-1-5225-3194-4.ch007

Reuter, C., Ludwig, T., Kaufhold, M. A., & Hupertz, J. (2017). Social Media Resilience during Infrastructure Breakdowns using Mobile Ad-Hoc Networks. Advances and New Trends in Environmental Informatics, 75-88. doi:10.1007/978-3-319-44711-7_7

Rousseau, L. (2008). The essential principles of graphic design. In Color (pp. 14-16). F+W Publications.

Sabnis, D., & Glick, R. L. (2012). Innovative community-based crisis and emergency services. In *Handbook of Community Psychiatry* (pp. 379–387). Springer New York. doi:10.1007/978-1-4614-3149-7_31

Sarshar, P., Nunavath, V., & Radianti, J. (2015). On the Usability of Smartphone Apps in Emergencies. An HCI Analysis of GDACSmobile and SmartRescue Apps. In M. Kurosu (Ed.), Human-Computer Interaction, Part II (LNCS 9170, pp. 765–774). Springer. doi:10.1007/978-3-319-20916-6_70

Sayed, A. H., Tarighat, A., & Khajehnouri, N. (2005). Network-based wireless location: Challenges faced in developing techniques for accurate wireless location information. *IEEE Signal Processing Magazine*, 22(4), 24–40. doi:10.1109/MSP.2005.1458275

Schleicher, R., Westermann, T., & Reichmuth, R. (2014). *Mobile Human Computer–Interaction Quality of Experience*. Heidelberg, Germany: Springer.

Schroeder, B. L., Whitmer, D. E., & Sims, V. K. (2017). Toward a User-Centered Approach for Emergency Warning Distribution. *Ergonomics in Design*, 25(1), 4–10. doi:10.1177/1064804616662420

Scott, R. L. (2000). Evaluation of a mobile crisis program: Effectiveness, efficiency, and consumer satisfaction. *Psychiatric Services (Washington, D.C.)*, 51(9), 1153–1156. doi:10.1176/appi.ps.51.9.1153 PMID:10970919

Sebillo, M., Vitiello, G., Paolino, L., & Ginige, A. (2016). Training emergency responders through augmented reality mobile interfaces. *Multimedia Tools and Applications*, 75(16), 9609–9622. doi:10.100711042-015-2955-0

Shah, S., Bao, F., Lu, C. T., & Chen, I. R. (2011). Crowdsafe: crowd sourcing of crime incidents and safe routing on mobile devices. In *Proceedings of the 19th ACM SIGSPATIAL International Conference on Advances in Geographic Information Systems* (pp. 521-524). ACM. 10.1145/2093973.2094064

Smith, L. (2017). Hajj 2017: Two million Muslim pilgrims from all over the world head to Mecca. *The Independent*. Retrieved March 13, 2018 from: http://www. independent.co.uk/news/world/middle-east/hajj-2017-muslim-pilgrimage-mecca-islam-pilgrims-saudi-arabia-a7917851.html

Snooks, H., Williams, S., Crouch, R., Foster, T., Hartley-Sharpe, C., & Dale, J. (2002). NHS emergency response to 999 calls: Alternatives for cases that are neither life threatening nor serious, *BMJ. British Medical Journal, 325*(7359), 330–333. doi:10.1136/bmj.325.7359.330 PMID:12169513

Suri, M., & Hofierka, J. (2004). A new GIS-based solar radiation model and its application to photovoltaic assessments. *Transactions in GIS, 8*(2), 175–190. doi:10.1111/j.1467-9671.2004.00174.x

Sutton, J., Palen, L., & Shklovski, I. (2008). Backchannels on the front lines: emergent uses of social media in the 2007 southern California wildfires. *Proceedings of the 5th International ISCRAM Conference*, 624-632.

Tapia, A. H., Giacobe, N. A., Soule, P. J., & LaLone, N. J. (2016). Scaling 911 texting for large-scale disasters: Developing practical technical innocations for emergency management at public universities. *International Journal of Public Administration in the Digital Age, 3*(3), 73–85. doi:10.4018/IJPADA.2016070105

Tashakkori, H., Rajabifard, A., & Kalantari, M. (2015). A new 3D indoor/outdoor spatial model for indoor emergency response facilitation. *Building and Environment, 89*, 170–182. doi:10.1016/j.buildenv.2015.02.036

Thompson, S., Altay, N., Green, W. G. III, & Lapetina, J. (2006). Improving disaster response efforts with decision support systems. *International Journal of Emergency Management, 3*(4), 250–263. doi:10.1504/IJEM.2006.011295

Thygerson, S. M., West, J. H., Rassbach, A. R., & Thygerson, A. L. (2012). iPhone apps for first aid: A content analysis. *Journal of Consumer Health on the Internet, 16*(2), 213–225. doi:10.1080/15398285.2012.673465

Tracy, K., & Tracy, S. J. (1998). Rudeness at 911 reconceptualizing face and face attack. *Human Communication Research, 25*(2), 225–251. doi:10.1111/j.1468-2958.1998.tb00444.x

Venable, J., Pries-Heje, J., & Baskerville, R. (2014). FEDS: A framework for evaluation in design science research. *European Journal of Information Systems*, 1–13.

Venkatesh, V. (2013). *Rankings based on AIS Senior Scholar's Basket Of Journals*, Retrieved September 27, 2014, from http://www.vvenkatesh.com/isranking/

Walls, J. G., Widmeyer, G. R., & El Sawy, O. A. (1992). Building an information system design theory for vigilant EIS. *Information Systems Research, 3*(1), 36–59. doi:10.1287/isre.3.1.36

Wang, Y., Hu, W., Wu, Y., & Cao, G. (2014). SmartPhoto: A Resource-Aware Crowdsourcing Approach for Image Sensing with Smartphones. *IEEE Transactions on Mobile Computing, 15*. doi:10.1145/2632951.2632979

Whalen, J., & Zimmerman, D. H. (1998). Observations on the display and management of emotion in naturally occurring activities: The case of hysteria in calls to 9-1-1. *Social Psychology Quarterly, 61*(2), 141–159. doi:10.2307/2787066

Winroither, E., & Kocina, E. (2014). *Donauinselfest will Gäste aus dem Ausland.* Retrieved September 27, 2014, from http://diepresse.com/home/kultur/popco/Festivals/donauinselfest/3827487/Donauinselfest-will-Gaeste-aus-dem-Ausland

Wood County 911. (2013). Retrieved September 27, 2014, from http://www.woodcounty911.com/calling.htm

Xu, H., Teo, H. H., Tan, B. C., & Agarwal, R. (2009). The role of push-pull technology in privacy calculus: The case of location-based services. *Journal of Management Information Systems, 26*(3), 135–174. doi:10.2753/MIS0742-1222260305

Yang, L., Su, G., & Yuan, H. (2012). Design principles of integrated information platform for emergency responses: The case of 2008 Beijing Olympic games. *Information Systems Research, 23*(3), 761–786. doi:10.1287/isre.1110.0387

Yeongtak, Jaehoon, & Youngjoon. (2015). Feedback algorithm for high-quality CPR based on smartphone. *Telemedicine & eHealth, 21*(1).

Yuan, Y., & Zhang, J. (2003). Towards an appropriate business model for m-commerce. *International Journal of Mobile Communications, 1*(1/2), 35–56. doi:10.1504/IJMC.2003.002459

Zapletal, B., Greif, R., Stumpf, D., Nierscher, F. J., Frantal, S., Haugk, M., ... Fischer, H. (2014). Comparing three CPR feedback devices and standard BLS in a single rescuer scenario: A randomised simulation study. *Resuscitation, 85*(4), 560–566. doi:10.1016/j.resuscitation.2013.10.028 PMID:24215730

## ADDITIONAL READING

Comfort, L. K. (2000). *Information technology and efficiency in disaster response: The Marmara, Turkey Earthquake, 17 August 1999*. Natural Hazards Center.

Kavitha, T., & Saraswathi, S. (Eds.). (2017). *Smart Technologies for Emergency Response and Disaster Management*. Hershey, PA, USA: IGI Global.

Nayak, S., & Zlatanova, S. (Eds.). (2008). *Remote sensing and GIS technologies for monitoring and prediction of disasters*. Springer Science & Business Media. doi:10.1007/978-3-540-79259-8

Potts, L. (2013). *Social media in disaster response: How experience architects can build for participation*. Routledge.

Valcik, N. A., & Tracy, P. E. (2017). *Case studies in disaster response and emergency management*. Taylor & Francis.

Van De Walle, B., Turoff, M., & Hiltz, S. R. (2014). *Information systems for emergency management*. Routledge.

Zlatanova, S., & Li, J. (Eds.). (2008). *Geospatial information technology for emergency response* (Vol. 6). Boca Raton: CRC Press.

## KEY TERMS AND DEFINITIONS

**Citizen Engagement:** Motivating and facilitating volunteers to participate in emergency response efforts.

**Geolocation:** Estimating geospatial location using collected sensor data.

**Location Analytics:** Deriving insights from geospatial data.

**PSAP:** A public-safety answering point, or call center, that dispatches police, fire, and ambulance services.

**Volunteer Expert:** A citizen that has specific knowledge or skills to support emergency response efforts, willing to provide expertise without monetary compensation.

**Volunteer First Responder:** A citizen that has been trained to respond to particular emergencies, willing to do so without monetary compensation.

# Chapter 2
# Live Video Communication in Prehospital Emergency Medicine

**Camilla Metelmann**
*Greifswald University, Germany*

**Bibiana Metelmann**
*Greifswald University, Germany*

## ABSTRACT

*Prehospital emergency medicine treats time-critical diseases and conditions and aims to reduce morbidity and mortality. The progression of emergency medicine is an important topic for governments worldwide. A problem occurs when paramedics need assistance at the emergency site by emergency doctors, who cannot be present. Video-communication in real-time from the emergency site to an emergency doctor offers an opportunity to enhance the quality of emergency medicine. The core piece of this study is a video camera system called "LiveCity camera," enabling real-time high quality video connection of paramedics and emergency doctors. The impact of video communication on emergency medicine is clearly appreciated among providers, based upon the extent of agreement that has been stated in this study's questionnaire by doctors and paramedics. This study was part of the FP7-European Union funded research project "LiveCity" (Grant Agreement No. 297291).*

DOI: 10.4018/978-1-5225-6204-7.ch002

# INTRODUCTION

Prehospital emergency medicine is a crucial part of all health care systems worldwide. The goal of emergency medicine is to treat time-critical diseases or conditions and thus reduce preventable disabilities and deaths. Citizens often judge their government by the quality of critical infrastructure regarding for instance security and emergency medicine (Hsia, Razzak, Tsai, & Hirshon, 2010; Razzak & Kellermann, 2002). One approach to further improve emergency medicine is to balance existing healthcare disparities by using telemedicine (Brokmann et al. 2015). Telemedicine are ICTs (information and communication technologies) in medicine enabling diagnostics and treatment of diseases over geographical distances (Kazley, McLeod, & Wager, 2012; WHO, 2011). Telemedicine is an important future topic as described in the "Global Observatory for eHealth" by the World Health Organization, and the implementation of telemedicine is one of the goals of the European Union (Economic and Social Committee, 2008; WHO, 2011). Telemedicine devices, using a high-definition video communication in realtime, offer the highest amount of information-transfer currently available (Metelmann & Metelmann, 2016).

This chapter is based on findings of the FP7- European Union funded research project LiveCity (Grant Agreement No. 297291). The LiveCity Project studied how high-definition video communication in real time can positively contribute to the quality of life of citizens or communities within the European Union in many different areas (Chochliouros, Stephanakis, Spiliopoulou, Sfakianakis, & Ladid, 2012; Weerakkody, El-Haddadeh, Chochliouros, & Morris, 2012). A special video camera, called "LiveCity camera" was developed to connect the different providers of emergency medicine in the European Union - the paramedics at the emergency site and a (remote) emergency doctor.

This chapter focuses on the impact of video communication on prehospital emergency medicine. In the first part the medical emergency systems worldwide and in Germany in particular are introduced, followed by a paragraph on the use of telemedicine in emergency medicine and the concept of a tele emergency doctor. In the next section the methodology of the study is described with information regarding the "LiveCity camera". A selection of results is presented. The discussion reflects on the results and how governments worldwide could benefit from implementing telemedicine in prehospital emergency medicine. Finally conclusions are drawn concerning the impact of video communication on emergency medicine.

# BACKGROUND OF STUDY

## Medical Emergency System Worldwide

Medical emergency systems are different constitutively or to some extent in every country worldwide (T. E. Callese et al., 2015). Sometimes even within one country there are different emergency systems, for example China had seven different emergency systems in 2007 (Huiyi, 2007). In some countries the urban areas can provide a higher developed system than rural areas (Vaitkaitis, 2008). And in many low- and middle-income-countries the existing emergency systems are used only insufficiently (Choi et al., 2017). To categorize the variety of systems four different types might be differentiated: (a) no organized structure, (b) basic life support, (c) advanced life support with paramedics and (d) advanced life support with physicians(Roudsari et al., 2007).

(a) Some developing countries in Sub-Saharan Africa or parts of Asia have no organized prehospital emergency system, for example Malawi (Chokotho et al., 2017). However in line with population growth, urbanization and industrialization there is an ongoing shift from infectious diseases towards medical conditions like cardiovascular diseases and vehicle accidents. Due to medical reasons this calls for a higher need of medical emergency systems (Suryanto, Plummer, & Boyle, 2017; WHO, 1996). One approach to improve the quality of emergency medicine in those countries is to teach volunteers of the community high quality first aid (Chokotho et al., 2017).

(b) Basic life support works without trained medical professionals at the emergency site and focuses on fast transport to a hospital and keeping the patient alive during transport, which is for instance the case in Kenya (Nielsen et al., 2012). Advanced life support systems in comparison work on a more sophisticated level of care at the emergency site and during the transport to a hospital, but depend upon well-educated and medically qualified providers (Roudsari et al., 2007).

(c) Advanced life support with paramedics as single providers at the emergency site is also called the Anglo-American model. It was developed in the United States of America (Wandling, Nathens, Shapiro, & Haut, 2016) and is also used e.g. in Ireland (Masterson et al., 2015), the United Kingdom (Clawson et al., 2017), Australia (Nehme, Andrew, Bernard, & Smith, 2014), Singapore (Lateef, 2006), and the Netherlands (Dib, Naderi, Sheridan, & Alagappan, 2006).

(d) Advanced life support with paramedics working together with physicians at the emergency site is called Franco-German model (Al-Shaqsi, 2010). It is for example used in Germany (Luiz, Dittrich, Pollach, & Madler, 2017), Finland (Kupari, Skrifvars, & Kuisma, 2017), Israel (Ellis & Sorene, 2008), Brazil (Timerman, Gonzalez, Zaroni, & Ramires, 2006), and in the urban areas of Lithuania (Vaitkaitis, 2008).

The main difference between the two advanced life support models is that the Anglo-American model brings the patient to the doctor and in the Franco-German model the doctor is brought to the patient (Dick, 2003).

## Medical Emergency System in Germany

The German Medical Emergency System as an example of the Franco-German model is a dual system with two partners, i.e. paramedics and emergency doctors (Harding et al., 2013). Paramedics receive a one- to three-year education in handling emergency situations (Becker, Hündorf, Kill, & Lipp, 2006). Emergency doctors are medical doctors with a special training in intensive care medicine and qualification in emergency medicine(Bundesärztekammer, 2011b).

Figure 1 shows the pathway of a patient, who experiences an emergency and alerts the medical emergency system.

The emergency call is answered by the emergency dispatcher, who will assess all relevant details. Based on that, the dispatcher will alert the paramedics and additionally an emergency doctor in cases of (potentially) life-threatening conditions. Approximately only one out of three to one out of four emergency situations require an emergency doctor (Roessler & Zuzan, 2006).

*Figure 1. Pathway of medical emergency system in Germany*

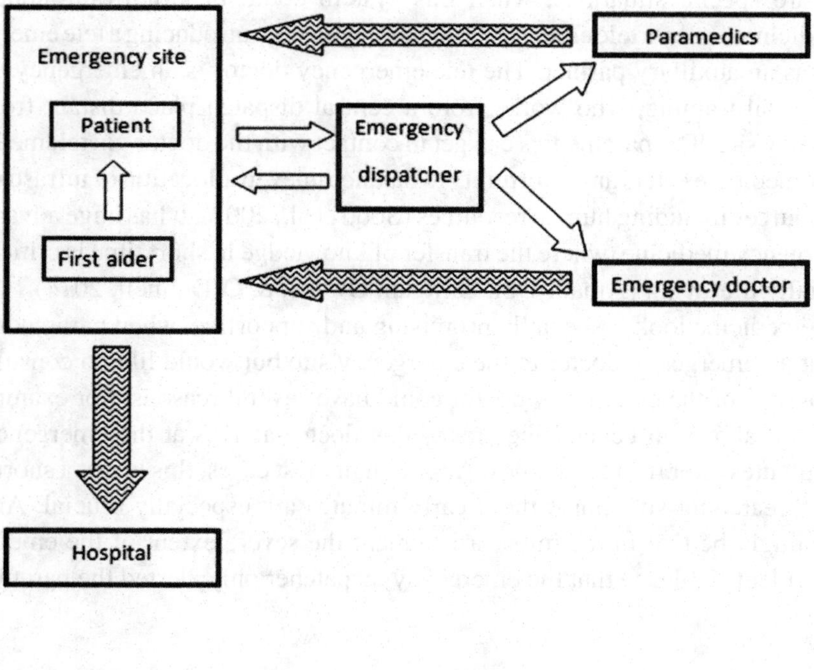

Because the paramedics are alerted in every emergency, there are more paramedics than emergency doctors. This allows a wider geographical spread of paramedics, which places the paramedics closer to potential sites of emergencies. The paramedics and the emergency doctors approach the emergency with different cars and meet only at the emergency site(DeutscherBundestag17.Wahlperiode, 2010; Schmiedel & Behrendt, 2011). This allows a high flexibility and leads to a substantial decrease in the time it takes for the first team of emergency personnel to arrive at the emergency site(Ellinger, 2011). Every federal state government in Germany is obliged by law to organize the required infrastructure for the emergency personnel to arrive within a predefined time(Becker et al., 2006; Binder, 1993). On average the paramedics in Germany arrive at the emergency site after 8.7 minutes and the emergency doctor after 12.3 minutes (Schmiedel & Behrendt, 2011).

At the emergency site doctor and paramedics establish a preliminary diagnosis and start the treatment. The treatment could be either completed at the emergency site, so that the patient can be left at home, which is the case in approximately 5% (Schmiedel & Behrendt, 2011). Or the patient has to be brought to the hospital. The transport of the patient to the hospital is done by the paramedics, often together with the emergency doctor. Once the patient is in the hospital, the hospital staff will continue the diagnostics and treatment and the paramedics and emergency doctor return to their different bases becoming available for the next emergency patient.

## Tele Emergency Doctor

There are special situations, when this system could benefit from support by telemedicine, e.g. by a tele emergency doctor. Figure 2 is introducing a tele emergency doctor as an auxiliary partner. The tele emergency doctor is an emergency doctor with special training, who works from a central dispatch place distant from the emergency site. The paramedics can get in contact with the doctor via telemedicine.

Telemedicine offers an opportunity to balance uneven allocation of infrastructure and resources including human resources (Sood et al., 2007). It has huge advantages in emergency medicine, where the transfer of knowledge in short time is critical and potentially lifesaving (Amadi-Obi, Gilligan, Owens, & O'Donnell, 2014).

Telemedicine looks especially promising and supportive, when paramedics are without an emergency doctor at the emergency site but would like to consult one. The absence of the emergency doctor could have several reasons. For example, as mentioned above, in general the emergency doctor arrives at the emergency site some minutes after the paramedics. Although in most cases, this is just a short time, in life-threatening situations, these early minutes are especially crucial. Another reason might be that in the initial assessment the severe extent of the emergency was not identifiable, so that the emergency dispatcher only alerted the paramedics.

*Figure 2. Pathway of medical emergency system in Germany with addition of a tele emergency doctor*

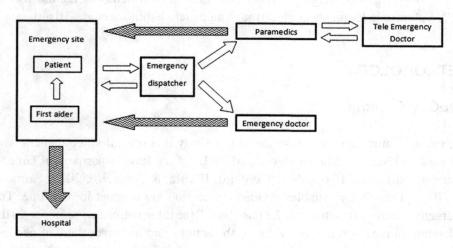

And in some emergencies the situation can worsen very quickly and unexpectedly, so that it develops into a situation, where an emergency doctor would be needed. Additionally there are emergencies, which are not life-threatening, but in which paramedics would like to have guidance by an emergency doctor. Those situations might be, for example, rare diseases or special circumstances, e.g. difficulties during pregnancy.

In all situations, in which paramedics are without an emergency doctor at the emergency site, but would like to consult one, telemedicine might be the solution. The prerequisite for that is that there is a real time connection for live communication between the paramedics and the tele emergency doctor.

For this contact to be efficient, helpful and according to legal regulations in medicine, the distant consultation has to transport more information than a mere telephone call can perform. The "Model Professional Code for Physicians in Germany" obligates physicians to an individual and direct treatment of patients also in telemedicine(Bundesärztekammer, 2011a; Katzenmeier & Schrag-Slavu, 2010).

Several different concepts of tele emergency doctors are currently under study or already implemented. One example is Telenotarzt in Aachen, Germany, where an ambulance car is equipped with a video camera, which sends high-definition videos in real-time to the tele emergency doctor. This concept was implemented as part of the medical emergency system in the city of Aachen in April 2014 (Felzen et al., 2016)(Brokmann et al. 2016a; Brokmann et al. 2016b; Brokmann et al. 2017a; Brokmann et al. 2017b)(Stevanovic et al. 2017). Based on these findings the tele emergency concept will be implemented and further analyzed within the project

Land|Rettung in the northern part of Germany. Another progressive project is PreSSUB in Brussels, Belgium (Yperzeele et al. 2014; Valenzuela Espinoza et al. 2017; Valenzuela Espinoza et al. 2016a; Valenzuela Espinoza et al. 2016b).

## METHODOLOGY

### LiveCity Camera

The central communicational device in this study is a special video camera with software and hardware newly developed by LiveCity Project-partners in Greece, Portugal and Ireland (Goncalves, Cordeiro, Batista, & Monteiro, 2012; Palma et al., 2013). This camera enables a video connection via internet in real time. The emergency doctor gives instructions based on all the information he got, observes the realization of the instructions, evaluates the actions and improves them, if needed. Hence a time lag is a huge hindrance and can result in such a poor communication, that no meaningful assistance by the emergency doctor is possible. At the same time the high legal standards regarding data security have to be met.

The LiveCity camera as shown in figure 3 consists of the video-camera itself, worn with a headband above the right ear, a headphone with mouthpiece to enable audio connection in both ways and a microPC, which builds the internet connection. The position of the camera above the right ear was chosen to transmit the same perspective the paramedic has to the emergency doctor. The transmitted video is dynamic and follows the head movements of the paramedics. One major advantage of the position of the camera is also, that the paramedic still has both hands free to work.

### Software of the LiveCity Camera

The transmitted video is received by the remote emergency doctor at a laptop provided with special software (Figure 4). This software allows the emergency doctor to adapt the transmitted video according to the particular needs, e.g. regarding light, contrast and sound level. A snapshot can be taken by the emergency doctor at any time and is a high definition photo transmitted independently from the video. Because of the high pixel count it allows the emergency doctor to analyze for instance a 12-lead-ECG in detail, where tiny elevations of lines can indicate a myocardial infarction. Because the interpretation of 12-lead-ECG is sometimes very challenging and needs a lot of experience, some authors state, that physicians have a higher success rate in detecting e.g. a heart attack than paramedics have (D. P. Davis et al., 2007).

*Figure 3. The LiveCity camera worn by a paramedic*

*Figure 4. Tele emergency doctor observing emergency site via LiveCity camera*

## Study Design

The aim of the study was to assess the impact of video communication on emergency medicine. The benefit of paramedics consulting a tele emergency doctor by use of the LiveCity camera was investigated in terms of professional work flow and outcome. To prevent potential harm for individuals the study was performed in the fully equipped medical simulation center of the Department of Anesthesiology at Greifswald University Medicine (Figure 5). A medical simulation center creates dynamic realistic routine or emergency scenarios with aid of computer-operated mannequins (Johannsson, Ayida, & Sadler, 2005). It is widely used in medicine for educational and research purposes (Cannon-Diehl, 2009; Kyle & Murray, 2010; Levine, DeMaria, Schwartz, & Sim, 2013).

To evaluate the co-operation of paramedics and doctors close to reality, ten typical emergency scenarios from five different categories were standardized and structured for a randomized two-armed protocol. These categories are: "Trauma", "Heart attack", "Stroke", "Rare diseases" and "Complications during pregnancy". For each category two cases with similar level of difficulty in terms of diagnosis and treatment were created to allow a cross-over design. Cross-over design was achieved by comparing the results and opinions of paramedics in action at the

*Figure 5. Paramedics at the emergency site treating a "patient" in the simulation center by use of LiveCity camera*

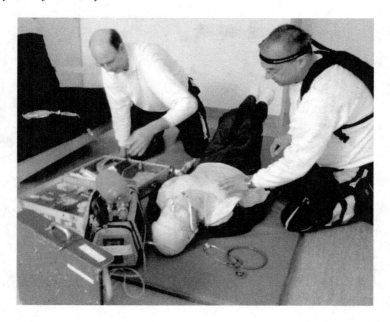

simulated emergency site: (a) *without* doctor´s support and (b) the same paramedics in corresponding cases another time *with* video-based consultation and contact to a tele emergency doctor. According to usual guidelines in German emergency medicine two paramedics worked together as a team. The sequence of the case scenarios and the assignment to the two cross-over categories was randomized.

To assess the outcome in practical, technical and psychological aspects, paramedics and doctors were interviewed by use of structured questionnaires developed together with the Department for Medical Psychology, Greifswald University Medicine.

## RESULTS

10 emergency doctors and 21 paramedics took part in a total of 110 simulated emergency scenarios. All participants (n =31) accomplished every scenario and completed all questionnaires. These are the results of the investigation in terms of "disagree", "partly disagree", "partly agree" or "agree" (ranked on a 4-point Likert scale) or concerning "yes" or "no" questions in the following sentences of the questionnaires:

"The scenarios were realistic."

Considering the total number of 10 emergency doctors, 1 partly disagreed, 5 partly agreed, 4 agreed. Considering the total number of 21 paramedics, 1 partly disagreed, 11 partly agreed and 9 agreed. No emergency doctor or paramedic disagreed (Table 1).

"The scenarios were relevant."

Considering the total number of 10 emergency doctors, 3 partly agreed, 7 agreed. Considering the total number of 21 paramedics, 7 partly agreed,14 agreed. No emergency doctor or paramedic disagreed or partly disagreed (Table 2).

"What kind of support would you especially like to get in an emergency situation?"

The paramedics were asked to choose between "help with practical and manual skills" or "help with diagnostics and treatment". 6 of 21 paramedics wished for practical or manual help. 13 of 21 paramedics wished for help with diagnostics and treatment. 2 paramedics could not decide (Table 3).

"I consider the tele emergency doctor as helpful."

*Table 1.*

|  | Agree | Partly agree | Partly disagree | Disagree |
|---|---|---|---|---|
| Doctors (10) | 4 | 5 | 1 | 0 |
| Paramedics (21) | 9 | 11 | 1 | 0 |

*Table 2.*

|  | **Agree** | **Partly agree** | **Partly disagree** | **Disagree** |
|---|---|---|---|---|
| *Doctors (10)* | 7 | 3 | 0 | 0 |
| *Paramedics (21)* | 14 | 7 | 0 | 0 |

*Table 3.*

|  | **Diagnostics/Treatment** | **Practical/Manual** | **undecided** |
|---|---|---|---|
| Paramedics (21) | 13 | 6 | 2 |

Considering the total number of 21 paramedics, 6 partly agreed and 15 agreed. No paramedic disagreed or partly disagreed (Table 4).

"Would you call a tele emergency doctor in cases you wouldn't normally call an emergency doctor?"

Considering the total number of 21 paramedics, 14 answered "yes" and 7 answered "no" (Table 5).

"A tele emergency doctor improves the quality of patient care."

Considering the total number of 10 emergency doctors, 7 partly agreed and 3 agreed. Considering the total number of 21 paramedics, 8 partly agreed and 13 agreed. No emergency doctor or paramedic disagreed or partly disagreed (Table 6).

"I perceive that the tele emergency doctor leads to a faster start of the therapy."

Considering the total number of 10 emergency doctors, 9 agreed (3 fully and 6 partly). 1 doctor disagreed partly, but no one to full extent. Of the paramedics, 20 of 21 agreed, in comparison more fully (11) than partly (9). 1 paramedic partly disagreed (Table 7).

"Is transmission of the vital signs without audio or video connection sufficient?"

Only emergency doctors were asked, 8 of 10answered "no" and 2 of 10 "yes" (Table 8).

"Is transmission of the vital signs with additional audio connection sufficient?"

Again only emergency doctors were asked, and again 8 of 10 answered "no" and 2 of 10 "yes" (Table 9).

"I can imagine working in a tele emergency doctor system."

Of the emergency doctors 9 of 10 agreed to the summarizing sentence of the study, 4 to full extent and 5 partly. Among the paramedics 16 of 21 agreed and 4 of 21 partly agreed. 1 paramedic and 1 emergency doctor partly disagreed (Table 10).

*Table 4.*

|  | Agree | Partly agree | Partly disagree | Disagree |
|---|---|---|---|---|
| Paramedics (21) | 15 | 6 | 0 | 0 |

*Table 5.*

|  | Yes | No |
|---|---|---|
| Paramedics (21) | 14 | 7 |

*Table 6.*

|  | Agree | Partly agree | Partly disagree | Disagree |
|---|---|---|---|---|
| Doctors (10) | 3 | 7 | 0 | 0 |
| Paramedics (21) | 13 | 8 | 0 | 0 |

*Table 7.*

|  | Agree | Partly agree | Partly disagree | Disagree |
|---|---|---|---|---|
| Doctors (10) | 3 | 6 | 1 | 0 |
| Paramedics (21) | 9 | 11 | 1 | 0 |

*Table 8.*

|  | Yes | No |
|---|---|---|
| Doctors (10) | 2 | 8 |

*Table 9.*

|  | Yes | No |
|---|---|---|
| Doctors (10) | 2 | 8 |

*Table 10.*

|  | Agree | Partly agree | Partly disagree | Disagree |
|---|---|---|---|---|
| Doctors (10) | 4 | 5 | 1 | 0 |
| Paramedics (21) | 16 | 4 | 1 | 0 |

## DISCUSSION

The impact of video communication on emergency medicine is very welcome among providers, based upon the amount of agreement of paramedics and emergency doctors in this study to a video-based consultation at the emergency site. This is an approach to increase quality of emergency treatment by applying telemedicine. The core piece of the concept is a special video camera, called LiveCity camera.

### External Validity of the Study

As Ammenwerth and coworkers have explained, there are three ways of testing a new health information technology. The first way is to evaluate it in a laboratory. But the results are limited by a low external validity. The second way is a field evaluation test, but for this both software and hardware have to be sufficiently mature to not possibly harm any person. So the solution is often the middle way: a simulation study, which combines good internal and external validity (Ammenwerth et al., 2012).

Simulation studies offer the opportunity to conduct experimental cross-over trials with high internal validity. The external validity depends on how realistic the simulated scenarios are. The perception of how realistic a scenario in a simulation center is, is influenced by three different aspects: the equipment fidelity, the environment fidelity and the psychological fidelity(Fritz, Gray, & Flanagan, 2008). The equipment fidelity is characterized by the used hard- and software. In the LiveCity Project the Laerdal mannequin Resusci Anne was used and the vital signs were dynamically simulated with the monitor iSimulate. The environment fidelity is mostly created by the appropriate surrounding for every scenario. In the LiveCity Project every scenario had different characteristic accessories, e.g. in one case of simulated heart attack a patient was watching sports sitting on a sofa with a football flag while eating potato crisps. Psychological fidelity is the ability of the individual participant to immerse into the simulated situation. Psychological fidelity can be increased by enhancing equipment and environment fidelity (Bauman, 2013).

After finishing all scenarios all participants were asked, if they perceived the simulated cases as realistic. The majority of both emergency doctors and paramedics rated the scenarios as realistic. Thus, the possibility of the participants behaving in the study environment similar to their normal behavior is high. This implies a good external validity.

## Relevance of the Selected Medical Emergencies

Furthermore, all emergency doctors and paramedics partly agreed or agreed that the chosen scenarios were relevant. This is also an indicator for a good external validity. To reflect the broad spectrum of emergencies, different scenarios were developed. The categories "Trauma", "Heart attack" and "Stroke" were chosen, because they belong to the "First Hour Quintet". This term was coined by the sixth European Resuscitation Council Meeting in Florence, Italy in 2002 and describes five emergencies, which are life-threatening diseases in which a fast treatment reduces morbidity and mortality (Krafft et al., 2003; Nilsen, 2012). Worldwide they belonged to the group of top 10 leading causes of death in 2004 and prognosis for 2030 predict them to be within the top 5 leading causes of death worldwide (WHO, 2010). Thus there are many approaches to improve the therapy, e.g. by telemedicine. The implementation of telemedicine in stroke treatment was recommended by the American Heart Association and American Stroke Association in 2009 (Schwamm et al., 2009). "Rare diseases" and "Complications during pregnancy" are a special challenge in medicine. Often there are no standard operating procedures and the paramedics might not have encountered a similar situation before, which increases the stress level. Another aspect in pregnancy is that the unborn child has to be considered, too e.g. in the application of drugs to manage the emergency. Therefore a video consultation of a tele emergency doctor might be helpful.

Since all paramedics and emergency doctors confirmed that the chosen scenarios were realistic and relevant, the simulation appears to be a suitable model and the findings of the LiveCity study might – at least partly – be transmitted from the simulation center into the existing medical emergency system.

## Wish for Telemedical Support

To further assess the need for a tele emergency doctor, the paramedics, were asked, what kind of support they usually would like to get in a "normal" emergency. More than 2/3 of all paramedics answered, that they would want assistance in diagnostics and therapy. Because telemedicine enables the transfer of knowledge, this is the main area, where the tele emergency doctor can support.

One of the main purposes of the tele emergency doctor concept is that the emergency doctor supports and helps the paramedics at the emergency site by providing expertise (Czaplik et al., 2014). After completing all 10 scenarios in the LiveCity Project, all paramedics rated the tele emergency doctor as helpful. Hence they confirmed that knowledge can be transferred via telemedicine to the emergency site. This concept of the tele-consultation via video might be also expanded into other fields of emergency medicine. For example emergency doctors with limited experience, who are at the emergency site, might want to get support by a more experienced emergency doctor. Since some emergencies only occur rarely, the young emergency doctor might not have encountered a similar situation before (Gries, Zink, Bernhard, Messelken, & Schlechtriemen, 2006). And young emergency doctors often have a huge awareness of the responsibility they have and feel the difference between working in a hospital, where help by senior doctors is within reach and being the only doctor at the emergency site (Groos, 2011). Thus the young emergency doctor might also perceive an experienced tele emergency doctor as helpful.

Another advantage of the tele emergency doctor is that support by an emergency doctor is easily accessible without the expensive mobilization of many resources. Additionally this tele emergency support starts without time delay the moment the telemedicine connection is built. In the current German medical emergency system, the paramedic calls the emergency dispatcher, who then alerts the emergency doctor. The "normal" emergency doctor would now start to travel to the emergency site. This whole procedure takes some time, which directly leads to a later start of transport to the hospital. As explained earlier, this time difference could be crucial. Thus paramedics are more likely, to call an emergency doctor. This would presumable lead to a higher quality of emergency medicine.

## Impact on Quality of Patient Care

Paramedics and emergency doctors were asked to rank the impact of a tele emergency doctor on the quality of patient care. All participants agreed or partly agreed that the tele emergency doctor improves the quality of patient care. Bashshur stated in 2002, that telemedicine has the potential to solve the existing problems in geographical differences in access to high standard medical care and might balance the uneven quality of care (Bashshur, 2002).So the improvement of patient care by the tele emergency doctor might be also used to enhance quality of diagnostics and therapies in geographical areas, where a high standard couldn't be achieved before. It would be very interesting to test the concept of a tele emergency doctor in countries outside of the European Union as well, which have not the medical emergency system of "advanced life support", but "basic life support" or "no organized structure". In these systems the transfer of expertise is even more important and can increase the quality of patient care immensely. Roughly 90% of all trauma-related death worldwide occur in low- and middle-income countries (Debenham, Fuller, Stewart, & Price, 2017). In these countries most trauma-related fatalities happen in the prehospital phase and some could be preventable through appropriate prehospital care (Anand, Singh, &

Kapoor, 2013). The World Health Organization has published a manual in 2005 how prehospital trauma care management worldwide could be improved(Sasser, Varghese, Kellermann, & Lormand, 2005). One concept for countries without an organized medical emergency system or with a low-grade medical emergency system was to teach volunteer citizens principles of basic life support. These volunteers could then work together to improve the prehospital care. One of the problems in teaching laypersons, who had not received a medical education before, is the low level of literacy(Tyler E. Callese et al., 2014). Therefore there is a need for special curricula, which uses the existing resources. A review by Callese and coworkers showed that trained volunteers can reduce the mortality after trauma. If the volunteers could get help by a remote emergency doctor via telemedicine, this could lead to an even higher increase in quality of care.

As mentioned above, rapid start of treatment in an emergency is crucial. It is also often used as an indicator for the quality of the medical emergency system (DeutscherBundestag17.Wahlperiode, 2010). One demand on telemedicine therefore is to not delay the therapy. As Rogers and coworkers presented, the implementation of a tele emergency doctor can decrease the time to start of therapy (Rogers et al., 2017). In the development of the LiveCity camera huge emphasis was put on reducing the time needed to build the connectivity. After working with the LiveCity camera the majority of paramedics and emergency doctors partly agreed or agreed that they perceived, that this tele emergency doctor concept leads to an earlier start of therapy. It can be concluded for the LiveCity camera that the early availability of medical expertise regarding diagnostics and therapy leads to such an early start of therapy, that it can outbalance any delay due to technical reasons.

## SPECIFIC CHALLENGES

As a consequence, one might argue, that reducing the technical complexity to a minimum might lead to a faster data transmission and thus to an earlier start of therapy. Additionally a complex system is often more failure-prone and requires a more stable and superior internet connection. To assess the possibility to eliminate expandable features, the emergency doctors were consulted, what information was necessary to evaluate the specific emergency situation. 80% of emergency doctors stated, that the sole transmission of vital signs (blood pressure, heart rate, oxygen saturation) would not have been enough. And even the addition of an audio connection would have not been enough for 80% of the emergency doctors to sufficiently treat the emergency patient. This means, that the telemedicine devise also needs to transmit video to enable the tele emergency doctor to successfully support the paramedics.

Despite great promises of telemedicine, the implementation of telemedicine projects into the existing medical systems is a huge challenge (Iakovidis, Maglavera, & Trakatellis, 2000; Zailani, Gilani, Nikbin, & Iranmanesh, 2014). Some very promising telemedicine projects were not as widely implemented as expected (Bont und Bal 2008). The reason for that is studied worldwide and several "enablers", e.g. well-working technology and training of the users, as well as "barriers", e.g. technical problems and lack of technical support, were discussed (Wade, Eliott, & Hiller, 2014). One main factor for successful implementation of telemedicine is a good acceptance of the idea and device by the users, e.g. doctors (Rho, Choi, & Lee, 2014). (Brewster et al. 2014). Wade and coworkers stated that acceptance by clinicians is the most important key factor and that if clinicians supported the telemedicine project, various technical problems were tolerated (Wade et al., 2014). The technology acceptance model (TAM) by Davis was applied to telemedicine and it could be shown that both the perceived usefulness and the perceived ease of use are significantly associated with the intention to use the system (F. D. Davis, 1989; Dünnebeil, Sunyaev, Blohm, Leimeister, & Krcmar, 2012; Kowitlawakul, 2011; Rho et al., 2014). In the LiveCity Project an impressive majority of emergency doctors and paramedics agreed, that they could imagine working in a tele emergency doctor system.

## FUTURE OUTLOOK

This concept to transfer knowledge in real time through video communication to distant places can improve the quality of medical emergency systems. With the arrival of the first members of the medical emergency team at the emergency site, a high quality in diagnostics and treatment can be achieved. This leads to an earlier beginning of high quality medicine. Polls among citizens showed that the timely access to high quality medical care was rated as the most important quality feature of a health care system (Soroka, 2007). The perceived achievement of this goal, influences the appraisal of the current government and the wish for political change (Soroka, 2007). It is essential, that the implementation of telemedicine in prehospital emergency medicine is in direct collaboration with the government. In the German county Vorpommern-Greifswald the project Land|Rettung introduces a tele emergency doctor into the existing emergency system. The project is coordinated by the county government. There will be a scientific evaluation of medical, economically and organizational aspects to allow a transferability to other counties and regions.

To achieve the highest benefit of a video consultation in emergency medicine, policy makers worldwide should adapt the concept according to the existing medical emergency system of their specific country.

# CONCLUSION

A common problem in emergency medicine worldwide is the lack of support by emergency doctors, when paramedics are at the emergency site without emergency doctors but need their assistance or back up. This chapter shows aim an approach to increase quality of emergency treatment by applying telemedicine. The core piece is a video camera system, enabling real time connection of paramedics and emergency doctors by high quality video. Emergency doctors and paramedics tested the work flow and outcome of this kind of communication in a medical simulation center with aid of computer-operated mannequins.

A structured questionnaire confirmed that, the majority of paramedics and emergency doctors considered the tele emergency doctor system (i) as helpful and (ii) an improvement regarding quality of patient care and could (iii) imagine working in a tele emergency doctor system. The impact of video communication on emergency medicine is clearly appreciated among providers, based upon the extent of agreement that has been stated in this study by doctors and paramedics. Thus, the concept of a video consultation of an emergency doctor is a good addition to the existing medical emergency system in Germany and the idea could be integrated into other medical emergency systems worldwide as well to enhance the quality of emergency medicine. Governments and policy makers play an integral role in introducing the benefits of live video communication in prehospital emergency medicine to their specific medical systems.

# ACKNOWLEDGMENT

The present article has been structured in the context of the LiveCity ("Live Video-to-Video Supporting Interactive City Infrastructure") European Research Project and has been supported by the Commission of the European Communities - DG CONNECT (FP7-ICT-PSP, Grant Agreement No.297291).

# REFERENCES

Al-Shaqsi, S. (2010). Models of International Emergency Medical Service (EMS) Systems. *Oman Medical Journal*, *25*(4), 320–323. doi:10.5001/omj.2010.92 PMID:22043368

Amadi-Obi, A., Gilligan, P., Owens, N., & O'Donnell, C. (2014). Telemedicine in pre-hospital care: A review of telemedicine applications in the pre-hospital environment. *International Journal of Emergency Medicine*, *7*(1), 29. doi:10.118612245-014-0029-0 PMID:25635190

Ammenwerth, E., Hackl, W. O., Binzer, K., Christoffersen, T. E., Jensen, S., Lawton, K., ... Nohr, C. (2012). Simulation studies for the evaluation of health information technologies: Experiences and results. *The HIM Journal*, *41*(2), 14–21. doi:10.1177/183335831204100202 PMID:22700558

Anand, L. K., Singh, M., & Kapoor, D. (2013). Prehospital trauma care services in developing countries. *Anaesthesia, Pain & Intensive Care*, *17*(1), 65.

Bashshur, R. L. (2002). Chapter 1: Telemedicine and health care. *Telemedicine Journal and e-Health*, *8*(1), 5–12. doi:10.1089/15305620252933365 PMID:12020402

Bauman, E. B. (2013). *Game-based Teaching and Simulation in Nursing and Healthcare*. Springer Publishing Company.

Becker, J., Hündorf, H-P., Kill, C., & Lipp, R. (2006). *Lexikon Rettungsdienst*. Stumpf + Kossendey Verlag.

Binder, G. (1993). *Hilfsfrist. In Rechtsbegriffe in der Notfallmedizin* (pp. 38–38). Springer Berlin Heidelberg. doi:10.1007/978-3-642-52350-2_38

Bundesärztekammer. (2011). *Übersicht Notarztqualifikation in Deutschland*. Retrieved from www.bundesaerztekammer.de

Callese, T. E., Richards, C. T., Shaw, P., Schuetz, S. J., Issa, N., Paladino, L., & Swaroop, M. (2014). Layperson trauma training in low- and middle-income countries: A review. *The Journal of Surgical Research*, *190*(1), 104–110. doi:10.1016/j.jss.2014.03.029 PMID:24746252

Callese, T. E., Richards, C. T., Shaw, P., Schuetz, S. J., Paladino, L., Issa, N., & Swaroop, M. (2015). Trauma system development in low- and middle-income countries: A review. *The Journal of Surgical Research*, *193*(1), 300–307. doi:10.1016/j.jss.2014.09.040 PMID:25450600

Cannon-Diehl, M. R. (2009). Simulation in healthcare and nursing: State of the science. *Critical Care Nursing Quarterly*, *32*(2), 128–136. doi:10.1097/CNQ.0b013e3181a27e0f PMID:19300077

Chochliouros, I., Stephanakis, I., Spiliopoulou, A., Sfakianakis, E., & Ladid, L. (2012). Developing Innovative Live Video-to-Video Communications for Smarter European Cities. In L. Iliadis, I. Maglogiannis, H. Papadopoulos, K. Karatzas, & S. Sioutas (Eds.), *Artificial Intelligence Applications and Innovations* (Vol. 382, pp. 279–289). Springer Berlin Heidelberg. doi:10.1007/978-3-642-33412-2_29

Choi, S. J., Oh, M. Y., Kim, N. R., Jung, Y. J., Ro, Y. S., & Shin, S. D. (2017). Comparison of trauma care systems in Asian countries: A systematic literature review. *Emergency Medicine Australasia*, *29*(6), 697–711. doi:10.1111/1742-6723.12840 PMID:28782875

Chokotho, L., Mulwafu, W., Singini, I., Njalale, Y., Maliwichi-Senganimalunje, L., & Jacobsen, K. H. (2017). First Responders and Prehospital Care for Road Traffic Injuries in Malawi. *Prehospital and Disaster Medicine*, *32*(1), 14–19. doi:10.1017/S1049023X16001175 PMID:27923422

Clawson, J. J., Gardett, I., Scott, G., Fivaz, C., Barron, T., Broadbent, M., & Olola, C. (2017). Hospital-Confirmed Acute Myocardial Infarction: Prehospital Identification Using the Medical Priority Dispatch System. *Prehospital and Disaster Medicine*, 1–7. doi:10.10171049023x1700704x PMID:29223194

Czaplik, M., Bergrath, S., Rossaint, R., Thelen, S., Brodziak, T., Valentin, B., ... Brokmann, J. C. (2014). Employment of telemedicine in emergency medicine. Clinical requirement analysis, system development and first test results. *Methods of Information in Medicine*, *53*(2), 99–107. doi:10.3414/ME13-01-0022 PMID:24477815

Davis, D. P., Graydon, C., Stein, R., Wilson, S., Buesch, B., Berthiaume, S., ... Leahy, D. R. (2007). The positive predictive value of paramedic versus emergency physician interpretation of the prehospital 12-lead electrocardiogram. *Prehospital Emergency Care*, *11*(4), 399–402. doi:10.1080/10903120701536784 PMID:17907023

Davis, F. D. (1989). Perceived Usefulness, Perceived Ease of Use, and User Acceptance of Information Technology. *Management Information Systems Quarterly*, *13*(3), 319–340. doi:10.2307/249008

Debenham, S., Fuller, M., Stewart, M., & Price, R. R. (2017). Where There is No EMS: Lay Providers in Emergency Medical Services Care - EMS as a Public Health Priority. *Prehospital and Disaster Medicine*, *32*(6), 593–595. doi:10.1017/S1049023X17006811 PMID:28797317

DeutscherBundestag17.Wahlperiode.(2010). *Bericht über Maßnahmen auf dem Gebiet der Unfallverhütung im Straßenverkehr 2008 und 2009 (Unfallverhütungsbericht Straßenverkehr 2008/2009)*. Author.

Dib, J. E., Naderi, S., Sheridan, I. A., & Alagappan, K. (2006). Analysis and applicability of the Dutch EMS system into countries developing EMS systems. *The Journal of Emergency Medicine*, *30*(1), 111–115. doi:10.1016/j.jemermed.2005.05.014 PMID:16434351

Dick, W. F. (2003). Anglo-American vs. Franco-German emergency medical services system. *Prehosp Disaster Med, 18*(1), 29-35.

Dünnebeil, S., Sunyaev, A., Blohm, I., Leimeister, J. M., & Krcmar, H. (2012). Determinants of physicians' technology acceptance for e-health in ambulatory care. *International Journal of Medical Informatics, 81*(11), 746–760. doi:10.1016/j.ijmedinf.2012.02.002 PMID:22397989

Economic and Social Committee, Section for Transport, Energy, Infrastructure and the Information Society. (2008). Opinion of the European Economic and Social Committee on the Communication from the Commission to the European Parliament, the Council, the European Economic and Social Committee and the Committee of the Regions on telemedicine for the benefit of patients, healthcare systems and society COM(2008) 689 final. Brussels: Author.

Ellinger, K. (2011). *Kursbuch Notfallmedizin: orientiert am bundeseinheitlichen Curriculum Zusatzbezeichnung Notfallmedizin*. Dt. Ärzte-Verlag.

Ellis, D. Y., & Sorene, E. (2008). Magen David Adom—The EMS in Israel. *Resuscitation, 76*(1), 5–10. doi:10.1016/j.resuscitation.2007.07.014 PMID:17767990

Felzen, M., Brokmann, J. C., Beckers, S. K., Czaplik, M., Hirsch, F., Tamm, M., ... Bergrath, S. (2016). Improved technical performance of a multifunctional prehospital telemedicine system between the research phase and the routine use phase - an observational study. *Journal of Telemedicine and Telecare*. doi:10.1177/1357633x16644115 PMID:27080747

Fritz, P. Z., Gray, T., & Flanagan, B. (2008). Review of mannequin-based high-fidelity simulation in emergency medicine. *Emergency Medicine Australasia, 20*(1), 1–9. doi:10.1111/j.1742-6723.2007.01022.x PMID:17999685

Goncalves, J., Cordeiro, L., Batista, P., & Monteiro, E. (2012). LiveCity: A Secure Live Video-to-Video Interactive City Infrastructure. In L. Iliadis, I. Maglogiannis, H. Papadopoulos, K. Karatzas, & S. Sioutas (Eds.), *Artificial Intelligence Applications and Innovations* (Vol. 382, pp. 260–267). Springer Berlin Heidelberg. doi:10.1007/978-3-642-33412-2_27

Gries, A., Zink, W., Bernhard, M., Messelken, M., & Schlechtriemen, T. (2006). Realistic assessment of the physican-staffed emergency services in Germany. *Der Anaesthesist*, *55*(10), 1080–1086. doi:10.100700101-006-1051-2 PMID:16791544

Groos, H. (2011). *Du musst die Menschen lieben: Als Ärztin im Rettungswagen, auf der Intensivstation und im Krieg*. Fischer E-Books.

Harding, U., Lechleuthner, A., Ritter, M. A., Schilling, M., Kros, M., Ohms, M., & Bohn, A. (2013). „Schlaganfall immer mit Notarzt?" – „Pro". *Medizinische Klinik, Intensivmedizin und Notfallmedizin*, *108*(5), 408–411. doi:10.100700063-012-0137-7 PMID:23010854

Hsia, R., Razzak, J., Tsai, A. C., & Hirshon, J. M. (2010). Placing emergency care on the global agenda. *Annals of Emergency Medicine*, *56*(2), 142–149. doi:10.1016/j.annemergmed.2010.01.013 PMID:20138398

Huiyi, T. (2007). *A Study on Prehospital Emergency Medical Service System Status in Guangzhou*. Hong Kong: University of Hong Kong.

Iakovidis, I., Maglavera, S., & Trakatellis, A. (2000). *User Acceptance of Health Telematics Applications: Education and Training in Health Telematics*. IOS Press.

Johannsson, H., Ayida, G., & Sadler, C. (2005). Faking it? Simulation in the training of obstetricians and gynaecologists. *Current Opinion in Obstetrics & Gynecology*, *17*(6), 557–561. doi:10.1097/01.gco.0000188726.45998.97 PMID:16258334

Katzenmeier, C., & Schrag-Slavu, S. (2010). *Einführung. In Rechtsfragen des Einsatzes der Telemedizin im Rettungsdienst* (Vol. 2, pp. 1–22). Springer Berlin Heidelberg. doi:10.1007/978-3-540-85132-5_1

Kazley, A. S., McLeod, A. C., & Wager, K. A. (2012). Telemedicine in an international context: Definition, use, and future. *Advances in Health Care Management*, *12*, 143–169. doi:10.1108/S1474-8231(2012)0000012011 PMID:22894049

Kowitlawakul, Y. (2011). The technology acceptance model: Predicting nurses' intention to use telemedicine technology (eICU). *Computers, Informatics, Nursing*, *29*(7), 411–418. doi:10.1097/NCN.0b013e3181f9dd4a PMID:20975536

Krafft, T., Garcia Castrillo-Riesgo, L., Edwards, S., Fischer, M., Overton, J., Robertson-Steel, I., & Konig, A. (2003). European Emergency Data Project (EED Project): EMS data-based health surveillance system. *European Journal of Public Health*, *13*(3Suppl), 85–90. doi:10.1093/eurpub/13.suppl_1.85 PMID:14533755

Kupari, P., Skrifvars, M., & Kuisma, M. (2017). External validation of the ROSC after cardiac arrest (RACA) score in a physician staffed emergency medical service system. *Scandinavian Journal of Trauma, Resuscitation and Emergency Medicine*, *25*(1), 34. doi:10.118613049-017-0380-2 PMID:28356134

Kyle, R., & Murray, W. B. (2010). *Clinical Simulation*. Elsevier Science.

Lateef, F. (2006). The emergency medical services in Singapore. *Resuscitation*, *68*(3), 323–328. doi:10.1016/j.resuscitation.2005.12.007 PMID:16503277

Levine, A. I., DeMaria, S., Schwartz, A. D., & Sim, A. J. (2013). *The Comprehensive Textbook of Healthcare Simulation*. Springer. doi:10.1007/978-1-4614-5993-4

Luiz, T., Dittrich, S., Pollach, G., & Madler, C. (2017). Kenntnisstand der Bevölkerung über Leitsymptome kardiovaskulärer Notfälle und Zuständigkeit und Erreichbarkeit von Notrufeinrichtungen. *Der Anaesthesist*, *66*(11), 840–849. doi:10.100700101-017-0367-4 PMID:29046934

Masterson, S., Wright, P., O'Donnell, C., Vellinga, A., Murphy, A. W., Hennelly, D., ... Deasy, C. (2015). Urban and rural differences in out-of-hospital cardiac arrest in Ireland. *Resuscitation*, *91*, 42–47. doi:10.1016/j.resuscitation.2015.03.012 PMID:25818707

Metelmann, B., & Metelmann, C. (2016). M-Health in Prehospital Emergency Medicine: Experiences from the EU funded Project LiveCity. In M. Anastasius (Ed.), *M-Health Innovations for Patient-Centered Care* (pp. 197–212). Hershey, PA: IGI Global. doi:10.4018/978-1-4666-9861-1.ch010

Nehme, Z., Andrew, E., Bernard, S., & Smith, K. (2014). The impact of partial resuscitation attempts on the reported outcomes of out-of-hospital cardiac arrest in Victoria, Australia: Implications for Utstein-style outcome reports. *Resuscitation*, *85*(9), 1185–1191. doi:10.1016/j.resuscitation.2014.05.032 PMID:24914831

Nielsen, K., Mock, C., Joshipura, M., Rubiano, A. M., Zakariah, A., & Rivara, F. (2012). Assessment of the Status of Prehospital Care in 13 Low- and Middle-Income Countries. *Prehospital Emergency Care*, *16*(3), 381–389. doi:10.3109/10903127.2012.664245 PMID:22490009

Nilsen, J. E. (2012). *Improving quality of care in the Emergency Medical Communication Centres (EMCC)*. Paper presented at the Konferanse for medisinsk nødmeldetjeneste, Sola, Norway.

Palma, D., Goncalves, J., Cordeiro, L., Simoes, P., Monteiro, E., Magdalinos, P., & Chochliouros, I. (2013). Tutamen: An Integrated Personal Mobile and Adaptable Video Platform for Health and Protection. In H. Papadopoulos, A. Andreou, L. Iliadis, & I. Maglogiannis (Eds.), *Artificial Intelligence Applications and Innovations* (Vol. 412, pp. 442–451). Springer Berlin Heidelberg. doi:10.1007/978-3-642-41142-7_45

Razzak, J. A., & Kellermann, A. L. (2002). Emergency medical care in developing countries: Is it worthwhile? *Bulletin of the World Health Organization*, *80*(11), 900–905. PMID:12481213

Rho, M. J., Choi, I. Y., & Lee, J. (2014). Predictive factors of telemedicine service acceptance and behavioral intention of physicians. *International Journal of Medical Informatics*, *83*(8), 559–571. doi:10.1016/j.ijmedinf.2014.05.005 PMID:24961820

Roessler, M., & Zuzan, O. (2006). EMS systems in Germany. *Resuscitation*, *68*(1), 45–49. doi:10.1016/j.resuscitation.2005.08.004 PMID:16401522

Rogers, H., Madathil, K. C., Agnisarman, S., Narasimha, S., Ashok, A., Nair, A., ... McElligott, J. T. (2017). A Systematic Review of the Implementation Challenges of Telemedicine Systems in Ambulances. *Telemedicine Journal and e-Health*, *23*(9), 707–717. doi:10.1089/tmj.2016.0248 PMID:28294704

Roudsari, B., Nathens, A., Cameron, P., Civil, I., Gruen, R., Koepsell, T., ... Rivara, F. (2007). International comparison of prehospital trauma care systems. *Injury*, *38*(9), 993–1000. doi:10.1016/j.injury.2007.03.028 PMID:17640641

Sasser, S., Varghese, M., Kellermann, A., & Lormand, J. D. (2005). *Prehospital trauma care systems*. Geneva: World Health Organization.

Schmiedel, R., & Behrendt, H. (2011). *Leistungen des Rettungsdienstes 2008/09*. Bonn: Dr. Schmiedel GmbH.

Schwamm, L. H., Holloway, R. G., Amarenco, P., Audebert, H. J., Bakas, T., Chumbler, N. R., ... Wechsler, L. R. (2009). A review of the evidence for the use of telemedicine within stroke systems of care: A scientific statement from the American Heart Association/American Stroke Association. *Stroke*, *40*(7), 2616–2634. doi:10.1161/STROKEAHA.109.192360 PMID:19423852

Sood, S., Mbarika, V., Jugoo, S., Dookhy, R., Doarn, C. R., Prakash, N., & Merrell, R. C. (2007). What is telemedicine? A collection of 104 peer-reviewed perspectives and theoretical underpinnings. *Telemedicine Journal and e-Health*, *13*(5), 573–590. doi:10.1089/tmj.2006.0073 PMID:17999619

Soroka, S. N. (2007). Canadian perceptions of the health care system. Toronto: Academic Press.

Suryanto, P., Plummer, V., & Boyle, M. (2017). EMS Systems in Lower-Middle Income Countries: A Literature Review. *Prehospital and Disaster Medicine, 32*(1), 64–70. doi:10.1017/S1049023X1600114X PMID:27938449

Timerman, S., Gonzalez, M. M. C., Zaroni, A. C., & Ramires, J. A. F. (2006). Emergency medical services: Brazil. *Resuscitation, 70*(3), 356–359. doi:10.1016/j.resuscitation.2006.05.010 PMID:16901612

Vaitkaitis, D. (2008). EMS systems in Lithuania. *Resuscitation, 76*(3), 329–332. doi:10.1016/j.resuscitation.2007.07.028 PMID:17822828

Wade, V. A., Eliott, J. A., & Hiller, J. E. (2014). Clinician Acceptance is the Key Factor for Sustainable Telehealth Services. *Qualitative Health Research, 24*(5), 682–694. doi:10.1177/1049732314528809 PMID:24685708

Wandling, M. W., Nathens, A. B., Shapiro, M. B., & Haut, E. R. (2016). Police transport versus ground EMS: A trauma system-level evaluation of prehospital care policies and their effect on clinical outcomes. *The Journal of Trauma and Acute Care Surgery, 81*(5), 931–935. doi:10.1097/TA.0000000000001228 PMID:27537514

Weerakkody, V., El-Haddadeh, R., Chochliouros, I., & Morris, D. (2012). Utilizing a High Definition Live Video Platform to Facilitate Public Service Delivery. In L. Iliadis, I. Maglogiannis, H. Papadopoulos, K. Karatzas, & S. Sioutas (Eds.), *Artificial Intelligence Applications and Innovations* (Vol. 382, pp. 290–299). Springer Berlin Heidelberg. doi:10.1007/978-3-642-33412-2_30

WHO. (1996). Report: Investing in health research and development; WHO reference number: TDR/Gen/96.1. Geneva: World Health Organization: Ad Hoc Committee on Health Research Relating to Future Intervention Options.

WHO. (2010). *Injuries and violence: the facts*. Geneva: WHO.

WHO. (2011). *Telemedicine – Opportunities and developments in Member States: report on the second global survey on eHealth 2009. In Global Observatory for eHealth series* (Vol. 2). World Health Oragnization.

Zailani, S., Gilani, M. S., Nikbin, D., & Iranmanesh, M. (2014). Determinants of Telemedicine Acceptance in Selected Public Hospitals in Malaysia: Clinical Perspective. *Journal of Medical Systems, 38*(9), 1–12. doi:10.100710916-014-0111-4 PMID:25038891

# Chapter 3
# Facebook Contradictions in Municipal Social Media Practices

**Lars Haahr**
*Aarhus University, Denmark*

## ABSTRACT

*The purpose of this chapter is to explore the emerging social media practices of governments and citizens. The study takes on the status of an exploratory case study and draws on a grounded research approach. The case study shows an emerging social media practice that is embedded in and driven by a diversity of contradictions. The study identifies the following three contradictions as the most significant: communicative contradictions between service administration and community feeling, organizational contradictions between central control and local engagement, digital platform contradictions between municipal website and social media. The chapter presents a single-case study, which is a small contribution to the initial understanding of the social media practices of governments and citizens. The analysis indicates how a local municipality in its social media practices on Facebook is embedded in and driven by contradictions, and hence offers insights into a new way of understanding the challenges and opportunities of government social media.*

DOI: 10.4018/978-1-5225-6204-7.ch003

## INTRODUCTION

Social media use by government organizations and citizens has undergone a significant uprise during the last decades and produced a manifold field of emerging practices. This uprise in government social media use has opened a highly interesting research area for understanding what is at stake in these emerging practices.

A special issue on social media in *Information Systems Research,* Vol. 24, No. 1, March 2013, points to opportunities for organizational innovation, but also to unexpected challenges, for example that involvement of communities in design innovation processes can lead to devaluation of the obtained results. The editorial concludes that many questions are not only unanswered, but unaddressed (Aral, Dellarocas, & Godes, 2013).

Likewise, a special issue on social media in *Government Information Quarterly, 29, 2012* points to great expectations for emerging practices in government social media practices, and for example includes a typology for citizen co-production (Linders, 2012) and a maturity model for social media based public engagement (Lee, Kwak, Gwanhoo, & Young Hoon, 2012). However, in the very same issue, empirical data document a low deployment degree of social media in local municipalities in the European Union (Bonsón, Torres, Royo, & Floresc, 2012), and likewise, a low level of activity on a government-run health portal (Andersen, Medaglia, & Henriksen, 2012). The special issue thereby points to a discrepancy between research highlighting expectations and best practices on the one hand, and empirical evidence of low use of social media on the other hand.

The discrepancy between the expectations of co-creation on the one hand, and the low degree of deployment on the other hand, illustrates what Andersen, Medaglia, and Henriksen (2012) point to in the very same special issue of *Government Information Quarterly*, namely that the first wave of research of emerging phenomena often reflects an enthusiasm for the innovation, while the actual practices lag behind or are never achieved.

This paper investigates an alternative route for understanding what is at stake in emerging social media practices. We suggest to understand emergent government social media practices less as a matter of progression than as a continued wrestling with inherent contradictions. The paper is therefore guided by the research question: *How is contradiction present in government social media practices?*

The paper thereby prolongs the dialectical tradition for studying contradictory drivers and effects in digital innovation (Robey & Boudreau, 1999). As empirical foundation for examining how these inherent contradictions are constitutive in the context of emerging government social media practices, the paper traces and analyzes contradictions in a case study of municipal social media practices.

The results of the study indicate three areas of contradictions: 1. The communicative contradiction between service administration and community feeling. 2.The organizing contradiction between central control and local engagement. 3. The platform contradiction between municipal websites and social media. In line with recent research on digital innovation, the paper argues that the future development of government social media practices is dependent on how government organizations manage these contradictions.

The study makes two contributions. First, it contributes to our understanding of emerging government social media practices by drawing on a conceptual framework of contradictions within digital innovation. Second, the study contributes to practitioners' understanding of the opportunities and challenges in their management of emerging government social media.

The argument is organized as follows: First, we present recent research on emerging government social media practices and a conceptual framework for understanding contradictions in these practices. Second, the empirical research setting, the data collection and the analytical approach are presented. Third, the findings of contradictions in emerging social media practices are presented. Fourth, these findings are discussed in perspective of recent research. Finally, the paper points to limitations, future research and concludes the study.

## RECENT RESEARCH AND CONCEPTUAL FRAMEWORK

Recent research on government information systems has investigated a variety of interesting aspects of emerging social media practices. Among the more fundamental questions we find a study of how organizational characteristics influence tasks and technologies, and thereby social media participation (Henrique, Oliveira, & Welch, 2013). More specifically, it is further studied how increased standardization of policies for social media use will enhance the promotion and adoption of these new information and communication technologies within government organizations (Bretschneider & Parker, 2016).

Social media has the potential to improve interactions and relationships between governments and citizens through dialogue, but studies of social media use in major U.S. cities indicate that local governments preferably use one-way 'push' strategies in their communication practices (Mossberger, Wu, & Crawford, 2013). Despite the potential for e-participation, one-way-information-based service was however the characteristics found in a study of the City and County of Honolulu's use of social media (Harris & Winter, 2013). Interactions and engagement with social media e-government is further investigated as conditioned by user-centered and in particular citizen-centered practices (Jaeger & Bertot, 2010). Public administration workers have adopted social media for a variety of activities ranging from policy making to campaigns, but despite these benefits, social media however also bring about additional challenges, and evaluation of benefits and risks therefore become a necessity (Sivarajah, Irani, & Weerakkody, 2015)

However, studies also reveal how government institutions deploy social media primarily to market activities, raise awareness and engage stakeholders (Campbell, Lambright, & Wells, 2014). This study by Campbell et al (2014) is in particular interesting because social media often are characterized as an arena for participation and thus a potential democratic public sphere (Linders, 2012). However, more studies indicate difficulties with regard to the engagement people. A significant finding indicates that actors with high salience participate less, and actors with low salience participate more in social media practices, and thereby problematize the often hyped democratic potentials of social media (Johannessen, Sæbø, & Flak, 2016). Contradictions and paradoxes in emerging social media practices are also found in a study of emerging social media practices in a large Danish municipality (Haahr, 2014a).

A special approach for understanding social media is represented by a stream of research develop maturity models and frameworks to evaluate emerging practices. Examples hereof is a maturity model (Lee et al., 2012) and an evaluation framework including technological, political and organizational perspectives (Ferro, Loukis, Charalabidis, & Osella, 2013).

In a study of how socio-economic characteristics influence the presence of social media in U.S. county governments, it is revealed that social media has a paradoxical role related to ineffectiveness (Cumbie & Kar, 2015). In line with this understanding, another study regards social media as an important intermediary for open and participatory practices, and despite ongoing adoption, nevertheless detects that a significant skepticism thrives among citizens (Khan, Swar, & Lee, 2014).

How adoption of social media changes the technology paradigm, and thereby standard operation procedures within organizations is highlighted in Mergel (2016). This study further points to how a strategic alignment and routinization leads convergence of central and decentral practices, and further to institutionalization of new technologies (Mergel, 2016). Focusing on exactly organizational characteristics of communication practices on Twitter, a study of Dutch Police indicates that although this Twitter practice is taking place on highly decentralized channels, the hyped digital transformation has to be nuanced. The study thus indicates that old bureaucratic practices are not dismissed, but still manifested in hybrid forms with new models as illustrated in Twitter communication practices (Meijer & Torenvlied, 2016).

A rather new research focus is the use social media analytics tools. It is suggested that the adoption of analytics tools possibly can play a vital role in relation to consequences of austerity, but also how analytics tools represent a democratic dilemma in times of cuts in the public sector (Moss, Kennedy, Moshonas, & Birchall, 2015).

While most research on social media has its point of departure in the western hemisphere, most recently studies of social media in for example China has contributed to our understanding. The potential of social media is for example framed as a matter of open innovation. A study of how the Haining Bureau of Justice uses microblogging investigates the opportunities and challenges such open innovation represents for governments in China, and suggests a framework and what factors that drive this innovation (Zhang, Zhao, Zhang, Meng, & Tan, 2017). Focusing on the relationship between external environment and internal capabilities, Zheng (2013) studied how Chinese governments use social media to disclose information and interact with citizens. A content analysis of emerging social media practices on Chinese microblogging accounts frame these practices as innovation. The analysis however indicates that a majority of these government messages are posted for self-promotion rather than service delivery, and therefore are characterized as insufficient and preliminary (Zheng & Zheng, 2014).

Another special area of research interest is students use of and attitudes towards social media. Selvi, (2016) find indications of divergent attitudes towards political statements on social media. Alhabash & Ma (2017) find that among the four platforms - Facebook, Twitter, Instagram and Snapchat – the most popular is Snapchat.

Summarizing these most recent research contributions about emerging government social media practices, we thus find several indications of contradictions. In order to highlight and take the first steps in understanding these contradictions, we suggest to draw on conceptual frameworks in information systems research that has focused on contradictions in digital innovation.

A fundamental reference is the dialectical approach (Benson, 1977) which points to contradictions in order to explain change and development in organizations (Van De Ven & Poole, 1995). The fundamental assumption in this stream of literature is that organizations exist in a world of colliding forces and contradictory values. Change is regarded as an effect of the contradictory forces, and the organizational wrestling with these contradictions is regarded as the activity that creates organizational innovation. In the dialectical tradition, the elements and relations in a contradiction are understood as a whole: The contradiction in a change process is inherent or – to use a term more pertinent in the dialectical tradition – immanent. In line with already well-established information systems research that draw on the dialectical tradition and its focus on contradictions (Carlo, Lyytinen, & Boland, 2012; Cho, Mathiassen, & Robey, 2007; Robey & Boudreau, 1999), this study adopts the dialectical approach in an effort to understand the emerging government social media practices.

A stream of organization literature initiated by among others Poole and van de Ven 1989 focuses on a special form of inherent contradictions, namely paradoxes. Although not originally conceptualized as a paradox, the conceptual pair of exploitation and exploration (March, 1991) is often regarded as an example of paradox in this stream of literature. This is for example the case in the comprehensive work by Smith & Lewis (2011), where exploitation and exploration is conceived as a paradox within the category of organizational learning. The paradox lens has been applied in a solid stream of organizational studies (Andriopoulos & Lewis, 2009; Berlinger & Sitkin, 1990; Eisenhardt, 2000; Luscher, Lewis, & Ingram, 2006; Lüscher & Lewis, 2008; Poole & van de Ven, 1989; Quinn & Cameron, 1988; Smith & Lewis, 2011; Sundaramurthy & Lewis, 2003).

In information systems research, the dialectical tradition and the focus on paradoxes are also present today (Carlo et al., 2012; Cho et al., 2007). Noteworthy studies of paradoxes in the field of information systems research include studies of how technological affordances are always already paradoxical (Arnold, 2003), how nomadic technologies have an embedded paradox of empowerment and enslavement (Jarvenpaa & Lang, 2005) and how the most significant paradox of virtual teamwork is that between physical and virtual presence (Dubé & Robey, 2009).

Relevant for the present study of government social media practices is also an analysis of the emerging digital infrastructures through a dialectical approach (Tilson, Lyytinen, & Sørensen, 2010). The emergence of an all-encompassing digital infrastructure is regarded and named as 'infrastructure turn', thereby alluding to 'linguistic turn' and 'literary turn'. It is hereby implied that e.g. social media is not merely a matter of a faster and more widespread digital infrastructure, but also a new infrastructure condition. The authors therefore argue that this emerging or new condition necessitates a rethinking within the information systems research community. It is in order to undertake that task that the authors employ a dialectical approach and a paradox lens. Important in relation to the present study are two contradictions or paradoxes. The first paradox is that of change. The paradox of change exists between the opposing logics of stability and flexibility and plays itself out across the infrastructural layers and elements. The second paradox is that of control. The paradox of control exists between the opposing logics around centralized and distributed control, and it includes the strategic actions of heterogeneous actors and their control preferences in relation to change processes.

Despite the interesting contributions from the stream of literature using the paradox lens, it is relevant to ask whether the trending focus on paradox is pertinent, or the more mundane term contradiction suffices. If the definition of paradox alone is 'inherent contradiction' (Smith & Lewis, 2011), then it is difficult to distinguish paradox from contradiction as this concept is used in the dialectical tradition. Often the terms are used interchangeably and as synonyms: "The paradox invites us to adopt a fresh stance on how change in digital infrastructures is driven by the dialectic of stability and flexibility and how it affects uses of IT in corporate environments"

(Tilson et al., 2010, p. 754). Furthermore, paradox as a special type of inherent contradiction is elusive because of its linguistic nature. The verbal phrasing is very important for obtaining the paradoxical quality. If what is perceived as a paradox, for example the paradox of centralized and distributed control (Tilson et al., 2010), is explained straight forward, the paradoxical quality melts into air.

The present study will draw on both the fundamental dialectical tradition for focusing on immanent contradictions as drivers of change and innovation, and also include the studies that focus on paradoxes, but only use the term contradiction.

## RESEARCH SETTING, DATA COLLECTION, AND ANALYSIS

The study followed the principles for interpretive field research (Klein & Myers, 1999) in the investigation of social media practices by the local government and its citizens in one of the five largest municipalities in Denmark. This empirical ground for the analysis was chosen because Denmark, according to Bonsón et al. (2012), is among the countries in the European Union with the most active municipalities in social media.

However, an initial contextualization revealed that there is no dedicated social media department or functions in the municipality, nor is there a special social media strategy or social media code of conduct. As one of the five largest municipalities in Denmark, one could expect that there was at least a formalized and central function to manage and govern the social media activities. But there was not even one person with the title of social media manager in the municipality. This basic field observation pinpoints the emerging and contradictory practices at stake. Although there was no formalized central organization in place, the directors of the six municipal departments did have social media as a focus area. During the period of the interviews, the directors had also formed a special tasks force, and the directors prioritized networking with other municipalities around social media practices.

Historically the selected municipality has a long tradition for prioritizing citizen dialogue. Already back in the 1990s, the municipality had web-based citizen dialogue initiatives. The city of the municipality has a high percentage of young inhabitants and students and has an innovative IT culture and industry.

Following the principles of interaction between researchers and participants (Klein & Myers, 1999), the empirical material was provided by interviews with directors tasked with social media activites in the municipality, by digital ethnography of the social media activity by the local government and citizens, and by gathering of documents related to emerging social media practices within the municipality. The interviewees were selected to ensure sensitivity to possible differences in interpretations among the directors of the different municipal departments and followed the principles and guidelines for qualitative interviews (Kvale, 1996; Myers & Newman, 2007). First, to establish a historical perspective and an overview of the practices within the municipality, we interviewed the director of communication in the mayor's office and at the same time made online observations of the municipality's social media practices. Next, to ensure variance and a deeper understanding in prolongation of the insights from the first interview, we interviewed the directors from the six main departments of the municipality. Finally, to test and saturate our analysis, we interviewed the director and manager responsible for one of the most active social media sites within the municipality. The interviews, observations and document gathering took place in 2013. The interviews lasted between forty five minutes and hundred and fifty minutes. The progression of the interviews were designed to facilitate a saturation of the analytical findings in observations and interviews and to clarify unclear issues.

The analysis took place as an iterative process of working with the empirical material combined with the focus on contradictions to tease out analytical insights (Golden-biddle & Locke, 1993; Klein & Myers, 1999) . The analysis followed three steps: First, we listened to the interviews, took notes, and went through the original notes from our online observations. The aim was to establish a general understanding of the case and to identify tentative focus points for the following iteration of interview and observation. Second, after the second and third iteration of interviews and observation, we carefully read through the transcribed interview data and conducted a coding of contradictions. This general coding resulted in a list of unordered contradictions found in the municipal's social media practices. Third, we drew on literature to sharpen our analytical understanding of the empirical material and considered the interdependent meaning of parts and wholes. To finalize the analysis with a parsimonious set of categories and elements, we classified only the most robust and relevant contradictions in our data. This resulted in three categories of contradictions. See Table 1.

## CONTRADICTIONS IN EMERGING MUNICIPAL SOCIAL MEDIA PRACTICES

The analysis discovered three categories of contradictions in municipal social media practices, each with its specific set of mutual relations and contradictory elements. The identified categories are 'communication', 'organization', and 'platform'. See Table 1.

*Table 1. Contradictions in municipal social media practices*

| Category and Elements | Description of Contradiction | Illustration From Interview and Observation |
|---|---|---|
| **Communication**<br>Contradiction between community feeling and service optimization. | Social media facilitate personal community feeling, but is intervened and exploited by professional service administration in a process where local social media actors in turn become dependent on municipal service administrators. | Interview quote # 2<br>"The Clean-City project has a Facebook site with more than thousand likes. A person here offered a sofa for free and got serveral hundred likes. Such spontanous municipal projects occur and function very well due to a professional effort. And the agenda of our task force is to ask: How can the municipality prolong and profit from this activity?"<br>Online observation # 2<br>Posts and comments by citizens on the Facebook site for 'Clean City' is intervened by a municipal moderator who posts news and responds to questions, and direct citizens to service functions on a municipal website. |
| **Organization**<br>Contradiction between local engagement and central control. | Local social media actors foster initiatives and engagement and thereby organizational autonomy, but are still subject to central governance and control which in turn depend on the local social media actors. | Interview quote # 1<br>"If we don't do something on the municipal level pretty fast, then the traffic department will go solo"<br>Online observation # 1<br>Indication of many Facebook sites for local or specific activities. No evidence of any social media sites that officially represent the municipality or any of the six main departments. Indication of temporary project sites and municipal campaign sites, for example 'bicycle city' and 'Clean City'. |
| **Platform**<br>Contradiction between municipal website and social media. | Social media functions as driver of change and challenger of proprietary municipal controlled IT, but are also met with imperatives about business directed IT integration from central municipal actors. | Interview quote # 3<br>"It is important that we can build on top of the initiatives of the engaged citizens and dedicated unsers [of the local social media sites], to the advantage of the whole business of the municipality."<br>Online observation # 3<br>Photos, comments and questions by citizens on Facebook site for 'Bicycle City'. Self-service forms and official public information relevant for 'Bicycle City' is only placed on municipal website. Visible traffic from Facebook site to municipal website, but not the reverse. |

## Communication

The first contradiction concerns the communicative modality of the social media practices. Digital ethnographic observations revealed the existence of Facebook sites that evolve around a community feeling, for example local municipal schools where participants share photos and personal experiences in relation to specific events and daily life in school. Other Facebook sites, for example 'Clean City', have a municipal administrator who responds to questions and comments and thereby establish a professional administrative service discourse in the midst of the community feeling that also exists on the Facebook-site. See observation #2 in Table 1.

Interviews indicate that the central municipal actors are aware of the local citizen actors being the drivers of community experience, and that the central actors would like to match and integrate this dimension as a part of the municipal service affairs. Interviews indicate this when the director of communication for the mayor's office expresses recognition for local engagement and success, but in the same sentence also says that it would be valuable for the central municipality to exploit this further. See interview quote #2 in Table 1.

On the basis of such contradictory relations of community feeling and service administration in the discursive practices, the analysis constructed the category 'communication'.

## Organization

The second finding concerns the organizing of the social media practices in the municipality. There is one striking finding concerning the organizing. On the one hand there is a presence of local initiatives and engagement, but often in unofficial forms. On the other hand, there is a lack of central presence and activity, but large concerns about control and exploitation of social media. Online observations indicate that Facebook facilitates many sites for local or specific educational, cultural and city infrastructure activities. However, we have not found any indication of one single social media site that represents the municipality as an integrated or official whole. Nor does an official website exist for any of the six main departments. See observation #1 in Table 1.

Interviews confirm that local Facebook-actors are the initiators and are regarded as successful, while central municipal actors express that they are concerned about municipal integration of the diverse local initiatives. For example, a central director expresses that local initiators are proactive and the central administration is lagging behind. Thereby local social media activities gain autonomous or 'solo' status within and beyond the organization. See interview quote #1 in Table 1. Grounded in such contradictory and interdependent elements of central control and local engagement, the analysis constructed the category 'organizing'.

## Platform

Online observations indicate activity of posts, photos, and comments on municipal social media sites, for example the Facebook site for 'Bicycle City'. However, when it comes to administrative service functions, for example self-service forms and official public information about road repair and bicycle lanes, these functions are under proprietary control from a municipal website. The website is fueled by a Facebook site, but the reverse is not the case. See observation 3 in Table 1.

Interviews indicate a central municipal recognition of the value of engaged participants on local social media sites, but also an imperative to integrate this activity into a website as a municipal 'business' project. See interview quote # 3 in Table 1. Grounded in such contradictory relations of public social media and proprietary municipal websites, the analysis constructed the category 'platform'.

## DISCUSSION

The emergent interactions between social media and existing government administration are an intriguing phenomenon that calls upon theoretically and empirically based investigation. Grounded in a case study, the purpose of this paper was to discuss the pertinence of dialectical theory to understand the contradictions present in municipal social media practices.

The analysis identified three categories of contradictions in municipal social media practices, each with their specific set of mutually related and contradictory elements. Figure 1 has been developed in order to better illustrate how the three categories are related and each one embeds contradictory elements: First, we traced contradictions in communication practices between service administration and community feeling. Second, we found contradictions in organizing between local engagement and central control. Third and finally, the study revealed contradictions related to the digital platform between municipal websites and social media. See Figure 1.

Concerning the contradictions inherent in communication practices, the present study detected a significant field of discursive practices evolving around community presence, engagement and feeling. This stream of practices was mainly apparent in very local social media practices, for example in a Facebook group for a local municipal primary school. These social media practices in some aspects resemble the "Do It Yourself Government" type in Linders (2012) classification of citizen co-production in the age of social media. Linders (2012) specifies that the "Do It

*Figure 1. Contradictions in municipal social media practices*

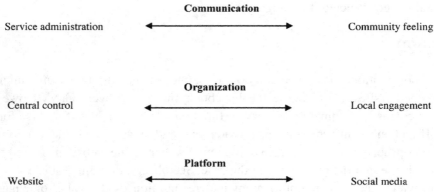

| | **Communication** | |
| Service administration | ←————————→ | Community feeling |

| | **Organization** | |
| Central control | ←————————→ | Local engagement |

| | **Platform** | |
| Website | ←————————→ | Social media |

Yourself Government" type of social media practices take place with little or no interference. However, Linders (2012) understands the activity within a service concept, for example when using the term 'self-service', and further also uses the term 'co-production'. In the present study, many local activities happened exactly as Linders' "Do It Yourself Government" without interference from central municipal authorities. However, the communication practices were also in many aspects outside the 'service' or 'co-production' logic, and rather to compare with a conversation for its own sake. We have therefore named the modality of this communication practice 'community feeling' to stress the difference to any discursive practice following a production or service administrative logic.

However, we also observed social media practices that had a professionalized tone and approach, and therefore labeled this communication practice 'service administration'. These social media practices were mostly apparent in relation to municipal institutions that directed their activity to a broader audience and were managed by employees who had it as a part of their professional portfolio of activities. These observations resemble the findings of one-way push strategies in the study of social media use in major U.S. cities (Mossberger, Wu, & Crawford, 2013) and the one-way information based services in the study of social media use in the City and County of Honolulu (Harris & Winter, 2013). Noteworthy about this stream of communication is that it often did not manage to address the citizens as citizens, but only as professional actors in the related industry. This professional service administration discourse executed on social media platforms by municipal employees, thus go beyond the other end of the scale of Linders' typology for citizen co-production (Linders, 2012). In comparison with Linders' interesting typology, the social media practices indicated in the present case study thereby falls outside both poles of citizen engagement; 'citizen sourcing' as well as 'Do It Yourself

Government'. According to our case study, the contradictions identified in current social media practices only involve citizen engagement to a very little degree.

The present study has only a few indications of 'citizen engagement'. The most evident examples are incidents related to activity on the 'Clean City' or 'Bicycle City' Facebook sites where spontaneous or 'self-organizing' citizen activity is staged or intervened by professional municipal service administrators. Thereby the present study points to a context of contradictions that differs considerably from the typology by Linders (2012) and the maturity model by Lee et al. (2012).

Concerning the contradictions in organization of local municipal social media practices, the study revealed a diverse landscape of local initiatives and central control. A part of the local municipal activity is very visible and recognized by the central authorities. In these situations, the central authorities express that it is desirable that the official municipality can benefit from these local activities. Other local activities are almost invisible or not recognized by others than the local community itself. In both situations, a dialectical approach, that focuses on contradiction, demonstrates its analytical pertinence by being attentive to how the municipality is wrestling with its own inherent contradictions, and how this wrestling plays a central role in the organizational change process (Van De Ven & Poole, 1995). Different from (Mergel, 2016), who found convergence of central and decentral practices, our study indicates an ongoing tension or contradiction between these organizational dimensions. Compared to studies of the deployment degree of government social media practices (Bonsón et al., 2012), the dialectical approach in the present study is capable of observing both the formal and official organizing and the tentative and informal activities of which the latter are not captured by the radar of the municipality itself.

As mentioned before the municipality despite being one of the five largest in Denmark, lacks a formal social media department. Never the less it acts as an organization that in certain ways is very attentive to and active in social media practices. Instead of understanding this situation as a lack of progression within a maturity scheme (Lee et al., 2012), the present paper suggests that it is more adequately understood as an example of municipal wrestling with contradictions. It is outside the scope of the present study to evaluate the wrestling itself, but it could turn out to be an example of resilience (Cho et al., 2007) or collective minding (Carlo et al., 2012).

The present study has also pointed to the fact that the municipality as an organization incorporates a wide variety of social media practices that are not officially recognized or even known. If these social media practices are not included in investigations, we are perhaps in a situation where the deployment degree of social media practices are considerably higher than current research points out (Bonsón, 2012), and may also include a wider variety of practice forms than anticipated so far.

Concerning the contradictions related to the digital platform, the dialectical approach in the present study has most importantly implied the inclusion of both proprietary municipal websites and social media platforms as the adequate object of analysis. In line with Tilson et al. (2010), the present study conceptualizes the digital platform as one whole 'affordance' that includes contradictory or paradoxical logics. We found indications of contradictions between the municipal website 'part' of the digital platform and the social media 'part' of the digital platform. This identification is in line with studies that also identified tensions between an existing organization and an emerging community being central for understanding the change process (Castello, Etter, & Morsing, 2012; Harri, Kalle, & Youngjin, 2010; Paramewaran & Whinston, 2007) . The present study highlighted the digital platform per se as an arena of contradictions, and how this impacts the way social media platforms become a natural working environment for municipal administrators. Whereas Bretschneider & Parker (2016) focuses on how standardization of policies enhances the promotion and adoption of social media, our study has emphasized how contradictions function as a driver of social media innovation.

## CONCLUSION

The paper took its point of departure in the discrepancy between current research in government social media practices that highlights expectations of co-creation and progression mirrored in typologies for citizen co-production (Linders, 2012) and maturity models (Lee et al., 2012) on one hand, and on the other hand research that documents low deployment degree of social media in local municipalities in the European Union (Bonsón et al., 2012). Extant literature on social media practices in both private and public contexts have detected inherent contradictions (Andersen et al., 2012; Aral et al., 2013) and the objective of the paper therefore becomes to prolong this literature. To this end, the paper draws on the dialectical tradition (Benson, 1977; Bjerknes, 1991) and the literature in which contradictions are understood as possible drivers of change and innovation (Poole & van de Ven, 1989; Smith & Lewis, 2011; Tilson et al., 2010) and asks how contradiction is present in government social media practices.

To theorize how contradiction is present in emerging government social media practices, the paper used a case study of social media practices in one of the five largest municipalities in Denmark. As the findings of the case study, the paper analyzes three related categories of contradictions in municipal social media practices, namely 'communication', 'organization' and 'platform'. In the category 'communication' the contradiction exists between community feeling and service administration. In the category 'organization' that contradiction exists between local initiatives and central governance. In the category 'platform' the contradiction exists between public social media and proprietary municipal information and communication technologies. The analytical findings are discussed in relation to extant literature on government social media practices (Bonsón et al., 2012; Lee et al., 2012; Linders, 2012).

The main theoretical contribution of the paper is therefore to theorize how emerging government social media practices are driven via three related categories of contradictions. More specifically the theoretical contribution of the paper is a conceptualization of the inherent contradictions of each category and how the organization in question copes with these contradictions. The paper hereby contributes to extant literature on contradictions in government social media practices (Andersen et al., 2012) and to theory on contradictions as drivers of change and innovation in organizations (Poole & van de Ven, 1989).

The practical contribution of the paper is the focus on social media practices as constitutively contradictory and organizational practice therefore a matter of coping with these contradictions. The dialectical approach of the paper suggests that practitioners understand this ambidextrous coping (Andriopoulos & Lewis, 2009; Smith & Lewis, 2011) less as a matter of progression – for example staged in maturity models – than as a continued wrestling with inherent contradictions.

The study acknowledges its limitations. First, despite single cases can provide a rich understanding of the studied phenomenon (Walsham, 1995), the studied case might have special characteristics. Future case studies can clarify this through comparison. Second, the study is also limited in only interviewing directors from the municipality administration and not citizens or groups of citizens. Future studies that include more relevant participants can establish a more complete material ground and critical context of interpretation (Klein & Myers, 1999). Third, the dialectical lens and the focus on contradictions might have become a part of what it describes and thereby constrained the attention to conflicting aspects in the empirical data (Golden-biddle & Locke, 1993; Klein & Myers, 1999). Future research in the contradictions of social media practices that employ alternative theoretical lenses are therefore desirable.

As a final critical reflection (Klein & Myers, 1999), it is worth noting that on the one hand the study found social media practices that bridge service administration and community feeling and thereby indicate a dawn of an 'integrated information environment' (Orlikowski, 1991), but on the other hand observations and interviews also point to social media as a digital infrastructure (Tilson et al., 2010) that can be used to exploit citizen engagement for municipal 'business' purposes. It is therefore pertinent to ask if municipal social media practices as part of an all-encompassing digital platform will facilitate citizen co-production (Linders, 2012) or rather will become a 'matrix of control'. The study by Johannessen, Sæbø, & Flak (2016) which indicates that actors with high salience participate less, and actors with low salience participate more in social media practices, and thereby problematize the often hyped democratic potentials of social media, thus points in the same direction. However, drawing on a dialectical tradition and understanding emergent social media practices as constitutively contradictory, the situation is rather to be understood as a both-and: social media practices will result in both citizen co-production and municipal matrix of control. Such a contradictory nature of social media practices can perhaps explain the lack of citizen participation in current municipal social media practices and perhaps exactly reflects a dialectics of collective mindfulness (Carlo et al., 2012). The paper therefore suggests a collective mindfulness in government social media practices as highly relevant for both researchers and practitioners.

# REFERENCES

Alhabash, S., & Ma, M. (2017). A Tale of Four Platforms: Motivations and Uses of Facebook, Twitter, Instagram, and Snapchat Among College Students? Social Media + Society, 3(1).

Andersen, K. N., Medaglia, R., & Henriksen, H. Z. (2012). Social Media in Public Health Care: Impact Domain Propositions. *Government Information Quarterly*, *29*(4), 462–469.

Andriopoulos, C., & Lewis, M. W. (2009). Exploitation-Exploration Tensions and Organizational Ambidexterity: Managing Paradoxes of Innovation. *Organization Science*, *20*(4), 696–717. doi:10.1287/orsc.1080.0406

Aral, S., Dellarocas, C., & Godes, D. (2013). Social Media and Business Transformation: A Framework for Research. *Information Systems Research*, *24*(1), 3–13. doi:10.1287/isre.1120.0470

Arnold, M. (2003). On the phenomenology of technology: The "Janus-faces" of mobile phones. *Information and Organization*, *13*(4), 231–256. doi:10.1016/S1471-7727(03)00013-7

Benson, J. K. (1977). Organizations: A Dialectical View. *Administrative Science Quarterly*, *22*(1), 1–21. doi:10.2307/2391741

Berlinger, L. R., Sitkin, S. B., Quinn, R. E., & Cameron, K. S. (1990). Paradox and Transformation: Toward a Theory of Change in Organization and Management. *Administrative Science Quarterly*, *35*(4), 740–744. doi:10.2307/2393523

Bjerknes, G. (1991). Dialectical Reflection in Information Systems Development. *Scandinavian Journal of Information Systems*, *3*, 55–77.

Bonsón, E., Torres, L., Royo, S., & Floresc, F. (2012). Local e-government 2.0: Social media and corporate transparency in municipalities. *Government Information Quarterly*, *29*(2), 123–132. doi:10.1016/j.giq.2011.10.001

Bretschneider, S., & Parker, M. (2016). Organization formalization, sector and social media : Does increased standardization of policy broaden and deepen social media use in organizations? *Government Information Quarterly*, *33*(4), 614–628. doi:10.1016/j.giq.2016.09.005

Campbell, D. A., Lambright, K. T., & Wells, C. J. (2014). *Looking for Friends, Fans, and Followers? Social Media Use in Public and Nonprofit Human Services.* Academic Press.

Carlo, J. L., Lyytinen, K., & Boland, J. R. J. (2012). Dialectics of Collective Minding: Contradictory Appropriations of Information Technology in a High-Risk Project. *Management Information Systems Quarterly*, *36*(4), 1081–A3.

Castello, I., Etter, M., & Morsing, M. (2012). Why Stakeholder Engagement will not be Tweeted: Logic and the Conditions of Authority Corset. In Academy of Management 2012, Boston, MA.

Cho, S., Mathiassen, L., & Robey, D. (2007). Dialectics of resilience: A multi-level analysis of a telehealth innovation. *Journal of Information Technology*, *22*(1), 24–35. doi:10.1057/palgrave.jit.2000088

Cumbie, B. A., & Kar, B. (2015). The Role of Social Media in U.S. County Governments: The Strategic Value of Operational Aimlessness. *International Journal of Electronic Government Research*, *11*(1), 1–20. doi:10.4018/IJEGR.2015010101

Dubé, L., & Robey, D. (2009). Surviving the Paradoxes of Virtual Teamwork. *Information Systems Journal*, *19*(1), 3–30. doi:10.1111/j.1365-2575.2008.00313.x

Eisenhardt, K. M. (2000). Paradox, Spirals, Ambivalence: The New Language of Change and Pluralism. *Academy of Management Review*, *25*(4), 703–705. doi:10.5465/AMR.2000.3707694

Ferro, E., Loukis, E. N., Charalabidis, Y., & Osella, M. (2013). Policy making 2.0 : From theory to practice. *Government Information Quarterly*, *30*(4), 359–368. doi:10.1016/j.giq.2013.05.018

Golden-biddle, K., & Locke, K. (1993). Appealing Work: An Investigation of How Ethnographic Texts Convince. *Organization Science*, *4*(4), 595–617. doi:10.1287/orsc.4.4.595

Haahr, L. (2014a). Wrestling with Contradictions in Government Social Media Practices. *International Journal of Electronic Government Research, 10*(1), 35–45. doi:10.4018/ijegr.2014010103

Haahr, L. (2014b). Wrestling with Social Media on Information Systems' Home Ground. In *Nordic Contributions in IS Research. 5th Scandinavian Conference on Information Systems, SCIS 2014, Ringsted, Denmark, 10-13 August, 2014. Proceedings.* Springer.

Harri, O.-K., Kalle, L., & Youngjin, Y. (2010). Social Networks and Information Systems: Ongoing and Future Research Streams. *Journal of the Association for Information Systems, 11*(2), 61–68. doi:10.17705/1jais.00222

Harris, C. S., & Winter, J. S. (2013). An Exploratory Study of Social Networking Services as a Potential Vehicle for E-Participation in the City and County of Honolulu. *International Journal of Electronic Government Research, 9*(2), 63–84. doi:10.4018/jegr.2013040104

Henrique, G., Oliveira, M., & Welch, E. W. (2013). Social media use in local government : Linkage of technology, task, and organizational context Technology Task Organizational context. *Government Information Quarterly, 30*(4), 397–405. doi:10.1016/j.giq.2013.05.019

Jaeger, P. T., & Bertot, J. C. (2010). Designing, Implementing, and Evaluating User-centered and Citizen-centered E-government. *International Journal of Electronic Government Research, 6*(2), 1–17. doi:10.4018/jegr.2010040101

Jarvenpaa, S. L., & Lang, K. R. (2005). Managing the Paradoxes of Mobile Technology. *Information Systems Management, 22*(4), 7–23. doi:10.1201/1078.10580530/455 20.22.4.20050901/90026.2

Johannessen, M. R., Sæbø, Ø., & Flak, L. S. (2016). Social media as public sphere : a stakeholder perspective. *Transforming Government: People. Process and Policy, 10*(2), 212–238.

Khan, G. F., Swar, B., & Lee, S. K. (2014). Social Media Risks and Benefits : A Public Sector Perspective. *Social Science Computer Review, 32*(5), 606–627. doi:10.1177/0894439314524701

Klein, H. K., & Myers, M. D. (1999). A Set of Principles for Conducting and Evaluating Interpretive Field Studies in Information Systems. *Management Information Systems Quarterly, 23*(1), 67–93. doi:10.2307/249410

Kvale, S. (1996). *Interviews: an introduction to qualitative research interviewing.* Thousand Oaks, CA: Sage.

Lee, G., Kwak, Y. H., Gwanhoo, L., & Young Hoon, K. (2012). An Open Government Maturity Model for Social Media-Based Public Engagement. *Government Information Quarterly, 29*(4), 492–503. doi:10.1016/j.giq.2012.06.001

Linders, D. (2012). From E-Government to We-Government: Defining a Typology for Citizen Coproduction in the Age of Social Media. *Government Information Quarterly, 29*(4), 446–454. doi:10.1016/j.giq.2012.06.003

Luscher, L. S., Lewis, M., & Ingram, A. (2006). The Social Construction of Organizational Change Paradoxes. *Journal of Organizational Change Management, 19*(4), 491–502. doi:10.1108/09534810610676680

Lüscher, L. S., & Lewis, M. W. (2008). Organizational Change and Managerial Sensemaking: Working Through Paradox. *Academy of Management Journal, 2*(2), 221–240. doi:10.5465/AMJ.2008.31767217

March, J. G. (1991). Exploration and exploitation in organizational learning. *Organization Science, 2*(1), 71–87. doi:10.1287/orsc.2.1.71

Medaglia, R., & Zheng, L. (2017). Mapping government social media research and moving it forward : A framework and a research agenda. *Government Information Quarterly, 34*(3), 496–510. doi:10.1016/j.giq.2017.06.001

Meijer, A. J., & Torenvlied, R. (2016). Social Media and the New Organization of Government Communications : An Empirical Analysis of Twitter Usage by the Dutch Police. *American Review of Public Administration, 46*(2), 143–161. doi:10.1177/0275074014551381

Mergel, I. (2016). Social media institutionalization in the U. S. federal government. *Government Information Quarterly, 33*(1), 142–148. doi:10.1016/j.giq.2015.09.002

Moss, G., Kennedy, H., Moshonas, S., & Birchall, C. (2015). Knowing your publics : The use of social media analytics in local government. *Information Policy, 20*(4), 287–298. doi:10.3233/IP-150376

Mossberger, K., Wu, Y., & Crawford, J. (2013). Connecting citizens and local governments? Social media and interactivity in major U. S. cities ☆. *Government Information Quarterly, 30*(4), 351–358. doi:10.1016/j.giq.2013.05.016

Myers, M. D., & Newman, M. (2007). The qualitative interview in IS research: Examining the craft. *Information and Organization, 17*(1), 2–26.

Orlikowski, W. (1991). Integrated Information Environment or Matrix of Control? The Contradictory Implications of Information technology. *Accounting Management and Information Technologies*.

Paramewaran, M., & Whinston, A. (2007). Research issues in social computing. *Journal of the Association for Information Systems*, *8*(6), 336–350. doi:10.17705/1jais.00132

Poole, M. S., & van de Ven, A. H. (1989). Using Paradox to Build Management and Organization Theories. *Academy of Management Review*, *14*(4), 562–578.

Quinn, R. E., & Cameron, K. S. (1988). *Paradox transformation: Toward a theory of change in organization and management*. Cambridge: Ballinger.

Robey, D., & Boudreau, M.-C. (1999). Accounting for the Contradictory Organizational Consequences of Information Technology: Theoretical Directions and Methodological Implications. *Information Systems Research*, *10*(2), 167–185. doi:10.1287/isre.10.2.167

Selvi, M. S. (2016). Attitudes of University Students Voters Towards Political Messages in Social Media. *International Journal of Electronic Government Research*, *12*(4), 67–89. doi:10.4018/IJEGR.2016100105

Sivarajah, U., Irani, Z., & Weerakkody, V. (2015). Evaluating the use and impact of Web 2. 0 technologies in local government. *Government Information Quarterly*, *32*(4), 473–487. doi:10.1016/j.giq.2015.06.004

Smith, W. K., & Lewis, M. W. (2011). Toward a Theory of Paradox: A Dynamic Equilibrium Model of Organizing. *Academy of Management Review*, *36*(2), 381–403.

Sundaramurthy, C., & Lewis, M. (2003). Control and Collaboration: Paradoxes of Governance. *Academy of Management Review*, *28*(3), 397–415.

Tilson, D., Lyytinen, K., & Sørensen, C. (2010). Digital Infrastructures: The Missing IS Research Agenda. *Information Systems Research*, *21*(4), 748–759. doi:10.1287/isre.1100.0318

Van De Ven, A. H., & Poole, M. S. (1995). Explaining Development and Change in Organizations. *Academy of Management Review*, *20*(3), 510–540. doi:10.2307/258786

Walsham, G. (1995). Interpretive case studies in IS research: Nature and method. *Organization Science*, (1973).

Zhang, N., Zhao, X., Zhang, Z., Meng, Q., & Tan, H. (2017). What factors drive open innovation in China ' s public sector? A case study of of fi cial document exchange via microblogging (ODEM) in Haining. *Government Information Quarterly*, *34*(1), 126–133. doi:10.1016/j.giq.2016.11.002

Zheng, L. (2013). Social media in Chinese government : Drivers, challenges and capabilities. *Government Information Quarterly*, *30*(4), 369–376. doi:10.1016/j.giq.2013.05.017

Zheng, L., & Zheng, T. (2014). Innovation through social media in the public sector : Information and interactions. *Government Information Quarterly*, *31*, S106–S117. doi:10.1016/j.giq.2014.01.011

# Chapter 4

# Strategic Overhaul of Government Operations:
## Situated Action Analysis of Socio-Technical Innovation in the Public Sector

**Hans J. Scholl**
*University of Washington, USA*

## ABSTRACT

*Field operations in municipal governments have undergone fundamental adjustments. This empirical study investigated the ramifications of the strategic shift in government field operations when mobile information and communication technologies (ICTs) were introduced for field crews in a multiyear process. The implementation had to overcome several serious socio-technical challenges. The data were collected using cognitive work analysis (CWA) and interpreted from a structurationist perspective. The study filled an important methodological gap: While structuration theory (ST) has been criticized for its paucity of guidance for empirical research, CWA has been denounced for its deterministic engineering approach to social systems. However, the subordination of the micro-meso-level CWA framework into the grand theory of ST resulted in an approach referred to as situated action analysis, which was found particularly useful for elucidating the observed feedbacks between human agency, the shaping of the information (technology) artifact, and the organizational structure.*

DOI: 10.4018/978-1-5225-6204-7.ch004

# INTRODUCTION

Like private-sector organizations, governments of the 21st century systematically pursue productivity gains, process streamlining, logistics optimization, and improved asset management. For example, as an early adopter, the City of Seattle experimented with mobile technology in its various guises beginning in the late 1990s. The City's public utilities (Seattle Public Utilities/SPU) embarked on a mobile pilot project in its field operations in 2003 with the intention of exploring the innovation potential of the most recent mobile and wireless technologies. The motivation was to study the effects of this particular innovation project in public-sector field operations, since those had not been systematically studied before, and the benefits of mobile technology use in public utilities field operations were not clear. A particular interest was directed toward understanding the role and effectiveness of the IT[1] artifact in these organizational and social transformation processes. In this project, huge productivity gains in field operations were documented along with improved asset and resource management as intended outcomes; however, also undesired side effects were witnessed in the transition and transformation, which were neither foreseen nor expected.

For studying the project in its various dimensions, the analytical framework known as *Cognitive Work Analysis* (CWA) was used (Fidel & Pejtersen, 2002; Rasmussen, 1986; Rasmussen, Pejtersen, & Goodstein, 1994; Rasmussen, Pejtersen, & Schmidt, 1990; Vicente, 1999), which has successfully been used in information system evaluation before (Fidel & Pejtersen, 2004). The framework is geared towards abstracting and delayering the rich context of a work domain under study by systematically observing and describing in detail what human actors in a specific domain do, what information they might need when they have to make decisions, and why they might act and decide as they do. CWA uses seven analytical layers for delayering organizational complexity. For understanding the organizational and socio-technical processes, the rich data were assessed and interpreted from a structurationist perspective (Giddens, 1984). In particular, the analysis of the structuring processes were a main focus as the system of interaction and the duality of structure, that is, the generative rules and resources (Bryant & Jary, 1991), at SPU's field operations upon introduction of mobile systems for crews and crew chiefs. As found in the process, the layered approach was of great utility in the structuration-oriented analysis.

This paper describes the mobile innovation project at SPU across multiple field cases. It has three aims:

1.  Document the challenges and opportunities of a major innovation project in the field operations of City government and the shaping/structuring of the social system in this process.
2.  Discuss the role of the information artifact in this project as a central part of both the structure and the interaction between contextually situated and knowledgeable human agents and structure from a structurationist perspective.
3.  Reflect on the effectiveness of using situated action analysis as an adaptation of Cognitive Work Analysis under the theoretical auspices of Structuration Theory

By so doing, this study contributes to the strand of empirical information systems (IS) research from a structurationist perspective intending to narrow the gap between structurationist concepts and empirical data (Silva, 2007).

The manuscript is organized as follows: First, taking into account the familiarity of the Information Systems and Electronic Government readerships with the dimensions and perspectives of Giddens' work, for example (Brooks, 1997; Gil-Garcia & Hassan, 2007; Puron-Cid, 2013; Walsham, 2005), the basic tenets of structuration theory are briefly recapped. Next, the research question is presented. Then, the unfolding of the *GoMobile* innovation project in the City's public utilities field operations is detailed, and the findings of this six-year research project are discussed; in particular, the roles of the mobile ICTs (the IT artifact) in human actors' actions and interactions are investigated, how those were influenced, and how the mobile systems were "shaped" and enacted structure through human agency. Next, the results and the approach are critically discussed. Finally, reflecting on the results, it is concluded that structuration-sensitive field studies might benefit from further explorations into using what has been referred to here as *situated action analysis*.

## THE STRUCTURATIONIST PERSPECTIVE AS THEORETICAL LENS

In the early 1990s Giddens' work (Giddens, 1984, 1991) began influencing studies on roles and structural properties of IT artifacts such as information systems (Bostrom, Gupta, & Thomas, 2009; Brooks, 1997; DeSanctis & Poole, 1994; Gopal, Bostrom, & Chin, 1993; Orlikowski, 1992; Orlikowski & Robey, 1991; Richardson & Robinson, 2007). However, as Silva asserted, as a consequence of its complexity Structuration Theory (ST) shows a serious lack in linking concepts to data making it difficult to use in empirical IS research (Silva, 2007). Yet, other contributions have been criticized for treating IT artifacts as immutable elements of structure, which maintain and perpetuate structural properties and predetermine human actors' action and interactions, and by so doing, not holding up the basic tenets of ST (Jones & Karsten, 2008, 2009). Those concerns notwithstanding ST has continued to attract IS researchers for over two decades, and a number of empirical studies have appeared, for example (Brooks, 1997; Chu & Smithson, 2007; Hussain & Cornelius, 2009). For the purpose of this study it appeared therefore appropriate to only briefly summarize those essentials of the structurationist perspective.

For analytical purposes, Giddens distinguished structure and human interaction (human agency) along three dimensions each, which he conceptualized as linked to each other via "modalities" or "modes" of structuring. The structure dimension of "signification" is linked to the interaction dimension of "communication" via the modality of "interpretive schemes." "Domination" as structure dimension links to the interaction dimension of "power" via "facility," while "legitimation" (structure) couples with "sanction" (interaction) via "norms" as their respective modalities. Understanding structuration rests on the study of these three modes of recursive and ongoing social-system production and reproduction (Giddens, 1984).

According to Giddens' Structuration Theory, human action and interaction, individual or group, are informed and guided by purpose; acting and interacting human agents are knowledgeable and act for a reason (Giddens, 1984, p. 25). Human activity, furthermore, unfolds on the premises of contextually situated human agents' discretion and choice; knowledgeable human agents have a great variety of choices and degrees of freedom when engaging in action and interaction and when determining their course of action (Giddens, 1984, p. 25; 1991, p. 215). Also, in action and interaction, contextually situated human agents impact the emerging context based on structural enablers and constraints, which are historically variable. The two sides of structure, enabling and constraining, "have to be studied together" (Giddens, 1984, p. 175). In Giddens' view, "physical constraints have no more fundamental influence over social activity than do other types of constraint" (Giddens, 1984, p. 175), such as legal or moral constraints. To make the point, he argues that even " the threat of death has no weight" (Giddens, 1984, p. 175) unless life is valued. Then, in choosing a course of action, which is reflective of and informed by structural enablers and constraints, contextually situated human agents draw on rules, resources, routines, instruments, artifacts, and other patterns of action, which represent traces of previous activities in the respective purpose-related time/space (Bryant & Jary, 1991; Giddens, 1984, p. 25). Whereas contextually situated human agents command only limited opportunity to change material constraints, thus significantly limiting their choices, in the case of both sanctions and structural constraints the choices human agents have might be more wide-ranging according to Giddens. As Jones and Karsten point out, "Giddens' agents are highly autonomous" (Jones & Karsten, 2008, p. 132). "How far these (structural properties of social systems—*insertion by the author*) are constraining qualities varies according to the context and nature of any given sequence of action or strip of interaction," Giddens emphasizes (Giddens, 1984, p. 176). Furthermore, reflective of and informed by structural enablers and constraints, contextually situated human agents create in action and interaction novel rules, routines, instruments, artifacts, and activity patterns as a matter of course, but also when dealing with new or unanticipated events and unintended consequences (Bryant & Jary, 1991; Giddens, 1984, p. 25). Finally, structure and human action/interaction couple recursively producing and reproducing each other (Bryant & Jary, 1991; Giddens, 1984, p. 25). This theorem of *Duality of Structure* is the main tenet of Structuration Theory: Knowledgeable action of contextually situated human agents, on the one hand, and structures, or "rules and resources, or sets of transformation relations, organized as properties of social systems" (Giddens, 1984, p. 25), on the other, interact and recursively co-evolve. Structuration then describes the conditions under which "the continuity or transmutation of structures and therefore the reproduction of social systems" (Giddens, 1984, p. 25) occurs. In that process of interaction and co-evolution, social systems emerge, which represent the "reproduced relations between actors or collectivities, organized as regular social practices" (Giddens, 1984, p. 25). Structure and human action are recursively intertwined and "not two independently given sets of phenomena" (Giddens, 1984, p. 25). In this sense, structure "is not 'external' to individuals" (Giddens, 1984, p. 25).

For Giddens, enablers and constraints are variable in space and time with regard to material and structural circumstances. However, since agents perceive enablers and constraints as 'objectively' given, "social phenomena become endowed with thing-like properties which they do not in fact have" (Giddens, 1984, p. 180). In fact, the "structural properties of social systems do not act, or 'act on,' anyone like forces of nature to 'compel' him or her to behave in any particular way" (Giddens, 1984, p. 181). Giddens is highly critical of any "reification" of enablement/constraint particularly when reproduced in academic discourse. Reification he suggests "should be seen as referring to forms of (academic-*insertion by the author*) discourse which treat such properties as 'objectively' given in the same way as are natural phenomena" (Giddens, 1984, p. 181).

In summary, Giddens' perspectives mark a clear departure from (a) understanding structure as pre-given, almost immutable, and rigid in general, and (b) information systems as embodied or embedded structure capable of directing agents' action in a deterministic fashion. However, this departure presents a challenge to identify the exact role of IT artifacts within the structuration process of a social system, the structure of which "is recursively implicated" (Giddens, 1984, p. 25). As Giddens remarks, "[a]nalyzing the structuration of a social system means studying the modes in which such systems, grounded in the knowledgeable activities of situated actors, who draw upon rules and resources in the diversity of action contexts, are produced and reproduced in interaction" (Giddens, 1984, p. 25). If the nature, role, use, utility, value, and impact of the IT artifact in structuration and its modes are to be studied, then research based on Giddens' ST needs to concern itself with studying the IT artifact in that very context and in the modes of structuring.

## CONNECTING GIDDENS' ST WITH CWA

In support of studying information artifact-related problems within organizations Information Systems Research has incorporated Giddens' ST as a grand theory with varying success (Klesel, Mokosch, & Niehaves, 2015; Orlikowski, 1992; Robey & Abdalla Mikhaeil, 2016; Veenstra, Melin, & Axelsson, 2014) and with various degrees of embracing the basic tenets of ST (Jones & Karsten, 2009; Pozzebon & Pinsonneault, 2005). One central problem facing researchers (besides the epistemological problem of ST's inherent circularity and recursivity, which poses an additional problem to positivist treatments (Robey & Abdalla Mikhaeil, 2016)) is the absence of any profound technology-related discourse in Giddens' work. Giddens is silent about what particular role information technology might play in structuration processes (Jones & Karsten, 2008). Moreover, Giddens provided little practical direction regarding the empirical study (of the dynamics) of human interaction and social structure (Pozzebon & Pinsonneault, 2005; Thrift, 1985), but rather presented the tenets of ST as merely 'sensitizing devices' (Giddens, 1982) in empirical research. Furthermore, ST was criticized for neglecting the impact of external structures on both human action and interaction and internal structures (Archer, 1995; Cohen, 1989; Parker, 2006; Whittington, 1992). For addressing these particular problems, Cognitive Work Analysis (CWA), was seen as a sound and practical framework, which has demonstrated its potential in delayering and decomposing the rich contexts of complex social systems and their inherent technology instantiations. CWA explicitly considers and investigates the external environment of a social system in its duality of enabler and constraint. In its lower layers, down to the tasks and activity layers, CWA also explicitly investigates actors' tools including the information (technology) artifact in its duality as enabler and constraint. CWA has been criticized for its hands-on engineering-type approach and its general theory-thinness as well as its lack of adequately representing dynamic systems, and its deterministic engineering approach when trying to design socio-technical systems (Cummings, 2006). However, the use of the CWA analytical hierarchy for delayering organizational and social system complexities facilitates and guides exactly what is missing in empirical ST, that is, the analysis of structuring processes. In particular, not only for the identity of terms, but rather for the shared understanding of the two concepts of (structural) "enablers" and "constraints" between ST and CWA, a strong conceptual bridge was identified connecting the high-level theory of ST with the analytical framework of

CWA. In a way, the incorporation and subordination of CWA into a structurationist analysis scheme seems to provide the grand theory of ST with the missing fine-grained empirical toolset, in particular, with respect to information technology and information artifacts, whereas ST emancipates CWA from its naïve and deterministic understanding of social and socio-technical system engineering. ST also relieves CWA from perceiving institutional structures as immutable and reified entities.

## THE OBJECTIVE OF THE STUDY, THE STUDY SITES, AND THE RESEARCH QUESTION

In the following, approach and findings of the study are laid out across multiple field cases in a multiyear study of an organizational innovation and change project, in which challenges and effects of implementing and using advanced mobile computing in the field operations of Seattle City Government's public utilities were studied. Previous studies had reported that process change projects in government were typically oriented towards tactical improvements (Scholl, 2005a), and such low-hanging fruit projects were mostly motivated by the desire to quickly improve service quality and cost-benefit ratios (Scholl, 2005b). Along similar lines, Seattle Public Utilities (SPU) had experimented with mobile equipment and applications for some time prior to the 2004 rollout of mobile devices (laptops for crew chiefs, small handhelds for crewmembers) to select field crews in the Water Operations Division (WOD) in the "*GoMobile*" project. SPU leadership intended to give online access to backend databases and geographical information to crews and supervisors working in the field. Also, work orders were to be dispatched online to workers in the field. The productivity gains and service improvements in this initial Field Force Automation (FFA) project with select crews at WOD were found so significant that SPU leadership hurried to expand the deployment of FFA technology into other SPU divisions (Bleiler, 2003). In fall of 2005, the *GoMobile* project was expanded to the Drainage and Waste Water Division (DWD), and in early 2006 the rollout began. Onsite observations and interviews at DWD commenced at about the same time. In 2008, the field study was extended to include the WOD. While the initial FFA pilot at WOD had unfolded in a "straightforward" (Newcombe, 2002, p. 2) fashion, the DWD rollout proved problem-stricken from the outset, suggesting that the pilot might have represented an ideal case.

This research project aimed to advance the understanding regarding both (1) requirements for and (2) organizational impacts of fully mobile, wirelessly connected (FMWC) (Gorlenko & Merrick, 2003), or mobile FFA applications in government (Scholl, Fidel, Liu, Paulsmeyer, & Unsworth, 2007; Scholl, Liu, Fidel, & Unsworth, 2007). The study also focused on more deeply understanding how the use of mobile

FFA applications impacted the business of government and the constituencies involved, and specifically, how that use changed field operations in government as well as crewmembers' and crew chiefs' roles, stances, and relations. Finally, the study sought to find out how the mobile IS and IT artifacts could be enhanced and which rollout strategies would work best in SPU's context.

As mentioned before the instrument development and data collection were guided by the seven-layer framework of Cognitive Work Analysis (CWA) (Rasmussen, 1986; Rasmussen et al., 1994; Vicente, 1999). However, the instrument was amended in a way to include structuration-oriented perspectives. The framework's seven hierarchical layers of analysis extend from the external environment through the level of work domain down to an individual worker's resources and values, which influence her or his on-the-job decision making. The layered approach to data collection over more than twenty field cases has been described elsewhere (Fidel, Scholl, Liu, & Unsworth, 2007; Liu, Unsworth, Fidel, & Scholl, 2007; Scholl, Fidel, et al., 2007; Scholl, Fidel, Mai, & Unsworth, 2006; Scholl, Liu, et al., 2007). For this study, the rich data and documentation collected were evaluated and interpreted from a structurationist perspective leading to the research question,

*(R) "What are the structuring effects found in the GoMobile field study data, that is, the specific structural challenges and effects of implementing and using advanced mobile ICTs in government field operations (the social system), and to what extent has the use of these mobile ICTs influenced the field operations' structures?"*

## METHODOLOGY

### Study Sites and Instrument

When the multiyear project was launched, the research team decided to focus first on DWD, because the rollout of the mobile ICTs had not begun allowing the research team to capture and document the status quo ex ante. The researchers intended to accompany, observe, and document the rollout and early use phases of the new systems. As soon as the mobile ICTs had become an integral part of the daily routine at DWD, the research team resumed its observations and interviews. Later it was decided to study separately two geographically separate units of DWD, which allowed for comparisons. Once the DWD study was completed, the mature implementation at WOD was studied. In order to inform SPU's leadership about the approach and to secure their commitment, the research team had engaged in a series of meetings with these leaders and had presented the approach in great detail. The two SPU leaders were very supportive of the undertaking and assigned a permanent liaison to the research team. This person was the technical specifier and initiator of the mobile project at the City, which turned out to be a highly fortunate circumstance, because this person was able to provide the team with unlimited access to documentation, mobile and backend IS and IT artifacts, field sites, crewmembers, and crew chiefs. As soon as the top leadership had given its full commitment to the research project, the research team conducted a meeting with the entire management team of SPU field operations in order to provide them with information about the research project. Because the team wanted free, around the clock access to information, sites, and people inside the organization, it was important to articulate to management of all levels and later to crews and crew chiefs that the research project was academic in nature and would not be a tool for performance evaluation by SPU's management team. These meetings led directly into meetings with crews and crew chiefs who were recruited as human subjects in the field study. In hindsight, it cannot be emphasized enough that the later success of the research project critically hinged upon this upfront comprehensive information sharing and systematic involvement of almost all managers and supervisors at SPU. During the half-year preparation and scanning phase, the research team conducted in-depth analyses of publicly available and internal documentation such as annual reports, strategy papers, organizational charts, process maps and workflows, business plans, procedures and routines, policies, work orders, job descriptions, and the IS and IT artifacts used. Based on these documents, the research team identified an initial set of purposes, operational objectives, priorities, enablers, constraints, functions, types of operations, and resources of the DWD.

A field case-tailored instrument was developed, that is, a comprehensive semi-structured questionnaire, which covers the seven nested layers of analysis as described above. Data collection started with a desk research phase, during which organizational documents were analyzed such as organizational charts, field manuals, documented organizational routines, rules, and work orders as well as the existing information system landscape and its connection to operations in the field, which further informed and helped targeting the questionnaire to the specific purpose and object of study.

## Sampling and Data Collection

In the purposive sampling approach, which was used, the team put a special emphasis on how close human agents were to the actual action/work and activity/task at hand (Ritchie, Lewis, & Gillian, 2003). In general, field crews were much closer to and immediately focused on the work tasks at hand than management or back office administrative and support staff. After all, it was the field crews who used the new mobile systems and not the managers or the administrative and support staff. Further, in the preparation and scanning phase, the research team had already found out that goals and priorities of the crews and crew chiefs were somewhat different from the goals and priorities of management. Therefore, the team decided to interview a significantly higher percentage of field crews and crew chiefs than management and other staff involved. The two latter groups mostly provided contextual information that complemented the overall picture but proved very useful in the later analysis. In the interviewee recruitment process, it became evident that field crews were fairly skeptical of SPU's management and of the research project, which was perceived as another managerial means to track field crews' individual productivity. It took the research team several months and quite a number of informational meetings with the field crews to establish that the study was an independent study effort and that sharing results with management would not compromise workers' anonymity. The researchers explained in great detail where and how they would lock away and access-control the recordings and transcripts at the University. Interview data and observations would be completely anonymized, and no personal identifiers would be published in the findings. For a total of 21 field cases, the team recruited and interviewed 28 field crew and crew chiefs, that is, more than 25 percent of SPU's field operations crews. Based on a comprehensive instrument comprising semi-structured and open-ended questions, the interviews with each human agent lasted for about 90 to 120 minutes and were followed by a 6-to-8-hour onsite observation session, during which researchers "shadowed" the human agents engaging in her/his daily routine. In this way, the team collected a very large set of rich data.

## Data Analysis

The interviews were audiotaped, transcribed, and then coded. For coding, the research team had developed and used an initial codebook before interviews and observations began, which was modified and enhanced in the course of the analysis. For coding the transcripts, Atlas TI was used as the coding tool. The twenty-one field cases were systematically documented mainly based on the interviews and were amended using the post-event notes from interviewers and observers. Detailed notes were recorded during the interviews. The notes were transcribed and summarized based on the field crew categories. A combination of pre-developed coding and open coding was used, where each unit of data was assigned to a category or sub-category whose dimensions and properties were further developed from the data (Strauss & Corbin, 1998). New categories and sub-categories were introduced, in case existing categories did not apply (Gorman, Clayton, Rice-Lively, & Gorman, 1997). An axial coding process was applied, during which the converged categories and subcategories were analyzed regarding their inherent structures and processes leading to paradigms, whose internal relationships were identified wherever possible (Strauss & Corbin, 1998). Finally, a selective coding process was performed, in which the resulting current practices concepts and theories were related to each other. Cross-case analyses were performed, which were conducted within and across along seven layers specified before.

## FINDINGS

In this presentation of results, the emphasis lies on the IS and IT artifact-related aspects of structuring. Partial results in other areas have been published elsewhere (Fidel et al., 2007; Scholl, Fidel, et al., 2007; Scholl et al., 2006; Scholl, Liu, et al., 2007). The seven analytical layers employed range from the external work environment (layer 7) over the work domain (layer 6) and the organizational/institutional domain (layer 5) to various activity levels (layers 4 to 2) to individual human actors' resources and values (layer 1). In the following the findings in each of these analytical layers are presented. For each layer, the specific areas of inquiry in the form of open-ended summary questions is covered. Please note that the actual interview questions were worded in a language better understandable to the target groups. The concepts were also broken down into smaller chunks.

### Findings in the Work Environment (Layer 7)

In this highest or outmost layer of analysis, the focus lies on the external environment. Questions were asked along the lines of "What elements external to the social system under study affect the human actors' activities where and when? And, what are the boundaries for the work or action time/space environment?" When it was decided to focus the study on the workers in DWD and WOD and their use of mobile ICTs as the work domains, by the same token this drew a boundary towards the external environment, which influences and is influenced by the work domain. In this case then, the external environment consists of other SPU divisions, the Utilities' leadership, and the structural frame and legal foundation of the Utilities as well as other City departments, the City leadership, and the City's political, administrative, legislative, jurisdictional, economical, and geographical frame, and last but not least, the general public, and more directly, the citizens and business customers receiving service from SPU. Because SPU commands a strong mandate as an independent City department, environmental enablers and constraints external to SPU were of minor importance with the exception that the City of Seattle prides itself as a leader in early and innovative technology adoption and diffusion. While the Department of Information Technology (DoIT) and its head, the City Chief Technology Officer (CTO), may determine the overall technology-related principles, standards, and policies, SPU was practically autonomous in its technology-related decision-making.

That notwithstanding, the SPU's *GoMobile* initiative was greatly acclaimed and supported by both the CTO/DoIT and the mayor, and it had high visibility throughout city agencies and departments. For SPU's leadership as well as for both the Utilities' management team and the field crews, the visibility of *GoMobile* throughout the City and the support from City leadership was perceived as helpful but also as an obligation to create a success story. Like other departments, SPU used and fed back to resources and databases citywide, such as the City's Geographical Information Systems. Both City and Utilities' leaderships expected the project to significantly improve the quality of asset management and the productivity of field operations. SPU leadership, while committed to "exceptional customer service," however, also tried to balance service standards with "financial, social and environmental impacts" and pursue a lean "capital investment strategy through asset management" as SPU's strategic goals revealed. The DWD field operations crews had their own view of the work environment and their role in it. For crews and their chiefs, the safe functioning of drainage and wastewater service along with customer satisfaction were the foremost priorities. As one crew member put it, "Looking at the other corners…to make sure they're working … that way I don't have to come back," and, "Customer service is a key to our success."

In summary, SPU's *GoMobile* project had few, if any, strings attached from the environment. It enjoyed full support from leadership across the City and had great visibility across other City departments and beyond. The City decision makers expected the project to run without major complications. So, from a structurationist perspective, existing interpretive schemes, facilities, and norms were not expected to change much in the unfolding of this project.

## Findings in the Work Domain (Purposes, Objectives, Enablers, Constraints, Priorities, Functions, Processes, and Resources: Layer 6)

This layer of analysis is the highest system-internal layer. On this level of analysis questions are asked such as, "What are the intentions, motivations, purposes, priorities, and constraints in human actors' action/interaction? And also, what are the functions and physical processes?" For both, DWD and WOD, equivalent high-level objectives guiding the two divisions, ("providing Seattle citizens with safe and reliable drainage, sewage, and waste water services" and "reliably providing Seattle citizens with safe and clean water") were found. Leadership and workforces of both divisions were united in pursuing these high-level objectives. In both divisions, work falls into the two categories of corrective and preventive maintenance. Work in the first category responds to reported problems in the field, while the second category involves ongoing routine asset inspection, repairs, and maintenance. For reasons of clarity of presentation, in the remainder of this report, the focus will lie on the DWD example. Furthermore, for space reasons one of twenty-one field cases is used for illustrating the structurationist interpretation on the lower levels of analysis.

DWD had experienced difficulties in organizing work for several years before the introduction of mobile technology. For seven years in a row, almost every year a new manager had been appointed to lead DWD prior to the launch of the *GoMobile* project, which was also the case when the systematic observations were started. The frequent changes in top leadership had left their traces; for example, workers were used to performing their tasks the way they considered most appropriate regardless of who was in charge. No clear and consistent priorities had been given; instead, workers defined priorities, as they deemed necessary. New or revised standard routines had not been developed for years. Worker turnover was relatively high and costly, since the training of novice workers had been (and still was, as observed during the study) lengthy and time consuming. Under such circumstances, it was surprising to find an intact work ethos among field crews who worked with great commitment and dedication to serve the citizens in the most effective way. Field workers expressed a strong sense of ownership in maintaining the infrastructure and keeping the critical assets in the best shape possible. Before the introduction to the field, management had repeatedly promoted and praised the new mobile technology for making decisions and organizing work in the field much easier. Consequently, at the outset field workers were very interested in using mobile devices and applications, since they expected that the mobile ICTs would enable them to perform a better job.

However, with the introduction of mobile ICTs, management also pursued two less promoted and less known objectives aimed at improving the management of assets and critical infrastructure and shifting from a traditional corrective/ preventive maintenance scheme to a leaner and more flexible reliability-centered (RCM) maintenance concept. The mobile ICTs were seen as a key element in that transition and were designed for comprehensive and up-to-date on-site information gathering necessary for RCM and lean asset management. Other than in the paper-based approach and with regard to the RCM, field crews were now expected to enter relatively large amounts of data into the mobile ICTs on a daily basis. For unit-wide compatibility reasons and shortly before the *GoMobile* launch, SPU's DWD had replaced one backend asset and logistics management system with another. The new backend system allowed for the introduction of its mobile systems variant, which disposed of functional and database integration into the backend system.

Typically, in DWD field operations, work was initiated via a detailed work order, which could consist of a scheduled repair job, an emergency repair job, or a new installation. The assets involved came in a wide variety and were highly specific to purpose. Many assets (for example, pumps, hydrants, catch basins, sewer lines, ditches, etc.) were long-lived and developed a highly specific maintenance history over a lifespan of several decades. Documentation of critical information on the specificity of such assets was mostly missing, while other important knowledge about those assets was found to be highly tacit. For example, field crews accumulated and used heuristics based on their own senses such as listening to sound, smelling the air at and around the asset, or looking at the watercolor to assess the state and condition of an asset. The clues from such human sensory assessment were never documented, and most workers were found unable to even express in words, how exactly they had made sense of the information they had gained this way. Most work in the field was found rich in detail complexity, had a high variability with many exceptions from the rule, and could hardly be preprogrammed from start to finish. In other words, work at DWD was found semi-structured at best. Despite planned and enforced job rotation and extensive apprenticeship programs, most workers held specific (tacit and explicit) knowledge about specific assets and also about specific processes, so that specific asset-actor couplets and specific task/process-actor couplets could be identified (for example, if pump A14 breaks, then it is Joe Smith who most effectively can carry out the repair job).

SPU used both ruggedized industry-standard laptops and PDA handhelds as hardware for the mobile ICTs. Both systems were capable of executing the work order-related applications, which connected to the backend systems via wireless connections. While crew chiefs used laptops, which allowed for accessing a whole host of applications on the backend systems including high-resolution Geographic Information Systems (GIS), the handheld users were not so lucky. The 6.5" display of the handheld was monochrome and could only display 40 lines per page. Under some conditions the screen was hard to read. Although it had a full QWERTY keyboard the key caps were fairly small, and some applications required the use of a stylus for operation. The mobile applications were adapted versions of those already in use on the backend systems. At times the connectivity between the mobile devices and the backend systems was shaky and unreliable depending on the location of work. However, in the course of the on-site observations, connectivity improved significantly due to enhanced wireless coverage.

By introducing *GoMobile* to the workforce as a tool to help make field crews' work easier and more productive, SPU leadership had established a high level of expectations among field workers. Early on in this study, the research team observed a disjoint with regard to "what they say" versus "what they mean" and "what they do" in the interpretive schemes used between the two groups. At the outset of the mobile ICTs rollout at DWD, despite some skepticism inside the field operations work force, crews expected the new systems to make their jobs easier and more productive. As mentioned before SPU leadership, however, had not communicated widely and clearly that with the introduction of *GoMobile,* several other goals were pursued that would impact the work situation in field operations. Field crews' and crew chiefs' involvement in the pre-implementation decision making process as well as in the mobile requirements elicitation process had been minimal. As a consequence, upon rollout a number of problems surfaced rather quickly, including in the communication between the two groups. In the way, it had launched *GoMobile*, SPU leadership used its allocative and authoritative resources rather single-handedly to advance its goals. In terms of enacted norms, field crews grudgingly accepted management's single-handed approach; however, the data show that more buy-in on part of the field force might have been obtainable, had management's approach been more participatory.

## Organizational/Institutional Analysis (Layer 5)

In this layer of analysis, answers were sought to questions such as, "What are the structural principles? What are the institutionalized structural properties and routines of the social system? How are these properties and routines changing over time? How is action divided among groups/teams of actors? What criteria are used? What are the values? And, how is action divided among team members?"

At the time the study was conducted, DWD was organized into a North and South District covering the territory of the City of Seattle. For this chapter observations and data were used that were collected in the North District. As mentioned above, DWD field operations had been plagued by a rapid change in leadership for quite a few years prior to *GoMobile*, and the North District was the most volatile in that regard. Field crews in that district were accustomed to working with great autonomy and little interference from outside their own span of control. Crew chiefs and field crews had performed a remarkable job of preserving and maintaining a high level of asset availability. Since field crews had accumulated vast amounts of tacit knowledge about processes and specific assets, this particular knowledge could not be transferred, but was rather recreated via a two-year individual apprenticeship program through which all novel field workers went. After completion of the apprenticeship program, workers were rotated through all field positions. On a rotational basis, field workers also assumed the role of crew chiefs for some time before they returned to regular crew assignments. While this rotational model provided SPU with great flexibility and a widespread distribution of skills and asset-specific know-how, the rotation also curtailed productivity and effective information sharing between field crews. Unsurprisingly, the frequent leadership and directional changes were not conducive to a smooth adoption of the mobile ICTs; due to the lack of leadership, field crews would not perceive the introduction of the mobile technology as something important in their work lives. Also, fairly soon after the implementation of the mobile ICTs, it became evident that the systems did not support important organizational procedures and field routines; furthermore, the mobile ICTs did not support preventive maintenance-oriented drive-by inspection procedures, which field crews had used for many years. The lack of sufficient mobile ICTs training further complicated a smooth rollout and implementation of the new systems.

In DWD's North District, a growing disconnect between the interpretive schemes of local leadership and field crews appeared upon the implementation of the mobile systems. Unlike in other units, DWD North leadership exposed little commitment to or engagement in making the new technology a success. As a consequence, the reception among field crews was lackluster. Crews at DWD North had great autonomy in their decision-making and had successfully filled the void created by lack of leadership had created and worked around the issues. Field crews in the North District enacted and maintained a work ethos that emphasized the smooth and safe functioning of the critical infrastructure and assets over any other priority, such as lean asset management or cost effectiveness. One crewmember's remarks represent the crews' views and self-understanding, after a malfunction reported by an elderly female citizen was fixed,

"If that lady is to come out to talk to me again, I will tell her that it is all fixed so she will be happy. That is kind of what this is about too, customer service, you know. I mean, they pay taxes, which pay our wages since we are city employees. Actually, I work for her. So, they are happy, my bosses are happy and I am happy, kind of big circle, you know what I mean?"

The spirit of these de-facto grassroots norms and their enactment in practice clearly flew in the face of several competing objectives that SPU's leaders pursued with *GoMobile*. Moreover, SPU leadership perceived workers' commitment and motivation as relatively low, which in their view called for more control.

## Activity Analysis in Work Domain Terms (Layer 4)

As indicated above when moving to the lower or inner layers, the analysis becomes more specific. In this analytical layer, questions were posed such as, "What are the current tasks? What are the purposes, intentions, and motivations underlying the activities, what are the constraints and functions involved? And, what is the technology used?"

For the purpose of this study the focus was put on the task of asset inspection at DWD's North District, in this case, a water inlet inspection.

Each morning crew chiefs handed out work orders for the day to field crews during an all-district early morning briefing. Before the *GoMobile* introduction, work orders were issued on paper; with *GoMobile,* crews now received work orders for the day on their handhelds. A work order for a water inlet inspection, for example, provides field crews with preprogrammed workflows, which the crews follow as long as no unanticipated circumstances arise.

In the case of a water inlet inspection, the overall *purpose* of inspection was identified as "Provide to the citizens of Seattle a reliable drainage system." The *enablers* and *constraints* for the particular task of water inlet inspection were found as (1) the weather and its effects on the drainage system, (2) the level of traffic near the site of inspection, (3) the level and extent of financial and human resources, and (4) the frequency of (inspection-schedule unrelated and superseding) emergency cases. Field crews assigned to the task of water inlet inspection followed a number of *priorities* such as (a) maintaining a regular scheme of inspection for catch basins, ditches, pipes, etc.; (b) inspecting sensitive sites outside the regular inspection schedule after severe weather situations and storms; (c) preparing and planning the inspection with caution considering the particular traffic situation, the proximity of buildings and other neighboring structures, as well as the safety of both workers and citizens; (d) using resources efficiently preventing waste; (e) casting a one-mile radius of inspection, and (f) minding the well-being of citizens at all times. The inspection then followed three *functional* steps of inspection preparation, performing the procedures of inspection, and inspection report writing.

Performing a water inlet inspection involved the process steps of diverting vehicle and pedestrian traffic (for example, setting orange cones, barricade taping), unloading task-related tools and equipment (metering and measuring devices), walking to and perusing the site, checking for irregularities in the drainage flow, observing the color and sensing the smell of water, testing the level of debris accumulation at the inlet (for example, by throwing a pebble into it and assessing the sound of the percussion). Resources used in the inspection process encompassed various tools and equipment including the mobile ICTs, which also provided important information about the history of the inspected site, field crews' general experience and specific knowledge about the site and task at hand, and the actual physical condition of the site.

Field crews consisted of two or more members who worked on the same work order. As outlined above, as long as no unanticipated circumstances occurred (including emergency calls), crews followed the pre-programmed workflow specified in the work order. However, at times, when crews traced the causes of defects or non-normal conditions, they needed to service and repair connected assets. In that case, the crew needed to issue a new work order on the spot. While such exception handling was easy with the paper-based system, the mobile ICTs did not make the creation of a new connected work order on the spot an easy task. As far as possible, field crews therefore performed the necessary tasks at hand without worrying about the lack of documentation of the additional work done. In their exchanges, field crews expressed their dissatisfaction with the mobile ICTs' lack of capability. "The mobile systems are cumbersome in certain important areas, but they (that is, management – *insertion by the author*) do not listen to us and our suggestions," the research team repeatedly heard from field crews when inquiring about the mobile systems' fit to purpose. So, what had already been found on higher levels of analysis could now be identified in more detail at the activity/task and other lower levels of analysis. At task level, it became even more apparent that field crews heavily relied on their task- and asset-specific knowledge, high degrees of which were tacit. To that extent, the new systems were of little help. Worse, unlike the phased-out paper-based system, (as *facilities*) the new mobile ICTs imposed a certain rigidity of procedure on the field crews, but nonetheless the crews carried out the tasks the way they thought was best. When performing a water inlet inspection, for example, crews employed and imposed on themselves standards and norms of high quality, which greatly facilitated the achievement of the overall purposes and objectives stated above. Also, at this layer of analysis, it became clear that despite the new ICTs suggesting otherwise crews would find and use workarounds for achieving the goals, to which they were committed, that is, keeping the infrastructure intact and serving their customers to the best of their ability.

## Activity Analysis in Terms of Choices Relative to Information Needs, Intentions, Motivations, and Purposes (Layer 3)

In this analytical layer, human actors' choices were investigated relative to the information at hand and also in terms of their intentions, motivations, and purposes. Answers were sought to questions such as, "What actions are taken based on what motivations, intentions, purposes, and how? What information is required, and how used? What information sources are useful? What information is used? What information is created? What information is shared? Among whom? And, what information is disseminated?"

In this field case of water inlet inspection, field crews were required to make numerous choices and decisions on the spot by themselves. For example, in the case of an identified irregularity, crews had to determine the methods to use for identifying the causes of the irregularity. Since the irregularity might have originated elsewhere, crews had to decide what radius of inspection they needed to cast in order to check other assets geographically collocated and connected to the inlet with the observed irregularity. Since causes of an irregularity at a water inlet could have been manifold, compound, and geographically dispersed, the detection procedure could take fairly varying pathways, which at best could only be pre-programmed in part. Furthermore, identifying the causes hinged upon heuristics and tacit knowing on the part of individual field crewmembers or field crews. Crew chiefs sometimes got involved in the analysis and decision-making processes; however, that was not the rule. Crews based their choices on information available to them, which comprised detailed asset descriptions and part breakdowns as well as historical data on the respective assets. Also, detailed and accurate geographical information was essential in determining the course of action. Some of that information was readily available to crews from their mobile ICTs, which provided asset-related details and also geographical information from the City's and Utilities' backend Enterprise Resource Planning (ERP) systems and Geographical Information Systems (GIS). Yet, the information presentation (particularly, the GIS data presentation) was poor, or even impractical to send to the handhelds over initially slow and undependable wireless networks. Later it was decided also to equip crewmembers with commercial-grade laptops, which appeared to work much better than the original handhelds. In addition to the detailed geographical and asset description (including the part breakdown and schematic asset blueprints), crews particularly sought historical data on the assets. This information helped them better understand the individual asset service needs. Unfortunately, the mobile ICTs would not provide such information, nor would they allow the capturing and entering of asset-specific comments after an inspection or a repair. Crews therefore frequently reverted to old paper records, which offset many gains in time the mobile systems could have provided. The highly structured and standard data-entry oriented mobile applications provided little, if any, functionality that could help capture and enter that vital information. Furthermore, mobile ICT developers and planners apparently erred in perceiving information that crews would enter to be of little value.

On the level of activity- and task-related choices and information needs, the system analysts and planners' lack of understanding of the specific needs and requirements of DWD field operations became highly visible. The formal system analysis had obviously not covered certain areas of field operations. While the mobile systems still helped improve and speed up the choosing process in some areas, the information provided was incomplete and led to double work involving the old paper-based information sources, and this mixed-media situation of new mobile systems and old paper-based systems significantly complicated the work situation for crewmembers and crew chiefs alike. To crews the new mobile ICTs were only partially conducive to receiving and providing relevant information, and hence, only partially helped improve making choices and decisions. Management, on the other side, considered the lackluster use of mobile ICTs at this level as some sort of resistance or unwillingness on part of the crews.

## Activity Analysis in Terms of Information Seeking Strategies Eligible for Use (Layer 2)

In this layer, human actors' information-seeking behavior was investigated. Answers were explored to questions such as, "What information seeking strategies are possible (e.g., browsing, the analytical strategy)? What information seeking strategies do the human actors in the domain prefer? What specific type of information is needed? What information sources does the human actor prefer?"

Within bounds, human agents have freedom when choosing a course of action and when selecting strategies for information seeking. In a structurationist perspective human actors' actual choices under a given set of circumstances cannot be predicted; however, what can be determined and also described with some confidence are the range of choices and, in particular, the information seeking strategies that human agents *can* employ or *can* choose from under a known set of circumstances. Five information-seeking strategies that human agents may employ can be distinguished: (1) browsing strategies, (2) analytical strategies, (3) empirical strategies, (4) known-site strategies, and (5) similarity strategies (see also, (Case, 2007)). The *browsing* strategy does not require much planning and employs an intuitive scanning approach that follows leads and clues by association. In using the *analytical* strategy, human agents explicitly consider the attributes of the information needs and the search system. The *empirical* approach relies on past experiences and uses rules and tactics that had proven successful. In the *known site* approach, human agents visit a site that they know holds the needed information. And finally, in the similarity approach to information seeking, human agents attempt to use previously successful methods that appear to be similar to the need at hand. Although these information-seeking strategies can be combined, human agents prefer the use of some strategies over others relative to their actual information need, the task at hand, and individual preferences. In the field case (water inlet inspection), crews combined the analytical with the known-site and similarity approaches. For example, crewmembers would not hesitate to locate and talk over the phone to other crewmembers that they thought would be able to provide the missing but critical historical information on an asset with an observed irregularity. Crewmembers also used the known-site approach when checking old paper-based maps of assets, onto which important notes had been added over time, and would pull all relevant information together in an analytical assessment of the irregularity. The research team found that crews were able to fairly quickly identify a problem and the choice-relevant information, and then choose on a course of action to be taken. The mobile ICTs were of some help whenever pre-programmable and pre-configurable scenarios occurred. They were of far lower utility in all non-standard situations, which are quite frequent.

## Analysis of Human Actors' Resources and Values (Layer 1)

In the innermost layer of analysis, the individual human actors' resources and values are studied relative to the task at hand. Here, the interest lies on answering questions such as, "What is your formal training? What is your specific area of expertise?

What is your experience with the subject domain and the work domain? What are your personal priorities? And, what are important personal values in this context?"

In structurationist understanding, resources (like structures) act as both enablers and limitations of human action and interaction. When analyzing the resources workers employed, the research team tried to understand and assess the dual nature of resources. In the DWD North District, crewmembers and crew chiefs alike received the same basic training. Major portions of the skills and knowledge relevant to successfully performing the jobs as field crews at DWD were also based on tacit knowing. The term used here reflects Polanyi's original understanding of something that cannot be expressed by words, and, hence, is not codifiable and is therefore not easily transferable (Polanyi, 1966; Polanyi & Grene, 1969). The Utilities had recognized the large portion of tacitness in the knowledge and skill base of field crews long ago, and, after some pressure from the labor unions, had put in place a compulsory two-year apprenticeship program for every newly hired crewmember. Furthermore, beyond their apprenticeship crewmembers were also required to rotate through all field positions including the position of crew chiefs. This rotational system and cross training not only assured the widespread buildup of critical knowledge and skills shielding the Utilities against sudden loss of important know-how, but also created an esprit-de-corps amongst crewmembers, which relied on peer feedback and collaboration and emphasized a strongly egalitarian culture. Most crewmembers and crew chiefs exposed creativity, strong self-esteem, a sense of responsibility, and an understanding of individual accountability as well as awareness of the prominent roles they played in maintaining a critical infrastructure indispensable for the wellbeing of all citizens in a major metropolitan area. At the same time, crews were highly critical of the Utilities' management for not comprehensively consulting with them before, during, and after the introduction of the new mobile ICTs. Interestingly, crews were willing to engage in learning and using the mobile ICTs as long as those systems helped them accomplish their mission in a more effective and efficient fashion. In other words, the notorious resistance to change frequently observed in similar projects did not play a role; on the contrary, crews tried hard and against all odds to make the new systems work to serving their ends. However, crews' frustration with the systems accumulated over time due to the lack of mobile system functionality and flexibility. While crewmembers did not express or show any opposition to the introduction and use of mobile ICTs, they felt that the lack of important functionality and flexibility could have been avoided had crews been involved in the requirements specification phase. Crews and crew chiefs had a well-developed capacity to solve complex problems, for which pre-programmed templates did not exist and for which the information base was incomplete. From a perspective of workers' resources and values, the interpretive schemes between management and field forces differed significantly. Therefore, while management predominantly expected a boost in worker productivity and asset management effectiveness from the mobile systems, field crews saw the mobile ICTs as tools in determining their course of routine and non-routine action and as sources of information, which would make their jobs easier to perform. While those two perspectives do not necessarily compete or even contradict each other, the Utilities' management failed to align the two perspectives sufficiently. In the egalitarian social system that the field crews had formed over time, the perceived mobile system deficiencies were instantaneously shared among its members, posing a challenge to the *GoMobile* implementation team and to management.

## DISCUSSION

### Information (IS/IT) Artifact, Information, and Contextuality

In the first part of the research question, the specific structural challenges and effects of implementing and using advanced mobile ICTs in government field operations (the social system) were in focus. So far, many context-sensitive study approaches in IS research assume IS/IT as pre-given (Alter, 2002, 2003; DeSanctis & Poole, 1994; Yuan, Archer, Connelly, & Zheng, 2010) and reified, which might be the case in the human agents' or even only in the researchers' own thinking, as Giddens points out (Giddens, 1984, pg. 180). From a structurationist perspective, however, knowledgeable human agents' action and interaction and the constrained use of resources including IS/IT co-create and occur within a unique context, which evolves and manifests itself in the process of structuring. When using a layered structurationist approach the analysis of structuring, the richness of analytical detail increases towards the lower or inner layers (for example, the activity/task and human-agent-related values and resource levels). The roles, uses, and interplays of resources including mobile ICTs within the emerging context of interaction can hence be determined at various levels of abstraction and particularly with regard to their influences and mediating effects on interpretive schemes, facilities, and norms (the modalities between interaction and structure). As an example, in the analytical layer of Organizational/Institutional Analysis, the research team found the disjoint of expectations and agendas regarding the use of the mobile ICTs. However, it was only in the lower analytical levels of the Work Domain, Activity/Task Domains and Domain of Human Agent's Resources and Values that the researchers saw the effects of that disjoint in a fairly detailed fashion. The researchers were also able to understand and trace how the interaction between the two groups was influenced by the disjoint, leading to suboptimal performance relative to the overall goal that both groups shared. The mobile ICTs apparently overly served management's desire of better control over workers and assets and underserved the workers' and task-related needs of supporting semi-structured and complex workflows and the ensuing necessity of autonomy in workers' reasoning and choosing. Interestingly, while management gained more and higher quality information on work orders and assets in real time, field crews did not enjoy an increase in the quality of information, at least not at the early stages of the innovation project. When using the mobile systems, field crews actually bemoaned the lack and even loss of information, which they believed they had had access to under the former paper-based system. When management decided to replace the backend assets and logistics management system in order to have the same platform for backend and mobile systems across SPU, large amounts of data could not be transferred from the old to the new backend system. Management traded this loss of data against the advantages of standardization and going mobile as a direct benefit from standardizing. However, the rationale for this trade-off was not sufficiently communicated to field crews. Through the layered structurationist analysis, the research team was able to understand the contextuality of human interaction, mobile IS/IT uses, and information at DWD at various levels of abstraction.

## Structure of Signification

Along with the mobile ICTs came new implicit rules and new interpretations of existing rules, which influenced and changed the interpretive schemes of the human actors involved. As mentioned above, when the new systems were introduced to field operations, the various stakeholders had diverging expectations regarding their immediate and long-term effects and benefits: While SPU leadership, first and foremost, expected to assume better operational supervision and control along with receiving substantially more and up-to-date asset-related data in near-real time, the crews and crew chiefs in the field expected more accurate and timely information relative to their respective tasks at hand. While either party's objectives and expectations were not mutually exclusive, they represented fairly different emphases in terms of operational goals. Crews soon found out that the discretion they had enjoyed when planning their workdays began to diminish, since management now was able to trace more accurately the progress of work on an hourly basis. Crews' times of relative slack previously used for running some errands or meeting colleagues over a cup of coffee suddenly became squeezed or even eliminated. Managerial control no longer was distant but far more immediate. From a relatively independent and self-steering work organization the crews found themselves closely monitored in ways never experienced before. Also, the administrative burden of manually entering into the mobile ICTs completed work order data at the end of a long workday was little appreciated, but rather perceived excessive. Much frustration arose among crews particularly with regard to the perceived challenge to their status of a highly trained expert and knowledge worker. Crews found the new tight controls as unnecessary as inappropriate. With these changes and the better grip of management on updated asset and work order information, the orientation of service was beginning to change ever so slightly from a preventive (and sometimes costly) maintenance philosophy to a lean, cost-conscious reliability-oriented maintenance philosophy, which rather tolerates an asset to break before replacing it than keeping it preventively maintained at higher overall cost. Of course, this change in meaning and service philosophy would not go without resistance on part of the crews. Interestingly, crews' resistance was not targeted against the mobile ICTs but rather against the managerial service re-direction and change in maintenance philosophy, which the mobile ICTs appeared to impose. Crews particularly resisted the idea of ignoring the maintenance of nearby assets when work was performed on other malfunctioning assets in the immediate vicinity. The interpretive schemes enacted by SPU leadership and field operation crews began to significantly diverge leading to a latent conflict as well as to much frustration on either side.

## Structure of Domination: Information and IS/ IT as Allocative and Authoritative Resources

In the second part of the research question, the extent, to which the use of mobile ICTs influenced the field operations' structures, in particular, the structures of domination were the main focus. As outlined before, the Utilities' management team, unwittingly or not, tried to shift the power balance between themselves and the field crews and become more dominant and also more controlling over outcomes than before. The way the mobile systems were set up as an extension of the backend asset management and logistics system attempted to impose a highly structured approach to the field operations, at least in terms of work order organization and asset information management. While the new systems were not designed to hold back information from the crews, the crews initially started with a tremendous loss of asset-related memory, because the information base of the old system was not preserved. As mentioned before, management required from field crews significantly more data entry than during times of the paper-based system. Under the new rule, the data had to be entered in certain formats, and the system made it impossible to capture the wealth of information available to the crewmember and necessary for a comprehensive report, which could be used by the next crew working on the same asset. The mobile applications, the hardware configuration of the handheld systems, and the information provided through the mobile systems initially did not improve the crewmembers' work situation in any significant ways. While some of these problems would disappear over time, others were of more systematic nature and needed to be addressed, such as relaxing the structured-process requirements prescribed by the new systems.

The image that SPU leadership held of field crews and their work ethos prior to the introduction of the new systems appeared to us not to be overly positive. Leadership seemed to believe that improved supervision and clear direction were needed to yield better productivity in field operations. The new systems were seen as instrumental in that regard. However, before the introduction SPU leadership had presented to crews the new technology mainly under the premise of making crews' work life easier and more effective. Field crews whole-heartedly embraced the idea of better, faster, and more effective workflows. Through the new systems they particularly expected to receive timelier, more accurate, and more task- and asset-specific information when working on site. Yet, shortly after the introduction crews began to realize that management had also advanced some unannounced items on the agenda, which the crews resisted. This resistance was not targeted against the mobile ICTs per se. Rather the initial deficiencies in the systems were used to reclaim the originally purported purpose of the mobile ICTs. Electronic records of work orders began piling up, and report writing as well as data entry were lagging. The crews understood their unique power as knowledge assets whose specific knowledge could only partially be captured by means of information systems. Soon management began to understand that effectively gaining tighter control of the crews would be illusory. In essence, tight control and supervision of these highly skilled subject matter experts, their decision-making, and their specific work progress proved not only impractical and unachievable, but also counterproductive. As a consequence, after months of struggle the status quo ante was re-established. However, over time the mobile ICTs had been improved, and field crews began enjoying the technologies' anticipated benefits. Management, in turn, was finally also able to benefit from the extended base of information, which improved the logistics and asset management of field operations measurably.

## Structure of Legitimation

As discussed management attempted to advance and sanction a particular way of executing work orders and a change of maintenance principles via the mobile ICTs. While the systems prescribed certain flows of work, in many instances, however, the situation required overwriting the pre-programmed paths. Crews needed to have enough discretion for doing so. While initially such deviations were difficult to accomplish, the systems were finally modified in a way that crews could more easily adjust to the situational necessities. Besides the system-specific adjustments, the shift from a preventive maintenance philosophy to a reliability-centered maintenance (RCM) philosophy caused concerns among field crews. Under RCM non-critical components may deliberately let be run to failure, a concept, which many field crews resisted as a matter of principle. Interestingly, voters in the neighboring City of Shoreline voted in late 2012 in favor of cutting loose from Seattle's public utilities water and sewer grid and go alone exactly for fear of over-aging and over-wearing their city's critical infrastructure. In other words, the crews did not stay alone in their concerns. Again, crews did not direct their resistance against the mobile ICTs but rather against the change in maintenance philosophy that the systems were supposed to help bring about.

## Reflecting on Using Situated Action Analysis

As outlined above, ST as a grand theory has not guided empirical research at any micro level of detail. Giddens himself suggested to use the concepts of ST as 'sensitizing devices' on a rather abstract or macro level in empirical study (Giddens, 1989, p. 294). He further suggested to use a 'methodological bracketing' approach, which distinguishes and separates the analysis of human actors' strategic conduct from the analysis of "structural properties as chronically reproduced features of social systems" (Giddens, 1984, p. 288). However, as both ST critical (Archer, 1995; Parker, 2006) and ST supportive accounts (Coad, Jack, & Kholeif, 2015; Elbasha & Wright, 2017; Feeney & Pierce, 2016; Stones, 2005) have shown, the study of structuration needs to engage on both micro and meso levels to be effective and have explanatory power. The proposed bracketing approach, however, proposes to study deeply intertwined phenomena in isolation, which neglects the dynamic interplay of structure and agency, that is the duality of structure. Methodological bracketing, hence, practically defeats ST's main tenet. In recent years, reformulations and faithful extensions of ST, for example, Strong Structuration Theory (SST) have been proposed to overcome these particular shortcomings (Elbasha & Wright, 2017; Feeney & Pierce, 2016; Jack, 2017; Jack & Kholeif, 2008; Stones, 2005).

CWA, while mainly used to help design information systems, uses a scalable and layered approach of analysis, which shows its particular strengths on micro and meso levels of empirical research. Most importantly, it does not study phenomena in isolation, but rather engages in decomposing static and dynamic complexity. Although the CWA originators (Rasmussen, 1986; Rasmussen et al., 1994; Vicente, 1999) employed a fairly mechanic and deterministic view of socio-technical systems, they nevertheless devised a sharp lens for delayering social systems, which not only includes the analysis of the external environment, but also encompasses the internal structures of the work and task domain down to the specific needs, strategies, and conduct of human actors-in-focus. Both ST and CWA are analytically highly sensitive to structural enablers and constraints. However, based on the analysis, whereas traditional CWA would try to "design" a social system, which fits the needs and the institutional requirements considering all identified enablers and constraints hoping for a highly predictable outcome in its ultimate enactment (Naikar, 2017; Naikar & Elix, 2016; Niskanen, 2017; Read, Salmon, & Lenné, 2012; Read, Salmon, Lenné, & Stanton, 2015), ST-inspired analysis would not follow that particular route.

Rather, Situational Action Analysis, which is the approach introduced here, that is, the adaptation of CWA as an analytical framework and its interpretative subordination to ST, helps research to capture, analyze, and interpret structuring processes including those that incorporate information (technology) artifacts. The study outcome is not the attempt to "design" a social system or a socio-technical system (an information artifact) but rather provide an informed and elaborate account of choices about (existing and proposed) artifacts, structures, and strategic conduct.

## Practical Impact of the Study

While conducting the study, various technical shortcomings, planning gaps, and organizational problems in the GoMobile project were detected. Based on the progressing study results both planners and implementers were given periodic feedback. Alternative approaches were identified that would maintain the organization's overall mission and strategic objectives while also addressing the needs of both management and field crews.

A comprehensive and detailed catalogue of functional and non-functional requirements for the mobile and stationary ICTs and made detailed recommendations was submitted to SPU, which would improve the fit between mobile ICTs and field crews' needs. For the mobile and backend systems, requirements were determined, which encompassed the hardware, the mobile application software, the human-computer interface, and the workflows themselves. Moreover, the research team was also able to make recommendations for the modification of organizational structures, crew training requirements, crew skills profiles, and novel approaches to the interaction and communication between management and crews. After the study was completed many of the study's recommendations were followed up upon. Still the lack of support for the tacit knowing of field crews, and how mobile ICTs would possibly support this dimension, remained an open issue. In this context, no solution had been identified for capturing, storing, searching, and retrieving on demand non-structured, free-format textual, audio, and video information. However, in the course of the *GoMobile* project SPU leadership and field crews discovered their shared and non-shared assumptions and interpretation of the organization's mission and each others' roles in accomplishing this mission. On both sides the project ultimately led to a better understanding and accepting of the validity of the views and interests of the other side. In essence, the IT artifact-based project was instrumental in increasing the alignment around a shared interpretation of the organizational mission.

## CONCLUSION

This article extends the strand of empirical studies employing the structurationist perspective in IS research. It adds to the understanding of the role of IT artifacts in organizational innovation and change projects, and in particular, in field operations in the public sector. The point of this contribution has been to present the shaping of a social system through human agency in the context of an information technology-based innovation project, its recursive structuring, and the important roles that innovative information artifacts and context-relevant information play in this regard. Stripping this shaping and reshaping of the social system through human agency from the analysis of the role and efficacy of the information artifact would explain its true impact only in part. Conversely, eliminating the information artifact from the analysis of the shaping of the social system through human agency would only partially explain the structuring processes and human interactions.

Over six years and in the course of implementation, use, and modification of mobile systems in field operations, the various stakeholders at the Utilities reshaped the social system in remarkable ways, aligned their agendas, created new routines, and finally all benefitted from the innovation and the adjustments in ways that no stakeholder had foreseen ex ante. Via twenty-one detailed field cases, it was possible to document and analyze these structuring processes in great detail. Ironically, the field crews and crew chiefs at the initially problem-stricken mobile-system introduction at the Drainage and Wastewater Division have turned into the most adamant advocates and enthusiastic proponents of the mobile systems in the field. "These systems have become absolutely indispensable," as one crewmember put it. Over time, when management and crews aligned their agendas, when system functionality and performance improved, wireless coverage increased, and information began flowing more openly between the groups, the acceptance, satisfaction, use of, and intent to use the mobile systems dramatically increased, reaping net benefits that neither group had anticipated at the outset. For example, productivity increased in triple-digit percentages over the old paper-based methods.

In the course of this empirical undertaking, the seven-layer frame from CWA was used, and it helped instill a structurationist perspective into the study's analysis. The findings suggest that when used in empirical research, the layered approach, which is referred to as *situated action analysis*, might have the capacity to increase the understanding of the multi-facetted roles and impacts of information artifacts within the rich context and the structuring of a social system. At the City of Seattle's public utilities, the approach enabled the research to effectively analyze the structuring of this particular social system in a non-reductionist fashion, in general, and in the action and interaction-related context, in particular. In the study, it has been shown that both information artifacts and information appeared as important allocative and authoritative resources. Employing the structurationist approach it was further possible to specify with fine granularity the requirements for information artifacts as they emerged from the specific contexts of human action and interaction. By so doing, the goals, enablers, constraints, priorities, functions, processes, and resources involved in the action and interaction were taken into account. Beyond functional and non-functional requirement specification for the information artifact, it was possible to specify requirements for resources and structures in general with fine granularity and context sensitivity, which provided human agents with a powerful handle to holistically understand and influence the shaping of the social system. While this contribution explicitly avoids and refutes a social engineering perspective with regard to the social systems, it is held that a deep understanding of the interplays and feedbacks in a social system would help human agents make more informed choices and better understand the options available to them in their interaction. Both information and IS/IT have become pervasive and even invasive in today's social systems. Both provide powerful enabling and limiting potentialities to the interaction of human agents. Understanding these potentialities in context is a premier focus of study in IS research. In future work the aspiration is to refine and (potentially further) develop the situated action analysis approach as presented here by analyzing other social systems undergoing ICT-based innovation.

## ACKNOWLEDGMENT

The research team greatly appreciates the support of the leadership and workers of the City of Seattle and of Seattle Public Utilities, in particular, whose open and welcoming attitude was fundamental to the success of this research project. Last and not least, the principal investigator is indebted to his co-investigator Prof. emerita Raya Fidel and to his research associates and former doctoral students Kari Holland, Shuhua (Monica) Liu, and Kristene Unsworth who conducted interviews, made observations, analyzed numerous documents and transcripts, and tremendously helped with the analysis.

## REFERENCES

Alter, S. (2002). Sidestepping The IT Artifact, Scrapping The IS Solo, And Laying Claim To "Systems In Organizations". *Communications of AIS, 2003*(12), 494–526.

Alter, S. (2003). The IS Core -- XI Sorting Out Issues About The Core, Scope, And Identity Of The IS Field. *Communications of AIS, 2003*(12), 607-628.

Archer, M. S. (1995). *Realist social theory: the morphogenetic approach.* Cambridge, UK: Cambridge University Press. doi:10.1017/CBO9780511557675

Bleiler, R. (2003). SPU Technology Project Post-Implementation Review: Water Operations Mobile Computing. Seattle, WA: Academic Press.

Bostrom, R. P., Gupta, S., & Thomas, D. (2009). A Meta-Theory for Understanding Information Systems Within Sociotechnical Systems. *Journal of Management Information Systems*, 26(1), 17–47. doi:10.2753/MIS0742-1222260102

Brooks, L. (1997). Structuration theory and new technology: Analysing organizationally situated computer-aided design (CAD). *Information Systems Journal*, 7(2), 133–151. doi:10.1046/j.1365-2575.1997.00011.x

Bryant, C. G. A., & Jary, D. (1991). Introduction: Coming to terms with Anthony Giddens. In C. G. A. Bryant & D. Jary (Eds.), *Giddens' theory of structuration: a critical appreciation* (pp. 1–31). London: Routledge. doi:10.1007/978-1-4613-9714-4_1

Case, D. O. (2007). *Looking for information: a survey of research on information seeking, needs, and behavior* (2nd ed.). Amsterdam: Elsevier/Academic Press.

Chu, C., & Smithson, S. (2007). E-business and organizational change: A structurational approach. *Information Systems Journal*, 17(4), 369–389. doi:10.1111/j.1365-2575.2007.00258.x

Coad, A., Jack, L., & Kholeif, A. O. R. (2015). Structuration theory: Reflections on its further potential for management accounting research. *Qualitative Research in Accounting & Management*, 12(2), 153–171. doi:10.1108/QRAM-01-2015-0013

Cohen, I. J. (1989). *Structuration theory: Anthony Giddens and the constitution of social life.* New York: St. Martin's Press. doi:10.1007/978-1-349-20255-3

Cummings, M. L. (2006). Can CWA inform the design of networked intelligent systems. *Proceedings of the 1st Moving Autonomy Forward Conference (MAF 2006)*, 1-6.

DeSanctis, G., & Poole, M. S. (1994). Capturing the complexity in advanced technology use: Adaptive structuration theory. *Organization Science*, 5(2), 121–147. doi:10.1287/orsc.5.2.121

Elbasha, T., & Wright, A. (2017). Reconciling structure and agency in strategy-as-practice research: Towards a strong-structuration theory approach. *M@n@gement*, 20(2), 107-128.

Feeney, O., & Pierce, B. (2016). Strong structuration theory and accounting information: An empirical study. *Accounting, Auditing & Accountability Journal, 29*(7), 1152–1176. doi:10.1108/AAAJ-07-2015-2130

Fidel, R., & Pejtersen, A. M. (2002). *Cognitive Work Analysis*. The Information School. Retrieved from http://projects.ischool.washington.edu/fidelr/RayaPubs/CWA-bookchapter.pdf

Fidel, R., & Pejtersen, A. M. (2004). From information behaviour research to the design of information systems: The Cognitive Work Analysis framework. *Information Research, 10*(1), 1–15.

Fidel, R., Scholl, H. J., Liu, S., & Unsworth, K. (2007). *Mobile Government Fieldwork: Technological, organizational, and social challenges*. Paper presented at the 8th Annual International Conference on Digital Government Research (DG.O 2007), Philadelphia, PA.

Giddens, A. (1982). A reply to my critics. *Theory, Culture & Society, 1*(2), 107–113. doi:10.1177/026327648200100212

Giddens, A. (1984). *The constitution of society: outline of the theory of structuration*. Berkeley, CA: University of California Press.

Giddens, A. (1989). A reply to my critics. In D. Held & J. B. Thompson (Eds.), *Social theory of modern societies: Anthony Giddens and his critics* (pp. 249–305). Cambridge, MA: Cambridge University Press. doi:10.1017/CBO9780511557699.013

Giddens, A. (1991). Structuration Theory: Past, present and future. In C. G. A. Bryant & D. Jary (Eds.), *Giddens' theory of structuration: a critical appreciation* (pp. 201–221). London: Routledge.

Gil-Garcia, J. R., & Hassan, S. (2007). Structuration Theory and IT-Based Organizational Change. In G. D. Garson & M. Khosrow-Pour (Eds.), *Handbook of Research on Public Information Technology* (pp. 371–375). Hershey, PA: Information Science.

Gopal, A., Bostrom, R. P., & Chin, W. W. (1993). Applying Adaptive Structuration Theory to Investigate the Process of Group Support Systems Use. *Journal of Management Information Systems, 9*(3), 45–70. doi:10.1080/07421222.1992.11517967

Gorlenko, L., & Merrick, R. (2003). No wires attached: Usability challenges in the connected mobile world. *IBM Systems Journal, 42*(4), 639–651. doi:10.1147j.424.0639

Gorman, G. E., Clayton, P., Rice-Lively, M. L., & Gorman, L. (1997). *Qualitative research for the information professional: a practical handbook*. London: Library Association Publishing.

Hussain, Z. I., & Cornelius, N. (2009). The use of domination and legitimation in information systems implementation. *Information Systems Journal, 19*(2), 197–224. doi:10.1111/j.1365-2575.2008.00322.x

Jack, L. (2017). Strong structuration theory and management accounting research. *Advances in Scientific and Applied Accounting, 10*(2), 211–223. doi:10.14392/asaa.2017100205

Jack, L., & Kholeif, A. (2008). Enterprise Resource Planning and a contest to limit the role of management accountants: A strong structuration perspective. *Accounting Forum, 32*(1), 30–45. doi:10.1016/j.accfor.2007.11.003

Jones, M. R., & Karsten, H. (2008). Giddens's structuration theory and information systems research. *Management Information Systems Quarterly, 32*(1), 127–157. doi:10.2307/25148831

Jones, M. R., & Karsten, H. (2009). Divided by a common language? A response to Marshall Scott Poole. *Management Information Systems Quarterly, 33*(3), 589–595. doi:10.2307/20650311

Klesel, M., Mokosch, G., & Niehaves, B. (2015). Maturing, Flagshipping and Piggybacking: On the Use of Structuration Theory in Information Systems Research. In *Proceedings of the 21st Americas Conference on Information Systems (AMCIS 2015)* (pp. 1-11). Fajardo, Puerto Rico: Association for Information Systems (AIS).

Liu, S., Unsworth, K., Fidel, R., & Scholl, H. J. (2007). Fully mobile wirelessly connected technology applications: Organizational communication, social, and information challenges. *Proceedings of the American Society for Information Science and Technology*. 10.1002/meet.1450440237

Naikar, N. (2017). Cognitive work analysis: An influential legacy extending beyond human factors and engineering. *Applied Ergonomics, 59*(Part B), 528-540. doi:10.1016/j.apergo.2016.06.001

Naikar, N., & Elix, B. (2016). Reflections on Cognitive Work Analysis and Its Capacity to Support Designing for Adaptation. *Journal of Cognitive Engineering and Decision Making, 10*(2), 123–125. doi:10.1177/1555343416654846

Newcombe, T. (2002, November). Mobile mapping, Report. *Government Technology*. Retrieved from http://www.govtech.net/magazine/sup_story.php?id=29377&story_pg=3

Niskanen, T. (2017). Implementation of a novel taxonomy based on cognitive work analysis in the assessment of safety performance. *International Journal of Occupational Safety and Ergonomics*. (accepted)

Orlikowski, W. J. (1992). The duality of technology: Rethinking the concept of technology in organizations. *Organization Science, 3*(3), 398–427. doi:10.1287/orsc.3.3.398

Orlikowski, W. J., & Robey, D. (1991). Information technology and the structuring of organizations. *Information Systems Research, 2*(2), 143–169. doi:10.1287/isre.2.2.143

Parker, J. (2006). Structuration's Future? From 'All and Every' to 'Who Did What, Where, When, How and Why?'. *Journal of Critical Realism, 5*(1), 122–138.

Polanyi, M. (1966). The tacit dimension (1st ed.). Garden City, NY: Doubleday.

Polanyi, M., & Grene, M. G. (1969). *Knowing and being; essays*. University of Chicago Press.

Pozzebon, M., & Pinsonneault, A. (2005). Challenges in conducting empirical work using structuration theory: Learning from IT research. *Organization Studies, 26*(9), 1353–1376. doi:10.1177/0170840605054621

Puron-Cid, G. (2013). Interdisciplinary application of structuration theory for e-government: A case study of an IT-enabled budget reform. *Government Information Quarterly, 30*(Supplement 1), S46–S58. doi:10.1016/j.giq.2012.07.010

Rasmussen, J. (1986). *Information processing and human-machine interaction: an approach to cognitive engineering*. New York: North-Holland.

Rasmussen, J., Pejtersen, A. M., & Goodstein, L. P. (1994). *Cognitive systems engineering*. New York: Wiley.

Rasmussen, J., Pejtersen, A. M., & Schmidt, K. (1990). *Taxonomy for Cognitive Work Analysis*. Retrieved from http://www.itu.dk/~schmidt/papers/taxonomy.pdf

Read, G. J. M., Salmon, P. M., & Lenné, M. G. (2012). From work analysis to work design: A review of cognitive work analysis design applications In *Proceedings of the human factors and ergonomics society annual meeting* (1st ed.; Vol. 56, pp. 368-372). Los Angeles, CA: SAGE Publications. 10.1177/1071181312561084

Read, G. J. M., Salmon, P. M., Lenné, M. G., & Stanton, N. A. (2015). Designing sociotechnical systems with cognitive work analysis: Putting theory back into practice. *Ergonomics*, *58*(5), 822–851. doi:10.1080/00140139.2014.980335 PMID:25407778

Richardson, H., & Robinson, B. (2007). The mysterious case of the missing paradigm: A review of critical information systems research 1991-2001. *Information Systems Journal*, *17*(3), 251–270. doi:10.1111/j.1365-2575.2007.00230.x

Ritchie, J., Lewis, J., & Gillian, E. (2003). Designing and selecting samples. In J. Ritchie & J. Lewis (Eds.), *Qualitative research practice: a guide for social science students and researchers* (pp. 77–108). London: Sage Publications.

Robey, D., & Abdalla Mikhaeil, C. (2016). Déjà Vu or Art Nouveau? A comment on Demetis and Lee's "Crafting theory to satisfy the requirements of systems science". *Information and Organization*, *26*(4), 127–130. doi:10.1016/j.infoandorg.2016.10.001

Scholl, H. J. (2005a). E-government-induced business process change (BPC): An empirical study of current practices. *International Journal of Electronic Government Research*, *1*(2), 25–47. doi:10.4018/jegr.2005040102

Scholl, H. J. (2005b). Motives, strategic approach, objectives & focal areas in e-Gov-induced change. *International Journal of Electronic Government Research*, *1*(1), 58–77. doi:10.4018/jegr.2005010104

Scholl, H. J., Fidel, R., Liu, S., Paulsmeyer, M., & Unsworth, K. (2007). E-Gov Field Force Automation: Promises, Challenges, and Stakeholders. In M. Wimmer, H. J. Scholl, & A. Groenlund (Eds.), *Electronic Government: Sixth International Conference, EGOV 2007* (*Vol. 4656*, pp. 127-142). Regensburg, Germany: Springer Verlag.

Scholl, H. J., Fidel, R., Mai, J.-E., & Unsworth, K. (2006). Seattle's Mobile City Project. *Proceedings of Euro mGov 2006: The Second European Conference on Mobile Government*.

Scholl, H. J., Liu, S., Fidel, R., & Unsworth, K. (2007). *Choices and Challenges in e-Government Field Force Automation Projects: Insights from Case Studies*. Paper presented at the ICEGOV, Macao, China. 10.1145/1328057.1328142

Silva, L. (2007). Epistemological and theoretical challenges for studying power and politics in information systems. *Information Systems Journal*, *17*(2), 165–183. doi:10.1111/j.1365-2575.2007.00232.x

Stones, R. (2005). *Structuration theory*. Wiley Online Library. doi:10.1007/978-0-230-21364-7

Strauss, A. L., & Corbin, J. M. (1998). *Basics of qualitative research: techniques and procedures for developing grounded theory* (2nd ed.). Thousand Oaks, CA: Sage Publications.

Thrift, N. (1985). Bear and Mouse or Bear and Tree? Anthony Giddenss Reconstitution of Social Theory. *Sociology, 19*(4), 609–623. doi:10.1177/0038038585019004009

Veenstra, A. F. v., Melin, U., & Axelsson, K. (2014). Theoretical and practical implications from the use of structuration theory in public sector information systems research. *Proceedings of the 22nd European Conference on Information Systems (ECIS 2014)*, 1-12.

Vicente, K. J. (1999). *Cognitive work analysis: toward safe, productive, and healthy computer-based work.* Mahwah, NJ: Lawrence Erlbaum Associates.

Walsham, G. (2005). Learning about being critical. *Information Systems Journal, 15*(2), 111–117. doi:10.1111/j.1365-2575.2004.00189.x

Whittington, R. (1992). Putting Giddens into action: Social systems and managerial agency. *Journal of Management Studies, 29*(6), 693–712. doi:10.1111/j.1467-6486.1992.tb00685.x

Yuan, Y., Archer, N., Connelly, C. E., & Zheng, W. (2010). Identifying the ideal fit between mobile work and mobile work support. *Information & Management, 47*(3), 125–137. doi:10.1016/j.im.2009.12.004

## ENDNOTE

[1] Please note that the terms "IT" for "information technology" and "ICT" for "information and communication technology" are used interchangeably. We further use the term "information artifact" as a summary term, which also includes their technology instantiations (information systems, applications, smart phones, etc.).

# Chapter 5
# Transformation of Government and Citizen Trust in Government:
## A Conceptual Model

**Mohamed Mahmood**
*Brunel University London, UK*

## ABSTRACT

*The continuing erosion of citizen trust and confidence in government has been attributed to a number of factors. This chapter examines the potential role of digital transformation of government in reversing this decline. Based on a systematic literature review, key factors that influence citizen trust and confidence in government as an institution are identified, including citizen satisfaction and expectations, government transparency and accountability, transformation of government, and government performance. The review of the literature also reveals a lack of knowledge and understanding of how transformation of government can influence the growing decline in citizen engagement with government. To address this gap, a conceptual model capturing the key constructs is proposed to support a better understanding of strategies for rebuilding trust and confidence in government administrations through transformation of government.*

DOI: 10.4018/978-1-5225-6204-7.ch005

# INTRODUCTION

Governments are implementing measures to improve their processes to provide more efficient and responsive services to their citizens. Rapid developments in information technology have radically altered the way government organizations interact with citizens, and e-government has become a mainstream service delivery method in the public sector. The transformation of the service delivery system by the Internet has enhanced government services and their operations for the benefit of citizens, businesses, employees, and other stakeholders. However, regardless of global enthusiasm for e-government, most endeavors have fallen short of their potential (Bannister and Connolly, 2011), particularly in developing countries. Among the challenges faced by governments around the world in implementing various e-government projects, the greatest is lack of adoption and use by citizens. Researchers have attributed this lack of willingness to use e-government to declining trust in government and government practices (Aljazzaf, Perry, & Capretz, 2010; Colesca, 2009; Teo, Srivastava, & Jiang, 2008). This chapter examines the influence of digital transformation of government on citizen trust and confidence.

Government authorities have sought to incorporate information technology into their operations to increase competitiveness, support economic development, reduce costs, increase transparency, improve accountability and reduce the unemployment rate, among other goals. In addition, citizens expect government or public servants to serve the public interest with fairness and manage public resources in an efficient manner. Fair and reliable public services can act as a catalyst to improve public trust and create a favorable environment for business. The Internet is viewed as a medium that can facilitate potential improvements in the performance of government agencies. Thus, proponents have argued that e-government can play an important role in rebuilding the loss of public confidence in government performance as well as improving citizen satisfaction with public services in a country (Morgeson, VanAmburg, & Mithas, 2011; Tolbert and Mossberger, 2006). However, a comprehensive understanding of the relevant drivers and factors for rebuilding citizen trust via the use of e-government practices remains lacking (Abu-Shanab and Al-Azzam, 2012; Alateyah, Crowder, & Wills, 2013; and Carter, 2008; Colesca, 2009).

To address this gap, this chapter identifies and examines factors that impact citizen trust related to e-government practices as well as citizen trust and confidence in government through digital transformation. This is pursued by critically reviewing various published research studies as well as secondary grey literature. Concepts related to trust in technology (or the Internet), e-government, and government are examined to develop a conceptual model based on appropriate theoretical underpinnings provided by the existing literature. Finally, based on the literature review, hypotheses are developed to test the relationships formulated in the conceptual model based on empirical data in a developing country context. Key challenges affecting the implementation of e-government practices that could lead to the development of citizen trust are also examined. The rest of this chapter is structured as follows: First, the methodology used for the study is outlined, followed by a broad overview of the literature. Next, the findings of the literature review on trust in the context of e-government are discussed, and the proposed conceptual model is presented. The chapter ends with concluding reflections.

## RESEARCH METHODOLOGY

Systematic literature reviews (SLRs) or reviews of the evidence-based literature have been used regularly in fields such as health, nursing, software engineering and psychology but have been limited in the Information Systems (IS) field (Oates, 2011). SLRs are a recognized, transparent and standardized methodology for conducting literature reviews (Okoli and Schabram, 2011). Consequently, an SLR was adopted here to examine the influence of trust within the context of e-government and to contribute towards advancing the understanding of e-government implementation and adoption. The SLR covered relevant academic papers, including peer-reviewed journal and conference papers, as well as grey literature, including white papers and reports. The SLR was divided into two phases. During the first phase, the search included three keywords, "e-government", "government" and "trust", and used Scopus as the primary searching index and Google Scholar and the Brunel University e-library as complementary databases. The initial pool of approximately 300 publications was then narrowed to 30 publications by conducting a number of filtration exercises in which the abstracts, conclusion sections, and main bodies of the papers were reviewed. In the second phase of the SLR, the same databases were searched with additional keywords related to the subject: "electronic government", "online government", "digital government" and "adoption". Of the approximately 100 publications retrieved, 33 remained after using the same filtration techniques described above. Ultimately, 63 papers were reviewed and analyzed.

## LITERATURE REVIEW

Citizen trust and confidence in government have declined over the last two decades (Bean, 2015; Edwards, 2015; McNeal, Hale, & Dotterweich, 2008; Morgeson et al., 2011; Pina, Torres, & Royo, 2010; Teo et al., 2008; Tolbert and Mossberger, 2006). Accordingly, the potential of implementation of e-government practices to reverse this decline has become a topic of considerable interest among researchers. A number of studies have focused on the factors that affect e-government practices in different countries (Bannister and Connolly, 2011; Morgeson et al., 2011; Colesca, 2009; Abu-Shanab and Al-Azzam, 2012). Avgerou, Ciborra, Cordella, Kallinikos, & Smith (2006) posit that e-government practices reflect the extent to which the government is able to establish its online presence in a country. Ba & Pavlou (2002) describe e-government as a model that helps governments transform their business function by integrating disparate processes and technology to enable one-stop service. However, Alateyah et al. (2013) suggest that e-government practices are also associated with uncertainty. Introducing a technological infrastructure for conducting transactions via new modes of communication, including government websites, poses a new set of challenges. These studies have identified a variety of external and internal factors that impact the introduction and implementation of e-government practices (Ulbig 2002; Sharma and Gupta, 2003). External pressures can have a major influence on the way organizations improve their processes and services to enhance quality and customer (in this case, citizens) satisfaction. Among these pressures, Powell and Heriot (2000) show that strong support for e-government by political leadership and implementation of legal and regulatory frameworks are significant factors affecting transformation within government institutions.

Although the factors identified in the literature are discussed with the objective of transforming government, there is no single definition of "transformation of government". According to Bannister and Connolly (2011), government transformation is expected to increase citizen perceptions and uptake of e-government through evident trust and confidence (Morgeson et al., 2011). However, the factors influencing transformation of government and the relationships between these factors have not been comprehensively discussed in the literature and represent a clear gap. For the purpose of this article, transformation of government is defined as major changes in the processes, procedures, functions, structure, and power of government (Bannister and Connolly, 2011; Waller and Weerakkody, 2016).

Numerous definitions of trust in the context of e-government are found in the literature. A straightforward description is provided by Bwalya (2009), who explains that trust occurs in an uncertain environment where there is the presence of risk. The level of trust may decrease if the trustor is unable to address unfulfilled expectations or harmful outcomes occurs. To develop an understanding of the mechanisms by which e-government practices impact citizen trust, Bwalya (2009) discusses factors directly related to e-government practices. Mishler and Rose (2005) identify perceived usefulness, ease of use and accessibility as factors impacting citizen trust in e-government practices. The literature also suggests that the level of trust may differ depending on user perception, which is related to user knowledge of and experience with the use of e-government. Literacy and knowledge related to e-government practices positively impact trust in e-government practices (Bannister and Connolly, 2011), and citizen adoption of and trust in e-government practices are also influenced by demographic factors such as age, gender, and education. However, a lack of technical infrastructure, especially in developing countries, can lead to a decline in e-government practices. Accordingly, different variables related to the competency of e-government services have been shown to influence citizen trust. Kamal and Alsudairi (2009) state that the competency and ease of use of e-government services are strongly related to the development of citizen perceptions and that good e-government practices can improve technical and organizational capabilities. Furthermore, Shih (2004) indicates that citizen trust in technology can be divided into different categories: trust in the competency of the government organization and perceived risk associated with using the Internet. Therefore, it is essential for government organizations to focus on improving service quality, reliability, speed of delivery and information quality to increase citizen confidence and trust when using e-government services. If the risk associated with e-government practices is not controlled and privacy is not maintained, the level of trust that citizens have in their government and e-government practices may be reduced (Al-Sobhi and Weerakkody, 2010; Ebrahim and Irani, 2005; Qaisar and Khan, 2010). Two security issues frequently cited in the literature are confidentiality of information and perceived risk.

In addition, research by Al-Sobhi and Weerakkody (2010) illustrates that the use of information technology plays an important role in promoting the diffusion of e-government practices and, in turn, improving interactions with citizens and between different government departments. Moreover, information technology can be used to introduce improvements to back office operations and improve workflow and efficiency, thus enhancing the front-end citizen experience and transforming the way government functions, works and serves citizens. Accordingly, a number of studies have emphasized that the adoption of information technology leads to enhancements of the provision of products and services (Abu-Shanab and Abu-Baker, 2011; Bannister and Connolly, 2011; Waller and Weerakkody, 2016; Wang and Benbasat, 2005; Welch, Hinnant, & Moon, 2005). Specifically, Wang and Benbasat (2005) posit that information technology has a major influence on the processes of e-government and online service provision. Therefore, a high level of trust in technology will ensure that citizens interact with a government that uses services supported by technology. Importantly, the adoption of new or innovative technologies should be supported by changes within the environment in which they are adopted to facilitate efficient and effective use.

A common factor discussed in several studies of the decline in government trust is the diminishing perception of government performance, particularly for the delivery of services to members of society (e.g., Cullen and Reilly, 2007; Karavasilis, Zafiropoulos, & Vrana, 2010; Morgeson et al., 2011; Welch et al.,

2005). E-government holds considerable potential for transforming government to improve service delivery to citizens (Teo et al., 2008; Tolbert and Mossberger, 2006) and citizen trust in government. Accordingly, many governments have recently developed websites with the aim of enhancing positive attitudes towards e-government and improving trust or confidence in government. Key outcomes of implementing e-government with the aim of transforming government and enhancing citizen trust are transparency and accountability (Bannister and Connolly, 2011; O'Neill, 2009; Tolbert and Mossberger, 2006; Waller and Weerakkody, 2016). Managing citizen expectations and demands is a critical task for enhancing the relationship between the government and its citizens (Morgeson et al., 2011; Nam, 2012). Government performance is an important criterion for citizen satisfaction with government and its services (Morgeson et al., 2011) and, in turn, enhanced citizen trust in government (Bean, 2015; Morgeson et al., 2011).

The literature also posits that the benefits of the use of e-government services can play a vital role in rebuilding trust among citizens. Lean, Zailani, Ramayah, & Fernando (2009) state that e-government services have the potential to reduce the cost of service delivery, which may increase citizen confidence in their government. The same study also posits that implementing and adopting e-government will be a hurdle unless the knowledge of citizens about their government and any associated political issues is increased. One of the greatest advantages of e-government is that it provides a direct channel for successfully communicating with government, which will attract citizens to the use of e-government practices. Similarly, research by Evans and Yen (2006) has shown that e-government practices bring about overall improvements in the processes, programs, plans, outputs and outcomes of government. However, authorities should ensure that necessary security measures are taken before disclosing information online (Alsaghier, Ford, Nguyen, & Hexel, 2009).

Over the years, governments have used information technology to hold meetings online, develop bulletin board systems, and create chat rooms and processes for e-rulemaking. The adoption of information technologies in their operations allows governments to fulfil their responsibilities to citizens more effectively and transparently (Hiller and Bélanger, 2001). Other benefits associated with the use of e-government practices include inward observability, active disclosure of information and external accessibility. With respect to transaction security in e-government practices, Carter and Bélanger (2005) note that governments or websites that are highly secure have the potential to attract a high level of trust from citizens, resulting in citizen uptake or adoption of the e-government service. Protection against unwanted access also improves the level of trust among citizens in the use of e-government practices. Therefore, it is important for the government to design a framework that is based on readiness and to precisely consider the basis on which an effective e-government model will be established to provide services to citizens.

The literature has also identified a number of challenges and barriers to the successful implementation of e-government practices. Failure can negatively impact citizen trust. Mishler and Rose (2005) find that e-government facilities remain insufficiently secure, with the threat of alteration or misuse of personal data by hackers. There is also a high degree of probability of theft of credit card data due to the disclosure of personal information. Accordingly, Al-Sobhi and Weerakkody (2010) report that implementation of e-government systems and citizen trust are also affected by financial risk, performance risk, psychological risk, social risk, convenience and overall risk. These risks must be overcome to encourage governments to implement e-government systems and to increase trust in such systems among citizens, including investors.

Many countries fail to recognize that the implementation of e-government practices involves several stages of evolution (from basic provisioning of information to more complex transactional services), with specific challenges that must be addressed in each stage. Consistent with this failure, numerous studies have revealed that governments have struggled to cope with certain issues in terms of implementation and service provisioning as well as adoption. Bannister and Connolly (2011) discuss some of these complex issues that undermine e-government service performance, including managerial, technological, and social issues and policy changes associated with the shift from conventional methods. Moon (2003) alludes to these issues by showing that the significant changes brought by e-government in the way services are provided to the public introduces uncertainty in service delivery and use.

The literature review clearly indicates that e-government services are used in many countries around the world. Previous studies have elucidated the impact of e-government on the performance of government agencies and revealed that e-government adoption is related to citizen trust in government. The majority of studies have indicated a positive relationship between e-government services and citizen trust in government. The identification of factors that affect trust in e-government and government raises the question of how these factors influence the restoration of trust in government. The conflicting conclusions in the literature indicate that e-government alone is insufficient to increase citizen trust and highlight the need for further understanding. A comprehensive discussion of the influence of transformation of government on trust and confidence is also lacking (Bannister and Connolly, 2011; West, 2004), and the factors influencing transformation of government and their interrelationships remain unclear. As a result, there is a lack of knowledge of how the transformation of existing practices and services can reverse the decline in citizen trust and confidence in government.

## PROPOSED CONCEPTUAL MODEL

Based on the literature review, a conceptual model is developed for the influence of a transformed government on citizen trust and confidence, taking into account factors such as technology, accountability, transparency, citizen expectations and satisfaction, and government performance. A number of models of declining citizen trust in government and the introduction of e-government regimes have been proposed in the literature (Morgeson et al., 2011; Teo et al., 2008), but none of these models have included the relationships between the identified factors and citizen trust in government. The model developed by Morgeson et al. (2011) is most closely related to the aim and objectives of this study as it discusses the relationships among e-government, citizen satisfaction, citizen expectations and citizen trust and confidence in government based on exit-voice theory (Hirschman, 1970). Within the boundaries of exit-voice theory, the model developed by Morgeson et al. (2011) is expanded by adding new factors and concepts as presented below.

According to Bannister and Connolly (2011), transformation is as a major variable determining e-government uptake. Technology, aspects of government, and trust in e-government have also been linked to e-government uptake. Because these factors are all discussed with the objective of transforming government, transformation of government here is considered a key variable influencing citizen trust and confidence in government. Transformation of government influences its performance, which impacts citizen satisfaction with government. In turn, satisfaction influences citizen trust and confidence in government, which is measured by the level of citizen engagement with government. According to the literature, the terms trust and confidence are closely related to each other and refer to the same meaning (e.g., Mungiu-Pippidi et al., 2016; Wolak and Palus, 2010; Gilmour, Coffey, & O'Toole, 2015; Khan, 2016; Edwards, 2015). Government transformation is therefore an independent variable in the proposed conceptual model, whereas citizen trust is a dependent variable. Government performance and citizen satisfaction are considered as mediator variables.

In addition, transformation of government is influenced by a number of variables, particularly e-government as a tool, technology adoption and use by government entities, and citizen expectations of government. As stated above, transformation refers to a major change in how government provides services to citizens. Two additional variables that influence this change are government transparency in providing services and government accountability to stakeholders. Here, transformation of government is considered a dependent variable, whereas the other five variables are independent variables.

Based on these relationships, the proposed conceptual model for evaluating the influence of digital transformation of government on citizen trust and confidence

*Figure 1. The proposed conceptual model for evaluating the influence of digital transformation of government on citizen trust and confidence*

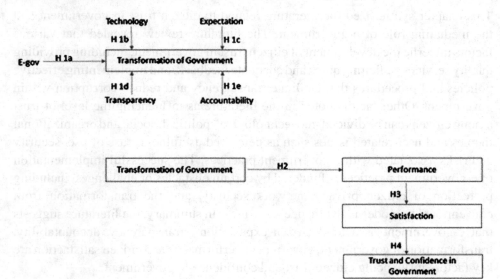

is outlined in Figure 1. The results and knowledge gained from this model could be used to at least partially reduce the decline of citizen engagement with government.

Based on the conceptual model and the arguments presented above, the following hypotheses are proposed:

**H1a:** E-government positively influences transformation of government.
**H1b:** Technology positively influences transformation of government.
**H1c:** Expectation positively influences transformation of government.
**H1d:** Transparency positively influences transformation of government.
**H1e:** Accountability positively influences transformation of government.
**H2:** Transformation of government positively influences performance of government.
**H3:** Performance of government positively influences citizen satisfaction with government.
**H4:** Satisfaction positively influences citizen engagement with government.

The next phases of this research will investigate the illustrated model and hypotheses to obtain information on the factors that affect trust in government. These phases will include the finalization of the research instruments, supporting theories and evidences, a pilot test and finally the main survey.

## CONCLUSION

This chapter synthesized the literature related to citizen trust in government and the mediating role of e-government. The literature review revealed that various factors underlie the development of citizen trust in government, including providing quality services, soliciting quick and adequate feedback, and implementing effective policies and procedures that facilitate transparency and reduce corruption within government. Other factors noted in the literature as influencing the level of trust among citizens can be divided into technological, political, social and organizational themes and user-related issues such as perceived usefulness, ease of use, security and risks associated with e-government practices. The successful implementation of e-government practices is hindered by certain obstacles or challenges, including protection of citizen privacy, network security, and the transformation from conventional to modern governance structures. In summary, the literature suggests that e-government as a tool, citizen expectations, transparency, accountability, transformation of government, government performance and citizen satisfaction are key factors influencing citizen trust and confidence in government.

This chapter argues that low uptake of e-government services by citizens may be due to insufficient knowledge of how transformation of government can improve services. A better understanding of this relationship could be used to enhance citizen trust and confidence in government and, in turn, at least partially reduce the decline in citizen engagement with government. However, the author recognizes that further review of the literature is needed to support the identified factors and gaps. For practitioners, the factors and challenges related to trust and confidence in government and e-government regimes highlighted in this chapter could be used to assist policymakers in their efforts to improve citizen uptake of digital services, digital participation and user satisfaction.

Finally, the findings of the literature review were used to develop a high-level conceptual model describing the factors influencing citizen trust and confidence in government related to digital transformation. The proposed conceptual model builds on the model of Morgeson et al. (2011) by adding new concepts based on the outcomes of other studies. This model and the associated hypotheses will be investigated further in the next phases of this research.

## REFERENCES

Abu-Shanab, E., & Al-Azzam, A. (2012). Trust dimensions and the adoption of e-government in Jordan. *International Journal of Information Communication Technologies and Human Development*, 4(1), 39–51. doi:10.4018/jicthd.2012010103

Abu-Shanab, E. A., & Abu-Baker, A. N. (2011). Evaluating Jordan's e-government website: a case study. *Electronic Government, an International Journal, 8*(4), 271-289.

Al-Sobhi, F., & Weerakkody, V. 2010. The role of intermediaries in facilitating e-government diffusion in Saudi Arabia. In *Online Proceedings of the European, Mediterranean & Middle Eastern Conference on Information Systems (EMCIS)*. Retrieved from http://emcis.eu/Emcis_archive/EMCIS/EMCIS2010/Proceedings/Accepted%20Refereed%20Papers/C97.pdf

Alateyah, S. A., Crowder, R. M., & Wills, G. B. (2013). Factors affecting the citizen's intention to adopt e-government in Saudi Arabia. *World Academy of Science Engineering and Technology International Journal of Social Science and Engineering, 7*(9), 2559–2564.

Aljazzaf, Z. M., Perry, M., & Capretz, M. A. (2010). Online trust: Definition and principles. In *Proceedings of the Fifth International Multi-conference on Computing in the Global Information Technology (ICCGI)* (pp. 163-168). Los Alamitos, CA: IEEE Computer Society Conference Publishing Services.

Alsaghier, H., Ford, M., Nguyen, A., & Hexel, R. (2009). Conceptualising citizen's trust in e-government: Application of Q methodology. *Journal of E-Government, 7*(4), 295–310.

Avgerou, C., Ciborra, C., Cordella, A., Kallinikos, J., & Smith, M. L. (2006, May). *E-government and trust in the state: lessons from electronic tax systems in Chile and Brazil* (London School of Economics and Political Science Department of Information Systems Working Paper Series No. 146). Retrieved from http://is2.lse.ac.uk/wp/pdf/WP146.PDF

Ba, S., & Pavlou, P. A. (2002). Evidence of the effect of trust building technology in electronic markets: Price premiums and buyer behavior. *Management Information Systems Quarterly, 26*(3), 243–268. doi:10.2307/4132332

Bannister, F., & Connolly, R. (2011). Trust and transformational government: A proposed framework for research. *Government Information Quarterly, 28*(2), 137–147. doi:10.1016/j.giq.2010.06.010

Bean, C. (2015). Changing citizen confidence: Orientations towards political and social institutions in Australia, 1983-2010. *The Open Political Science Journal, 8*(1), 1–9. doi:10.2174/1874949601508010001

Bélanger, F., & Carter, L. (2008). Trust and risk in e-government adoption. *The Journal of Strategic Information Systems, 17*(2), 165–176. doi:10.1016/j.jsis.2007.12.002

Bwalya, K. J. (2009). Factors affecting adoption of e-government in Zambia. *The Electronic Journal on Information Systems in Developing Countries*, *38*(4), 1–13. doi:10.1002/j.1681-4835.2009.tb00267.x

Carter, L., & Bélanger, F. (2005). The utilization of e-government services: Citizen trust, innovation and acceptance factors. *Information Systems Journal*, *15*(1), 5–25. doi:10.1111/j.1365-2575.2005.00183.x

Colesca, S. E. (2009). Understanding trust in e-government. *Inzinerine Ekonomika -. The Engineering Economist*, *3*, 7–15.

Cullen, R., & Reilly, P. (2007). Information privacy and trust in government: A citizen-based perspective from New Zealand. In *Proceedings of the 40th Hawaii International Conference on System Sciences* (pp. 109-114). Los Alamitos, CA: IEEE Computer Society Conference Publishing Services. 10.1109/HICSS.2007.271

Ebrahim, Z., & Irani, Z. (2005). E-government adoption: Architecture and barriers. *Business Process Management Journal*, *11*(5), 589–611. doi:10.1108/14637150510619902

Edwards, M. (2015, April 8). *The trust deficit - concepts and causes of low public trust in governments*. Retrieved from http://workspace.unpan.org/sites/Internet/Documents/UNPAN94464.pdf

Evans, D., & Yen, D. C. (2006). E-government: Evolving relationship of citizens and government, domestic, and international development. *Government Information Quarterly*, *23*(2), 207–235. doi:10.1016/j.giq.2005.11.004

Gilmour, P., Coffey, B., & O'Toole, K. (2015). Trust and knowledge exchange in coastal settings. *Australian Journal of Maritime and Ocean Affairs*, *7*(1), 66–74. doi:10.1080/18366503.2015.1014013

Hiller, J. S., & Bélanger, F. (2001, January). *Privacy strategies for electronic government*. Retrieved from http://www.businessofgovernment.org/sites/default/files/PrivacyStrategies.pdf

Hirschman, A. O. (1970). *Exit, voice, and loyalty: Responses to decline in firms, organizations, and states*. Cambridge, MA: Harvard University Press.

Kamal, M. M., & Alsudairi, M. (2009). Investigating the importance of factors influencing integration technologies adoption in local government authorities. *Transforming Government: People, Process and Policy*, *3*(3), 302–331.

Karavasilis, I., Zafiropoulos, K., & Vrana, V. (2010). Factors affecting the adoption of eGovernance by teachers in Greece. In *Proceedings of the 10th European Conference on e-Government* (pp. 221-229). Reading, UK: Academic Publishing Limited.

Khan, A. (2016, February). *Central bank governance and the role of nonfinancial risk management* (International Monetary Fund Working Paper No. 16/34). Retrieved from https://www.imf.org/external/pubs/ft/wp/2016/wp1634.pdf

Lean, O. K., Zailani, S., Ramayah, T., & Fernando, Y. (2009). Factors influencing intention to use e-government services among citizens in Malaysia. *International Journal of Information Management, 29*(6), 458–475. doi:10.1016/j.ijinfomgt.2009.03.012

McNeal, R., Hale, K., & Dotterweich, L. (2008). Citizen–government interaction and the Internet: Expectations and accomplishments in contact, quality, and trust. *Journal of Information Technology & Politics, 5*(2), 213–229. doi:10.1080/19331680802298298

Mishler, W., & Rose, R. (2005). What are the political consequences of trust? A test of cultural and institutional theories in Russia. *Comparative Political Studies, 38*(9), 1050–1078. doi:10.1177/0010414005278419

Moon, M. J. (2003). Can IT help government to restore public trust? Declining public trust and potential prospects of IT in the public sector. *Proceedings of the 36th Hawaii International Conference on System Sciences*. 10.1109/HICSS.2003.1174303

Morgeson, F. V. III, VanAmburg, D., & Mithas, S. (2011). Misplaced trust? Exploring the structure of the e-government-citizen trust relationship. *Journal of Public Administration: Research and Theory, 21*(2), 257–283. doi:10.1093/jopart/muq006

Mungiu-Pippidi, A., Dadašov, R., Fazekas, M., Tóth, I. J., Kocsis, G., Jancsis, D., Kortas, A.-M., ... Skolkay, A. (2015, January 1). *Public Integrity and Trust in Europe*. Retrieved from https://www.government.nl/documents/reports/2016/01/18/public-integrity-and-trust-in-europe

Nam, T. (2012). Citizens' attitudes toward Open Government and Government 2.0. *International Review of Administrative Sciences, 78*(2), 346–368. doi:10.1177/0020852312438783

O'Neill, R. (2009). The transformative impact of e-government on public governance in New Zealand. *Public Management Review, 11*(6), 751–770. doi:10.1080/14719030903318939

Oates, B. (2011). Evidence-based information systems: A decade later. *ECIS 2011 Proceedings*. Retrieved from http://aisel.aisnet.org/ecis2011/222

Okoli, C., & Schabram, K. (2010). A guide to conducting a systematic literature review of information systems research. *Sprouts: Working Papers on Information Systems, 10*(26). Retrieved from http://sprouts.aisnet.org/10-26

Pina, V., Torres, L., & Royo, S. (2009). E-government evolution in EU local governments: A comparative perspective. *Online Information Review, 33*(6), 1137–1168. doi:10.1108/14684520911011052

Qaisar, N., & Khan, H. (2010). E-government challenges in public sector: A case study of Pakistan. *International Journal of Computer Science Issues, 7*(5), 310–317. Retrieved from http://www.ijcsi.org/papers/7-5-310-317.pdf

Sharma, S., & Gupta, J. (2003). Building blocks of an e-government: A framework. *Journal of Electronic Commerce in Organizations, 1*(4), 34–48. doi:10.4018/jeco.2003100103

Teo, T. S., Srivastava, S. C., & Jiang, L. (2008). Trust and electronic government success: An empirical study. *Journal of Management Information Systems, 25*(3), 99–132. doi:10.2753/MIS0742-1222250303

Tolbert, C. J., & Mossberger, K. (2006). The effects of e-government on trust and confidence in government. *Public Administration Review, 66*(3), 354–369. doi:10.1111/j.1540-6210.2006.00594.x

Ulbig, S. (2002). Policies, procedures, and people: Sources of support for government? *Social Science Quarterly, 83*(3), 789–809. doi:10.1111/1540-6237.00115

Waller, P., & Weerakkody, V. (2016, June). *Digital government: Overcoming the systemic failure of transformation* (Brunel University London Working Paper No. 2). Retrieved from http://bura.brunel.ac.uk/handle/2438/12732

Wang, W., & Benbasat, I. (2005). Trust in and adoption of online recommendation agents. *Journal of the Association for Information Systems, 6*(3), 72–101. doi:10.17705/1jais.00065

Welch, E. W., Hinnant, C. C., & Moon, M. J. (2005). Linking citizen satisfaction with e-government and trust in government. *Journal of Public Administration: Research and Theory, 15*(3), 371–391. doi:10.1093/jopart/mui021

Wolak, J., & Palus, C. K. (2010). The dynamics of public confidence in U.S. state and local government. *State Politics & Policy Quarterly, 10*(4), 421–445. doi:10.1177/153244001001000407

## ADDITIONAL READING

Ashaye, O. R., & Irani, Z. (2014). E-government implementation benefits, risks, and barriers in developing countries: Evidence from Nigeria. *US-China Education Review B*, *4*(1), 13–25.

Dalton, R. J. (2005). The social transformation of trust in government. *International Review of Sociology*, *15*(1), 133–154. doi:10.1080/03906700500038819

Gilbert, D., Balestrini, P., & Littleboy, D. (2004). Barriers and benefits in the adoption of e-government. *International Journal of Public Sector Management*, *17*(4), 286–301. doi:10.1108/09513550410539794

Gunawong, P., & Gao, P. (2017). Understanding e-government failure in the developing country context: A process-oriented study. *Information Technology for Development*, *23*(1), 153–178. doi:10.1080/02681102.2016.1269713

Kampen, J. K., Van de Walle, S. V., & Bouckaert, G. (2006). Assessing the relation between satisfaction with public service delivery and trust in government: The impact of the predisposition of citizens toward government on evaluations of its performance. *Public Performance & Management Review*, *29*(4), 387–404.

Kim, S., Kim, H. J., & Lee, H. (2009). An institutional analysis of an e-government system for anti-corruption: The case of OPEN. *Government Information Quarterly*, *26*(1), 42–50. doi:10.1016/j.giq.2008.09.002

Omar, A., Weerakkody, V., & Sivarajah, U. (2017). Digitally enabled service transformation in UK public sector: A case analysis of universal credit. *International Journal of Information Management*, *37*(4), 350–356. doi:10.1016/j.ijinfomgt.2017.04.001

Rodríguez Bolívar, M. P., Alcaide Muñoz, L., & López Hernández, A. M. (2016). Scientometric study of the progress and development of e-government research during the period 2000–2012. *Information Technology for Development*, *22*(1), 36–74. doi:10.1080/02681102.2014.927340

Weerakkody, V., Janssen, M., & Dwivedi, Y. (Eds.). (2009). *Handbook of research on ICT-enabled transformational government: A global perspective*. Hershey, PA: Information Science Reference. doi:10.4018/978-1-60566-390-6

Zhang, J. (2013). *Towards a citizen-centered e-government: Exploring citizens' satisfaction with e-government in China* (Doctoral dissertation). Retrieved from ProQuest. (Accession 3596682)

## KEY TERMS AND DEFINITIONS

**Accountability:** The responsibility of government to its stakeholders (i.e., citizens).

**E-Government:** Government-related information and services that are delivered via the internet or other digital means.

**Expectations:** The beliefs held by citizens about the services the government will perform or provide.

**Information Technology:** The use of computers to manage data or information, including storage, retrieval, transmission, manipulation, and analysis.

**Performance:** The effective and efficient use of resources.

**Satisfaction:** An individual's overall sense of fulfilment with an experience.

**Transparency:** An operating style that allow outsiders to assess the true position or activities of an organization, such as a company or government.

# Chapter 6
# Debating Digitally–Enabled Service Transformation in Public Sector:
## Keeping the Research Talking

**Amizan Omar**
*Brunel University London, UK*

**Craig Johnson**
*University of Bradford, UK*

**Vishanth Weerakkody**
*University of Bradford, UK*

## ABSTRACT

*Digitally-enabled service transformation (DEST) in the public sector (PS) offers a unique opportunity for public administration (PA) and information systems (IS) disciplines to interlace. Such uniqueness has enabled a deviance in the theoretical selection from the adoption of native PA/IS theories to imported social sciences theories including institutional and structuration. Institutional theory provides a way of viewing and explaining why and how institutions emerge in a certain way within a given context, but it falls under the criticism of structural bias as it avoids explanations situated at individual or same level of analysis. Such a gap is filled with structuration theory adoption, focusing on how institutional structures arise, or are maintained through the interplay process. The fusion of such concepts would potentially enrich the debates on DEST in PS by provoking new insights to keep the "research talking."*

DOI: 10.4018/978-1-5225-6204-7.ch006

# INTRODUCTION

*Only attention to what solves concrete problems as defined by user communities might allow organisation studies to rise above multiparadigmaticism (McKelvey, 2003).*

The Digital Darwinism Era has plotted a completely different institutional landscape within both domains of public and private sectors, demanding fierce competition against unforeseeable future crafted by fast-pace of technology and social evolution. Abruptly, such evolution has molded a new template for people's behavior and expectations, which is the reason that underpins digitally-enabled service transformation (DEST) in many organizations. DEST refers to the use of ICT to change an existing service radically, in pursuance of achieving dramatic improvement in any critical measure of performance, including cost, quality and speed (Omar & Weerakkody, 2016). In the domain of public sector, DEST is attributable to the e-Government (eGov) phenomenon. While the economics reason appeared as the main motivation driving the changes in private institution, the public institutions perceived DEST (and eGov) as the solution to fundamentally improve their services through enhancement of interactions with citizens. Having said so, plenty of digitally-enabled changes were applied in both transactional and complex government services, from the tax payments to the healthcare and benefit system. Along the line, the obsessive races against Digital Darwinism had produced both – successes as well as disappointments. Such phenomenon had enticed the attentions of many, especially the scholars in the domain of Public Administrations (PA) and Information System / Technology (IST) who attempted to rationalize the derailments of the DEST cases. To the PA advocators, much of the arguments raised were constructed against the public policy design and delivery. Meanwhile, the paradigm of IST academia was largely clustered into two perspectives of behavioral and design science of such transformation. While these issues inhibit and dominated the discussions, much of the proposed recommendations rarely revealed the practical insights to assist better DEST adoption and diffusion in the future.

Although various theories have been utilized to study the eGov phenomenon, plenty of DEST's dogmas remain unchallenged (see Janowski, 2015; Majchrzak, Markus & Wareham, 2016; Omar & Elhaddadeh, 2016; Omar, El-Haddadeh, & Weerakkody, 2016; Omar & Osmani, 2015). Hence, it was said that the scope for potentially better theories to discover more about the e-government phenomena are limitless (Bannister and Connolly, 2015). To discuss the validity of this assertion in any detail is well beyond the scope of our discourse here, but indubitably the argument that the DEST researchers need to be exploring beyond both views is conceivable. Having said so, the opportunity to escape the PA and IST paradoxes stays open. Besides, our disagreement on the claim that eGov is a finite academic domain has reinforced such belief. Rather, eGov is an artefact with hybrids of identities – which is heavily infused by the IST and PA disciplines that cause the interlaces between social and technological aspects inseparable (Amenta & Ramsey, 2010; Heugens & Lander, 2016; Omar et al. 2014; Outhwaite 1987; Pinsonneault & Pozzebon 2001; Poole 2009; Van Veenstra, Janssen & Tan, 2010; Welch & Feeney 2014). As such, we suggest that the hunt for its native theory is a complex struggle. This point reminds us to Weber's argument about how an authority for a certain discipline to be recognised as a field is questionable upon the absence of a coherent theory. Nevertheless, an argument on a coherent theory is a merely subjective and contestable due to the 'research aim'- 'theory purpose' nexus. Considering this, a new ground for theoretical deviances in eGov research was formed. That being said, perhaps the hunt for a perfect theory or a deep theorisation of the field that leads to the claim that eGov is undertheorized is less than true. Furthermore, since the separation of socio-technological relationship in eGov is illogical, there is a depriving need for an analytical lens that would enable the elucidation of insights on such relationship in the context of DEST adoption and diffusion in a PS context. The critical point that the authors would like to put forward is that – unless the roles of actors and structures in structuring and institutionalising change within the context of institution were explored and understood – the adoption and diffusion of DEST will constantly be impeded by persisting and escalating challenges. Not just that, the authors also posit that by employing a conceptual lens that expands afar ordinary context could unearthed some practical and theoretical contributions.

Hence, this chapter assesses if utilisation of both Institutional and Structuration Theory concepts in exploring the institutionalisation of DEST in PS would facilitate the scholarly discourses and widened the perspectives towards how e-government research could be approached. To do so, the authors examine the nature of such duo by prescribing our focus on the questions of coherence and utilisation if they were used as an analytical lens to explore DEST in PS. The authors contest that there is no need for the domination of one treatment towards a theory over another (e.g. good theory vs. incoherent theory) in a large and diverse discipline dealing with equally diverse versions of DEST in PS. It is nevertheless obvious that advocates of rational choice approach in choosing theory(s) attempts to impose orthodoxy on the discipline. The question then becomes whether institutionalism and structuralism has sufficient analytic power to be a worthy counterpoint to that one attempt to create dominance.

In elucidating this matter, our arguments are structured as follow: First, the authors provide explanation on the significance of theory in research by understanding its contribution and how to recognise good theory for any research. This is followed by the explanations about the existing DEST research paradigm, including the common theories that were used in e-Government research and the different levels of them.

Then, the authors uncovered the potential of combined concepts of Institutional and Structuration Theory as lens for DEST research, before finally reflects and concludes how they could empower the DEST debates in the backdrop of PS institutions.

## THEORIZING AND STUDYING THE ADOPTION AND DIFFUSION OF DIGITALLY-ENABLED SERVICE TRANSFORMATION IN PUBLIC INSTITUTIONS

*Scientific research in its various branches seeks not merely to record particular occurrences in the world of our experience: it tries to discover regularities in the flux of events and thus to establish general laws which and explanation may be used for prediction, post diction, and explanation. (Hempel, 1958)*

The authors begin this section by quoting Hempel's argument that they think underpins our arguments through this chapter. Agreeing with Hempel, the authors suggest that theory is important in research for at least two reasons. First, theory serves as a mean for the scholars to communicate with others, or even among themselves about their research, in order to accumulate knowledge, as well as to legitimise (and acknowledge) certain field as a discipline (see Bannister and Connolly, 2015; Walsham and Han, 1991; Walsham, 1995) Second, the use of theory will help the researcher to answer the questions of who, what, when, where, how, why, could, should and would in a particular context of study (see Dubin, 1978Naor, Bernardes & Coman, 2012). Nonetheless, the use of theory in research also gives rise to a phenomenon known as 'Hempel's theoretician dilemma'. In 1958, Hempel argues that the use of theory in science induces the growth of paradoxical-related catechism – questioning the justification for the purposive use of theory in research to derive hypothetical assumptions, rather than to establish predictive and explanatory nexus of the observables. A question was also raised about sufficiency of the 'plain vocabulary' utilisation in reporting the observable rather than the use of 'extravagant general statements' in accomplishing research purpose. The main critique that he pointed out of these argument is – the dysfunctional of many 'general statements in terms of their applicability and conventions parameters had proved that "they are not true general statements" (Hempel, 1958, pp.43).

In practice, since the demarcation line separating the theoretical and observation languages is hardly visible, the authors assert that the researchers realise the 'antecedent meanings' of theories that McKelvey (2009) suggests as *"neither totally unconnected nor perfectly synonymous with the meanings of observation terms"*. After all, it is part of the science agenda to find the working connections between theoretical constructs and observable phenomena. Having said so, the authors agree with the use of theory in research is vital, for a good one will not just elucidate new facts when it was tested in different context, but also elevate understanding of the relationships, mechanisms, models, and concepts in the quest of providing a roadmap for the future avenues. But searching for a general term describing a (good) theory is a daunting challenge. Nonetheless, Campbell's (1990) and Shalley's (2012) description (at least) can be used as the "Ecclesiastical" of a (good) theory. Both of them suggest that a theory is capable in facilitating the identification of important variables or events buried in the investigated phenomenon. They also added that a theory is also able to provide the underpinning description of such phenomenon by justifying how the variables or events are interrelated, as well as the context that constitutes or conditions them. As such, theories are particularly useful in providing multitude of answers to a single phenomenon across range of perspectives (Reeves, Albert, Kuper, & Hodges, 2008). A theory could transport an individual's personal insights towards a wider significant context, enabling better understanding and applicability of a particular phenomenon (Billig, 2015). This is relevant to the quoted statement at the beginning of this chapter – i.e. to give rise to multipragmatism, implying that the use of theory will also enrich the body of knowledge of the associated discipline. So much so, the importance of theory in research is undoubted. A good theory-based research is immediate, insightful, and applicable in practice. But to be able to achieve all of these promises, a good theory is needed – which leads us to the quest for a good theory's characterisation.

## The Characteristics of a Good Theory for Research

In the previous section, the authors illustrated various tones of the scholars' views towards the importance of theories in research. As people say – the ends justify the means. Such aims inflict their opinions on the characters of a good theory. Since our attempt is to provide a valuable insight on the subject, here the authors had gathered some of the well-known principles or definitions describing the characters of a good theory.

In discussing how to derive a prediction and make an optimal decision, Churchman (1961) explains that a theory should be able to indicate its measurement approaches for the empirical works. Opposing the view is Shubik's (1987) suggestion on a good theory, with a claim that a good theory is unnecessarily applicable; rather it is potentially abstract in nature as much as non-applicable. Adopting a different view is Lindblom (1987), who posits that a 'good' theory should be discovered through unscientific, ordinary practices, rather than structured investigation– which makes him question about the benefit of scientific investigation and theory building in the field of social science and management research. His argument had proved a deeper thought on the issue of abstraction and its nexus with good theory characterisation.

On such thought, Wacker (1998) counter argues the classification of good theory and its opposite is relatable to the theory' definition, which also contributes towards the degree of its abstraction and non-applicability. Wacker also shares Lindblom's view that a good theory is discoverable through daily practices, rather than scientific process. But unlike Linsblom, Wacker added that such discoverability is also conditioned by the theory's definition. Wacker's provocative view had aroused a serious criticism for its inference on the theory utilisation and contribution. Such inference equal to the opinion that a theory needs not to be applied, neither it makes substantial progresses in the external world, nor it emerges due to definition measurement scarcity (i.e. every theory reflects certain degree of reality that enables the measurement). Here the authors contest that the criticism – however, relies on the praxis of theory definition and what makes it good.

To continue, the authors look at the work of Naor et al. (2012) that associate a good theory character with its ability to rationalise relationships of the variables or events by indicating how and why such relationships occur. This view resonates with Wacker's (2008) view that a good theory should be able to illustrate if a relationship or hypothesis is a theory or just assumptions through specific tests – which amplifies his earlier work of 1998. In such work, Wacker argues that a good theory should indicate the analysis framework, clear explanations on reality and provide efficient method for evidence gathering. The later characteristic – echoes Churchman's (1961) view that the authors had specified earlier on. It was apparent that all of these characteristics had employed different perspectives in defining a 'good theory'. These perspectives were then beautifully summarised by Bannister and Connolly (2015) – i.e. a good theory should enable rigorous explanation and understanding, and helps to predict future evolution through pattern recognition, where Wacker's eight characteristics of good theory was outline as shown in Figure 1

In the list - while the terms uniqueness, generalizability and internal consistency are self-explanatory, other terms assert the following meanings:

- 'Conservatism' - the theory is the best one available, and can only be replaced by something better;
- 'Fecundity - the theory provide 'a good source of hypotheses and possibly other theories;
- 'Parsimony' - the theory should not have too many variables, constructs or relationships (i.e. it should have minimum number of assumptions);
- 'Empirical riskiness' - the theory should allow examination where there is potential for it to be proven wrong;
- 'Abstract' - the theory it is contextually dependent and applicable across time and boundary.

*Figure 1. Characteristics of good theory*

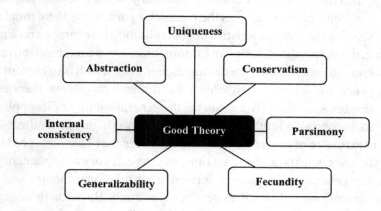

Far from agreeing with all the characteristics that they highlight, Bannister and Connolly (2015) call for accentuation on the "generalisability" character of a good theory, claiming that it competes Popper's (1959) argument that a scientific theory should be verifiable – i.e. if strictly applied possibly negates some categories of theory. As such call complicates our understanding; the authors turn to the definition of theory outlined by Gregor (2006). Gregor defines theory as *"…an abstract entity that aims to describe, explain and enhance understanding of the world and in some cases to provide predictions of what will happen in the future and to give a basis for intervention and action"*- which derives us to the conclusion that characteristics of a good theory are determined by its purpose of discovery or utilisation.

It is also worth to note that theories are largely classifiable into two clusters of native and imported theories. In this respect, the native theory cluster represent theories that were originated or developed for specific discipline or what described as reflecting disciplinary identity. Meanwhile, the cluster of 'imported theory' embodies the theories that are borrowed from, and introduced to other discipline as alternative approach to understanding certain phenomena (Moody, Iacob & Amrit, 2010; Benbasat & Zmud 2003, Weber, 2003). Fawcett and Downs (1986) argue that the relationship between theory and research is dialectic transaction. A theory in any research would indicate what empirical data need to be collected and how to go about (i.e. research design), so that the theory can be challenged. Besides such classification, Hence, theories can also be categorised further into three categories according to the research design, purpose and method – and they are known as descriptive (prescriptive), relational, and explanatory – as summarised in Table 1. (Moody et al., 2010).

Notably, their differences were defined by the purposes of (the theory's) existence. Such purposes consequently serve as the parameter guiding the theoretical aim and objectives shaping their characteristics of generalisability, accuracy and simplicity. For instance, the purpose of descriptive (or sometimes known as prescriptive) theory is to provide detail descriptions of a certain dimensions, which is to explain how the events happened and what to do to achieve the research objectives, theories in this category are more specific. Having said so, the generalisability of its application is fairly limited. In contrast, the relational theory category is highly generalizable, due to the constant existence of general relationships between the observable predeveloped constructs across contexts. at the same time, the last category of explanatory theory is also highly generalizable, as it is derived from relational theory, and used to predict the dimensions or differences between constructs. Based on these arguments of conflicting opinions and different nature of theories that serve different purpose, definition of a good theory is merely subjective (and often controversial). Another argument that adds into this status is the claim that the verdict if a theory is good also depends on the legitimacy and recognition of the research field as an academic discipline (Bannister & Connolly, 2014; Bannister & Connolly, 2015; Heeks & Bailur, 2007).

If such is true, then the field of e-government could be subjected to a critical good theory deficiency. As mentioned in our earlier narrations, e-government is a field that embodies two established academic disciplines of Information Technology and Public Administrative (Bannister & Connolly, 2015; Heeks & Bailur, 2007). As the result, an objective continuum depicting the most relevant theories to the less relevant ones hardly exists. In this context, the selection of theory to study any subject in the field of e-government could be a challenging decision. Nonetheless, Outhwaite's (1987) argument elucidates some insights in mitigating such doubt. He argues that despite of the idea that the candidate theory should be simple and testable, there appears to be no common grounds for rational preferences in theoretical selection. He then suggests if one would like to explore more on certain subject, i.e. beyond reductionist view, then a holism theory should be good to keep the research talking. His perspective was then employed as the basis in examining if the e-government field is under-theorised, or suffers what the authors term as 'good-theory deficiency syndrome', which was detailed in the following section.

In the introduction, the authors have highlighted the claims that e-government field is suffering from theoretical depletion in research. A few studies such as Moody et al. (2010) and the most recent Bannister and Connolly (2015) had made counter-points for such claim. Before embarking on the important remarks made by such studies, the authors think that it is worthy to recall and synthesis the definition of imported and native theories as mentioned in previous section – i.e. if such definition was mapped against the backdrop of e-government field, imported theory represent

*Table 1. Types of theories*

| Descriptions | Descriptive Theory | Relational Theory | Explanatory Theory |
|---|---|---|---|
| **Research Design** | Descriptive or Exploratory | Correlational | Experimental |
| **Purpose** | To describe or classify specific dimensions or characteristics of phenomenon by summarizing the commonalities (what is) found in discrete observations. When it will be used? When nothing or very little is known about the phenomenon. | To specify relations between dimensions or characteristics of certain subject (i.e. how they are related to each other), after they have been descriptively developed and validated. | To predict precise causal relationships between dimensions or differences between groups, addressing questions such as "What will happen if…" and "Is treatment A different from treatment B?" |
| **Research Methods** | **Empirical** (I.e. case studies, surveys, grounded theory, ethnographies, observations, and phenomenological studies). **Non-empirical** (I.e. Philosophical enquiry, where earlier phenomena were described through critical discussion or historical research). | Empirical – as the dimensions required to be measured in their natural states (i.e. interviews and surveys). | Empirical, involving manipulation of quantifiable data, to determine its effect on certain dimensions (i.e. experiment – pre-test post-test, quasi-experiments, and true experiments). |

Source: Omar et.al, 2016

any theory that is used to study e-government, but comes have different field of origins. Meanwhile, native theory means a theory that is significant and developed for e-government studies.

Moody et al., (2010) are among the earlier scholars that had made attempts to validate if the field of e-government suffered from lack of theoretical foundation, through the approach of citation analysis in their research. Their findings provide invalidity to the claim – as it was discovered that e-government is a well theoretically grounded field, where native theories have greater influence than imported theories. Although the authors agree with their finding, they strongly suggest that such analysis to be re-deployed according to current situation, since the evolution of theory cluster is vulnerable towards paradigm extension that occurs over time and context. Nonetheless, such study still holds an admissible remark that both native and imported theories form a legitimate part of a field's theoretical foundations- where the native theories contribute to e-government disciplinary identity, while imported theories help root the research in more established disciplines.

Using a different approach, Bannister and Connolly (2015) later discovered that e-government research had utilised numerous theories that could be clustered into imported and native theories. Since the evidence indicates that the use of imported theory has been prevalent, an experiment was used as approach to unveil the real situation, where common theories from IS and the broader social sciences were listed and matched with the scholarly articles after 2003 that utilised the respective theories. Although it was admitted that many more theories that could be included in such analysis, it was claimed that their arbitrary selections are sufficient to back their arguments. Unsurprisingly, their study also discovers that large numbers of papers exist for each listed theory from the imported category (non-native e-government theory). Although it seems absurd just to base our claim on these two studies, the rigorousness of the analysis conducted by such studies enable us to rest the premise that e-government field is under-theorised. Instead, the authors suspect that a huge gap of misconception on the meaning of theory exists among the claimants. They assert that a broadly interpreted meaning would account for concepts, frameworks and non-generalizable explanatory research that create a perception that the e-government field is under-theorised or experience lack of good theory. Nevertheless, if the meaning refers to 'strong' or 'grand' theory (i.e. theory that enables explanation and prediction and consequently testable), then the claim might be partly true. It is worth mentioning that in the constraint of the later interpretation, several native theories of e-government, especially the concept of an e-government stage or maturity model, De Lone and McLean's Information System Success Model (ISM), Technology Acceptance Model (TAM) and Unified Theory of Acceptance and Use of Technology (UTAUT), have been widely cited and developed extensively post 2000.

Despite of these agreements, both studies have conflicting opinion on the identity of 'e-government' as a discipline on its own. Moody et al. (2010) firmly state that there is no identity crisis in the field as it has its own native theories, which have double influence over imported theories in research. Meanwhile, Bannister & Connolly (2015) argued this decision, however relies on how the field was defined i.e. e-government is the availability of government services on-line 24/7, or e-government covers all use of Information Communication Technology (ICT) in government or at least in the formulation of policy and the delivery of services. If the first was employed, then e-government is a unique field. However if how it was perceived fits into the second definition, then e-government is subjected to hybrids of identities, infused by both the IS and PA disciplines.

Regardless of this identity issue, e-government offers plenty of explanatory and predictive theories to choose when conducting research. Again, it is worthy to note Weber's remark about the absence of a coherent theory, the entitlement of something to be called as a field is questionable. Nevertheless, the authors still argue that Weick's (1979) criteria for good theory – namely generalisability, accuracy and simplicity, are simultaneously unattainable in a field with multitude of disciplines. Since a deep theorisation of a field that constitutes many discipline may be unachievable (Bannister & Connolly, 2015), the hunt for the perfect theory in e-government research should be approached with caution. As it may be as good as it gets, there remains more to discover by deploying the rich vein of the existing theories, instead of searching for a grand theory of e-government.

Based on the findings of our previous studies that Institutional and Structuration theories concepts have a promising potential in surfacing new issues related to the e-government phenomenon, the authors propose that the viability of their usage in studying e-government should be considered (see Omar and El-Haddadeh, 2016; Omar and Osmani, 2015; Omar et al., 2014).

## INSTITUTIONAL AND STRUCTURATION THEORY IN DEST RESEARCH: A NEW PERSPECTIVE

In the previous sections, arguments were presented justifying that numerous theories exist and substantial for any research in the field of e-government. In addition, it was noted that since e-government is a field that constitutes other disciplines (i.e. IS and PA), there might not be a perfect theory for the field. Therefore, against this context, this study is attempting to explore the potential contributions of utilising Institutional and Structuration Theories in fulfilling Wacker's good theory criteria.

### The Missing Part

As field that embodies two disciplines of Information System (IS) and Public Administration (PA), e-government is inescapable from some of the claims suffered by both disciplines. This includes the claim that both were lack of good theory, made by many scholars including Heeks & Bailur, 2007; Meijer & Bekkers, 2015. Agreeing with Bannister & Connolly (2014) the authors postulate that perhaps, these deficiencies raised the arguments of under-theorization in e-government research. Nevertheless, the fact that such discrepancies had somehow contributed towards the extensive development of theories in e-government research as proven by Rocheleau (2007) is unneglectable. This brought us to a speculation that should the absence of coherent theory or grand theory in IS and PA not hamper the development of theories in both fields, it potentially brings no impairment to the status of e-government. Our thoughts then shifted to the question of – if no harm was done in such field, then what is missing?

The implementation of DEST in public sector usually been proposed as an objective of e-government after the provision of online information and transactions of government services. In most cases, such transformation entails the high-level policy decisions that were designed to enhance productivity of the public institution besides increasing public value. Although this begs the serious questions of should 'digital' be the only mean of the policy instruments and how the public value is going to be measured – the concerted efforts that have taken place in digitalizing public services had mocked the society that DEST is a crucial way to transform public service. In such scenario, often the process of rationalizing why ICT was chosen as the policy instrument comes after the selection decision. Perhaps, these manipulation and misunderstanding are the roots for the turmoil that are often observable in the major public service digitalization programs such as National Program for Information Technology (NPfIT) and Universal Credit in the United Kingdom, as well as the Air Force Expeditionary Combat Support System (ECSS) in the United States.

Before going further, the authors think that it would be useful to remind the foundational role of the government. As quoted from the UK Parliament, "The Government is responsible for deciding how the country is run and for managing things, day to day. They set taxes, choose what to spend public money on and decide how best to deliver public services…" (UK Parliament, n.d.). An insight from Hood and Margetts (2007) elucidates more about this. It was suggested that the government's foundational roles both internal and external. The internal refers to the process of decision making or addressing policy; and the external are what entails after that – including the selection of "tools" to as an effective means to interact with the public and the environment in achieving the policy goals. The last description represents the notion of *policy instruments. Hence, selection of 'policy instrument' is part of the government roles.* Hence, the authors we propose that the points that would be highlighted throughout this discourse would be relevant to facilitate the exploration if DEST (as a policy instrument) would help the government to exercise its roles effectively.

Although issues similar to these have been examined, they found that the studies have largely constrained their focuses on two questions of why DEST was introduced and what are the challenges that impede DEST adoption/diffusion. While the answer to the first question generally pinpoint to the environment as the main change inducer, the answer to the second questions often reveals that technology and managerial issues are the two factors impeding DEST success. This includes faulty IT/IS design, mismatched system specification, complicacies in integrating various legacies systems/platforms, and weak managerial approach to the project management.

The overt focus on such questions had largely buried the critical aspects that sticking the internal-external nexus of the government's role, which is their interplays and subsequent outcomes. Such aspects include interconnectedness of roles between the institutional actors and the artefacts guiding their practices, known as institutional structures. A systematic literature review that the authors conducted in 2015 highlights that the focus on how the interplay between institutional actors and structures facilitate/impede the DEST institutionalisation process in PS remains scarce. Instead of analysing the processual accounts of change institutionalisation, majority of the papers inclined to explain the discrete events, hence unable to bring about new facts about the cases. As such, the authors hypothesised that: (1) The fact that research was conducted in very specific contexts and the retrospective studies (instead of longitudinal) had elucidated the generalisability of the study findings (i.e. Diniz et al., 2012; Luna-Reyes & Gil-Garcia, 2013); (2) The utilisation of single theory in studies had limited the arguments and failed to elucidate new facts; and (3) The interactions between institutional actors and structures that contribute towards the development of actions or other structures underpinning DEST were under-represented – thus, not contributing towards better understanding of the institutionalisation process. (i.e. Heinze & Hu, 2005; Meneklis & Douligeris, 2010; (van Veenstra, Melin, & Axelsson, 2014).

A significant gap was found in the study of DEST institutionalisation process, suggesting further studies should consider the utilisation of sociology theory(s)to enrich the knowledge and understanding on the repercussion of the interplays and its associated elements. Although many studies had employed Institutional Theory as their analytical lens, its inescapable limitation in explaining how structures emerge and passed-through time had constraints its effectiveness. As such, it needs assistance from the Structuration Theory.

## Potential Contributions From the Mixed Concepts

Institutional Theory provides a way of viewing how 'institution' emerge and diffused in a certain way within a given context. It also provides explanation on the penetration of the external environment into an institution through the three concepts of institutional pressures, namely coercive, normative, and mimetic. The theory has long rooted history and has been re-born for at least twice. In its original shape, the theory asserts that both institution and actors shape each other through special relationship that was described as 'interplay'. Early institutional theorists argued that institutions are 'socially constructed templates for action, generated and maintain through reciprocal interactions' (Zucker, 1977; Meyer & Rowan, 1977), while Barley and Tolbert (1997) defined institutions as "shared rules and typifications that identify categories of social actors and their appropriate activities or relationships". All of the arguments implied that any structure or behaviours that emerged in an institution are the product of historical negotiations, or interplays that happened between institutional actors and structures. In short, actions and structures recursively shape each other by constraining certain behaviour and permitting others. The situation resembles the notion of 'structure' in Gidden's Structuration Theory (1984). Giddens (1984) argued that albeit structure (institutions) is a product of action, it also has capacity to constraint action. Although similar in many aspects, the theories differ in how the creation, alteration, and reproduction of institutions are perceived.

With the passage of time, the original notion of IT fades. This is due to the excessive focus given to the institutional homogenization process, or isomorphism that refers to organizational conformity towards environmental pressures – ignoring the focus on how such structures emerge or are maintained. Therefore, in an explanation on institutionalization process, Institutional Theory acknowledges the emergence and diffusion of DEST through association of institutional pressures – a concept that explains how environment pressures penetrate the organization through conformity exercise (isomorphism) (Meyer & Rowan, 1977 cited in Barley & Tolbert, 1997). Despite emphasizing the role of normative and taken-for-granted assumptions during the isomorphism process, little attention was given to the process of how structure is reaffirmed or altered, which is a crucial phenomenon in the institutionalization process. As such, institution receives obsessive power in shaping actions and in contrasts – actors were viewed as passive. It was such period that the term of institutional field was introduced to mark the parameter of an institution. Later, the concept of 'actor's agency' that represents actor's capacity to perform action and shape institution was retaliated to IT. It was proposed that agency could be constructed through ones' knowledge and social position. Such concept mimics and brings back the original notion of IT that institution shapes and being shaped by actions – which are relatable to the key concept in Structuration Theory (ST), which is duality of structures.

Institutionalists such as DiMaggio & Powell (1983) and Greenwood & Hinings (1996) propose that the adoption of isomorphic templates for organizing (e.g. through mimetic mechanism) has a positive effect on organizations' substantive performance. Such hypothesis, however is rarely tested due to research design constraints. This study however has been designed to provide evidence and deeper understanding on such claims through the concepts of 'micro foundations of institutional diffusion mechanism and diffusion moderators' (see Heugens & Lander, 2009). Such concept allows explanations that are consistent with the story of what agent(s) do and why they do it (e.g. why do they choose certain templates in organising or complying to certain regulations or demands).Further, the concept of isomorphism was introduced by DiMaggio and Powell (1983) to represent the process which constraints heterogeneity of organizations within a specific institutional environment. This statement supports the structuralists' views on the constraining effect of institutions on organizational agency, in respect of how such effect produces stability and recognisability in organizational structures and strategies (i.e. through isomorphic mechanisms). However, the agency theoreticians argue that the effect of isomorphism on social structures do not completely determine organizational behaviours and may even be a sources of deviance, such as improvisation (see Hoffman, 1999; Washington & Ventresca, 2004). Thus to enrich understanding, institutional pressures can examined as potential forces which had given rise to endogenous pressures for change, causing deviance by the field's occupants, instead of 'bounding' them as proposed in majority of the existing research.

Next, Institutional Theory also postulates that organizations requires the endorsement of cultural and political authorities, who can grant them "licence to do what they do", instead of just material resources and technical information if they are to survive and thrive in their social environments (Scott, Ruef, Mendel, & Caronna, 2000: 237). The concept of cultural and political authorities in contemporary societies are visualised in organisations such as the state, professional, associations, unions and also critics – as sources to gain endorsement i.e. by conforming to their prescriptions. This would explicitly highlight the role of these authorities in the processual account of DEST institutionalisation. Nevertheless, in assessing the effect of isomorphism on symbolic and substantive performance, Institutional Theory illustrates distinguish characteristic to disentangle institutional isomorphism from competitive isomorphism – a rarely accounted level of analysis. The inability to classify between the two could lead to inflated or deflated assessment of the institutional isomorphism's contribution to substantive performance (Lee & Pennings, 2002; Heugens & Lander, 2009). The micro-institutionalisation process (Barley & Tolbert, 1997) highlighted three stages of institutionalisation: 'Pre-institutionalisation', 'Semi Institutionalisation' and 'Total Sedimentation'. The semi institutionalization stage is the most critical stage determining success of DEST institutionalization process, as it encapsulates intense structuration processes, where production of actions and structures as reaction towards DEST implementation takes place (Barley & Tolbert, 1997; Tolbert & Zucker, 1996; Scott, 2014).

Although IT has many to offers, it is also being subjected to criticism due its structural biasness in avoiding both individual-level explanations and explanations situated at the same level of analysis. The same feature has distinctive explanatory advantages. Claiming that something which is identified at a higher level will explain processes and outcomes at a lower level of analysis, the theory focus on cultural and ideational causes in exerting influence either at within or beyond organisational-field level. As mentioned earlier, the initial idea of Institutional Theory laid on the principle that actions and structures are intrinsically linked, and shaping each other – which is shared by Structuration Theory (Giddens, 1984). However, for more insights on how structures (institutions) are created, altered, and reproduced, the authors turn to Structuration Theory.

Structuration theory (ST) focuses mainly on the dynamics or how structures are created, altered, and reproduced – the main issue neglected by Institutional Theory (Barley & Tolbert, 1997). Based on the concept of "duality of structure", ST views structure is both the product of and constrains action (Giddens, 1984; Barley & Tolbert, 1997). Gidden's ST model gives attentive focus on the intersection of two realms - structure and action realms - known as modality. The three modalities are known as 'Interpretive Scheme', which determines how the actor understands the structure; 'Facility', which determines how the actors could exercise their power; and Norm, which determines how the actors perceive the acceptable behaviour.

As explained by Zuurmond (1998), the introduction of DEST would cause temporary instability in the institution. This is because such innovation at certain points of the implementation timeline – demands for the discontinuation of certain old practices. Having said so, actors would seek for the best solution to mitigate the situation by overserving others. In Institutional Theory, this stage is known as 'inter- organization monitoring', where the actors are prone to imitate readily available solutions by monitoring and imitating patterns of reactions performed by others. Post observation, the actors would conceptually outlines the actions and structures that are required to stay align with the proposed solution. This stage is called as theorization. As suggested by structuration theory, actors' backgrounds would influence the pattern of solutions proposed (Giddens, 1984). The outcome here is very much attributable to the institutional field, where a highly diverse field would result into highly diverse solutions. The more diverse the proposed solution, the less chance of having a common agreeable solution, and the more vulnerable such institutionalisation process is. The outcome of these two stages is identification of the solution that fits the context. In reaching such outcome, understanding and consensus among the actors is required to facilitate adoption of the proposed structure. The structuration theory concept of 'interpretive scheme' is a micro-process where proposed structure or actions are justified and rationalized through communication (action). All of these processual accounts are encapsulated in the habitualisation stage of Institutional Theory.

In the next stage of Institutional Theory, the actors would conduct benchmarking exercise to enhance the value of new structure – known as 'monitoring'. Actors would exercise their power by utilizing available structures or resources to govern actions of others – a process explained by Structuration Theory (Giddens, 1984; Barley & Tolbert, 1997). Actions will gradually become norms after they were well distributed – the concept of Institutional Theory. The actors then would reproduce or modify the structures, based on the findings from the benchmarking exercise.

From structuration process point of view, this stage resembles the modality of 'norm', where the actors' actions would be rewarded or sanctioned accordingly to increase structural legitimacy. These processes emerged during the objectification stage, where the ultimate aim is to achieve consensus among the actors on the value of structures, which would increase adoption of DEST. The completion of habitualisation and objectification stage would lead to sedimentation stage – where DEST is institutionalized.

The focus on exogenous attributes of Institutional Theory had diverted its view from 'inherent duality' (indicating that structure arise from and constrain actions) to compliance towards environmental characteristics and its consequences in the context of DEST research in the PS. Nonetheless, Structuration Theory concepts explanations how actors produce structures that enable or constrain the DEST implementation. Hence, the combination of concepts from both Institutional and Structuration Theories generate more rigorous explanation and understanding on institutionalisation of DEST in public institution. This offers a new reference point for practitioners and researchers within the domain of e-government to better understand the past, existing, and future programs, leading to better practices. If such combination was evaluated against Weick's (1979) criteria for good theory– then again, it will fail to check all boxes simultaneously. Nevertheless, if evaluated against Gregor's definition of good theory, the combination just perfectly matched with the criteria that enable description, explanation and enhancing understanding of the world, besides providing predictions of what will happen in the future, allowing intervention and action.

## CONCLUSION

The question asked at the outset of this paper is whether Institutional Theory and Structuration Theory concepts would help to elucidate new facts in the context of public sector DEST research i.e. to keep the 'research talking'. The answer has turned out to be satisfactory. But to derive the answer, the question of 'what is the philosophy and objectives underpinning such research and what defines the research context?' should be asked. As the research becomes more interdisciplinary, theory generalisability, accuracy and simplicity become more difficult, if not impossible. As such, Weick's (1979) criteria for good theory are rather inadmissible. Hence, different measures such as Wacker's (1998) notion on "substantive significance" should be given priority, rather than "statistical significance" – because good theory will not just be contextually independent, but will be able to reveal new facts which are transferrable to better practices. In this perspective, Institutional and Structuration Theory are two highly abstract social theories that are able to disclose rarely sighted dimensions of DEST, opening new paradigm of debates within both the body of knowledge and practice of e-government. With caution on counsel of perfection, it can be concluded that utilisation of Institutional Theory and Structuration Theory concepts together - as a single analytical lens in exploring the DEST phenomenon - will keep e-government research 'talking'.

# REFERENCES

Amenta, E., & Ramsey, K. M. (2010). Institutional Theory. In K. T. Leicht & J. C. Jenkins (Eds.), Handbook of Politics: State and Society in Global Perspective, Handbooks of Sociology and Social Research (pp. 15–40). Springer Science+Business Media. doi:10.1007/978-0-387-68930-2_2

Bannister, F., & Connolly, R. (2014). ICT, public values and transformative government : A framework and programme for research. *Government Information Quarterly*, *31*(1), 119–128. doi:10.1016/j.giq.2013.06.002

Bannister, F., & Connolly, R. (2015). The great theory hunt : Does e-government really have a problem? *Government Information Quarterly*, *32*(1), 1–11. doi:10.1016/j.giq.2014.10.003

Barley, S. R., & Tolbert, P. S. (1997). Institutionalization and Structuration: Studying the Links between Action and Institution. *Organization Studies*, *18*(1), 93–117. doi:10.1177/017084069701800106

Benbasat, I., & Zmud, R. W. (2003). The identity crisis within the IS discipline: Defining and communication the discipline's core properties. *Management Information Systems Quarterly*, *27*(2), 183–194. doi:10.2307/30036527

Billig, M. (2015). Kurt Lewin's Leadership Studies and His Legacy to Social Psychology: Is There Nothing as Practical as a Good Theory? *Journal for the Theory of Social Behaviour*, *45*(4), 440–460. doi:10.1111/jtsb.12074

Fawcett, J., & Downs, F. (1986). Types of Theory and Research. *The Relationship Between Theory and Research*, 4–7. Retrieved from http://www.indiana.edu/~educy520/readings/fawcett86.pdf

Heeks, R., & Bailur, S. (2007). Analyzing e-government research: Perspectives, philosophies, theories, methods, and practice. *Government Information Quarterly*, *24*(2), 243–265. doi:10.1016/j.giq.2006.06.005

Hempel, C. G. (1958). The Theoretician's Dilemma: A Study in the Logic of Theory Construction. In Concepts, Theories, and the Mind-Body Problem (pp. 37–98). Academic Press.

Heugens, P. P. M. A. R., & Lander, M. W. (2016). *Structure! Agency! (And Other Quarrels): A Meta-Analysis of Institutional Theories of Organization.* Academy of Management. Retrieved from http://www.jstor.org/stable/40390276

McKelvey, B. (2009). Organisation Studies: Discipline or Field. In R. Westwood & S. Clegg (Eds.), Debating Organization: Point Counter-point in Organisation Studies (pp. 47–66). Blackwell Publishing Ltd.

Meijer, A., & Bekkers, V. (2015). A metatheory of e-government : Creating some order in a fragmented research fi eld. *Government Information Quarterly*, *32*(3), 237–245. doi:10.1016/j.giq.2015.04.006

Moody, D., Iacob, M., & Amrit, C. (2010). In Search of Paradigms: Identifying the Theoretical Foundations of the IS Field. *Ecis*, (2010), 15. Retrieved from http://aisel.aisnet.org/ecis2010/43/

Naor, M., & Bernardes, E. S., & Coman, A. (2012). Theory of constraints: is it a theory and a good one? *International Journal of Production Research*, *51*, 1–13. doi:10.1080/00207543.2011.654137

Omar, A., & El-Haddadeh, R. (2016). Structuring Institutionalization of Digitally-Enabled Service Transformation in Public Sector : Does Actor or Structure Matters? Full paper. *Twenty-second Americas Conference on Information Systems*, 1–7.

Omar, A., El-Haddadeh, R., & Weerakkody, V. (2016). Exploring Digitally Enabled Service Transformation in the Public Sector. *Would Institutional and Structuration Theory Concepts Keep the Research Talking*, *12*(4), 1–18. doi:10.4018/IJEGR.2016100101

Omar, A., & Osmani, M. (2015a). Digitally Enabled Service Transformations in Public Sector. *International Journal of Electronic Government Research*, *11*(3), 76–94. doi:10.4018/IJEGR.2015070105

Omar, A., & Osmani, M. (2015b). Digitally Enabled Service Transformations in Public Sector: A Review of Institutionalisation and Structuration Theories. *International Journal of Electronic Government Research*, *11*(3), 76–94. doi:10.4018/IJEGR.2015070105

Omar, A., Weerakkody, V., & El-Haddadeh, R. (2014). The Institutional And Structuration Dimensions Of Ict Enabled Public Sector Transformation: A Systematic Literature Review. *European, Mediterranean & Middle Eastern Conference on Information Systems*.

Omar, A., Weerakkody, V., & Sivarajah, U. (2017). Digitally enabled service transformation in UK public sector: A case analysis of universal credit. *International Journal of Information Management, 37*(4), 350–356. doi:10.1016/j.ijinfomgt.2017.04.001

Outhwaite, W. (1987). *New Philosophies of Social Science: Realism, Hermeneutics, and Critical Theory* (A. Giddens, Ed.). Macmillan Education Ltd. doi:10.1007/978-1-349-18946-5

Poole, M. S. (2009). Response to Jones and Karsten, "Giddens's Structuration Theory and Information Systems Research. *Management Information Systems Quarterly, 33*(3), 583–587. doi:10.2307/20650310

Reeves, S., Albert, M., Kuper, A., & Hodges, B. D. (2008). Why use theories in qualitative research? *BMJ (Clinical Research Ed.), 337*(September), a949. doi:10.1136/bmj.a949 PMID:18687730

Van Veenstra, A. F., Janssen, M., & Tan, Y. H. (2010). Towards an understanding of e-government induced change-drawing on organization and structuration theories. Lecture Notes in Computer Science, 6228, 1–12. doi:10.1007/978-3-642-14799-9_1

van Veenstra, A. F., Melin, U., & Axelsson, K. (2014). Theoretical and Practical Implications From the Use of Structuration Theory in Public Sector Is Research. *Twenty Second European Conference on Information Systems*, 1–12.

Wacker, J. G. (1998). A definition of theory research guidelines for different-theory building research methods in operations management. *Journal of Operations Management, 16*(4), 361–385. doi:10.1016/S0272-6963(98)00019-9

Wacker, J. G. (2008). A conceptual understanding of requirements for theory-building research: Guidelines for scientific theory building. *The Journal of Supply Chain Management, 44*(3), 5–15. doi:10.1111/j.1745-493X.2008.00062.x

Walsham, G. (1995). Interpretive case studies in IS research: Nature and method. *European Journal of Information Systems, 4*(2), 74–81. doi:10.1057/ejis.1995.9

Walsham, G., & Han, C. K. (1991). Structuration theory and information systems research. *Journal of Applied Systems Analysis, 15*(1), 77–85.

Weber, R. (2003). Editor's Comments: Theoretically Speaking. *Management Information Systems Quarterly*, *27*(3), 3–12. doi:10.2307/30036536

Weerakkody, V., Omar, A., El-Haddadeh, R., & Al-Busaidy, M. (2016). Digitally-enabled service transformation in the public sector: The lure of institutional pressure and strategic response towards change. *Government Information Quarterly*, *11*. doi:10.1016/j.giq.2016.06.006

Weick, K. E. (1979). *The Social Psychology of Organizing* (2nd ed.). Reading, MA: Addison-Wesley.

Welch, E. W., & Feeney, M. K. (2014). Technology in government : How organizational culture mediates information and communication technology outcomes. *Government Information Quarterly*, *31*(4), 506–512. doi:10.1016/j.giq.2014.07.006

Zuurmond, A. (1998). From bureaucracy to infocracy: Are democratic institutions lagging behind. In I. T. M. Snellen & W. van de Donk (Eds.), *Public administration in an information age; A handbook* (pp. 259–272). Amsterdam: IOS Press.

# ADDITIONAL READING

Omar, A., & El-Haddadeh, R. (2016). Structuring Institutionalization of Digitally-Enabled Service Transformation in Public Sector : Does Actor or Structure Matters? Full paper. In *Twenty-second Americas Conference on Information Systems* (pp. 1–7). San Diego.

Omar, A., El-Haddadeh, R., & Weerakkody, V. (2016). Exploring Digitally Enabled Service Transformation in the Public Sector. *Would Institutional and Structuration Theory Concepts Keep the Research Talking*, *12*(4), 1–18. doi:10.4018/IJEGR.2016100101

Omar, A., & Osmani, M. (2015b). Digitally Enabled Service Transformations in Public Sector: A Review of Institutionalisation and Structuration Theories. *International Journal of Electronic Government Research*, *11*(3), 76–94. doi:10.4018/IJEGR.2015070105

Omar, A., Weerakkody, V., & El-Haddadeh, R. (2014). The Institutional And Structuration Dimensions Of Ict Enabled Public Sector Transformation: A Systematic Literature Review. In *European, Mediterranean & Middle Eastern Conference on Information Systems*.

Omar, A., Weerakkody, V., & Sivarajah, U. (2017). Digitally enabled service transformation in UK public sector: A case analysis of universal credit. *International Journal of Information Management, 37*(4), 350–356. doi:10.1016/j. ijinfomgt.2017.04.001

Van Veenstra, A. F., Melin, U., & Axelsson, K. (2014). Theoretical and Practical Implications From the Use of Structuration Theory in Public Sector Is Research. *Twenty Second European Conference on Information Systems*, (October), 1–12.

Weerakkody, V., Omar, A., El-Haddadeh, R., & Al-Busaidy, M. (2016). Digitally-enabled service transformation in the public sector: The lure of institutional pressure and strategic response towards change. *Government Information Quarterly, 11.* doi:10.1016/j.giq.2016.06.006

# Chapter 7
# Empowering Society Participation in Public Service Processes

**Bruna Diirr**
*Federal University of the State of Rio de Janeiro (UNIRIO), Brazil*

**Renata Araujo**
*Federal University of the State of Rio de Janeiro (UNIRIO), Brazil*

**Claudia Cappelli**
*Federal University of the State of Rio de Janeiro (UNIRIO), Brazil*

## ABSTRACT

*Several discussions enforce the need for a greater engagement of society in public issues and show how ICTs can enhance it. This chapter presents the idea of conversations about public services. It is argued that by making society aware of how a service is provided—its process—citizens may develop a better attitude for interacting with government and other service users. Both society and governmental service providers can discuss problems, correct available information, and increase their knowledge about the processes, thus providing closer ties between them. This chapter also presents a tool designed to support these conversations and the results obtained with a case study of its use. The results suggest that conversations have stimulated interaction among citizens and services providers as well as allowed service improvement opportunities.*

DOI: 10.4018/978-1-5225-6204-7.ch007

# INTRODUCTION

The increasing adoption of ICTs has been enforcing discussions on how these technologies could increase society involvement and participation in the practice of Democracy (Grönlund, 2009). It is expected that ICTs allow the government to be open to citizens, offer new channels for disseminating information, and improve operations and integration within and between governments. In society's perspective, ICTs could increase citizens' awareness, trust and participation in public issues and decision-making (Allen, 2004; Bryant, 2006; Charalabidis & Loukis, 2012; Hague, 1999; Mahmood, 2016; Oates, 2008; Shirky, 2008).

E-Democracy and e-Government initiatives argue that society's involvement through ICT follows an increasing scale of relationship between government and citizens (Arnstein, 1969; Femers & Wiedemann, 1993; Gomes, 2004; OECD, 2001). At lower levels, government and citizens have distinct roles and responsibilities, while roles and responsibilities are interchanged at higher levels. It is discussed that closer ties between government and society, i.e. greater interaction and collaboration among them, a better understanding about the public information and issues, interchange of roles and responsibilities etc., must start from the most basic levels of participation and continuously evolve towards higher participation levels.

However, claims still arise about the challenges for ICTs wide adoption (Andersen, Medaglia & Henriksen, 2011; Classe, Araujo & Xexéo, 2017; Mahmood, 2016; Tavares, Soares & Estevez, 2016; Winters, Karin & Martawardaya, 2014). Despite the efforts made to increase public services quality, it seems that citizens feel uncomfortable to use online services due to the lack of information about how it is executed and by whom – usually "invisible" to citizens. The way that information is presented to citizens, with an excess of bureaucracy, complexity of rules and lack of transparency, also affects citizens' ICTs adoption. In addition, government cannot always monitor service execution from citizens' perspective to address their specific needs. This can cause misinformation, lack of confidence in the service and indifference to the practice of Democracy, creating a "distance" between service providers and users.

This work presents an approach based on conversations about public services that encourages closer ties between service providers (government) and citizens. Public services are explained to citizens using process models, about which citizens and service providers can discuss, exchange information and increase shared knowledge about the service provision. A tool was designed to support this dialogue and to organize and analyze relevant information obtained from it, serving as a basis for the service improvement as well as an artifact for empowering citizens' participation. The proposed approach is evaluated in the context of a democratic public institution and obtained results suggest that it has stimulated the interaction between citizens and services providers as well as allowed service improvement opportunities.

The paper proceeds as follows: Section 2 describes proposals for society and government interaction through ICTs; Section 3 details different levels for bringing together society and government through the use of public services; Section 4 presents the approach for conversations about public services; Section 5 describes the case study conducted in a public institution to evaluate the proposal applicability; Section 6 discusses research findings and the practical implication of them; finally, Section 7 concludes the paper.

## SOCIETY AND GOVERNMENT INTERACTION IN PUBLIC AFFAIRS

Literature describes different frameworks to classify citizen participation in democratic contexts using ICTs (Andersen, 2012; Arnstein, 1969; Femers & Wiedemann, 1993; Gomes, 2004; Grönlund, 2009; OECD, 2001). It is common sense that citizen participation follows an increasing scale, with variations in citizens' participation power, discussion level and decision-making in public issues. Thus, the participation levels can be summarized as:

- **Information Provision:** Government uses websites to provide citizens both institutional information (history, contact information, and functional structure; links to social networks; news; agenda; government actions in progress etc.) as well operational information, such as budget execution. Examples are found in government institutional websites and websites as the Transparency Portal of the Brazilian Federal Government (Portal of Transparency, n.d.), which details the use of public resources obtained from taxes by Brazilian Government, besides information about the budget execution, indicators, and statistics;
- **Citizen Consultation:** Government provides mechanisms for gathering public opinion about information and services provided. An example is Ombudsman online offices which may be available on government websites such as "Contact us". Online polls are another approach to secure feedback from citizens, such as e-Citizenship Portal (Portal e-Cidadania, n.d.), where Brazilians can vote on several projects that will be discussed in the Senate;
- **Services Provision:** Public entities provide detailed information about services and procedures to require them, and citizens can request these services using online tools. Examples are found in (a) the Brazilian Department of Motor Vehicles website (DETRAN-RJ), where citizens have access to services (e.g.

"schedule of the annual vehicle inspection", "renewal of driver's license", "taxes payment" etc.), important forms and the procedure to use these services; and (b) 1746 (Portal 1746, n.d.), provided by the City Hall of Rio de Janeiro, where citizens can request public lighting repairs, pothole repairs, illegal parking complaints etc.;

- **Public Debate:** Citizens become active participants in public debate. Some examples: (a) CitizenScape (CitizenScape), a website which aggregates several blogs and sends information via Twitter to registered users; (b) VoteWatch.eu (VoteWatch, 2018), which allows the tracking of votes in European Parliament; (c) the Dring13 project (DRING13), where the inhabitants of Paris can post their opinions, comment on other citizens' reviews and see the votes received for each opinion; (d) the e-Democracy Portal (Portal e-Democracia, n.d.), which encourages Brazilians to discuss about public issues, agenda setting and prioritization of projects, using forums, chats and social networks; and (e) Plataforma Brasil (ITS RIO, n.d.), which aims to discuss and propose solutions for social issues.

The barriers to providing access to citizen participation at each level involve technological, social, cultural and economic aspects (Baller, Dutta & Lanvin, 2016; CGI.br, 2010). Moreover, research on e-Democracy indicates that it is still difficult to find effective solutions encouraging civil society participation in public affairs (Roman & Miller, 2013). Few initiatives for a more active participation by citizens are found when compared to the predominance of proposals which focus on government-to-citizen interactions, i.e. solutions focusing on providing information/services, electronic voting or collecting opinion on pre-established matters. Additionally, considering that Democracy is bound to participation, sharing and contribution between citizens and government, collaboration is still a subject of little attention within the initiatives found.

The limited provision of information, possibilities of use and mechanisms for interacting to the government can lead to a gap between who is responsible for setting and monitoring public issues (government institutions) and who is directly affected by the application of these public issues (society). This gap limits the interaction possibilities between these parties, especially those regarding the collaboration between citizen to citizen and between society and government, as a source of information which can be used for government issues discussion and decision-making.

# UNDERSTANDING CITIZEN-GOVERNMENT TIES THROUGH PUBLIC SERVICES

Government and society have closer ties when there is collaboration among them, a better understanding about the public information and issues, interchange of roles and responsibilities, and a greater participation of society in public issues and decision making. When ICTs are applied to increase these ties, it is argued that one must follow a continuous ladder of participation levels, as explained above. In this work, the focus is on information provision by the government – the basic level of participation – and how to obtain comments from society about public services. It is argued that any change made in public services is more visible and directly affects the lives of citizens who use them, which can be an aspect to encourage their participation and involvement in public issues.

Therefore, it was designed a scale to establish closer ties between citizens and between society and government through public services (Figure 1). This scale pieces together the ideas presented by the democratic participation frameworks and the conclusions obtained from a literature survey (Diirr, Araujo & Cappelli, 2011).

The *availability of online services* is the simplest type of approximation. Government discloses information about the public services and their execution via an online tool, and society can understand services details, request their use and follow its requests without having to go to a government agency. The possibility of citizens' participation is still limited.

Following this idea, Hwang and Manandhar (2009) propose a tool where a set of public services is provided to society. Citizens may request the use of these services and follow up their requests by using this tool. The authors argue that online services can improve the public service delivery in terms of availability, ease of use and lower

*Figure 1. Government-citizen approximation scale through services*

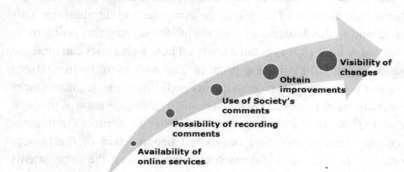

costs, besides increasing transparency and accountability, which helps to build trust between the government and citizens.

Classe et al (2017) and Pflanz et al (2016) propose the use of digital games based on public service processes. These authors argue that games allow citizens to live and understand a provided service in a playful way. Games can help players to acquire a vision and awareness about the goals and challenges of the service, both from the user's and from the providing institution's point of view, thus bringing their visions closer together.

Citizens also have the *possibility to comment* about public services. Usually, citizens express themselves via links like "Contact us" at government sites, or via Ombudsman online offices provided by public agencies responsible for the service provision. Citizens can send pre-classified messages (suggestions, praises, criticism, etc.) which will be received an internal public agent. The problem is that these messages may be answered or not, according to the agency relationship policy. The most import thing at this level is the possibility to retain public opinion or suggestions, different from the first level.

Berntzen (2013) presents a perspective of public participation in society is not only a consumer of public services but also a resource which can add value to the government and should be involved in all stages of the lifecycle of an eGovernment service. It is argued that the government is responsible for providing the infrastructure (servers, databases, software, etc.) and a basic set of public service information, and society can provide or consume information about these services using this infrastructure.

Miah, Gammack & Greenfield (2009) propose a user-centered service infrastructure for online participation, where citizens can access a range of public services and request their use. They can also enter to forums for discussing the services and vote on topics on government agenda.

Reuver, Stein, Hampe & Bouwman (2010) introduce a mobile platform that allows citizens to obtain and contribute with new information and unknown problems to those responsible for the information, such as a blocked passage identified by a citizen who indicates the location of the blockage using the mobile platform. This information will be sent to the department responsible for solving this problem.

Sajjad, Lee, Kamal & Irani (2011) detail a study on how workflows can increase society participation in the policy-making process. The authors argue that citizen participation improves policy-making process quality and effectiveness, and produces a reduction of conflicts, more constructive debates and a strategic vision of process. In addition, the workflow allows the creation of a citizens' feedback database; stimulates citizens to identify important issues and become part of the policy-formulation process; acts as a communication channel between the departments responsible for the policy-making process; and increases the citizens' perception about political issues.

Closeness among citizens is increased at the *use of society' comments* level since they can interact through comments about the service. This type of interaction can be found in chat rooms and forums available to citizens to discuss the services provided by government (Palace of the City, n.d.).

Loukis, Xenakis & Tseperli (2009) present an approach using visualizations in legislative procedure discussions and aims to increase society's participation in decision making. A set of IBIS-based visualizations was created, which aim to help the society's understanding about the subject at issue and encourage its participation.

Sell (2016) designed a tool to assist citizens to understand the business rules in public services. These rules are described in declarative language so that citizens can understand them and share experiences and information about the service with other citizens.

Araujo & Taher (2014) propose another way to use society's comments for bringing government and citizens together: IT requirements. They discuss an approach to identify requirements for citizen engagement support in public service design and delivery, according to desired participation levels. In this way, citizens will progressively be able to perform their role, as participative agents in the public service design and delivery, more consciously.

Government uses citizens' comments as a source for improving public services at the *obtain improvements* level. At this point that all suggestions and opinions made by citizens are retrieved, analyzed and implemented in the process. At the *visibility of changes* level, the government shows to society that has used citizen's comments to perform changes in public services. These changes should be tracked, so society can assess how its contribution has affected the public service. Although predicted on the government-citizen approximation scale through services, it was not possible to identify existing proposals to illustrate these levels.

Despite the potential for using services to establish closer ties between government and society, the available solutions are mainly interested in how to allow online service requests to reduce existing bureaucracy and provide agility to the process. The solutions attempting to maintain a closer dialogue between society and government have a special attention on how to provide mechanisms allowing voting on pre-established matters and mechanisms through which society can provide information about the service. Government has no obligation to consider the information provided by society for service improvement, and if this information is used, the government does not explain how it was used.

This work argues that is important to advance at this level of participation. The main challenges are how to help governments to evolve from an authority to a service provision relationship with citizens; and how to improve citizens' cooperation and commitment with decision making, acquiring continuous education on democratic practices. From the government side, benefits arise if it is aware of citizens' point of view while using the service and problems that may be invisible to the government. It allows the provision of services closer to the citizens' needs. To the society, benefits are expected when they face opportunities to participate more actively, collaborating to improve the service and minimizing faced problems. It increases trust and possibilities for the service improvement and innovation.

## TALKING ABOUT PUBLIC SERVICES

This work proposes the use of conversations about public services for a closer relationship between society and service providers (government). Here, conversations are defined as narratives made by those who are involved in discussions about public services. These conversations are a common practice, especially in Brazilian culture, being identified inside public agencies but also in social interactions, such as bar tables, parties, and work. For instance, while standing in line for requesting a service (e.g. annual vehicle inspection), people use to talk to one another while waiting. Problems in service provision, the way that attendees perform their work, lack of information about the required documentation, and problems with the information system used to request the service, are a set of the most common narratives. And these conversations usually cross the borders of the public agency. It is common that people talk to their friends about the difficulties faced. They discuss their own experiences (*"I did my inspection last month and it took me 2 hours because the system was too slow"*), opinions (*"I cannot understand why we have to do it every year! Why the vehicle control department inspects vehicles every two years as in other cities?"*), information (*"Do you know that vehicle control department send you an SMS to warn about the period in which you must do the annual inspection?"*) and what they did to avoid problems (*"Before going to the inspection, I went to a mechanic to check whether everything was ok with my car."*), and will probably take this information and use it when their turn comes to have the same service provided.

The main problem here is that, in these situations, people usually talk, complain or discuss with no familiarity with service details. The execution flow and rules about how it can or must be provided by the public institution – the service process model – are not visible to the citizens. If citizens are not aware of why the service must be provided or if the organization is facing problems to provide it that way, complaints might be not useful and will require extra effort from the staff and from the public institution to handle them. It is important to make the service details visible, so its users can discuss and analyze the service provided with greater basis.

Additionally, people who need to use a specific service usually prefer to ask other citizens in place for information, rather than going out for someone responsible for service provision. Thus, government representatives or the public institution staff are not physically present or near enough to correct or explain any wrong view or information. It increases the chances of leading to information inconsistencies and dissatisfaction, being important to bring government representatives or the public institution staff into the citizens' interaction to minimize these problems.

Finally, the knowledge sharing is restricted to those who are physically present during the conversation and may be lost. It is important to keep what was discussed during the conversation to benefit others who cannot participate in conversation but are interested in or use the public service.

Therefore, it is proposed the establishment of a virtual environment where these interactions may occur, minimizing these limitations and getting advantage of conversations, i.e. to increase participants' understanding about the service; to increase the number of participants in discussions; to bring government to citizens' interaction; to keep a conversation log which can be used for others; and to explain relevant information to improve the public service provided.

## SUPPORTING CONVERSATIONS ABOUT PUBLIC SERVICES

Web and social software (wikis, blogs, social bookmarking and so on) (Allen, 2004; Bryant, 2006; Oates, 2008; Shirky, 2008) have comprised the fundamental platforms for enabling actions into communities and social networks due to their simplicity and flexibility. Although allowing high connectivity among participants, these tools still require adjustments to enable effective collaboration further than publishing, liking, and twitting. More than that, further studies are necessary to understand how governments have been adopting these tools for promoting participation of society in public issues (Alryalat et al, 2017; Charalabidis & Loukis, 2012; Ferro, Loukism, Charalabidis & Osella, 2013).

The challenge of designing tools with these features increases due to issues related to the democratic process, such as conflicts between secrecy-transparency of information (Holzner & Holzner, 2006), diversity of participants (Shirky, 2008) and the need to manage and preserve knowledge produced as social memory (Sunstein, 2006). In this work, three main aspects are considered important for Electronic Democracy support, and must be addressed as requirements for tools specification and development (Diirr, Araujo & Cappelli, 2009):

- Transparency of information, actions, and decisions – Democracy is a model of truth and equality and cannot be fully implemented in a misinformation environment. Transparency is a way to provide accessibility, usability, informativeness, understandability, and auditability of organizational information (Cappelli, Oliveira & Leite, 2007). Thus, having visibility of how public service is executed, citizens understand how it can or must be provided by the public institution, thereby reducing complaints and enhancing trust and confidence (Khosrowjerdi, 2016; Mahmood, 2016);

- Collaboration among participants – Democracy is based on participation, sharing, equality and public contribution to actions and decisions. New mechanisms for doubts removal and service improvements identification are created when government encourages the interaction between citizens and between citizens and government;

- Memory of discussion and deliberation – Discussion and decisions of public issues must rely on past memory. From this, citizens and government can make good decisions, have a wider view of discussion and learn from different points of view.

Diirr et al (2009) present an approach to systematize the specification, development, and deployment of virtual environments to support e-Democracy (Figure 2). If an organization aims to support e-Democracy initiatives, it is necessary that the organization (a) knows how to run its activities, (b) assess the acceptance of the proposed solution considering the existing cultural values; and (c) defines the desired democratic participation level. Using this information and considering the aspects of collaboration, transparency, and memory, it is possible to identify a set of requirements which can be implemented in e-Democracy support for that context.

*Figure 2. ICT-based approach for defining e-democracy support*

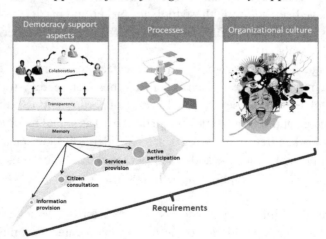

In this work, the "services provision" was selected as the desired democratic participation level to establish closer ties between government and society. The process of talking about public service provision was defined through three steps: (a) *provision of public services*, where society has visibility about the public service details, allowing it to know the public service better; (b) *possibility of talking about public services*, where citizens can interact with other users and service providers, by sharing experiences, opinions, problems, suggestions, etc.; (c) *conversations analysis*, where Government can retrieve conversations and extract information for the public service improvement. Regarding cultural issues, talking and sharing information about public services provision is a common practice, especially in societies where service provision lacks information. Thus, some requirements for transparency, collaboration and memory have been identified from this information. They were used to design an online tool to support conversations about public service processes (Figure 3).

This tool is accessible by the general public and allows people to know the public service through models and textual descriptions explaining how it works. The main aspect of the developed tool is to make available the public service process model (Figure 4) so that citizens can acquire a better understanding of the service operation (in our example, the travel funding process), thus guiding their comments. Citizens have access to the information flow, events, activities, actors, and artifacts in the process. Those process elements are considered relevant to the service users' understanding because they represent process triggers, the necessary steps to use the public service, people responsible for performing each step of the service, and which documents are necessary and processed during public service performance.

*Figure 3. The online tool to support conversations about public services processes*

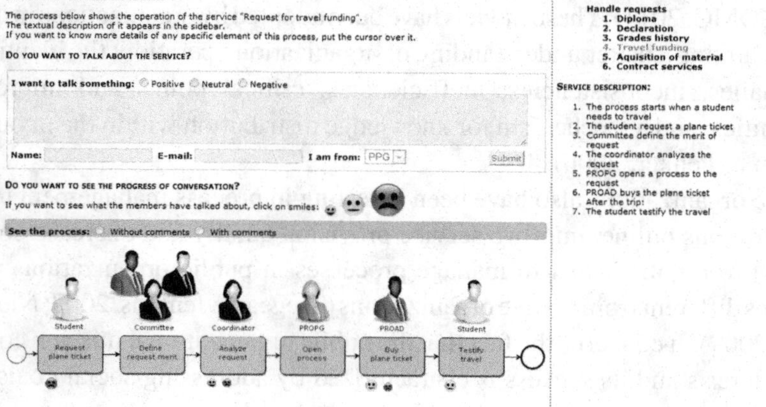

*Figure 4. Process model describing service details*

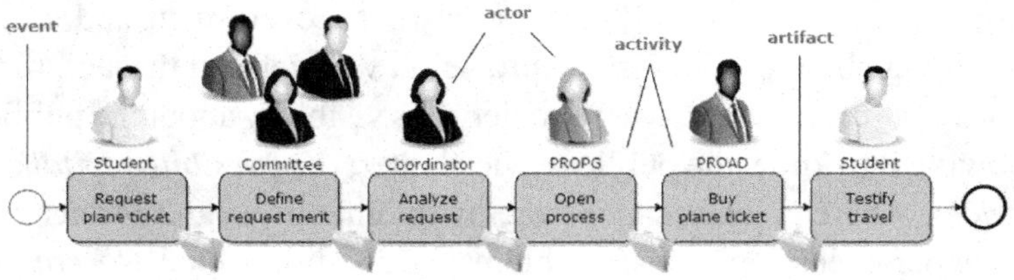

The tool allows participants to share experiences, opinions, questions, problems, suggestions etc., about the services provided. Each participant can pose contributions for the service/process as a whole or he/she can talk about specific elements of this process – an activity, an actor etc. They can also interact with other participants to add relevant information, correct something said and answer questions. The service manager can analyze this interaction and, according to certain criteria, identify information for the service improvement.

The identified features are presented below. They are organized according to the democratic participation support aspects, and it is also presented how these features were implemented in the designed tool to illustrate them.

## Transparency Features

This proposal relies on the use of process models to promote visibility about public services. Process models show simplified views of the organization's complex reality (Eriksson & Penker, 2000) and are comprised of the following elements: goal (why the process exists), actor (who performs each process activity), activities (process steps), artifacts (activity inputs and outputs), resources (equipment or systems supporting activities), events (triggers elements of the process), business rules (laws governing the process) and possible flow (decisions and alternatives in process)(OMG, 2011). These models have been adopted by organizations in different contexts, aiming a better understanding of organization operation; the identification of anomalies, inconsistencies, inefficiencies, critical points and improvement opportunities; and a mechanism for knowledge distribution within the organization (Eriksson & Penker, 2000).

Public organizations also have been investing in process management to render their operations online, improve service provision quality and decrease costs. It is important to highlight that to manage processes in public organizations presents challenges different from private organizations (Tregear & Jenkins, 2007; Niehaves & Malsch, 2009). It concerns the fact that the public organizational mission comprises public interests and its success is characterized by addressing social goals. Public organizations must deal with a complex variety of "clients" and their results have a higher impact on their lives.

Thus, participants have access to detailed information for process execution. For example, by positioning the cursor over a specific activity, a description is shown. It details the process elements that are necessary to execute this activity, such as event triggers, the actor who performs it, artifacts required, necessary resources, business rules, products generated etc. (Figure 5).

One important aspect here is that the public sees the process model in its definition form, i.e. the operation flow that was defined by the organization to accomplish the service. It is not expected to present to citizens the flow of activities of their own process instance or execution. The reason is that, as described below, to make citizens collaborate among them and with public organizations representatives, they should share the same process model definition. Although for each individual case the process could follow different process branches and citizens will prefer to comment on specific portions of the process they took part, the basis for discussion and further analysis is the same for all participants. Furthermore, citizens that have never used the process can also participate in the discussion, if they want to contribute with comments and suggestions for process/service improvement.

## Collaboration Features

Following the finds of other researchers (Chun & Cho, 2012; Niehaves & Malsch, 2009), this work argues that collaboration among citizens and public institutions through process management is an alternative to shorten the distance between these agents. It is a way to improve processes/services and to promote the role of these agents as co-participants in a Government structure, thereby improving their synergy.

Collaboration support can be designed concerning three main aspects: communication, coordination, and awareness (Araujo, Borges & Dias, 1997).

*Figure 5. Activity description*

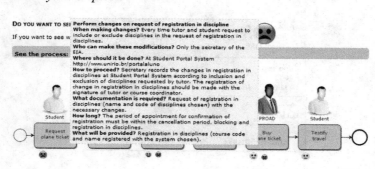

Concerning communication facilities, mechanisms were designed to enable communication between citizens and between citizens and government through the process model (their shared space) so that the distance among these participants are minimized. The first mechanism is to comment about the public service (Figure 6). This feature allows participants to point out their issues, complaints, experiences, opinions, suggestions, and information about services.

Other mechanisms which encourage society's dialogue are "Like", "Reply", "Share", which are used on social networks like Facebook and Twitter. They comprise a useful approach for fast interaction among people, increasing knowledge about the service and encouraging discussions (Figure 7).

Coordination means articulating participants to prevent loss of decisions made. Thus, it is proposed that comments be oriented to the process elements. For this, while using the tool, by clicking on a process activity, the box represented in Figure 8, appears and participants can comment on it. This comment will be associated with this specific activity.

Regarding *awareness* facilities, it is necessary to make participants aware of collaborative interaction, concerning information about who is participating and participation progress. The tool provides a set of mechanisms to understand the

*Figure 6. Posting comments about the public service*

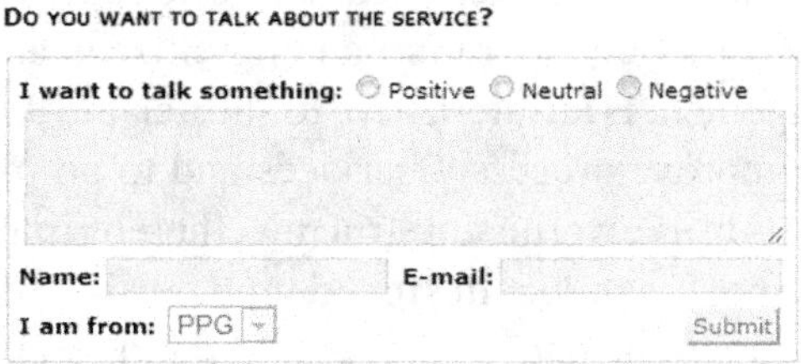

*Figure 7. Interaction mechanism in comment details*

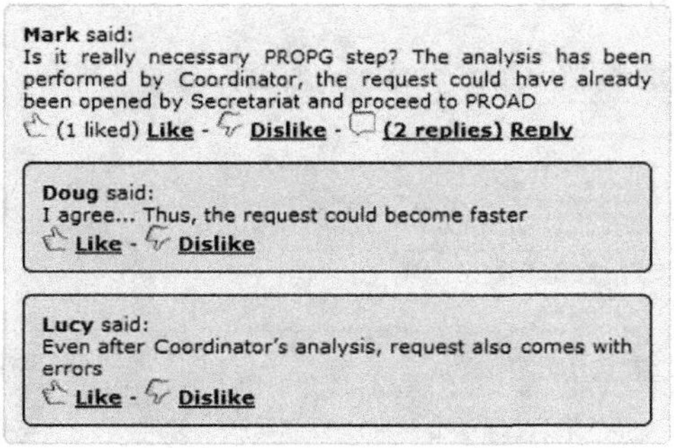

*Figure 8. Association between a comment and an activity*

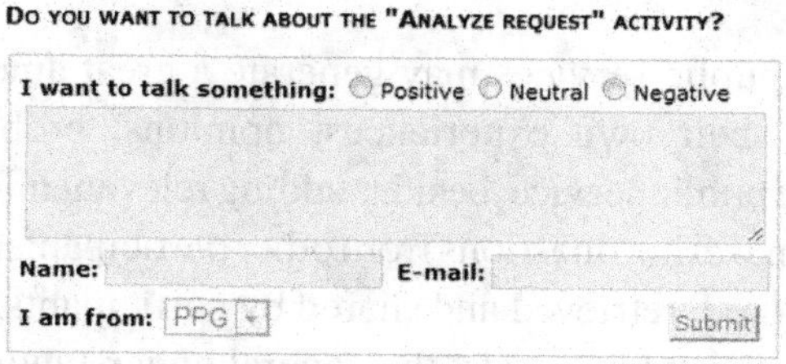

**Do you want to talk about the "Analyze request" activity?**

**I want to talk something:** ○ Positive ○ Neutral ○ Negative

**Name:**      **E-mail:**

**I am from:** PPG ▾      Submit

conversation flow. First, participants can follow the existence and number of comments associated with different process elements. There are colored icons organized by type of comment (positive – green; neutral – yellow; negative – red), which size changes according to the number of comments made by participants – the greater the number of comments, the bigger the icon is (Figure 9).

Besides that, "Like", "Dislike" and "Reply" mechanisms help participants to understand how the conversation is evolving. The tool shows the number of participants who agreed, disagreed and replied to each comment made (Figure 10).

*Figure 9. Visualization of comments for process elements*

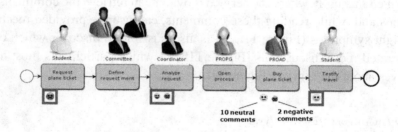

*Figure 10. Participants' use of interaction mechanisms*

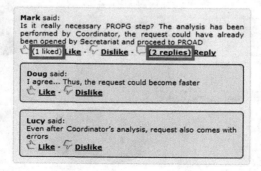

## Memory Features

Conversations about public services may generate a great amount of information. Participants provide their own experiences, opinions, problems, improvement suggestions etc. on the public service, besides adding relevant information, correcting something said and answering questions from other participants. All this information must be organized, stored, retrieved and shared by participants, so the accumulated knowledge of past situations can assist the general understanding of the group and build a group memory from past experiences (Hedberg, 1981; Conklin, 1997).

However, the great volume of information makes it difficult to monitor the conversations, both by society, which needs to understand what is being discussed to start participating, and by the government, which needs to capture and organize the information which can be relevant to public service improvement. Thus, it is necessary for the information to be organized and recorded.

The previously-recorded information about the public service, when combined with comments made by participants, can be used as input for symptom identification during government's conversation analysis. Symptoms are parts of comments which indicate aspects of public service which need to be rethought (Oliveira, Araujo & Borges, 2007), and may lead to service provision improvement. Figure 11 shows an example of the analysis which can be done in the developed tool. This analysis is performed manually where the service provider can retrieve the comments made by citizens and, while reading these comments, can use the provided mechanism to highlight symptoms (Figure 11a). It is also possible to discover which content has generated more discussions (Figure 11b) or which participants most express themselves about the service (Figure 11c).

*Figure 11. Conversation analysis*

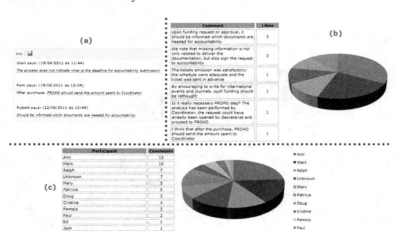

The proposed approach and supporting tool differs from other proposals to encourage closer relationship between society and government in three aspects: (a) the use of processes to disclose service details for society and to contribute to service transparency, (b) the application of an usual mechanism (conversations) that allow the interaction between citizens and between government and citizens to exchange experiences, opinions, problems, suggestions, and information about the public service; (c) the explicit association between comments and process elements, which helps both citizens – who may find more information about a specific aspects of public service – and government – which identifies the specific points of public service which may require improvement.

## CASE STUDY

A case study was designed to investigate the applicability of conversations about public service processes to encourage interaction between service providers and society. It was performed in the Federal University of the State of Rio de Janeiro (UNIRIO), which is a public organization with the main characteristics and needs of a public environment and has an initiative for modeling its organizational processes (CGCP-UNIRIO, 2012). For this case study, researchers have selected the service "Apply for PROAP-CAPES funding", which aims to spend the government-granted fund on the university graduate programs. This service purports many problems during its execution, has difficulties for accountability to external organizations, and generates numerous complaints from those who need to use this fund (students, teachers and administrative staff of the different graduate programs). It is believed that this problem occurs because the service details are unknown – people involved/ interested in this service only have a partial view of the service operation, i.e. they only know the activities under their responsibility – and the communication during service performance also faces difficulties.

This service is used by all graduate programs in UNIRIO, which may have specific and distinct needs from each other, and needs to be performed by many people at different departments. Thus, it characterizes the scenario which the proposal aims to meet since this service provision creates a context encouraging interaction between different university departments (Government) and members of graduate programs, the beneficiaries of the funding (Citizens).

### Case Study Design

This research posits the hypothesis that citizens and government representatives talking about the process model of a public service can improve the dialogue, mutual understanding and to leverage the democratic practice among these actors. I.e. citizens are encouraged to talk and the government is open to interacting. As a first step to validate this, the case study aims to investigate if and how the tool could support the conversation about the process and if the conversation results could lead to relevant inputs for the public service improvement. Therefore, information gathered from the case study should answer the following research questions:

**RQ1:** *Does the presentation of public services through process models guides participants' comments about the service?*

To assess how the adoption of process models guides users' comments about the public service. Variables to evaluate this question: the number of comments made on each process element type (flow, activity or role); and the number of comments content of which is related to the associated process element.

**RQ2:** *Do collaborative mechanisms provided by the tool enable interaction among those involved with the service?*

To evaluate how the provided collaborative mechanisms stimulate interaction among those involved with the service provided. Variables to evaluate this question: the number of citations to participants' name; the number of citations to other participant's comment; the number of "likes"; and the number of "replies".

**RQ3:** *Do conversations among those involved with the service provide bring inputs for service improvement identification?*

To assess how conversations about the process models can be used as input for identifying service improvements. Variables to evaluate this question: number of symptoms identified; and relevance of symptoms.

As the application of PROAP-CAPES funding has several subprocesses, the service "Request for travel funding" was chosen to be used in the designed case study. The process model representing this service was reviewed to simplify it, reducing its flow complexity as well as focusing on relevant elements to be understood by citizens (actors, activities, start and final events) (Figure 12).

## Case Study Execution

The tool was made available to the general public via the internet, but people directly involved or interested in this particular service performance (students, teachers, and administrative staff) were encouraged to participate in the case study. An email was

*Figure 12. Process for requesting travel funding*

sent requesting participants to access the tool and, if they so wished, they could interact with one another and discuss the process that represents the process for the "Request for travel funding" service. Participants were not required to have used before or to be using the service to take part in the study. They could send emails to the researcher for help if needed.

The case study was performed remotely and was available for three weeks. 17 people accepted the invitation to participate, and 71 comments about the service were identified. Among these 17 participants, it was possible to identify all profiles involved in "Request for travel funding" performance: teachers, students, committee for merit assignment, graduate program coordinator and administrative staff. Result analysis for each research question is presented below.

## Result Analysis

**RQ1:** *Does the presentation of public services through process models guides participants' comments about the service?*

All the 71 comments were made to some process element (flow – 23 comments – or activity – 48 comments). This result helps us argue that the use of processes to give visibility of public services assists in guiding participants' comments. Process availability provides visibility to information about service operation, allowing participants to discuss the service through process elements. All comments were associated, explicitly or implicitly, to some process element and the comment content reflects reports of experiences, opinions, suggestions, and explanations about the related process element.

The process element "Actor" had no explicit comment associated. It was expected in the context of UNIRIO administration since there is not a well-defined characterization of the roles responsible for performing tasks or responsibilities assigned to those roles. For instance, when a student needs information about the progress of his/her request, the orientation is to speak with "Carl" from PROPG; if any problem in buying a ticket arises, the orientation is to contact "Joan" from PROAD. Thus, the absence of explicit comments to the process element "Actor" is expressed by not questioning/understanding the responsibility needed to undertake a specific activity.

Moreover, it was possible to identify implicit associations to process elements, i.e. comments indirectly mentioning some process elements: *"The process does not indicate what **the deadline for accountability submission** is"* – rule; *"After purchase, PROAD should send **the amount spent to Coordinator**"* – information; *"It should be informed **which documents are needed for accountability**"* – document etc.

In addition, the contents of 4 comments were not directly related to the process element for which it was made. They should be associated with the element "Activity" instead of the element "Process". This is not considered problematic since these comments were associated with the element "Process", which by definition includes a set of activities.

**RQ2:** *Do collaborative mechanisms provided by the tool enable interaction among those involved with the service?*

The interaction among participants showed citations to other participants' name (in 10 comments) and to other participants' comments (in 34 comments). These citations were used either to enhance a comment made by the participant quoted or remove doubts on what another participant had talked about.

The mechanisms "Like" and "Reply" were also used 47 times throughout the conversation. "Citizens" used them to interact with other users, and the service provider could use them to correct information previously provided, explaining their ideas and views, promoting discussion and increasing service awareness.

An example of conversation which this situation occurred in case study can be seen below:

*Teacher:* "This step at PROPG is really necessary? The analysis has been performed by the Coordinator, the request could have already been opened by Secretariat and proceed to PROAD"
*Student:* "I agree... Thus, the request could move faster"
*PROPG Employee:* "Even after Coordinator's analysis, the request also comes with errors"

It is possible to see that participants have interacted with other users and service providers, by pointing a service problem, explaining their ideas and points of view, and adding information which may be invisible to other participants. This allows an increase of information about the service.

**RQ3:** *Do conversations among those involved with the service provide bring inputs for service improvement identification?*

Regarding service improvements identification, it was possible to identify 53 symptoms from the 71 comments. These symptoms dealt with different types of service improvements such as deadline review; delays caused by request processing; misunderstanding regarding some previous descriptions; lack of information about the process; the difficulty of accessing information; agility achieved by automating the process; difficulty in requests monitoring; review of funding responsibility scope etc.

The comments have mentioned process elements which did not allow explicit comments, so it was possible to identify symptoms related to "Documents", "Information", "Systems" and "Rules".

It was also possible to classify the symptoms according to their criticality. From the 53 identified symptoms, 37 symptoms were considered critical, i.e. cause significant changes in the process, as a change of rules, review of available information, definition of new documents, process automation and so on.

These results show that the information provided by participants serves as input for service improvement identification. When comments were analyzed, they generated a set of symptoms related to different process elements, which can be used as input to improve these aspects of the public service. For example, by identifying comments about requests delay due to paper processing, the lack of expense control, the lack of information for accounting etc., it is possible to think about service improvements such as the use of a system which enables the automation of requests, the creation of reports to control the expenditures made, the creation of a useful documents repository etc.

## Limitations

The first limitation of the case study concerns participants' profile. The intellectual level of the "citizens" in the university is high. In addition, most participants were members of the Graduate Program in Information Systems, having great familiarity in using technologies and more systematic thinking when compared to members of other areas. It is necessary to evaluate how results behave when other profiles are involved and if problems may arise in understanding the information provided, analysis of process models, establishment of different forms of interaction and argumentation etc.

Another limitation is related to the service used in the discussion. Although "Request for travel funding" service has a certain complexity and there are demands for its use, the complexity and scope of this service are limited when compared to other public services. The increase of complexity and number of participants demand to rethink how information should be presented for better understanding of the service by citizens, the way information is analyzed and how symptom identification is carried out.

## DISCUSSION

Conversations are interesting mechanisms for a closer relationship between society and service providers. It is a practice that is part of people's daily lives, whether while standing in line, at a bar table or in social media. The challenge is to bring this social interaction to virtual environments that promote greater participation in public issues (Alryalat et al, 2017; Charalabidis & Loukis, 2012; Ferro et al, 2013; Shirky, 2008).

It is necessary to support the collaboration, transparency and memory aspects, which are important pillars for the practice of democracy and consequent support for e-Democracy (Diirr, Araujo & Cappelli, 2009). The representation of public services through process models stimulates the visibility of the hitherto "unknown", leading to a greater understanding of the public service details as well as greater confidence in its operation. Such models, combined with collaboration mechanisms, enable and guide the interaction between citizens and between citizens and government. Moreover, not only using the process models that adequately define the provided services but also recording the experiences of using these services, allow an improvement of the knowledge about the public service.

In terms of practical implications, both service providers (government) and society can benefit from conversations about public service processes. From the government perspective, structuring public services through process models assists the service review. Services providers can identify problems and increase the efficiency of service operation (Tregear & Jenkins, 2007; Niehaves & Malsch, 2009). In addition, the knowledge gained from citizens' point of view helps the identification of problems that may be invisible to the service providers. On the other hand, society acquires a greater knowledge about the service, thus reducing uncertainties and criticisms about it, as well as exchange experiences that may prove useful when the service is necessary. It leads to citizens' satisfaction and trust increase (Khosrowjerdi, 2016; Mahmood, 2016). All this leads to higher levels of democratic participation.

Besides all the benefits arising from the proposal application and support tool, some aspects must also bear an in-depth study. It is pointed out the influence of participation culture in proposal adoption. This proposal invests in Brazilians' characteristic, which is people who enjoy interacting with others besides not displaying an active political participation, to encourage society's participation and to bring it closer to the government. The impact of socio-cultural aspects must be considered when attempting to extrapolate the proposal to other fields. Medina & Rufin (2015) have already addressed this concern, especially regarding transparency and perceived trust in public services.

Process model presentation is another issue. The developed tool explicitly represents the flow, activities, and actors, beyond describing other process elements (events, resources, artifacts, and rules). However, there is no guarantee that this presentation is more appropriate for discussion in democratic contexts. Discussions regarding the definition of an approach enabling process models creation/adaptation, so that citizens can know, understand and talk about the details of the public service provided were addressed by researchers' group (Engiel, Araujo & Cappelli, 2014; Iglesias, 2014; Martins, 2015; Carvalho, Santoro & Cappelli, 2016), besides being an investigation topic from other researchers (Sell, 2016).

Information quality and volume must also be handled. Noise can be created by participants who use the tool to sell services or detract the conversation about the public service. In addition, comments, which may have been answered by other participants or have used during service analysis and improvement, should be archived so as not to impair participants' interaction. Moreover, as the number of services provided and comments related increases, manual analysis is not the most appropriate way for symptoms identification. Thus, it is necessary to create mechanisms, such as moderation, to minimize noises; procedures that assist archiving obsolete comments, as well as retrieving relevant information from it, such as text mining; automation of symptoms identification through text mining and creation of a symptoms classification, which leaves the changes that need to be made clearer (creation of new artifacts; changes to actor responsibilities; exclusion of rules etc.).

The developed tool may be improved in terms of usability to assist in improving the participation of those involved with the public service. In addition, it is important that this tool is integrated with the organizational process repository, so as the process models to be easily imported to the tool, speeding up the dynamics of presenting process versions or variations to the public.

## CONCLUSION

This work has proposed the use of conversations about public service processes to encourage better interaction and establishes closer ties between society and government. This proposal is motivated by the existence of conversations in the real world, which are common in various public contexts, and attempting to reconstruct them in virtual environments.

The main subject of conversations among citizens and service providers are the process models of public services. Being an artifact for internal organizational communication of procedures and an instrument for operation improvement, this proposal expects to broaden business process models communication capability to the external environment. The concern of public organizations in explaining their processes to citizens may be proportional to the extent that it is interested and prepared to be transparent to the public, or if they are obliged to do so. In some countries, for instance in Brazil, there are federal rules indicating that public organizations must publish their processes to the citizens (Brasil, 2009; Brasil, 2011). A big effort is being done by organizations to improve their process management and modeling practices, as well as to find different ways of presenting it to the public.

The developed tool to support the conversations provides access to a process model of a given public service, which is used as the basis for participants to share their experiences, opinions, problems, suggestions, and information. The process guides the conversation through its elements providing visibility on service execution, which are often unknown by citizens. Participants can interact with other users and service providers using the offered collaborative mechanisms, thereby promoting discussions and increasing knowledge about public service. Moreover, comments may provide information that, when analyzed, generate a set of symptoms which can be used by the government to service improvement.

The case study has demonstrated that the proposal has the potential to encourage "citizens" and "service providers" to have closer ties from a public service discussion in an organization. Users had visibility about service details, thus reducing the lack of knowledge about its operation and allowing for the possibility of inquiring about the reasons why the service worked in that way. Service providers could understand the service from the users' perspective and experience their problems. This increases the range of ideas to improve service provision.

Further research would comprise the tool enhancements and its use in different public contexts, organizations, and processes. It will provide a broader understanding of proposal successes and failures, besides a better insight into the extent of its practical implications.

## ACKNOWLEDGMENT

Renata Araujo is supported by the Brazilian National Council for Scientific and Technological Development (CNPq) [305060/2016-3]. This work had been part of the project "Democracy, Transparency and Public Administration – Reflections and Implementations of Government Systems through ICTs" (http://www.uniriotec. br/~agora), supported by the Coordination for the Improvement of Higher Level Personnel (CAPES) and CNPq (2009-2014). It has also been part of the Brazilian Webscience Institute, supported by CNPq [557.128/2009-9] and the Research Support Foundation of State of Rio de Janeiro (FAPERJ) [E-26/170028/2008].

# REFERENCES

Allen, C. (2004). *Tracing the evolution of Social Software*. Retrieved from http:// www.lifewithalacrity.com/2004/10/tracing_the_evo.html

Alryalat, M., Rana, N., Sahu, G., Dwivedi, Y., & Tajvidi, M. (2017). Use of Social Media in Citizen-Centric Electronic Government Services: A Literature Analysis. *International Journal of Electronic Government Research, 13*(3), 55–79. doi:10.4018/ IJEGR.2017070104

Andersen, K., Henriksen, H., & Medaglia, R. (2012). Beyond the Layne & Lee Legacy. Public Administration in the Information Age: Revisited, 205-220.

Andersen, K., Medaglia, R., & Henriksen, H. (2011). Frequency and costs of communication with citizens in local government. *International Conference on Electronic Government and the Information Systems Perspective* (LNCS 6866, pp. 15-25). Toulouse, France: Springer. 10.1007/978-3-642-22961-9_2

Araujo, R., & Taher, Y. (2014). Refining IT Requirements for Government-Citizen Co-participation Support in Public Service Design and Delivery. *Conference for E-Democracy and Open Government, 1*, 61–72.

Araujo, R. M., Borges, M. R. S., & Dias, M. S. (1997). A Framework for the Classification of Computer Supported Collaborative Design Approaches. *III CYTED-RITOS International Workshop on Groupware*.

Arnstein, S. (1969). A ladder of citizen participation. *Journal of the American Institute of Planners, 35*(4), 216–224. doi:10.1080/01944366908977225

Baller, S., Dutta, S., & Lanvin, B. (2016). The global information technology report 2016 – Innovating in the Digital Economy. *World Economic Forum*.

Berntzen, L. (2013). Citizen-centric eGovernment Services: Use of indicators to measure degree of user involvement in eGovernment service development. *International Conference on Advances in Human-oriented and Personalized Mechanisms, Technologies and Services*, 132-136.

Brasil. (2009). *Lei complementar n° 131 – Disponibilização em tempo real de informações* (Supplementary Law no. 131 – Real-time provision of information). Retrieved from https://www.planalto.gov.br/ccivil_03/Leis/LCP/Lcp131.htm

Brasil. (2011). *Lei n° 12.527 – Lei de acesso à informação* (Law no. 12,527 – Law on information access). Retrieved from http://www.planalto.gov.br/ccivil_03/_ato2011-2014/2011/lei/l12527.htm

Bryant, T. (2006). Social Software in Academia. *Educate Quarterly, 6*, 61-64.

Cappelli, C., Oliveira, A., & Leite, J. C. (2007). Exploring Business Process Transparency Concepts. *IEEE International Requirements Engineering Conference*, 389-390. 10.1109/RE.2007.35

Carvalho, L. P., Santoro, F., & Cappelli, C. (2016). Using a Citizen Language in Public Process Models: The Case Study of a Brazilian University. *LNCS, 9831*, 123–134.

CGCP-UNIRIO. (2012). *Coordenadoria de Gestão Corporativa de Processos da UNIRIO* (Coordination of Corporate Process Management). Retrieved from http://www2.unirio.br/unirio/cgcp/projetos/internos/proap-1/produtos

CGI.br. (2010). *TIC Governo Eletrônico*. Retrieved from http://www.cetic.br/tic/egov/2010/index.htm

Charalabidis, Y., & Loukis, E. (2012). Participative Public Policy Making Through Multiple Social Media Platforms Utilization. *International Journal of Electronic Government Research, 8*(3), 78–97. doi:10.4018/jegr.2012070105

Chun, S. A., & Cho, J. (2012). E-participation and transparent policy decision making. *Information Polity, 17*(2), 129–145.

CitizenScape. (n.d.). Retrieved from http://www.citizenscape.net

Classe, T., Araujo, R., & Xexéo, G. (2017). *Desaparecidos RJ – Um Jogo Digital para o Entendimento de Processos de Prestação de Serviços Públicos [Disappeared RJ – A Digital Game for Understanding the Public Service Provision Processes]*. Curitiba: Simpósio Brasileiro de Jogos e Entretenimento Digital.

Conklin, E. (1997). *Designing Organizational Memory: Preserving Intellectual Assets in a Knowledge Economy*. Retrieved from http://cognexus.org/dom.pdf

DETRAN-RJ. (n.d.). Retrieved from http://www.detran.rj.gov.br

Diirr, B., Araujo, R., & Cappelli, C. (2009). An Approach for Defining Digital Democracy Support based on ICT. *International Conference on Computer Supported Cooperative Work in Design*, 203-208. 10.1109/CSCWD.2009.4968059

Diirr, B., Araujo, R., & Cappelli, C. (2011). Propostas para aproximação entre Sociedade e Governo por meio de discussões apoiadas por TICs [Proposals for closer ties between society and government through discussions supported by ICTs]. *DIA-UNIRIO Technical Report (RelaTe-DIA)*. Retrieved from http://www.seer.unirio.br/index.php/monografiasppgi/article/view/1730

DRING13. (n.d.). Retrieved from http://www.dring13.org

Engiel, P., Araujo, R., & Cappelli, C. (2014). Designing Public Service Process Models for Understandability. Electronic. *Journal of E-Government*, *12*, 95–111.

Eriksson, H., & Penker, M. (2000). *Business Modeling with UML: Business Patterns at Work*. New York: Wiley Publishers.

Femers, S., & Wiedemann, P. (1993). Public participation in waste management decision making: Analysis and management of conflicts. *Journal of Hazardous Materials*, *33*(3), 355–368. doi:10.1016/0304-3894(93)85085-S

Ferro, E., Loukis, E., Charalabidis, Y., & Osella, M. (2013). Policy making 2.0: From theory to practice. *Government Information Quarterly*, *30*(4), 359–368. doi:10.1016/j.giq.2013.05.018

Gomes, W. (2004). *Transformações da política na era da comunicação de massa [Politics transformation in the mass communication era]*. São Paulo: Paulus.

Grönlund, A. (2009). ICT is not Participation is not Democracy – eParticipation Development Models Revisited. *International Conference on eParticipation*, 12-23. 10.1007/978-3-642-03781-8_2

Hague, B. (1999). *Digital Democracy: Discourse and Decision Making in the Information Age* (1st ed.). London: Routledge.

Hedberg, B. (1981). How organizations learn and unlearn. In P. Nystrom & W. Starbuck (Eds.), *Handbook of Organizational Design* (pp. 3–27). New York: Oxford University Press.

Holzner, B., & Holzner, L. (2006). *Transparency in global change: The vanguard of the open society*. Pittsburgh, PA: University of Pittsburgh Press.

Hwang, J., & Manandhar, S. (2009). Cost-benefit analysis of OPEN system: A case study for Kathmandu Metropolitan City, *International Conference on Computer Sciences and Convergence Information Technology*, 1425-1430. 10.1109/ICCIT.2009.252

Iglesias, C. (2014). *Promovendo o entendimento de cartas de serviços ao cidadão* [Promoting the understanding of service letters to citizens] (Dissertation). Federal University of the State of Rio de Janeiro.

Khosrowjerdi, M. (2016). Trust in People, Organizations, and Government: A Generic Model. *International Journal of Electronic Government Research, 12*(3), 55–70. doi:10.4018/IJEGR.2016070104

Loukis, E., Xenakis, A., & Tseperli, N. (2009). Using argument visualization to enhance e-participation in the legislation formation process. *International Conference on eParticipation*, 125-138. 10.1007/978-3-642-03781-8_12

Mahmood, M. (2016). Enhancing Citizens' Trust and Confidence in Government through Digital Transformation. *International Journal of Electronic Government Research, 12*(1), 99–110. doi:10.4018/IJEGR.2016010105

Martins, L. (2015). *Ambiente de discussões sobre normas jurídicas nos processos de negócio da administração pública* [Environment for discussions about legal norms in business processes of public administration] (Dissertation). Federal University of the State of Rio de Janeiro.

Medina, C., & Rufin, R. (2015). Social Media Use and Perception of Transparency in the Generation of Trust in Public Services. *Hawaii International Conference on System Sciences*. 10.1109/HICSS.2015.290

Miah, S., Gammack, J., & Greenfield, G. (2009). An infrastructure for implementing e-participation services in developing countries. *IEEE International Conference on Digital Ecosystems and Technologies*, 407-411. 10.1109/DEST.2009.5276686

Niehaves, B., & Malsch, R. (2009). Democratizing Process Innovation? On Citizen Involvement in Public Sector BPM. *IFIP Conference on Electronic Government* (LNCS 5693, pp. 245-256). Springer-Verlag Berlin Heidelberg.

Oates, S. (2008). *Introduction to media and politics*. London: Sage Publications.

OECD. (2001). *Citizens as partners, Handbook on information, consultation and public participation in policy-making*. Paris: OECD Publications.

Oliveira, A. C., Araujo, R. M., & Borges, M. R. S. (2007) Telling Stories about System Use: Capturing Collective Tacit Knowledge for System Maintenance. *International Conference on Software Engineering and Knowledge Engineering*, 337-342.

OMG. (2011). *Object Management Group Business Process Model Notation*. Retrieved from http://www.bpmn.org

Palace of the City. (n.d.). *Prefeitura Do Rio De Janeiro*. Retrieved from http://www.rio.rj.gov.br/web/relacoesinternacionais/contato

Pflanz, N., Classe, T., Araujo, R., & Vossen, G. (2016). Designing Serious Games for Citizen Engagement in Public Service Processes. *Workshop on Social and Human Aspects of Business Process Management*.

Portal 1746. (n.d.). *Ligue 1746*. Retrieved from http://www.1746.rio.gov.br

Portal e-Cidadania. (n.d.). *ecidadania*. Retrieved from https://www12.senado.leg.br/ecidadania

Portal e-Democracia. (n.d.). *Camera dos Deputados*. Retrieved from http://edemocracia.camara.gov.br

Portal of Transparency. (n.d.). *Portal da Transparencia*. Retrieved from http://www.portaltransparencia.gov.br

Reuver, M., Stein, S., Hampe, F., & Bouwman, H. (2010). Towards a service platform and business model for mobile participation. *International Conference on Mobile Business*, 305-311. 10.1109/ICMB-GMR.2010.57

Rio, I. T. S. (n.d.). *Plataforma Brasil*. Retrieved from http://plataformabrasil.org.br/?/

Roman, A., & Miller, H. (2013). New Questions for E-Government: Efficiency but not (yet?) Democracy. *International Journal of Electronic Government Research*, *9*(1), 65–81. doi:10.4018/jegr.2013010104

Sajjad, F., Lee, H., Kamal, M., & Irani, Z. (2011). Workflow technology as an e-participation tool to support policy-making processes. *Journal of Enterprise Information Management*, *2*(24), 197–212. doi:10.1108/17410391111106301

Sell, M. (2016). *Regra clara: Uma proposta de design de artefato para compreensão de regras de negócios em processos de prestação de serviços públicos* [Regra Clara: An artifact design proposal for understanding business rules in public services] (Dissertation). Federal University of the State of Rio de Janeiro.

Shirky, C. (2008). *Here comes everybody: The power of organizing without organization*. The Penguin Press.

Sunstein, C. (2006). *Infotopia: How Many Minds Produce Knowledge*. New York: Oxford University Press.

Tavares, A., Soares, D., & Estevez, E. (2016). Electronic Governance for Context-Specific Public Service Delivery: A Survey of the Literature. *International Conference on Theory and Practice of Electronic Governance*, 135-138. 10.1145/2910019.2910110

Tregear, R., & Jenkins, T. (2007). Government Process Management: a review of key differences between the public and private sectors and their influence on the achievement of public sector process management. *BPTrends*. Retrieved from www.bptrends.com

VoteWatch. (2018). *Vote Watch Europe*. Retrieved from http://www.votewatch.eu

Winters, M., Karim, A., & Martawardaya, B. (2014). Public Service Provision under Conditions of Insufficient Citizen Demand: Insights from the Urban Sanitation Sector in Indonesia. *World Development*, *60*, 31–42. doi:10.1016/j.worlddev.2014.03.017

## ADDITIONAL READING

Anderson, D., Wu, R., Cho, J.-S., & Schroeder, K. (2015). *E-Government Strategy, ICT and Innovation for Citizen Engagement*. Springer New York. doi:10.1007/978-1-4939-3350-1

Araujo, R., Cappelli, C., Diirr, B., Engiel, P., & Tavares, R. (2011). Democracia Eletrônica (Electronic Democracy). In *Sistemas Colaborativos* (pp. 110–121). Rio de Janeiro: Elsevier.

Brooks, L., Henriksen, H., Janssen, M., Papazafeiropoulou, A., & Trutnev, D. (2014). Public sector information systems (PSIS): How ICT can bring innovation into the policymaking process. *European Conference on Information Systems*, Panel, Tel Aviv.

Kreiss, D. (2015). *The Problem of Citizens: E-Democracy for Actually Existing Democracy*. Social Media + Society (pp. 1–11). July-December.

Kumar, V. (2017). *E-Democracy for Smart Cities*. Springer Nature Singapore. doi:10.1007/978-981-10-4035-1

Manoharan, A., & Holzer, M. (2012). *E-Governance and Civic Engagement: Factors and Determinants of E-Democracy*. USA: IGI Global. doi:10.4018/978-1-61350-083-5

Meier, A. (2012). *eDemocracy & eGovernment: Stages of a Democratic Knowledge Society*. Springer-Verlag Berlin Heidelberg.

Qvortrup, M. (2007). *The Politics of Participation: From Athens to E-Democracy*. Manchester: Manchester University Press. doi:10.7228/manchester/9780719076589.001.0001

## KEY TERMS AND DEFINITIONS

**Collaboration:** The situation of two or more people working together to produce something or achieve the same thing. Its support is designed concerning three main aspects: communication (exchange of information from one person to another that result in understanding), coordination (ability to make different parts work together) and awareness (knowledge that something exists).

**Conversations:** Narratives made by those who are involved in discussions about public services, comprising information about participants' experiences, opinions, additional information, problems, and suggestions.

**E-Democracy/E-Government Initiatives:** Initiatives that aims to increase the scale of participation and relationship between government and citizens through the use of ICTs.

**Memory:** The information generated from conversations about public services that must be organized, stored, retrieved and shared by participants, so the accumulated knowledge of past situations can assist the general understanding of the group and build a group memory from past experiences.

**Public Service Process:** The services provided by the Government, comprising information about them, the way citizens can require this service and detailed procedures of how they are executed.

**Social Software:** Tools that enable users to interact and share data to each other based on the Internet, such as wikis, blogs, social bookmarking and so on.

**Transparency:** Provides accessibility, usability, informativeness, understandability, and auditability of organizational information, thus allowing citizens to understand how a public service can or must be provided by the public institution, thereby reducing complaints and enhancing trust and confidence.

Chapter 8

# Smart Government and the Maturity Levels of Sociopolitical Digital Interactions:
## Analysing Temporal Changes in Brazilian E-Government Portals

**Herman Resende Santos**
*Independent Researcher, Brazil*

**Dany Flávio Tonelli**
*Universidade Federal de Lavras, Brazil*

## ABSTRACT

*The emerging concept of smart government has a deep connection with the capacity to equalize high levels of performance and responsiveness in order to promote and enable development and prosperity. The expansion of public space towards the digital environment and increasing contextual complexity push governments to new perspectives concerning political and administrative dimensions. The capacity to interact virtually with citizens leads to the concept of sociopolitical digital interactions and the exploration of a conceptual framework called sociopolitical digital interactions' maturity (SDIM) directed the conducting of this study through a qualitative methodological approach. A comparative content analysis of the 27 Brazilian states' government websites was structured on 2013 and 2018 verifications. In this lapse time, the poor adoption of crowdsourcing digital tools denoted low governmental capacity to explore collective intelligence as well as an unwillingness concerning the adoption of citizen-centric models and a lack of openness to co-creative interaction processes.*
DOI: 10.4018/978-1-5225-6204-7.ch008

# INTRODUCTION

In order to deal with the increasing complexity of today's context, some governments are developing new mindsets and to some extent reshaping administrative and political dimensions.

Far beyond the digitalisation of public administration processes and the adoption of innovative practices for the conducting of public policies, the capacity to orchestrate complex, open and self-organising systems is consolidated as a core competency required to promote and enable development and prosperity.

The increasing adoption of information and communication technologies (ICTs), as well as of SMACT (Social Media, Mobile, Analytics, Cloud and the Internet of Things) technologies, pushes governments to learn how to extract advantage from these tools in order to generate actionable intelligence and increase their performance and response levels.

The growing movement by governments towards a citizen-centred model (Citizen-Centric-Government), which refers to the conducting of priorities and services based on the needs of society, is inducing governments to rethink and reshape their political interactions with citizens and could provide a broad range of benefits (Arunachalam & Sarkar, 2013; Clark & Guzman, 2016), leading to the concept of sociopolitical interactions.

Following this perspective, collaboration and co-creation have the potential to improve democracy and public management processes; to empower people in the defense of public interests; and to foster democratic engagement through the promotion of civic culture, education, social participation and politicisation of society.

According to Janowski, Pardo and Davies (2012, p. S1), governments can no longer afford to address increasingly complex and interdependent public goals alone or step back and rely on the markets. Instead, they have to work through networks of state and non-state actors to organize existing resources, knowledge and capabilities in the pursuit of public goals. This reiterates Bertot, Jaeger, Munson and Glaisyer (2010, p. 5), who observed the need to rethink traditional boundaries between individuals, the public, communities, and levels of government concerning how the public and government interact, develop solutions, and deliver services.

Governmental ability to interact with society and other non-state actors consists of a very important skill, which guides the processes of identification of problems/gaps, of perception of the desired/needed outcomes/results and, most important, of collaborative and co-creative processes that lead to the concepts of social capital and collective intelligence. Although an increasing number of governmental agencies are implementing practices of citizen sourcing (Bronk & Smith, 2010) and other co-creative practices, there has been a gap between the reality and the conceptions of the potential of democratic participation.

According to Rød and Weidmann (2015), the advance of Internet technologies does not necessarily mean that decision-making processes will be more democratic. Currently, scholars are less optimistic about the role of Internet technologies in the consolidation of deliberative regimes. It is uncertain that the extension of the Internet will contribute to the performance of new repertoires of action and increase the quality of the public service delivery (Alonso & Barbeito, 2016). However, while the democratic process remains a challenge, Porwol, Ojo and Breslin (2016) comprehend that there are other possibilities. These different options refer to the understanding of electronic participation as a sociotechnical system and as a project (Porwol, Ojo & Breslin, 2016). This fact encourages research on new perspectives concerning the adoption of administrative and political tools and processes as 'Sociopolitical Digital Interactions'.

The goal of this research is to address the gap identified by Alonso and Barbeito (2016), which refers to the role of mechanisms of e-participation to improve the quality of the democratic process, with regard to the importance of an analysis of government actions in the digital environment. This reiterates the gap pointed out by Cegarra-Navarro et al. (2012) concerning the ICTs' impact on government-citizen relations.

The immediate objective of this work was to explore a useful conceptual framework (SDIM), both for theoretical reflections on the theme and for the analysis and design of electronic tools for government websites. Using the SDIM, the contents of Brazil's 27 state government websites were analysed on two different occasions.

The central questions in this study were as follows: (1) What is the current developmental stage of digital sociopolitical interactions in Brazilian states' governmental websites? (2) How have Brazilian states' governmental websites evolved in the time between 2013 and 2018?

The relevance of this research resides in the following: a comparative analysis using the SDIM framework permits the identification of governmental progress concerning the digital instrumentalisation of democratic processes of e-participation, the evaluation of participative architecture and the possibility of promoting discussions and exchanges between researchers and government agents.

This article is structured as follows: after reviewing the literature, explaining the theoretical setting and presenting the conceptual scheme of SDIM, the methodological approach is defined. The 27 Brazilian states' government websites previously analysed in 2013 are re-analysed in 2018 and the results are compared; final thoughts are then offered on the points discussed.

## LITERATURE REVIEW

The constant debate between organisational and democratic theory, between New Public Management and New Public Service (Denhart & Denhart, 2015) between, on the one side, strategy, performance, efficiency, effectiveness and efficacy, and on the other side, citizen-centricity, social responsiveness, civic engagement, political participation and social capital pervades studies of public administration. The entire process of formulation and delivery of responsive public values by governments, as well as their efficiency and performance in implementing public policies, are at the centre of several contradictory and conciliatory positions and lead to reflections about the very nature of the state.

As an organisation, governments may be understood as a system of activities or forces consciously coordinated (Barnard, 1948). Early studies of intergovernmental relations (Rhodes, 1986), governmental actors and patterns of exchange among interest groups (John, 2001) led to the idea that both the agenda and the outcome policies are outlined by networks (policy networks). According to Castells et al. (2000), networks consist of nodes connecting systems, and the distinct and overlapping mechanics of the network's dynamics (centralised, decentralised and distributed) (Baran, 1964) regulate the interrelationships between context, actors, processes and results – the CAPR model (Santos, 2014), defining possible approaches to public administration issues.

Governmental organisations are structured on fundamental dimensions. Thompson (2017) points out that in every organisation it is possible to identify three basic organisational levels, namely, the technical, the managerial and the institutional. In order to provide an integrated perspective on the concept of Smart Government, a brief description has been provided below concerning the two basic main dimensions of any government, namely, the political dimension and the administrative dimension. The administrative dimension, in turn, is classified under four distinct structuring models: the institutional, organisational, processual and technological.

## Political Dimension

The political dimension concerns the interactive ability to negotiate interests, visions and priorities, to define control and influence the course of actions. These related terms lead to the idea of governance, as well as to the concepts of responsiveness to social and market interests, civic engagement, political participation and democracy. The relationships between society, market and the state are one of the core objects of study of public administration. It contemplates a vast field of research and touches upon themes such as power relations, government regimes, governance networks and public management models. The growing trend towards a citizen-centred model (Citizen-Centric-Government) is leading governments to rethink and reshape their political interactions with citizens (Arunachalam & Sarkar, 2013) and other actors, steering the design of new priorities and services based on transparency, accountability, responsiveness, etc.

## Administrative Dimension

The administrative dimension concerns the formulation of development strategies, the implementation of public policies and the prioritisation of actions that focus on the coordination of efforts in order to generate and make public values available. That dimension leads to the ideas of strategy, performance, efficiency, effectiveness, efficacy and the adequacy of governmental actions with the principles of legality, impartiality, morality and publicity. In this dimension, state and government planning are formulated and executed. Managerial goals and performance metrics are defined, visions of the future are designed and policies are operationalised. Everyday operations are conducted in parallel with the construction of long-term projects.

### Institutional Model

The relations between a government, other governments and non-state actors are regulated by specific laws, rules, guidelines and legal structures. The regulation of constitutional power among the executive, legislative and judiciary branches, as well as of bureaucratic systems define the governance networks, power hierarchy and command chain and all its nuances and specificities. At this level, the rules of the game among actors and powers are defined and balanced. A rational design of this model streamlines the resolution of power contests and eliminates legal deadlocks.

### Organisational Model

Government organisations are structured around defined organograms and organisational architectures. In the array of sub-systems/sub-organisations, the organisational design consists of a fundamental structuring mechanism that has a direct influence on administrative processes. The definition of key activities, functions and competencies has a direct impact on organisational design and the speed of the decision-making process.

### Processual Model

The modeling of courses of action is closely related to organisational performance levels. The design of the processes of management of relationships, assets, resources, information, projects and programmes defines how well and how fast everything works inside a government, a city, a province or a country. The executive capacity to implement public policies reflects the levels of efficiency, effectiveness and efficacy concerning the delivery of public values and the transformation of social life.

## Technological Model

SMACT technologies and related terms, such as interoperability frameworks, legacy systems, software and hardware infrastructure, data collection, big data, data storage, data retrieval, security and privacy, are increasingly defining important new technological and administrative functionalities of public administration.

According to Gil-Garcia (2012, p. 64-65) *Sensors, virtualizations, geographic information technologies, social media applications, and other elements could function like a brain to manage the resources and capabilities of government, but also the participation of social actors, the physical infrastructure, and the machines and equipment using that infrastructure. This could potentially lead to a new form of electronic governance – a Smart State.*

Nowadays, governments tend to understand that increasing computational power and Big Data Analytics capacity are essential to deal with the huge amount of digital data generated by society on a daily basis. In this emerging informational space, smart machines and artificial intelligence (AI) are enabling significant changes in processual models of extraction of actionable intelligence from raw data, crowd sourcing and crowd sensing methods (Bellavista, Cardone, Corradi, Foschini & Ianniello, 2015), steering the adoption of evidence-based decision-making processes.

These practices include the use of software for facial analysis in crime detection, mobility monitoring systems to optimise traffic flows, electric energy demand prediction and citizen categorisation/ranking mechanisms based on online individual behaviour, such as the Chinese Social Credit System (SCS). Other examples are the UK government's Behavioural Insights Team; the Regulations.gov platform in the USA; Iceland's participative drafting of a new constitution in 2010; participatory budgeting in Cologne, Germany; the Open 311 platform in New York, San Francisco and Chicago; the SeeClickFix platform; the Office of New Urban Mechanics in Boston and Philadelphia; the Challenge.gov platform; and the Datapaloozas.

In this context, observing the 'no turning back' trend in which governments increasingly become a kind of 'Big Brother' controller, with a huge processing capacity, it is probably naive to believe that if society does not agree or desire it, governments will stop the process of becoming 'comprehensive brains' capable of processing and analysing any single datum of individual behaviour and using this information to rule society.

In parallel with several ethical questions concerning the use Social Big Data by private and public organisations, powerful algorithms are increasingly capable of detecting human and market behavioural trends and patterns, leading to the rise of 'algorithmic public policies' instrumentalised through machine learning mechanisms.

While, on the one hand, this may result in useful tools for the design of public policies (government actions), on the other hand, it might be used to enable 'persuasive computing', 'big nudge' technologies and 'choice architecture mechanisms' capable of steering social behaviour and even undermining cultural systems, compromising the democratic process itself.

## E-Government

The advance of ICTs led to the expansion of public space towards the digital environment and in this context the concept of e-government arose and was followed by several upgraded versions.

According to Janssen and Estevez (2013, p. S3), the three distinct *waves of e-Government research* are based on the dislocation from a techno-centric to a citizen-centric approach and consist of electronic government (e-Government), transformational government (t-Government) and lean government (l-Government).

E-government *involves a complex web of relationships between technological, organizational, institutional, and contextual variables* (Luna-Reyes, Gil-Garcia & Romero, 2012, p. 324) and the four areas of application for electronic government are i) e-services, ii) e-management, iii) e-democracy and iv) e-public policy.

T-Government consists in an *ICT-enabled and organization-led transformation of government operations, internal and external processes and structures to enable the realization of citizen-centric services that are cost effective and efficient* (Weerakkody, Janssen & Dwivedi, 2011, p. 327).

L-Government consists of a *smaller government utilizing ICT to connect, engage and involve the public in solving societal problems, resulting in changes in traditional roles* (Janssen & Estevez, 2013, p. S4).

These concepts, in addition to Government 2.0 (Eggers, 2007), Open government (Downey, 2012), Government as a platform (O'Reilly, 2009), Wiki government (Noveck, 2009), Networked government (Goldsmith & Eggers, 2005), Government 3.0, etc., may be understood as complimentary features of the general idea of Smart Government, which not only comprises a new generation of electronic and citizen-centric governments but also synthesises the convergence of several qualities that governments should incorporate in order to promote and enable development and prosperity.

## Smart Government

In the context of human-machine networks, cognitive computing is increasingly used in order to generate actionable intelligence through the processing and mining of structured and un-structured data. Collective intelligence may also be extracted through crowdsourcing and crowdsensing methods. The use of artificial intelligence in data analysis provides relevant insights oriented to the increasing automation of processes and to informational support for evidence-based decisions. The emergence of the concept of Smart Government may be understood as a natural unfolding of the concept of Smart Cities and, following this rationale, Smart Governments are essential to the administration of Smart Cities.

Gil-Garcia et al. (2014, p. I1) point out that *Smart government is used to characterize activities that creatively invest in emergent technologies coupled with innovative strategies to achieve more agile and resilient government structures and governance infrastructures.* Jiménez et al. (2014, p.8) conceive Smart Government as *the highest modernization phase of the public organizations, evolved from Open Government.* According to Gil-Garcia et al. (2016, p. 525), fourteen components account for smartness in governments, namely: *integration, innovation, evidence-based, citizen-centricity, sustainability, creativity, effectiveness, efficiency, equality, entrepreneurialism, citizen engagement, openness, resiliency, and technology savviness.*

The concept of Smart Government has a deep connection with the capacity to generate and employ actionable intelligence, and to equalise high levels of performance and responsiveness in order to promote and enable development and prosperity.

The most fundamental characteristics of a Smart Government comprise the state's capacities

1. To generate actionable intelligence and be able to use it to promote and enable development and prosperity efficiently;
2. To configure and optimise political and administrative designs (that include institutional, organisational, processual and technological models) with the prerogatives of being a prosperity-oriented, performance- and responsiveness-focused, evidence-based and data analysis–led organisation; and
3. To orchestrate complex, open and self-organising systems and their entangled dimensions of relationships among the context, itself and non-state actors, aligning top-down directives of strategic planning (administration performance) and bottom-up, non-state inputs (political responsiveness) around accountable political and administrative architectures.

## THEORETICAL SETTING

### Actor-Network Theory and Co-Creation: The Foundations for the SDIM Conceptual Framework

Several studies have been shaped concerning co-creation processes and the consequent narrowing of relations between state and society. Examples of these kind of studies are found in the literature of participative policies concerning public transport (Nunes & Cunha, 2014), science and technology (Rogers-Hayden & Pidgeon, 2008), and urban planning (Izvercianu, Seran, & Branea, 2014). The maturity level of sociopolitical interaction, called co-creation, reiterates this kind of approach and is defined by Szkuta et al. (2014) as the collaborative involvement of citizens on the co-production of public services and policies. In recent years, a significant increase of studies in this field coincided with the advancement of the Web 2.0 trend (Szkuta et al., 2014).

One important difference between this article's perspective and the approach of other papers relates to the co-creation conception, not only as a result of interaction between people, but as a result of the articulation of various constituent elements of collectivities, that reiterates Latour (2005), who breaks with the modern view based on the separation between nature and society. According to the previous assumption there is no ontological difference between materiality and humanity, which inculcates the notion that reality is formed and the performed by heterogeneous and symmetric elements, human and non-human, called actor-network (Latour, 2005; B. Latour & Woolgar, 1986; Tonelli, Brito, & Zambalde, 2011). In this sense, the co-creative activity in the relationship between state and society presupposes the construction of the actor-network, such as the Web 2.0 plataform of sociopolitical interactions.

Through the Actor-Network Theory (ANT) lens, the analysis of action leads to the perception that it (the action) is not restricted by specific actors. The action is always distributed, shared, and performative. Actors are not isolated but constitute simultaneous associations of people and physical artifacts, which assume an important role in the narratives. Usually, the actor and the action clearly assume human characteristics of intentional conduct. On the other hand, the actant could better describe the construction of macro-actors such as corporations, societies, and institutions (Czarniawska, 2009).

Based on the ANT, the co-creation approach relies on a firm commitment to abstain from a unilateral domain of action, be it intended by the state or the society. In the real world, there is no possibility that this large dominance occurs by any predefined actor. As stated by Latour (2001), no one was ever able to dominate the results of an action. It is common for the scientist or architect to be surprised by the results of his action (Latour, 2001; Tonelli, Brito, & Zambalde, 2011). Through co-creation, predictability is given up to allow innovation, arising from the interaction between heterogeneous elements derived from the state, the society, and the several other spheres of reality, which creates associations and institutions that are not defined only by a single sphere but by hybrid, heterogeneous and multifaceted corporations.

## Proposal of the SDIM Conceptual Framework: Adaptation and Reframing

In order to conduct this study, the concept of sociopolitical digital interactions was elaborated (Santos, Tonelli and Bermejo, 2014), which here is understood as the bottom-up and top-down dynamics of a government-citizen democratic relationship instrumentalized by the information and communication technologies (ICTs).

Sociopolitical Digital Interactions' Maturity (SDIM) categorization represents a possible way to analyze, design and improve formal and informal horizontal arrangements of democratic participation mediated by electronic tools, which can optimize informative, communicative and collaborative interaction processes between government and society. Understanding digital multi-stakeholders engagement platforms remits to the ideas of *network-state*, *network society* and *governance-networks* built upon the relationship between human and non-human, between state and non-state actors.

The concept of maturity in reference to the sociopolitical digital interactions refers to the complexity level of the digital government-society relations. The main ideas that structure the understanding of sociopolitical digital interactions' complexity delineate a route for action based on:

1.  The provision, dissemination and access to information as an initial condition for interactions;
2.  The establishment of connection between human and non-human (state and non-state) actors through communicative exchanges and dialogue; and
3.  The collaborative interactions that may culminate in co-creation processes.

The conceptual framework of SDIM led to understanding the maturity levels of sociopolitical interaction related to its inherent information-flow dynamics and associated with its corresponding digital interactive tools.

## Maturity Levels

The maturity levels of sociopolitical digital interactions were conceived from the combination of Vedel's democratic process sequences classification (information, discussion, and decision); the three strategic thrusts that structure the vision of a *Collaborative Government* according to the Singaporean Government's eGov2015 Masterplan of the Singapore Government (2013) (which are Co-creating for Greater Value; Connecting for Active Participation; and Catalysing Whole-of-Government Transformation); and government-citizen relations in policy-making discussed by the Organisation for Economic Co-operation and Development (OECD, 2001) (information, consultation, and active participation). By combining these categorizations, it was established that the production, dissemination and access to information corresponds to the basic level of interaction; discussion was related with communication processes and determined the connection level; and decision was associated with consultation, collaboration, and active participation, and thus the co-creation level was established.

## Information Flow Dynamics

The idea of the information flow dynamics was developed from the categorization of government-citizen relations in policy-making discussed by the Organisation for Economic Co-operation and Development (OECD, 2001), which stated that information consists of a one-way relation, consultation and active participation (a relation based on partnership) consists of a two-way relation. The classification of the government-citizen interaction dynamics observed in the conceptual scheme of SDIM was based on the sense of informational flows. These were classified into the following: (1) unilateral (government information to citizen); (2) bilateral (communication between government and citizens, and between one individual to many); and (3) multilateral (collaboration between government and citizens, between one individual to many, and many individuals to one), (see Figure 1).

*Figure 1. Information flow dynamics*

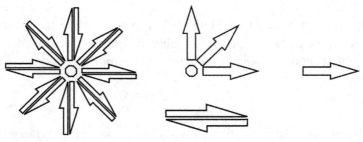

A) multilateral, B) bilateral, and C) unilateral

## Digital Interactive Tools

In order to explore possible forms of promoting an alignment between democratic processes and the web 2.0 platforms of e-participation, this approach of sociopolitical interactions' electronic modalities remits to the idea of *Government Information Networks* (Janowski, Pardo, & Davies, 2012) focusing on the information flow dynamics intrinsic to digital tools, which instrumentalize the relations between state and non-state actors.

The establishment of associations between maturity levels and digital interactive tools was inspired by the ideas about the correlations between Web 2.0 applications in government websites and information work provided by Chua et al. (2012). The authors identified four levels of information work (acquisition, dissemination, organization, and sharing) that were reshaped in the conception of sociopolitical digital interactions.

From this categorization, associations between sociopolitical interaction and digital tools were established, taking into account the information flow dynamics that characterize each one of the digital interactive tools. In this way, the tree correspondent maturity levels and information flow dynamics were associated with each one of the following tools:

- **Co-Creation (Level 3):** E-vote, e-petitions, opinion polls, challenges, wikis, discussion forums, applications, open channel for suggestions, open data.
- **Connection (Level 2):** Social networks, professional networks, chat, contact forms/email, multimedia sharing services, comment boxes.
- **Information (Level 1):** Blogs, microblogs, RSS feed, newsletter, downloading information availability, search engine.

These schemes structured relevant aspects of virtual interfaces, guidelines for e-government, and sociopolitical interactions, from which a conceptual scheme of SDIM was formulated that combined maturity levels, information flow dynamics, and digital tools of government-citizen interaction (See Table 1).

# RESEARCH METHODOLOGY

To conduct this study, a qualitative methodological approach was adopted. The content analysis of the 27 Brazilian states' government websites was structured on the conceptual scheme of SDIM, which allowed the verification and classification of digital interactive tools used in e-government portals. The research was conducted in the steps described below.

*Table 1. Conceptual framework of Sociopolitical Digital Interactions' Maturity (SDIM)*

| Maturity Levels | Description | Information Flow Dynamics | Digital Interactive Tools |
|---|---|---|---|
| **CO-CREATION**<br>Level 3 | Consultation; Collaboration; Participative Construction; Collective Intelligence. | Multilateral Flow | e-vote; e-petitions; opinion polls; challenges; wikis; discussion forums; applications; open channel for suggestions; open data |
| **CONNECTION**<br>Level 2 | Communicative Exchanges Dialogue; Discussion and Sharing. | Bilateral Flow | social networks; professional networks; chat; contact forms / e-mail; multimedia sharing services; comment box |
| **INFORMATION**<br>Level 1 | Production; Dissemination and Access | Unilateral Flow | blogs; microblogs; RSS feed; newsletter; downloading information availability; search engine |

## Definition of the Research Universe

The research universe was defined as the 27 states of Brazil. The study proceeded to diagnose the current stage of development of sociopolitical interactions mediated by digital tools observed in the institutional websites of each of the federation's member states and to compare, through a lapse time content analysis, how e-gov portals evolved between 2013 and 2018.

## Verification of Sociopolitical Interaction Digital Tools on Government Websites

In part, the methodological procedures used by Chua et al. (2012) were replicated in terms of the approach to verifying digital tools on government websites. The first content analysis of the 27 Brazilian states' government websites was performed and recorded from December 18–21, 2013. The second content analysis of the same websites was performed and recorded from January 8–11, 2018. The presence or absence of 21 electronic tools of sociopolitical interactions (blogs, microblogs, RSS feed, newsletter, downloading information availability, search engine, social networks, professional networks, chat, contact forms / e-mail, multimedia sharing services, comment box, e-vote, e-petitions, opinion polls, challenges, wikis, discussion forums, applications, open channel for suggestions, open data) was checked and the identified tools were classified according to a verification table (see Table 2) adapted from Mossberger et al. (2013). From the fulfillment of one table for each governmental website and according to the scoring criteria, the SDIM Ranking was established.

*Table 2. Roadmap for digital interactive tools verification*

| CO-CREATION TOOLS (Level 3) Y/N | CONNECTION TOOLS (Level 2) Y/N | INFORMATION TOOLS (Level 1) Y/N |
| --- | --- | --- |
| e-vote | social networks | blogs |
| e-petitions | professional networks | microblogs |
| opinion polls | chat | RSS feed |
| challenges | contact forms / e-mail | newsletter |
| wikis | multimedia sharing services | downloading information availability |
| discussion forums | comment box | search engine |
| applications | | |
| open channel for suggestions | | |
| open data | | |

Source: Adapted from Mossberger et al. (2013)

## Scoring Criteria

The categories shown in Table 2 were assigned numeric values depending on the sociopolitical interaction dynamics' maturity (complexity) levels. Thus, every co-creation digital tool pertaining to participatory construction (Level 3) is assigned the value of a point in the hundreds; every connection digital instrument relating to communicative exchanges (Level 2) is assigned the value of a point in the tens; and every information electronic tool regarding the information production and distribution activities (Level 1) is assigned the value of a point in the units place;

Although the availability of data can be classified as a one-way information flow and therefore as a information tool (level 1), the fact that the data meets in an open format affords it a characteristic of co-creation (level 3). Also, it consists of an invitation to collaborative forms of sociopolitical interaction that may culminate in applications, challenges, and wiki platforms of shared work between government and citizens. Therefore, the availability of Open Data has been classified as a co-creative digital tool (level 3).

## An Example of the Scoring Procedure: Rio Grande do Sul Government Website

Based on the scoring criteria directives, each one of the Brazilian states' government websites were analyzed. The verification procedure consisted of noting the presence or absence of the digital interactive tools and web 2.0 applications listed in Table 3. Following the checklist, the verification table was filled. For each observed listed item a value of 1 point was attributed, and for each absent (non-observed) item the value of 0 was assigned in the corresponding line of the table.

According to the scoring criteria, different values were related to each maturity level of sociopolitical digital interactions. In this way, each co-creation tool (Level 3) was attributed the value of 100 points; each connection tool (Level 2) was attributed the value of ten points; and each information tool (Level 1) was attributed the value one point. Then the sum of the corresponding layer values established the position rankings.

According to the 2013 analysis of Rio Grande do Sul's state government website (http://estado.rs.gov.br/), four co-creation tools (Level 3) were identified (e-vote, opinion polls, wikis and open data), equaling 400 points. Four connection tools (Level 2) were identified (social networks, contact forms/email, multimedia sharing services and comment boxes) totaling 40 points. Four information tools (Level 1) were observed (microblog, RSS feed, downloading information availability and search engine) totaling four points.

*Table 3. Verification table (checklist): Rio Grande do Sul e-gov website – 2013*

| Digital Interactive Tools and Web 2.0 Applications | Yes/No 1/0 |
|---|---|
| **CO-CREATION TOOLS (Level 3)** | **1 = 100** |
| e-vote | 1 |
| e-petitions | 0 |
| opinion polls | 1 |
| challenges | 0 |
| wikis | 1 |
| discussion forums | 0 |
| applications | 0 |
| open channel for suggestions | 0 |
| open data | 1 |
| Sub-total | 4.0.0 |
| **CONNECTION TOOLS (Level 2)** | **1 = 10** |
| social networks | 1 |
| professional networks | 0 |
| chat | 0 |
| contact forms / e-mail | 1 |
| multimedia sharing services | 1 |
| comment box | 1 |
| Sub-total | 0.4.0 |
| **INFORMATION TOOLS (Level 1)** | **1 = 1** |
| blogs | 0 |
| microblogs | 1 |
| RSS feed | 1 |
| newsletter | 0 |
| downloading information availability | 1 |
| search engine | 1 |
| Sub-total | 0.0.4 |
| **TOTAL** | **4.4.4** |

The total value of the tree strands [Co-creation (400) + Connection (40) + Information (4)] of the Rio Grande do Sul state government website equaled 4.4.4 points. The SDIM ranking was established comparing this value with the other government websites.

## FINDINGS

This study represents a specific point in the analysis of digital interactive tools between society and state, classifying the nature of government-citizen relations. The modes of democratic participation, mediated by electronic tools, configure interactive processes of communication and collaboration between government and society, and insert new codes in the 'Network State' software, which can result in governmental innovations (Bloch & Bugge, 2013).

The Brazilian federation's states' government websites were ranked according to the scoring criteria established in the methodological procedures section. A lapsed time analysis, comparing 2013 and 2018 e-Gov portals, was conducted in order to evaluate how SDIM evolved over time.

Comparing the 2013 and 2018 analyses, it was observed that several government websites' positions changed in the general ranking, as was an overall increase in the number of digital tools available in e-gov portals. As the government website of the state of Sergipe was not available on the occasion of the 2018 analysis, its ranking valuation was left blank.

In Table 5, sociopolitical interaction electronic tools on government websites are organised and arranged by category.

In both 2013 and 2018, the same most widely adopted mechanisms and digital tools were identified: 'search engines', 'downloading information availability', 'microblogging' (Twitter), 'multimedia sharing services' (YouTube), 'contact forms/ email' and 'social networking tools' (Facebook).

In both 2013 and 2018, the less commonly detected tools (and in some cases not detected at all) were 'e-voting', 'e-petitions', 'opinion polls', 'challenges', 'wikis', 'discussion forums', 'professional networks', 'chat' and 'comment boxes'. Here, the absence of permanent 'discussion forums' in electronic portals represents an unwillingness and/or the inability to manage differing opinions and opposition criticisms that may affect the political image of the government.

In 2018, two relevant changes concerning the adoption of digital tools were observed, consisting in the increased availability of 'open data' – from 1 to 10 tools (available through the Portals of Transparency) and of 'open channel for suggestions' – from 4 to 24 tools (available through Ombudsman Portals).

*Table 4. Comparative ranking of the 27 Brazilian federation's states' government websites (2013/2018)*

| Ranking 2013 | State | SDIM | Tool Quantities | Ranking 2018 | State | SDIM | Tool Quantities |
|---|---|---|---|---|---|---|---|
| 1º | Rio Grande do Sul | 4.4.4 | 12 | 1º | São Paulo | 3.4.6 | 13 |
| 2º | São Paulo | 1.4.5 | 10 | 2º | Paraná | 3.4.5 | 12 |
| 3º | Pernambuco | 1.3.5 | 9 | 3º | Minas Gerais | 3.3.5 | 11 |
| 4º | Maranhão | 1.3.4 | 8 | | Ceará | 3.3.5 | 11 |
| 5º | Espírito Santo | 1.3.3 | 7 | 4º | Rio Grande do Sul | 2.4.4 | 10 |
| | Roraima | 1.3.3 | 7 | 5º | Pernambuco | 2.3.5 | 10 |
| 6º | Rio de Janeiro | 1.2.4 | 7 | 6º | Santa Catarina | 2.3.4 | 9 |
| 7º | Ceará | 1.1.4 | 6 | | Mato Grosso | 2.3.4 | 9 |
| 8º | Minas Gerais | 0.3.5 | 8 | 7º | Rio de Janeiro | 2.3.3 | 8 |
| | Mato Grosso | 0.3.5 | 8 | | Espírito Santo | 2.3.3 | 8 |
| | Rio Grande do Norte | 0.3.5 | 8 | | Roraima | 2.3.3 | 8 |
| | Piauí | 0.3.5 | 8 | | Bahia | 2.3.3 | 8 |
| 9º | Paraná | 0.3.4 | 7 | 8º | Distrito Federal | 1.3.5 | 9 |
| | Distrito Federal | 0.3.4 | 7 | 9º | Mato Grosso do Sul | 1.3.4 | 8 |
| | Amazonas | 0.3.4 | 7 | | Amazonas | 1.3.4 | 8 |
| | Goiás | 0.3.4 | 7 | | Paraíba | 1.3.4 | 8 |
| 10º | Santa Catarina | 0.3.3 | 6 | | Pará | 1.3.4 | 8 |
| | Paraíba | 0.3.3 | 6 | | Maranhão | 1.3.4 | 8 |
| | Amapá | 0.3.3 | 6 | | Alagoas | 1.3.4 | 8 |
| 11º | Mato Grosso do Sul | 0.2.3 | 5 | 10º | Tocantins | 1.3.3 | 7 |
| | Acre | 0.2.3 | 5 | | Rondônia | 1.3.3 | 7 |
| 12º | Pará | 0.2.2 | 4 | | Rio Grande do Norte | 1.3.3 | 7 |
| 13º | Rondônia | 0.2.1 | 3 | | Piauí | 1.3.3 | 7 |
| 14º | Tocantins | 0.1.3 | 4 | 11º | Goiás | 1.3.2 | 6 |
| | Sergipe | 0.1.3 | 4 | | Amapá | 1.3.2 | 6 |
| 15º | Bahia | 0.1.1 | 2 | 12º | Acre | 0.2.3 | 5 |
| 16º | Alagoas | 0.0.2 | 2 | | Sergipe | - | - |

*Table 5. Digital interactive tools quantity by category*

| | CO-CREATION | | | | | | | | | | CONNECTION | | | | | | | INFORMATION | | | | | | | |
|---|---|---|---|---|---|---|---|---|---|---|---|---|---|---|---|---|---|---|---|---|---|---|---|---|---|
| Year | e-vote | e-petitions | opinion polls | challenges | wikis | discussion forums | applications | open channel for suggestions | open data | Tool Subtotal | social networks | professional networks | chat | contact forms / e-mail | multimedia sharing services | comment box | Tool Subtotal | blogs | microblogs | RSS feed | newsletter | downloading information availability | search engine | Tool Subtotal | Tool Quantities |
| 2013 | 1 | 4 | 1 | | | 1 | 4 | | | 11 | 20 | | 1 | 25 | 18 | 2 | 66 | 3 | 21 | 14 | 6 | 26 | 25 | 95 | 172 |
| 2018 | | 1 | 1 | | | 1 | 4 | 10 | 24 | 41 | 26 | 1 | 1 | 26 | 25 | 1 | 80 | 2 | 25 | 11 | 9 | 25 | 26 | 98 | 219 |

Source: Adapted from Chua and Goh et al. (2012)

Given the great complexity involved in the responsiveness process, the importance of 'open data' and 'open channels for suggestions' is a fundamental requirement for the promotion of practical, co-created results based on citizen sourcing and the provision of actionable data/information. In this sense, the increased adoption of these tools in 2018 shows that basic levels of participative architecture aligned with co-creative processes are being constructed.

In 2013, 172 government-citizen interaction tools were detected in the 27 e-gov portals: 95 'level 1' tools (55.2%), 66 'level 2' tools (38.4%) and 11 'level 3' tools (6.4%).

In 2018, 219 government-citizen interaction tools were detected in 26 e-gov portals: 98 'level 1' tools (44.7%), 80 'level 2' tools (36.5%) and 41 'level 3' tools (18.7%).

There is a growing global trend towards citizen-centred government practices, caused in part by rising citizen expectations concerning public governance processes and government-society partnerships (Chua et al., 2012). It was observed in this analysis that the presence of co-creation tools (level 3) is still low, at less than one-third.

Even if the amount of level 3 tools indicates a significant increase (from 6.4% in 2013 to 18.7% in 2018), the predominance of information tools (level 1) and connection tools (level 2) on governmental websites is to the detriment of co-creation tools (level 3).

## CONCLUSION

The digital interfaces of government and society interactions generate continuous causes and effects in policy network transformations. In the context of human-machine networks, cognitive computing and big data analysis are instrumentalising the design of 'algorithmic public policies' that are capable of steering social behaviour and even undermining cultural systems, compromising the democratic process itself.

The capacity to configure and optimise political and administrative designs with the prerogatives of being a prosperity-oriented, performance- and responsiveness-focused, evidence-based and data analysis–led organisation touches the very core of government modeling and demonstrates the levels of commitment to the strategic promotion of development.

In pursuing the generation of actionable intelligence, some governments have realised the huge potential of collective intelligence, which may be extracted through crowdsourcing and crowdsensing methods. Through the analysis of SDIM levels, it is possible to infer the depth of the governmental capacity to instrumentalise the co-creation process in alignment with the generation and capture of collective intelligence.

Reiterating the gaps presented by Alonso and Barbeito (2016) and Cegarra-Navarro et al. (2012), the study addressed issues related to understanding how sociopolitical digital interaction mechanisms compose governmental participative architecture and its relation with citizen-centric models.

Analysis of the current stage of development of digital sociopolitical interactions observed in the government websites of Brazilian states showed that most of the electronic tools provided by e-gov portals focus on level 1 (information) and have a tendency to shy away from the instrumentalisation of interactions on level 3 (co-creation).

In spite of the increased adoption of 'open channel for suggestions' by 2018, digital tools such as 'e-votes', 'e-petitions', 'opinion polls', 'challenges', 'wikis' and 'discussion forums' were, in practice, not adopted by Brazilian governments. The absence of these crowdsourcing tools, which could be used to improve the processes of the public policy cycle, reinforces the current tendency towards highly centralised political power and denotes weak governmental commitment to some of the fundamental characteristics of a Smart Government, including the quality of being a responsiveness-focused organisation and of being sensitive to the use of collective intelligence. This fact indicates low governmental openness to the adoption of citizen-centric and co-creative models.

With regard to the limitations of this study, it must be stressed that the universe analysed was a narrow one, restricted to the government websites of Brazilian states. It must also be mentioned that the 2013/2018 analysis of government websites was undertaken by the same person on both occasions, which prevented the cross-referencing of reviews and limited the revision of the results.

Future studies could expand the scope of analysis to other contexts and generate comparisons between sociopolitical, economic and technological indicators between countries, regions, continents, etc. This could help to verify possible hypotheses about the correlation between e-participation, the levels of SDIM and other categories of analysis. A specific methodological approach could also be adopted in order to validate SDIM as a theoretical model.

The practical contributions of this study concerning the exploration of the conceptual framework of SDIM are related to its capacity to support the processes of analysis, design and improvement of participative architectures in government websites.

The theoretical contributions of this paper are related to the reinforcement of the co-creative, collaborative and co-productive approaches, which relies, though not exclusively, on the expansion from a techno-centric to a citizen-centric model, as well as on the understanding that opening information, discussion and collaboration channels for co-creation relies on the capacity to orchestrate complex, open and self-organising systems.

Thus, co-creation is a continuous source of transformation of and improvement to the public sector and the ability to explore it is a core capacity of Smart Governments. The ability to extract and use collective intelligence is essential for the formulation of responsive and strategic processes of conception and delivery of public values, as well as being central to states' competency concerning the promotion and enabling of development and prosperity.

# REFERENCES

Alonso, A. I., & Barbeito, R. L. (2016). Does e-participation Influence and Improve Political Decision Making Processes? Evidence From a Local Government. *Lex Localis-Journal of Local Self-Government*, *14*(4), 873–891.

Arunachalam, R., & Sarkar, S. (2013). The New Eye of Government: Citizen Sentiment Analysis in Social Media. *Sixth International Joint Conference on Natural Language Processing*.

Baran, P. (1964). On Distributed Communications Networks. *Communications Systems. IEEE Transactions on, 12*(1), 1–9. doi:10.1109/TCOM.1964.1088883

Barnard, C. I. (1948). *The Functions of the Executive*. Boston: Harvard University Press.

Bellavista, P., Cardone, G., Corradi, A., Foschini, L., & Ianniello, R. (2015). Crowdsensing in Smart Cities: Technical Challenges, Open Issues. Handbook of Research on Social, Economic, and Environmental Sustainability in the Development of Smart Cities, 316.

Bertot, J., Jaeger, P., Munson, S., & Glaisyer, T. (2010). Engaging the public in open government: Social media technology and policy for government transparency. *Computer, 43*(11), 53–59. doi:10.1109/MC.2010.325

Bloch, C., & Bugge, M. M. (2013). Public Sector Innovation—From Theory to Measurement. *Structural Change and Economic Dynamics, 27*(0), 133–145. doi:10.1016/j.strueco.2013.06.008

Bronk, C., & Smith, T. (2010). Diplopedia Imagined: Building State's Diplomacy Wiki. In *Collaborative Technologies and Systems (CTS), 2010 International Symposium on*. IEEE.

Castells, M. (2000). *A sociedade em rede*. Paz e Terra São Paulo.

Cegarra-Navarro, J.-G., Pachón, J. R. C., & Cegarra, J. L. M. (2012). E-government and Citizen's Engagement with Local Affairs through E-websites: The Case of Spanish Municipalities. *International Journal of Information Management, 32*(5), 469–478. doi:10.1016/j.ijinfomgt.2012.02.008

Chua, A. Y. K., Goh, D. H., & Ang, R. P. (2012). Web 2.0 applications in government web sites: Prevalence, use and correlations with perceived web site quality. *Online Information Review, 36*(2), 175–195. doi:10.1108/14684521211229020

Clark, B. Y., & Guzman, T. S. (2016). Does Technologically Enabled Citizen Participation Lead to Budget Adjustments? An Investigation of Boston, MA, and San Francisco, CA. *American Review of Public Administration.*

Czarniawska, B. (2009). Emerging Institutions: Pyramids or Anthills? *Organization Studies, 30*(4), 423–441. doi:10.1177/0170840609102282

Denhardt, J. V., & Denhardt, R. B. (2015). The New Public Service Revisited. *Public Administration Review, 75*(5), 664–672. doi:10.1111/puar.12347

Downey, E. (2012). *Public Service, Governance and Web 2.0 Technologies: Future Trends in Social Media: Future Trends in Social Media.* Information Science Reference. doi:10.4018/978-1-4666-0071-3

Eggers, W. D. (2007). *Government 2.0: Using Technology to Improve Education, Cut Red Tape, Reduce Gridlock, and Enhance Democracy.* Rowman & Littlefield.

Gil-Garcia, J. R. (2012). Towards a smart state? Inter-agency collaboration, information integration, and beyond. *Information Polity, 17*(3-4), 269–280.

Gil-Garcia, J. R., Helbig, N., & Ojo, A. (2014). Being smart: Emerging technologies and innovation in the public sector. *Government Information Quarterly, 31*, I1–I8. doi:10.1016/j.giq.2014.09.001

Gil-Garcia, J. R., Zhang, J., & Puron-Cid, G. (2016). Conceptualizing smartness in government: An integrative and multi-dimensional view. *Government Information Quarterly, 33*(3), 524–534. doi:10.1016/j.giq.2016.03.002

Goldsmith, S., & Eggers, W. D. (2005). *Governing by Network: The New Shape of the Public Sector.* Brookings Institution Press.

Izvercianu, M., Şeran, S. A., & Branea, A.-M. (2014). Prosumer-oriented Value Co-creation Strategies for Tomorrow's Urban Management. *Procedia: Social and Behavioral Sciences, 124*(0), 149–156. doi:10.1016/j.sbspro.2014.02.471

Janowski, T., Pardo, T. A., & Davies, J. (2012). Government Information Networks-Mapping Electronic Governance cases through Public Administration concepts. *Government Information Quarterly*, *29*, S1–S10. doi:10.1016/j.giq.2011.11.003

Janowski, T., Pardo, T. A., & Davies, J. (2012). Government Information Networks-Mapping Electronic Governance cases through Public Administration concepts. *Government Information Quarterly, 29*, S1-S10.

Janssen, M., & Estevez, E. (2013). Lean government and platform-based governance—Doing more with less. *Government Information Quarterly*, *30*, S1–S8. doi:10.1016/j.giq.2012.11.003

Jiménez, C. E., Falcone, F., Solanas, A., Puyosa, H., Zoughbi, S., & González, F. (2014). Smart government: Opportunities and challenges in smart cities development. In Ć. Dolićanin, E. Kajan, D. Randjelović, & B. Stojanović (Eds.), *Handbook of research on democratic strategies and citizen-centered e government services* (pp. 1–19). Hershey, PA: IGI Global.

John, P. (2001). Policy Networks. *The Blackwell Companion to Political Sociology*, 139-148.

Latour, B. (2001). *A Esperança de Pandora: ensaios sobre a realidade dos estudos científicos*. Bauro: Edusc.

Latour, B. (2005). *Reassembling the Social: An Introduction to Actor-Network-Theory*. Oxford University Press.

Latour, B., & Woolgar, S. (1986). *Laboratory Life: The Construction of Scientific Facts*. Princeton University Press.

Luna-Reyes, L. F., Gil-Garcia, J. R., & Romero, G. (2012). Towards a multidimensional model for evaluating electronic government: Proposing a more comprehensive and integrative perspective. *Government Information Quarterly*, *29*(3), 324–334. doi:10.1016/j.giq.2012.03.001

Mossberger, K. (2013). Connecting Citizens and Local governments? Social Media and Interactivity in Major U.S. Cities. *Government Information Quarterly*.

Noveck, B. S. (2009). *Wiki Government: How Technology Can Make Government Better, Democracy Stronger, and Citizens More Powerful*. Brookings Institution Press.

Nunes, A. A., Galvão, T., & Cunha, J. F. e. (2014). Urban Public Transport Service Co-creation: Leveraging Passenger's Knowledge to Enhance Travel Experience. *Procedia: Social and Behavioral Sciences*, *111*(0), 577–585. doi:10.1016/j. sbspro.2014.01.091

O'Reilly, T. (2009). *What is Web 2.0: Design Patterns and Business Models for the Next Generation of Software. Communications & Strategies, (1), 17* .

OECD. (2001). *Engaging Citizens in Policy-making: Information*. Consultation and Public Participation.

Porwol, L., Ojo, A., & Breslin, J. G. (2016). An ontology for next generation e-Participation initiatives. *Government Information Quarterly*, *33*(3), 583–594. doi:10.1016/j.giq.2016.01.007

Rhodes, R. A. (1986). *European Policy-Making, Implementation and Subcentral Governments: A Survey*. European Institute of Public Administration Maastricht.

Rød, E. G., & Weidmann, N. B. (2015). Empowering activists or autocrats? The Internet in authoritarian regimes. *Journal of Peace Research*, *52*(3), 338–351. doi:10.1177/0022343314555782

Rogers-Hayden, T., & Pidgeon, N. (2008). Developments in nanotechnology public engagement in the UK: 'upstream' towards sustainability? *Journal of Cleaner Production*, *16*(8–9), 1010–1013. doi:10.1016/j.jclepro.2007.04.013

Santos, H. R. (2015). E-democracy and sociopolitical digital interactions: analysing co-creation in public sector innovation (Mestrado em Administração Pública). Universidade Federal de Lavras, Brazil.

Santos, H.R., Tonelli, D.F., & Bermejo, P.H. (2014) Sociopolitical digital interactions' maturity: analyzing the brazilian states. *Int. J. Electr. Gov. Res., 10*(4), 76–93. doi:10. 4018/ijegr.2014100104

Singapore. Government. (2013). *e-Gov2015 Masterplan (2011-2015). Vision & Strategic*. Available: http://www.egov.gov.sg/egov-masterplans-introduction;jsess ionid=542A47297AB7144B00189EF45E04FA67

Szkuta, K., Pizzicannella, R., & Osimo, D. (2014). Collaborative approaches to public sector innovation: A scoping study. *Telecommunications Policy*, *38*(5–6), 558–567. doi:10.1016/j.telpol.2014.04.002

Thompson, J. D. (2017). *Organizations in Action: Social Science Bases of Administrative Theory*. Taylor & Francis.

Tonelli, D. F., de Brito, M. J., & Zambalde, A. L. (2011). Empreendedorismo na Ótica da Teoria Ator-Rede: Explorando Alternativa às Perspectivas Subjetivista e Objetivista. *Cadernos EBAPE.BR*, 9.

Weerakkody, V., Janssen, M., & Dwivedi, Y. (2011). Transformational change and business process reengineering (BPR): Lessons from the British and Dutch public sector. *Government Information Quarterly*, *28*(3), 320–328. doi:10.1016/j.giq.2010.07.010

Chapter 9

# A Quantitative Evaluation of Costs, Opportunities, Benefits, and Risks Accompanying the Use of E-Government Services in Qatar

**Karim Al-Yafi**
*Qatar University, Qatar*

## ABSTRACT

*Providers of e-government systems and policymakers recognize that usability and adoption are key success indicators of e-government services. Borrowed from the field of e-commerce, several models were proposed and tested in the literature to evaluate users' adoption of e-government services in different contexts. This chapter examines users' satisfaction with e-government services in Qatar reflected by the cost, opportunity, benefit, and risk of using these e-services. After a quick review on research works done on evaluating e-government services in the Middle East region, quantitative data collected from three e-government services in Qatar is presented and analyzed using structural equation modelling techniques. Results revealed that while the hypotheses linking cost and opportunity to satisfaction were rejected, benefits and risk were significantly able to explain the level of users' satisfaction with e-government services.*

DOI: 10.4018/978-1-5225-6204-7.ch009

# INTRODUCTION

Undoubtedly, Web 2.0 technologies have significantly contributed to users' Internet adoption as a mean to fulfil different purposes. These purposes range from entertainment, learning, networking and professional productivity to formal administrative engagement in governmental transactions. This has been facilitated by the recent technological developments such as faster and more reliable network infrastructures and the spread of smartphones and other mobile devices. Another antecedent of users' huge buy in for technology lies in network externalities (Bouni et al., 2017; Tucker, 2017) and the global culture that does not consider the "e-" channel optional anymore but complementary and sometimes mandatory (Leidner and Kayworth 2006). Meanwhile, Qatar demonstrated an interesting and particular aspect of how technology has quickly spread and been accepted (Al-Yafi et al., 2016; Al-Yafi et al., 2014). These developments can be attributed to different factors: global, local and economic. The global propagation of technology and the quasi-instantaneous availability of new technologies in Qatar triggered a high interest in exploiting it optimally. The local context of Qatar is also characterized by a particular social and cultural composition. The population of Qatar includes a high rate of expatriates from different backgrounds where, at the time of this writing, it outnumbers local citizens. This phenomenon constantly motivates policy makers in Qatar to adopt modern technologies for better administration and optimal resource allocations. Finally, the economic factor certainly has a central effect on the proliferation of technology in Qatar. Despite the great efforts in diversifying the local economy, Qatar resources are mainly relying on oil and gas. This secured to Qatar over the past two decades a progressive place in the list of the world's wealthiest countries. Therefore, the cost of innovation remains marginal compared to the utility provided by implementing new solutions based on technologies. This chapter focuses on evaluating the adoption and adaptation of e-Government services offered in Qatar given its recent developments in the field of e-Government. We therefore examine the readiness and maturity of e-Government services from a users' satisfaction point of view. To measure satisfaction, we consider the factors presented in the COBRA model developed by Osman et al. (2014). The model hypothesizes the effects of cost, opportunity, risk and benefit of using e-Government services on the overall users' satisfaction. The aim would therefore be to understand whether these factors are as influential as they proved to be in other contexts and whether the COBRA model is an appropriate instrument to evaluate the modern e-Government services in Qatar. We refer in this study to the term "users" or "residents" rather than "citizens" in order to properly reflect on the actual usage of the services offered, or controlled, by the legal authorities and to do justice to the composition of the society in the country.

## TECHNOLOGY IN QATAR'S PUBLIC SECTOR

e-Government initiatives started in Qatar in the early 2000's as part of a larger effort to modernize the public sector such as health and education (Al-Shafi and Weerakkody 2007). Despite the fact that Qatar is categorized as a developing country, considerable efforts have been undertaken to advance the nation's economy and welfare. As opposed to many developing countries where the diffusion of technology is slow, Qatar pioneered a number of initiatives to exploit the latest technological developments (Al-Yafi et al. 2016; Faisal and Talib 2015). For instance, and according to Gremm and colleagues (2017), Doha has the highest potential of becoming an information city among the cities in the GCC. Financial investments and governance reforms were done to secure a sustainable base for implementing public e-Services such as e-Government, e-Health and e-Learning. Nevertheless, it has been estimated that these e-Services are yet under-utilized and the adoption rate can be boosted (Al-Yafi et al. 2014; Al-Shafi and Weerakkody 2008).

At the time of this writing, "Hukoomi", the Qatar's e-Government service portal aggregates over 1000 services carried out by over 230 entities. These services target a variety of user categories such as citizens and residents (G2C), businesses (G2B), government (G2G) and others. Given their highest rates of e-Government usage, we limit our study in this paper to examine only the services offered to users under the G2C model. To fulfil this objective, we have selected the three most commonly used e-Services: the traffic violations electronic service offered by the Ministry of Interior, the automated service for renewal of health cards offered by Hamad Medical Corporation (HMC), and the online payment of utility bills provided by the Qatar General Electricity and Water Corporation (Kahramaa).

Traffic violation e-Services aim to provide road users and the traffic police department with detailed and timely information about violations breaches of road rules. To improve the effectiveness of these services, main roads have been equipped with radars directly connected to headquarters' information systems that process and store image feeds. When a violation is filed, the owner of the vehicle is dynamically informed by an SMS alert through Metrash2 (a mobile app companion for the suite of e-Government services). Drivers may later view and pay online, either directly through the MOI official website, via the Hukoomi e-Services gateway, or directly using the mobile application. The second e-Service examined in this study is the renewal of health cards provided by HMC. This service allows users to issue new health cards required to have access to the medical and healthcare services at the HMC hospitals and clinics. Health cardholders are also entitled to have prescription filled at government-run pharmacies at discounted prices. Finally, the online payment of water and electricity bills service offered by KahraMaa is the third service we included in this research. This service is among the most common transactional services used in Qatar.

From these three representative e-Services, it is possible to understand users' perceptions about public e-services in Qatar in general and to examine the reasons behind users' low adoption compared to the high investments done by government.

Irani et al (2012) reviewed the research methods employed in e-Government research from a users' viewpoint. A comprehensive classification of e-Government users' literature is done in Weerakkody et al. (2013). The authors classified their findings according to the categories of the analytical work presented in Osman et al. (2011): Cost, Opportunity, Risk and Benefit. Founded on an empirical study conducted in Turkey, Osman et al. (2014) produced the COBRA framework based on factors relevant to the cost, opportunity, benefit and risk of using e-Government services. In this paper, we are interested in continuing the same line of research and investigate the possibility to generalize the COBRA framework when applied on different e-services in the context of Qatar. Based on the COBRA framework, this research seeks to evaluate quantitatively users' satisfaction with the available public e-Service. User satisfaction will accordingly be assessed by the perceived costs, opportunities, benefits and risks (COBRA) encountered by users when using the e-Services. In this study, we consider citizens, residents or whoever who have used at least one of the offered e-Services as users. Using an e-Service can either be directly from the website of the respective provider of the e-Service, through the Hukoomi portal, or via the respective mobile apps.

The remaining of this chapter is organized as following: the next section overviews the literature related to the evaluation of e-Services and users' satisfaction. It also covers relevant studies conducted in the Middle East contexts. This is followed by a description of the COBRA model and the research hypotheses of this study. The methodology section explains how the research instrument was adapted and how data was collected and handled. The results and study findings contain subsections presenting participants' demographics along with descriptive statistics of respondents' overall satisfaction with the e-Services according to the COBRA framework. Results also present findings of the structural equation modelling analysis examining the goodness of data fit against the COBRA model as suggested by Osman et al. (2014). Finally, the paper concludes with the theoretical and practical contributions as well as recognizing its limitations and proposing venues for future research.

## EVALUATION OF E-SERVICES AND USERS' SATISFACTION

Examining electronic services and assessing their efficacy has been a quite flourishing research topic since a while now. Besides the quality and advantages offered by a new e-Service (Sharma et al., 2013), achieving high rates of adoption and user's satisfaction are synonyms for success (Gatian, 1994). Aiming at evaluating e-Services in an objective approach, several research works focused on suggesting models and theories to develop metrics for evaluating e-Services. The initial attempts to understand how to measure and to improve services date back to the influential work of Shostack (1982), Parasuraman et al. (1985) and the service quality model in Grönroos (1984). The output of these studies resulted in the development of the SERVQUAL framework (Parasuraman et al., 1985). Along with the wide spread of the internet, many services were migrated online extending the traditional offline customer services as well as new services saw the light of day. This exponential increase in the number of e-Services paved the way towards the development of specialized models to evaluate the quality of e-Services (Parasuraman et al. 2005). eTailQ (Wolfinbarger & Gilly, 2003), SiteQual (Webb and Webb 2004), E-S-QUAL (Parasuraman et al. 2005), and WebQual (Loiacono et al., 2007) may all be regarded as updates to the original SERVQUAL framework.

Since e-Government is mostly about providing governmental and administrative services to citizens, which greatly differs from e-Business and e-Commerce in terms of goals (Grimsley and Meehan, 2007), evaluation of e-Government solutions emerged as a hot research topic in the early 2000's and is still considered as multi-disciplinary field of knowledge (Alcaide–Muñoz et al. 2017). Most of those studies started by focusing on evaluating e-Government services from a providers' perspective (Wirtz & Kurtz, 2016; Sharma et al., 2013). This wave of research might have been guided by two major forces. First, most public e-Services initiatives are started and guided by the supply side (i.e. governments) and second, the ICT technology developments (Verdegem & Verleye, 2009). Public agencies had to consider and assess several reforms to its bureaucratic processes in order to enact their e-Government initiatives (Abu-Shanab, 2015). Such changes may involve updating decision-making mechanisms, re-engineering business processes and considering users' preferences (Abu-Shanab, 2015; van Dijk et al., 2008; Lee-Kelley & Kolsaker, 2004). On the other hand, the availability of technology and issues related to implementation that may neglect users' real expectations of the new e-Services (Weerakkody et al., 2016; Bertot & Jaeger, 2008; van Dijk et al., 2008).

Since the establishment of e-Government services infrastructure, research exploring the evaluation of these e-Services from users' perspectives has emerged (Alcaide–Muñoz et al., 2017). This research stream focuses and discusses topics related to citizens' adoption and active participation in using these e-Government services instead of having them imposed by policy makers (Wirtz & Kurtz, 2016). This shift of addressing e-Government stakeholders' interests by considering users' needs and satisfaction attributes resembled to a great extent to how users evaluate CRM systems in enterprises (Seng, 2013; Tat-Kei Ho, 2002; Verdegem & Verleye,

2009). Following a chronological review of the literature to understand the origins of studies addressing technology acceptance, the Diffusion of Innovation theory by Rogers (2003) appears as a theoretical root. Even though it was too generic to be applied in a practical context to assess technology adoption or to measure users' satisfaction towards an e-Service (van Dijk et al., 2008; Verdegem & Verleye, 2009), it motivated many scholars to propose models based on this theory. Several seminal extensions appears in the literature examining how technology can be evaluated from a users' perspective. For instance, the Theory of Reasoned Actions (TRA) by Ajzen (1985) and the Technology Acceptance Model (TAM) by Davis and colleagues (1989). The Unified Theory of Acceptance and Use of Technology (UTAUT) developed by Venkatesh et al. (2003) aggregates constructs related to expected performance, effort, social influence and other facilitating conditions that directly influence users' behavior. UTAUT also suggest psychometric factors, such as age and gender, to moderate the influence of the independent variables on the intention to use and users' behavior.

These models were extensively used by researchers as "theoretical seeds" to build on top of them customized models. These customized models were driven by research contexts (e.g. countries), inclusion of new factors (e.g. website design), and technology developments (e.g. mobile devices). This led to a large number of published models and theories that may puzzle policy makers and other stakeholders in deciding which one to employ. This has recently motivated Dwivedi and colleagues (2017) to review these models and to propose a unified model of e-Government adoption (UMEGA). This model was tested and validated empirically by its creators stating it outperformed all the previous models.

## E-GOVERNMENT RESEARCH IN THE MIDDLE EAST

The introduction of e-Government initiatives in the Middle East in the early years of 2000 has motivated many scholars to research the topic of e-Government in the Arabic context. Recent research can be categorized into three main streams: Barriers and enablers influencing the diffusion of e-Government, application of new technology in the public sector, and the evaluation of e-Government services.

Research belonging to the first stream investigated the socio-cultural factors affecting the diffusion, use and adoption of e-Government services in the Middle East. For example, the effects of digital divide in the Arab society was extensively studied in Abu-Shanab (2017a), Abu-Shanab and Khasawneh (2014), Al-Shafi and Weerakkody (2010) and Al-Sobhi et al. (2010). Similarly, the effects of word-of-mouth, favoritism (*wasta*), and resistance to change on the adoption of e-Government were discussed in Alomari et al. (2014). In Qatar, El-Haddadeh et al. (2010) empirically examined the main barriers to implement e-Government solutions in the GCC area represented by Qatar. Weerakkody et al. (2011) studied the complexities accompanying e-Government implementation in developing countries taking Qatar as a representative example. From a providers' perspective, Sarrayrih and Sriram (2015) examined the main challenges to implement e-Government projects and developed a prescriptive model to assist local authorities to achieve e-Government initiatives successfully in Oman. Recently, Abu-Shanab (2017b) evaluated the benefits of e-Government projects in Jordan from a providers' viewpoint. He concluded that campaigns aiming at promoting e-Government solutions should be initiated by providers to increase awareness. This in turn may affect current processes and practices followed to fulfill public operations, leading to changes that should accordingly be managed.

The second stream of research included efforts examining ways to apply modern technology in public sector applications. For instance, mobile government (m-Government) (e.g. Abu-Shanab & Haidar, 2015; Alssbaiheen & Love, 2015; Faisal & Talib, 2015), big data (e.g. Saxena & Sharma, 2016), cloud computing (e.g. Mohammed et al., 2016) and open government (e.g. Al-Jamal & Abu-Shanab, 2016).

The last research stream, which most of the e-Government literature in the Middle East belongs to, is dedicated to evaluate the usage and adoption of e-Government services in different contexts. The major part of these studies employed original or extended versions of well-established theories and models. These included the Diffusion of Innovation (DOI) theory, the Technology Acceptance Model (TAM) and the Unified Theory of Acceptance and Use of Technology (UTAUT) (e.g. Anagreh & Abu-Shanab, 2017; Kurfalı et al., 2017; Alathmay et al., 2016; Alraja et al., 2016; Ahmad & Campbell, 2015; Abu-Shanab, 2014; Sharma et al., 2013; Weerakkody et al., 2013). The main conclusions of these studies converge roughly towards the same conclusions. That is, the significant effect of almost all the constructs covered by these evaluation models on the usage level of e-Government. Ease of use, perceived usefulness, social influence, trust, security and awareness were all found to be factors influencing users' adoption of e-Government services, yet, e-Government is still regarded as underutilized in the Arab world compared to the investments done by the providing governments (Al-Yafi et al., 2014). This may indicate the *saturation* of these models when it comes to evaluate modern e-Government services. On one hand, technology and Internet literacy is increasingly developing in the Arabic population due to the presence of technology in all modern life aspects. On the other hand, governments are significantly shifting their services to be online and the visibility and accessibility of these e-Services is becoming getting higher. These facts would naturally confirm the hypotheses proposed by the basic TAM and UTAUT models. So, in order to evaluate modern e-Government services, a new model may be needed to capture other relevant factors that are more adapted to recent techno-social developments. The present study is filling this gap by exploring users' satisfaction in terms of cost, benefits, opportunity and risk from using e-Government services in Qatar.

## THE COBRA MODEL FOR E-SERVICES' EVALUATION AND STUDY'S HYPOTHESES

The COBRA model was initially proposed in Osman et al. (2011). The proper formulation of COBRA came as an outcome of a systematic literature review by Weerakkody et al. (2013) that focused on the factors influencing e-Government service users' satisfaction. Consequently, the COBRA model suggests that cost, opportunity, benefits and risk are the most relevant factors affecting users' satisfaction. The following subsections explain those factors along with the hypotheses suggested by the COBRA model and tested in this study.

### Cost

Apart from the work in Lee et al. (2011) in the G2B context, cost was mainly regarded from a providers' perspective. Carter et al. (2016) is a recent example of this. The COBRA model is the first e-Government model considering cost as a factor affecting users' satisfaction. The cost construct is considered both in its tangible and intangible forms. According to Osman et al. (2014), the COBRA model considers tangible costs by the money amount needed to pay to use an e-Service as compared to its offline counterpart; whereas, intangible costs are mainly reflected by the time and efforts required to find and complete a transaction using the e-Service.

**Hypothesis 1:** Cost has a negative impact on users' satisfaction with an e-Service.

### Opportunity

During the development of the COBRA model, Osman et al. (2014) argued that encouraging factors to use e-Government services are the "*Opportunities presented by the government or country within which the e-Government service operates*". Transparency, electronic e-Services integration, 24/7 access to governmental services and the ability to share experience on social media are all examples about opportunity. Consequently, opportunity stands for the advantages users may experience by using the electronic version of the service as compared to using its offline counterpart. Osman et al. (2014) regarded opportunity from two complementary angles: *e-service support* and *technical support*. The former form of opportunity stands for the advantages of having access to the service offered via electronic channels such as accessing the service any time and from a variety of smart devices. In addition, users' perception of the e-Service visibility on social media and the ability to communicate with other users directly from the e-Service are included in this dimension of opportunity. The technical support opportunity refers to the more technical benefits of using the e-Service. The ability to view the transaction history, to track progress, or to receive confirmation notification are all examples of the technical support form of opportunity.

**Hypothesis 2:** Opportunity has a positive effect on user's satisfaction with an e-Service.

## Benefit

Benefit mainly refers to the set of benefits the user of an e-Service may take advantage of as compared to offline version of the same service. The previous constructs, cost and opportunity, may already include some *tangible benefits* to users such time and money savings. However, the perception of the COBRA model on this constructs extends to include the *intangible benefits* of using an e-Service. The information quality in terms of relevance and timeliness (Alenezi et al. 2015) and system quality in terms of ease of use and perceived usefulness (Rana et al. 2015; DeLone and McLean 2016; Venkatesh et al. 2016) are contained in the COBRA benefit construct.

**Hypothesis 3:** Benefit has a positive effect on user's satisfaction with an e-Service.

## Risk

As any online operation necessitating the transaction of sensitive information, using an e-Service may face security issues and users' estimation of the severity of the risks arising from these issues would definitely impact their trust (Venkatesh et al., 2016), and thus their satisfaction. The COBRA model examines risks based on two complementary dimensions: *personal risks* and *financial risks*. The former form of risks include concerns about privacy, identity theft and fraud (Al-Jamal & Abu-Shanab, 2015; Wu, 2014), while the latter form examines threats to the financial side of transactions such as stealth of banking details, money loss and uncompleted payments (Fonseca, 2014). This construct is therefore targeting users' perceptions of cyber security issues and their trust in technology as well as in the authority providing the service.

**Hypothesis 4:** Risk has a negative impact on users' satisfaction with an e-Service.

Based on the description of the above constructs formulating the main hypotheses of the COBRA model, Figure 1 graphically depicts the structure of the theoretical model employed in this study. It is worth noting that the COBRA model acknowledges the inter-correlations among the exogenous constructs. For instance, costs of using an e-Service may affect users' perception of the benefits, risks or opportunities gained by using that e-Service. The combination of all factors consequently reflects the overall level of satisfaction.

## RESEARCH DESIGN AND DATA COLLECTION

This research followed pretty much the same process as reported in Osman et al. (2014) in terms of methodology and data collection. Since the purpose of this work is to test an existing model for generalizability in a GCC context, employing a survey-based quantitative method is thought to be the most appropriate (Jackson 2011). The survey targeted an audience of users of any of the e-Services covered in this research. The survey questionnaire was designed using scale and multiple-answer questions organized into respective sections followed by few subjective questions to capture e-Government users' feedback. The first section asked respondents about the service they recently used and are about to fill in the survey for. In few cases, respondents who used more than one e-Service filled more than one questionnaire (one per each e-Service they used). The second section contained questions related to measuring the COBRA constructs while the third section was to capture the demographic data of the responder.

The questionnaire used is identical to the one employed in Al-Yafi et al. (2014), which is an adapted version of the original one developed in Osman et al. (2014). Few

*Figure 1. The COBRA model*

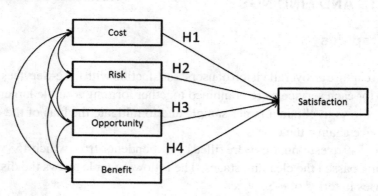

items were revised to ensure consistency with the local culture while preserving the objective of each item. The questionnaire consisted of forty-nine seven-point Lickert scale questions addressing the four examined variables, two open-ended questions and seven questions on subjects' demographic data, computer skills and overall internet usage. The questionnaire was made available online as well as a printer-friendly version was also produced to distribute the questionnaire as hardcopies. For both online and offline questionnaires, they were distributed in both English and Arabic as per respondents' preferences. However, it was noted during the distribution of the paper-based questionnaires that the length demotivated some respondents from completing it. An issue that made the data collection process quite challenging and during data screening, some observations had to be discarded for this reason.

Collected data was imported and cleaned in MS-Excel. The data cleaning processes consisted of two stages. Firstly, questionnaires with less than 35% of answered questions were eliminated from the sample. From the remaining responses, a second stage of cleaning was applied. Only responses having answers for more than 80% of the questions per construct (e.g. Cost) were kept, the remaining responses were discarded. From the remaining sample and for SEM analysis, missing values were calculated based on the median value of the same item across all the other questionnaires. This ensured the data has no missing values and is in an appropriate form to extract descriptive statistics and to conduct a comprehensive SEM analysis. SEM is then used to validate the COBRA model against the data collected in Qatar for the considered e-Services.

As a last step of analysis, a basic thematic analysis was conducted to analyze the free text answers to the open-ended items (Boyatzis 1998). This was only to understand whether users had comments or issues to report that may had not captured by the quantitative items.

## RESULTS AND FINDINGS

## Demographics

In order to capture an overall vision of users' satisfaction with the e-Services, the data collected for each service were combined together forming a single larger sample. Doing so allows to obtain a larger sample and to mitigate the bias of the data of a given service against the others.

In total, 549 questionnaires were filled by respondents, from which 458 were kept after having passed the cleaning stages. The following table shows the distribution of responses in terms of e-Services.

*Table 1. Distribution data per e-Services*

| Service Name | Acronym | Percentage |
|---|---|---|
| MOI (Ministry of Interior): Traffic violations and car fines. | MOI | 59.38% |
| SCH/HMC (Supreme Council of Health, Hamad Medical Corp): Renewal of health cards, replace damaged/lost health cards, schedule medical commission appointment. | HMC | 18.58% |
| Electricity and Water: Pay Utility Bills. | KahraMaa | 17.49% |
| No answer | | 4.55% |

It is clear that the MOI traffic violation e-Service is the most commonly used service compared to the other two e-Services. This might be attributed to the high usage of cars in Qatar as it is considered the transportation mean by default. The other two e-Services have almost an equivalent popularity that is significantly lower than the first. The periodical need to use these two e-Services (monthly or annually) may justify the relatively lower usage rate compared to the traffic violation e-Service, which some respondents reported using it every day.

From the 458 respondents, 44% were males, 50.82% were females, and 5.28% did not specify their gender. Table 2 summarizes the respondents' demographic data.

From an age point of view, it is worth mentioning that the sample does justice to the composition of the population using ICT. Most respondents are young users

*Table 2. Summary of the sample demographics*

| Age Group | | Education Level | | Income | | Internet Experience | | Usage | |
|---|---|---|---|---|---|---|---|---|---|
| <25 | 38% | Secondary or less | 2% | < $10,000 | 33% | Beginner (less than 3 Years) | 4% | Every day | 16% |
| 25-34 | 23% | High School | 12% | $10,000-$19,999 | 11% | Fair (3-6 Years) | 13% | Several times weekly | 14% |
| 35-44 | 18% | Undergrad Education | 45% | $20,000-$49,999 | 25% | Good (6-10 Years) | 35% | Once a month | 19% |
| 45-54 | 14% | Postgrad Education | 24% | $50,000-$69,999 | 9% | | | Several times a month | 15% |
| 55-64 | 3% | Doctorate | 8% | $70,000-$99,999 | 5% | Excellent (over 10 Years) | 44% | Once a year | 7% |
| >65 | 1% | Other Professional Qualifications | 3% | >$100K | 9% | | | Several times a year | 25% |
| N.A | 4% | N.A. | 5% | N.A. | 9% | N.A. | 4% | N.A. | 4% |

aged under 34 years old. Furthermore, most respondents reported having completed undergraduate or postgraduate education. In terms of internet literacy, the majority of respondents affirmed being experienced in using the internet with more than six years of continuous use. This may indicate that TAM conventional constructs could be of marginal utility in this case as the users may positively perceive the usefulness and ease of using these e-Services.

## Descriptive Analysis of COBRA Variables

The following subsections briefly describe each of the COBRA framework constructs and how they were measured in the survey. They also provide descriptive statistics of each construct by looking at the answers offered by respondents to the "overall satisfaction" question for each of the constructs. Thereafter, the results of a detailed SEM analysis are discussed.

## Cost

This construct is evaluated through 14 independent items. Intangible costs were measured by 8 items related to the time needed to find the e-Service, to upload or download data, to receive confirmation, the complexity and the number of steps required to complete a task by using the e-Service. As for the tangible costs, 6 questions about registration costs and internet subscriptions were proposed.

Apart from the internet subscription, all other material costs for using any of the e-Services covered in this research are free. About 60% of respondents positively scored the overall cost of using an e-Service and agreed to the statement that the cost of using an e-Service, in terms of money and time, is reasonable. About 20% of respondents, however, gave a negative feedback about the overall cost and about 4% did not provide any answer.

## Opportunity

Users' opportunity of using an e-Service was measured using an overall satisfaction question as well as through thirteen independent items. Eight items were for the e-Service opportunity and five items for the technical opportunity. These items asked users on issues about potential corruption, service access at anytime from anywhere, support for personalization, delivery options, alerts, availability of technical support, payment methods, transaction history, integration with social networks, and localization. 67% of respondents expressed their positive feedback about the overall opportunity obtained from using the e-Services, about 14% were not satisfied and about 4.4% of respondents did not provide feedback on opportunity.

## Benefit

The benefits users may have experienced by using any of the e-Services were evaluated through 11 items, in addition to an item to capture the overall benefit evaluation. These items asked respondents' opinions about the time and money savings. They also covered attributes regarding the information necessary to complete a service such as information lookup, presentation, completeness, accuracy, ease of navigation and use. Collected data showed relatively few respondents (12.6%) rating the overall benefits of the e-Services negatively. In fact, the majority of respondents positively rated the overall benefits from using an e-Service with a score of 68.3%, of which 26% strongly agreed with the e-Services' overall benefits. 14.4% of respondents expressed a neutral opinion whereas about 4.75% did not give an answer.

## Risk

Perceived risk associated with using an e-Service was measured by eleven independent questions in addition to an overall question. For the financial risks, these questions targeted the opinion of respondents about their perception of the risk of becoming victims of fraud, facing errors in payment, and the risk of facing additional hidden cost. As for the personal risks, the questions covered topics such as trust in public agencies, risk of social isolation, abuse of information privacy, and the risk of using personal information for purposes not related to the service in question.

Collected data showed that most respondents were concerned with the overall risk of using an e-Service (57.2%). It is also noticeable that there is a relatively higher rate of neutrality (17.7%) and only 21.7% of respondents did not express concerns about overall risk in using an e-Service. This may lead to conclude that respondents are quite aware of the risks associated with the sharing of sensitive information online and still have their own trust and security concerns when it comes to payment transactions.

## Model Validation With Structural Equation Modelling Analysis

Following the descriptive analysis of the COBRA indicators, a confirmatory factor analysis (CFA) using structural equation modelling (SEM) is applied (Bollen, 1989). SEM is therefore applied to verify the validity and to evaluate the COBRA model fit to the data sampled from Qatar.

As opposed to Exploratory Factor Analysis (EFA), CFA evaluates hypotheses proposed in advance and is largely driven by theoretical reasoning. Therefore, CFA is mainly about examining the factors' structure of a set of manifest variables (Tarhini et al. 2015). SEM has been described as a combination of CFA and multiple regression (Ullman, 2001). SEM can be used more as a CFA technique, but it can also be used for EFA (Schreiber et al. 2006). SEM does also specify the direction of causal relationships between factors and variables (Arbuckle, 2009), and this is of particular interest to understand if the level of e-Services users' satisfaction is really provoked by perceived costs, opportunity, benefits and risks.

Before applying SEM to the cleaned data, several steps were applied to ensure reliable SEM results. The first step was to ensure the data was following a normal distribution. For this, a Jarque-Bera test of normality was applied to all examined items and it was found that the data is actually normally distributed with a P-value >0.05; thus rejecting the null hypothesis that the data is not following a normal distribution. Consequently, a Cronbach Alpha test was applied on the data to ensure the reliability of the used instruments. The output of the Cronbach Alpha tests suggested the elimination of some survey items. Table 3 shows the results of the Cronbach Alpha test on the users' data. Except for the construct Cost-Time, all values are above the threshold of 0.7 indicating a good reliability of the survey items measuring each construct.

IBM SPSS AMOS v22 was used to conduct the SEM analysis. Figure 2 shows the structured model of COBRA used in the analysis phase of this study. In addition to the four constructs shown in the theoretical model, the sub-dimensions of each construct are depicted as well. These sub-dimensions are consistent with the definition of each construct and have respective items in the questionnaire items. The results of the SEM analysis were based on reporting the values of six indicators, these are the relative Chi-squared (CMIN/DF), the root mean residual (RMR), goodness of fit (GFI), the normed-fit index (NFI), the comparative-fit index (CFI), and the root mean squared error approximation (RMSEA). Table 4 shows the obtained results along with the recommended values for each indicator.

*Table 3. Results of the first round of Cronbach's Alpha test for reliability*

| Construct | Cronbach Alpha |
|---|---|
| Overall | **0.953** |
| Cost-Time | 0.609 |
| Cost-Money | **0.717** |
| Risk-Finance | **0.78** |
| Risk-Personal | **0.73** |
| Benefit-Information | **0.865** |
| Benefit-Service | **0.787** |
| Opportunity-Technical | **0.751** |
| Overall | **0.953** |

*Figure 2. COBRA Structural Path Model*

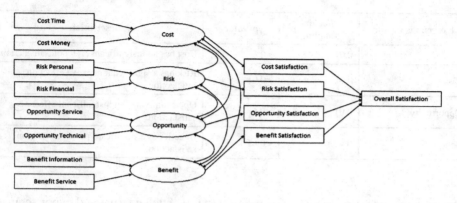

*Table 4. Model fit indices results summary*

| Index | Model's Index Values | Recommended Values |
|---|---|---|
| CMIN/DF | 1.69 | <5 |
| RMR | 0.049 | <0.1 |
| GFI | 0.976 | >0.9 |
| NFI | 0.982 | >0.9 |
| CFI | 0.992 | >0.9 |
| RMSEA | 0.04 | <0.08 |

From the fit indices, the data demonstrate a significant fit with the COBRA structural path model. Though the model was able to explain 63% of the total variance of the endogenous satisfaction variable, only two hypotheses from the COBRA model were confirmed. As shown in Table 5, results suggest rejecting hypothesis 1 and hypothesis 2 due to statistical insignificance. The standardized factor loadings between satisfaction and the exogenous factors along with their respective p-values are given in Table 5.

Given the insignificant negative effect cost has on satisfaction ($\beta=0.01$ and p-value $>0.5$), Hypothesis 1 is rejected. Similarly, hypothesis 2 is rejected due to the insignificant positive effect of opportunity on satisfaction ($\beta=0.01$ and p-value $>0.5$). On the other hand, hypothesis 3 is accepted as benefit proved to have a significant positive impact on satisfaction ($\beta=0.42$ and p-value $<0.01$). Similarly, hypothesis 4 is accepted given the significant negative effect risk has on satisfaction ($\beta=-0.4$ and p-value $<0.01$). These results suggest that meanwhile the cost and the opportunity of using e-Government services do not affect users' satisfaction, the benefits and the risk encountered are almost equivalently influencing users' satisfaction. This may

*Table 5. Standardized factor loadings between Satisfaction and COBRA variables*

| Exogenous Factor | Factor Loading | p-Value | Description |
|---|---|---|---|
| Cost | 0.01 | >0.5 | Cost has an insignificant effect on satisfaction. |
| Risk | -0.4 | <0.01 | Risk has a significant negative effect on satisfaction. |
| Opportunity | 0.01 | >0.5 | Opportunity has an insignificant effect on satisfaction. |
| Benefit | 0.42 | <0.01 | Benefit has a significant positive effect on satisfaction. |

imply users' concerns about issues relating to risk, such as trust and cyber security, that may significantly decrease satisfaction. Even if the cost and the opportunity of using an e-Service is reduced and increased, respectively, perceiving risk may still be a hurdle facing satisfaction. On the other hand, the benefits gained by using an e-Service has more credit for achieving satisfaction than it is for costs or opportunity. Perhaps the apparent aspects of benefits, the free cost of using these e-services and the non-applicability of some opportunity aspects contribute to this conclusion.

## Qualitative Observations

Respondents' qualitative feedback was caught through two open-ended questions. The first question asked respondents to explain whether the e-Service met their expected needs whereas the second question aimed at collecting comments about the e-Service. It worth noting that most questionnaires having these two questions answered belonged to respondents who have used the traffic violation e-Service. A reason can be due to the relatively higher number of users in the selected sample. Overall, the subjective answers complemented and confirmed the positive quantitative results, though some exceptions were observed.

The answers to the first subjective question were mainly positive. Most respondents who answered this qualitative question reported satisfaction towards the e-Services they used. Furthermore, this satisfaction was mostly related to topics covered by the benefit dimension of the COBRA model. Ease of access, information quality and time to fulfill administrative were all positively reflected in the positive answers. On the other hand, statements relating to the ease of use of the e-Service were relatively less mentioned. This may imply that either users using the e-Services have a minimum level of technical skills, the design of the e-Services is very user friendly, or both altogether. Surprisingly, few features belonging to the opportunity construct were also frequently highlighted as "useful features". Most of the mentioned features were the ability to fulfil administrative tasks electronically at any time of the day and avoiding the burden of traveling to the respective public agencies. Even though this contradicts the quantitative results (since hypothesis 3 were rejected), these features seemed to be the most useful ones belonging to the opportunity factor. Some respondents reported few concerns about privacy and possible errors in payment. Security issues were mentioned occasionally particularly regarding the share of private data and during payment transactions. This corresponds to the quantitative results confirming hypothesis 4. Finally, a theme that was not caught in the COBRA constructs was identified. Some respondents claimed the occasional need to physical presence to complete some administrative steps. These comments were essentially concerning some services (other than those examined in this study) that are partially or fully not available online yet. Therefore, this type of answers were more like a feedback than a regular answer regarding an existing e-Service they used.

The second subjective free question recorded suggestions and recommendations. These recommendations consisted of improving the way e-Services are organized in an e-Government portal where all public services can be integrated (this issue has already been considered through the Hukoomi e-Services gateway). Additionally, periodical reviewing of information accuracy was among the reported recommendations as occasional inconsistencies occurs between the online and offline versions. Third and most importantly, the need to increase the number of payment methods (currently limited to credit cards only). This concern becomes of importance as not every user may have or qualify for a credit card. This results in the exclusion of a considerable number of potential users and thus accentuating the effect of digital divide on the e-Government usage.

## DISCUSSION AND CONCLUDING REMARKS

This study examined three of the most mature and popular e-Services in the State of Qatar provided by three different public agencies. It has attracted many users by improving the way citizens and expatriate residents can fulfil their administrative tasks. Despite the spread of different e-Services in Qatar provided by almost every public agency in the country, studies to evaluate users' satisfaction with some of the mostly used e-Services are scarce, apart from a descriptive study done by Al-Yafi et al. (2014). The particularity of the present research is its aims of generalizing the application of the COBRA model within a single context, but on e-Services provided by different agencies. Therefore this study sought to understand and measure users' satisfaction and to investigate the reasons encouraging users to keep using an e-Service. Based on opinions collected from 458 users across three e-Services provided by different agencies, satisfaction data was examined based on the four main dimensions taken from the COBRA model (Osman et al. 2014): cost, opportunity, benefit and risk of using the e-Service. Descriptive statistics showed the traffic violation e-Service topped the ranking in terms of usage as compared to the other two e-Services. This can be attributed to the high number of car users compared to the HMC health cardholders and utility bill payers. While the results of the SEM analysis showed an excellent model fit with the data, it showed that the model could explain 63% of users' satisfaction. Additionally, two hypotheses out of the four proposed by the COBRA model were confirmed.

The hypothesis examining the effect of cost on satisfaction was rejected for insignificance. This might be attributed to the non-applicability of the cost construct in the studied context. In fact, all three e-Services examined in this research are free of charge and the processing time for fulfilling a service online is insignificant for the users to judge them as time costs. In addition, the internet subscription fee is low compared to the average income of users regularly using these e-Services. Regarding users' perception of risk, the hypothesis suggesting that risk may have a negative impact on satisfaction was accepted. Users' awareness of cyber security issues such as fraud and occasional data breaches may have made them conscious about the threats of using the internet for serious transactions. This awareness and prudence was reflected in respondents' quantitative as well as qualitative feedback.

Regarding the hypotheses about the benefits and opportunities of using the e-Services, only the one pertaining to benefits was accepted whereas the other was rejected for statistical insignificance. This might be due to the similarity of some concepts between benefit and opportunity. Both constructs are looking at the advantages users may perceive when using the online version of a service compared to its traditional offline counterpart. In other words, they both look at the quality of e-Services' support, the availability of multi-option service delivery, and the quality of information to complete the service. Therefore, a clearer separation of concepts might be needed and a reformulation of the COBRA framework may solve this issue. However, contrary to the benefit construct, opportunity covers additional issues that are irrelevant to most e-Services currently provided in Qatar. Ability to access transactions history, update of personal information, integration with social media are all issues not applicable to the e-Services considered in this study.

While the quantitative results revealed an objective overview of the general satisfaction with e-Services, qualitative feedback confirmed users' satisfaction with the electronic versions of their administrative services provided through the web. The feedback also included suggestions to improve the effectiveness of e-Services. The integration of public e-Services in one gateway, compatibility with modern smart devices and multiplying the number of payment methods were all among the most frequently mentioned themes in the qualitative responses.

Though not mentioned in the results section, but an interesting observation was noted that a significant number of respondents reported having used an e-Service through their smartphones. Therefore, it is worth highlighting the importance of the technical abstraction of e-Services to ensure reusability and to keep up with the rapid pace of technological innovations. In other words, the accessibility of a modern e-Service should not be limited to a single endpoint neither to a single type of devices. Instead, the same e-Service should be sufficiently flexible to be accessed by different gateways through either websites or mobile applications. Besides, modern e-Services should be easily and quickly adaptable for integration with new types of devices. This feature is particularly important as new devices enter the market and are quickly used by users. Smart watches is a good example of this phenomenon.

It is worth mentioning that public e-Services in the State of Qatar has witnessed recent innovations in terms of accessibility from mobile devices. The majority of public services are now available through mobile applications running on the most popular platforms. For instance, Metrash 2 is a mobile application developed by the Ministry of Interior as a minified mobile gateway aggregating several e-Services like traffic violation, visas, and application status tracking. Metrash 2 also integrates with SMS notifications to inform users dynamically about events requiring attention such as a traffic violation. Similarly, KahraMaa recently offered an innovative mobile application helping users to not only track their water and electricity consumption and pay bills, but to assist households on optimizing the use of resources and to become more "green". Thus, shifting the utility of e-Government solutions to cover not only the functional aspects but also to deliver social and ethical messages. Furthermore, KahraMaa bills payment e-Service has become a good example of technical abstraction in terms of integration with other websites or mobile applications. For example, KahraMaa utility bills can be paid via most e-banking systems proposed by Qatari banks or through telecommunication providers' websites and mobile apps.

## Study's Implications

This study suggests several theoretical and managerial contributions. First, it contributes to the research literature on evaluating e-Government systems, notably when it comes to assess users' satisfaction. The COBRA model and its questionnaire were employed as the main instruments to capture users' perception based on cost, opportunity, benefit and risk. Therefore, the Arabic version of the questionnaire was validated and successfully applied in the GCC context, thus improving and generalizing the usage of the COBRA model. This research is also novel in the way it evaluates e-Services since it does not evaluate users' satisfaction of a single e-Service but rather of three e-Services provided by three different providers representing a fair sample of the e-Government solutions currently offered in

Qatar. This gives a general overview of users' overall experience with the Qatari e-Government services instead of scattered evaluations of individual e-Services. This is of significant importance as e-Services vary in maturity. The coverage of three e-Services in our study resolves the probable bias and inaccurate view of the overall e-Government. Last but not least, this research contributes to the body of the e-Government literature studying the evaluation of e-Services in the Arab world context. This is the first study considering users' satisfaction towards e-Government services. This differentiates itself in terms of aim (users' satisfaction versus users' adoption) as well as in terms of the employed theoretical model (COBRA versus older models such as TAM and UTAUT).

The major practical implication of this study is addressed to policy makers and other relevant stakeholders. Policy makers and technical providers of e-Services may exploit the results and observations of this study in order to improve the quality of e-Services. Particularly the fact that new types of devices enter the market and users quickly adopt them, e-Services should demonstrate flexibility and portability to be accessed through these new channels. The quantitative results revealed the main factors affecting users' satisfaction. That is minimizing risks and increasing benefits would lead to better user satisfaction and therefore higher usage rates. The qualitative feedback may also serve stakeholders in addressing issues reported by users in order to broaden the acceptance and continuity of use of e-Services.

## Limitations and Future Work

This study has few limitations that need to be acknowledged. Firstly, data was collected according to a cross-sectional design resulting in obtaining users' opinions over a limited period. Furthermore, data collection was challenging due to the relatively long questionnaire. Consequently, convenient sampling was used and respondents understanding the value of such a research were primarily targeted. The sample mainly consisted of university students, academics and administrative staff; nevertheless, some random respondents took the survey too. Therefore, generalizing the findings of this study should be treated cautiously. Additionally, this study examined only three e-Services out of many available. Including more e-Services and to cover a wider range of users in the research sample are important factors to generalize the findings initiated by this study.

The COBRA model was applied in different contexts to evaluate users' satisfaction with different e-Services in Turkey and the UK. It is worth conducting a comparison study to check whether COBRA would catch cultural and social differences as well as e-Service maturity contrasts. Finally yet importantly, testing the COBRA model to evaluate e-Services only when accessed through mobile devices and to compare the results with their desktop web-based peers also seems as a promising venue for future research.

# REFERENCES

Abanumy, A., Al-Badi, A., & Mayhew, P. (2005). e-Government Website accessibility: In-depth evaluation of Saudi Arabia and Oman. The Electronic. *Journal of E-Government*, *3*(3), 99–106.

Abu-Shanab, E. A. (2014). Antecedents of trust in e-government services: an empirical test in Jordan. Transforming Government: People. *Process and Policy*, *8*(4), 480–499.

Abu-Shanab, E. A. (2015). Reengineering the open government concept: An empirical support for a proposed model. *Government Information Quarterly*, *32*(4), 453–463. doi:10.1016/j.giq.2015.07.002

Abu-Shanab, E. A. (2017). E-government familiarity influence on Jordanians' perceptions. *Telematics and Informatics*, *34*(1), 103–113. doi:10.1016/j.tele.2016.05.001

Abu-Shanab, E. A. (2017). E-government contribution to better performance by public sector. *International Journal of Electronic Government Research*, *13*(2), 81–96. doi:10.4018/IJEGR.2017040105

Abu-Shanab, E. A., & Haidar, S. (2015). Major factors influencing the adoption of m-government in Jordan. Electronic Government. *International Journal (Toronto, Ont.)*, *11*(4), 223–240.

Ahmed, K. M., & Campbell, J. (2015). Citizen Perceptions of E-Government in the Kurdistan Region of Iraq. *AJIS. Australasian Journal of Information Systems*, 19.

Ajzen, I. (1985). *From Intentions to Actions: A Theory of Planned Behavior*. In P. D. J. Kuhl & D. J. Beckmann (Eds.), *Action Control* (pp. 11–39). Springer Berlin Heidelberg.

Al-Aama, A. Y. (2014). Technology knowledge management (TKM) taxonomy: using technology to manage knowledge in a Saudi municipality. *VINE: The Journal of Information and Knowledge Management Systems, 44*(1), 2-21.

Al-Jamal, M., & Abu-Shanab, E. (2015). Privacy Policy Of E-Government Websites: An Itemized Checklist Proposed And Tested. *Management Research and Practice*, *7*(3), 80.

Al-Jamal, M., & Abu-Shanab, E. (2016). The influence of open government on e-government website: The case of Jordan. *International Journal of Electronic Governance*, *8*(2), 159–179. doi:10.1504/IJEG.2016.078131

Al-Sebie, M., & Irani, Z. (2005). Technical and organisational challenges facing transactional e-government systems: an empirical study. *Electronic Government, an International Journal, 2*(3), 247-276.

Al-Shafi, S., & Weerakkody, V. (2007). Implementing and managing e-government in the State of Qatar: a citizens' perspective. *Electronic Government, an International Journal, 4*(4), 436–450.

Al-Shafi, S., & Weerakkody, V. (2008). The Use of Wireless Internet Parks to Facilitate Adoption and Diffusion of E-Government Services: An Empirical Study in Qatar. Presented at the *14th Americas Conference on Information Systems*, Toronto, Canada.

Al-Shafi, S., & Weerakkody, V. (2010). *Factors affecting e-government adoption in the state of Qatar*. Presented at the European and Mediterranean Conference on Information Systems (EMCIS) 2010, Abu Dhabi, UAE.

Al-Sobhi, F., Weerakkody, V., & Kamal, M. M. (2010). An exploratory study on the role of intermediaries in delivering public services in Madinah City: Case of Saudi Arabia. *Transforming Government: People, Process and Policy, 4*(1), 14–36.

Al-Yafi, K., Osman, I. H., & Hindi, N. M. (2014). *Exploring user satisfaction of the public e-services in the State of Qatar: case of traffic violations e-service provided by the Ministry of Interior*. Presented at the *20th Americas Conference on Information Systems (AMCIS'14)*, Savannah, GA.

AlAwadhi, S., & Morris, A. (2009). Factors Influencing the Adoption of E-government Services. *Journal of Software, 4*(6), 584–590. doi:10.4304/jsw.4.6.584-590

Alcaide–Muñoz, L., Rodríguez–Bolívar, M. P., Cobo, M. J., & Herrera–Viedma, E. (2017). Analysing the scientific evolution of e-government using a science mapping approach. *Government Information Quarterly, 34*(3), 545–555. doi:10.1016/j.giq.2017.05.002

Alenezi, H., Tarhini, A., & Sharma, S. K. (2015). Development of quantitative model to investigate the strategic relationship between information quality and e-government benefits. Transforming Government: People. *Process and Policy, 9*(3), 324–351.

Alomari, M., Woods, P., & Sandhu, K. (2012). Predictors for e-government adoption in Jordan: Deployment of an empirical evaluation based on a citizen-centric approach. *Information Technology & People, 25*(2), 207–234. doi:10.1108/09593841211232712

Alomari, M. K., Sandhu, K., & Woods, P. (2014). "Exploring citizen perceptions of barriers to e-government adoption in a developing country," Transforming Government: People. *Process and Policy, 8*(1), 131–150.

Alraja, M. N., Hammami, S., Chikhi, B., & Fekir, S. (2016). The Influence of Effort and Performance Expectancy on Employees to adopt e-Government: Evidence from Oman. *International Review of Management and Marketing*, *6*(4), 930–934.

Anagreh, L. F., & Abu-Shanab, E. A. (2017). Voter's intention to use electronic voting systems. *International Journal of E-Business Research*, *13*(3), 67–85. doi:10.4018/IJEBR.2017070105

Arbuckle, J. (2009). *Amos 18 User's Guide*. Armonk, NY: SPSS Incorporated.

Ashrafi, R., & Murtaza, M. (2010). ICT adoption in SME in an Arab GCC Country Oman. E-strategies for Resource Management Systems: Planning and Implementation, 371-376.

Athmay, A. L., Al, A. A., Fantazy, K., & Kumar, V. (2016). E-government adoption and user's satisfaction: An empirical investigation. *EuroMed Journal of Business*, *11*(1), 57–83. doi:10.1108/EMJB-05-2014-0016

Bener, A., & Bhugra, D. (2013). Lifestyle and depressive risk factors associated with problematic internet use in adolescents in an Arabian Gulf culture. *Journal of Addiction Medicine*, *7*(4), 236–242. doi:10.1097/ADM.0b013e3182926b1f PMID:23666321

Bertot, J. C., & Jaeger, P. T. (2008). The E-Government paradox: Better customer service doesn't necessarily cost less. *Government Information Quarterly*, *25*(2), 149–154. doi:10.1016/j.giq.2007.10.002

Bollen, K. (1989). *Structural equations with latent variables*. New York: Wiley. doi:10.1002/9781118619179

Bounie, D., François, A., & Van Hove, L. (2017). Consumer payment preferences, network externalities, and merchant card acceptance: An empirical investigation. *Review of Industrial Organization*, *51*(3), 257–290. doi:10.100711151-016-9543-y

Boyatzis, R. E. (1998). *Transforming qualitative information: Thematic analysis and code development* (Vol. xvi). Thousand Oaks, CA: Sage Publications, Inc.

Carter, L., Weerakkody, V., Phillips, B., & Dwivedi, Y. K. (2016). Citizen Adoption of E-Government Services: Exploring Citizen Perceptions of Online Services in the United States and United Kingdom. *Information Systems Management*, *33*(2), 124–140. doi:10.1080/10580530.2016.1155948

Charbaji, A., & Mikdashi, T. (2003). A path analytic study of the attitude toward e-government in Lebanon. *Corporate Governance*, *3*(1), 76–82. doi:10.1108/14720700310459872

Davis, F. D., Bagozzi, R. P., & Warshaw, P. R. (1989). User Acceptance of Computer Technology: A Comparison of Two Theoretical Models. *Management Science, 35*(8), 982–1003. doi:10.1287/mnsc.35.8.982

DeLone, W.H., & McLean, E.R. (2016). Information Systems Success Measurement. *Foundations and Trends® in Information Systems, 2*(1), 1-116.

Dwivedi, Y. K., Rana, N. P., Janssen, M., Lal, B., Williams, M. D., & Clement, M. (2017). An empirical validation of a unified model of electronic government adoption (UMEGA). *Government Information Quarterly, 34*(2), 211–230. doi:10.1016/j.giq.2017.03.001

El-Haddadeh, R., Weerakkody, V., Al-Shafi, S., & Ali, M. (2010). E-Government implementation Challenges: A Case study. Presented at the *16th Americas Conference on Information Systems.*

Faisal, M. N., & Talib, F. (2015). E-government to m-government: A study in a developing economy. *International Journal of Mobile Communications, 14*(6), 568–592. doi:10.1504/IJMC.2016.079301

Feuilherarde, P. (2013, October 8). Winning the hearts and minds of GCC public transport users. *MENA Rail News.*

Fonseca, J. R. (2014). e-banking culture: A comparison of EU 27 countries and Portuguese case in the EU 27 retail banking context. *Journal of Retailing and Consumer Services, 21*(5), 708–716. doi:10.1016/j.jretconser.2014.05.006

Gatian, A. W. (1994). Is User Satisfaction a Valid Measure of System Effectiveness? *Information & Management, 26*(3), 119–131. doi:10.1016/0378-7206(94)90036-1

Gremm, J., Barth, J., Fietkiewicz, K. J., & Stock, W. G. (2017). *Transitioning Towards a Knowledge Society: Qatar as a Case Study.* Springer.

Grimsley, M., & Meehan, A. (2007). e-Government information systems: Evaluation-led design for public value and client trust. *European Journal of Information Systems, 16*(2), 134–148. doi:10.1057/palgrave.ejis.3000674

Grönroos, C. (1984). A Service Quality Model and its Marketing Implications. *European Journal of Marketing, 18*(4), 36–44. doi:10.1108/EUM0000000004784

Gupta, M. P., & Jana, D. (2003). E-government evaluation: A framework and case study. *Government Information Quarterly, 20*(4), 365–387. doi:10.1016/j.giq.2003.08.002

Irani, Z., Weerakkody, V., Kamal, M., Hindi, N. M., Osman, I. H., Anouze, A. L., ... Al-Ayoubi, B. (2012). An analysis of methodologies utilised in e-government research: A user satisfaction perspective. *Journal of Enterprise Information Management*, *25*(3), 298–313. doi:10.1108/17410391211224417

Jackson, S. (2011). *Research Methods and Statistics: A Critical Thinking Approach*. Cengage Learning.

Khatri, S. (2013, December 9). Official: Qatar's population could grow another 15 percent by 2015. *Doha News*.

Kurfalı, M., Arifoğlu, A., Tokdemir, G., & Paçin, Y. (2017). Adoption of e-government services in Turkey. *Computers in Human Behavior*, *66*, 168–178. doi:10.1016/j.chb.2016.09.041

Lee, J., Kim, H. J., & Ahn, M. J. (2011). The willingness of e-Government service adoption by business users: The role of offline service quality and trust in technology. *Government Information Quarterly*, *28*(2), 222–230. doi:10.1016/j.giq.2010.07.007

Lee-Kelley, L., & Kolsaker, A. (2004). E-government: the 'fit' between supply assumptions and usage drivers. *Electronic Government, an International Journal*, *1*(2), 130–140.

Leidner, D. E., & Kayworth, T. (2006). Review: a review of culture in information systems research: toward a theory of information technology culture conflict. *Management Information Systems Quarterly*, *30*(2), 357–399. doi:10.2307/25148735

Loiacono, E., Watson, R., & Goodhue, D. (2007). WebQual: An Instrument for Consumer Evaluation of Web Sites. *International Journal of Electronic Commerce*, *11*(3), 51–87. doi:10.2753/JEC1086-4415110302

Mansour, A. M. (2012). E-Government in the Gulf Cooperation Council Countries: A Comparative Study. *Journal of the Social Sciences*, *40*(1), 2102.

Mohammed, F., Ibrahim, O., & Ithnin, N. (2016). Factors influencing cloud computing adoption for e-government implementation in developing countries: Instrument development. *Journal of Systems and Information Technology*, *18*(3), 297–327. doi:10.1108/JSIT-01-2016-0001

Osman, I., Anouze, A., Irani, Z., Lee, H., Balcı, A., Medeni, T., & Weerakkody, V. (2011). A new COBRAS framework to evaluate e-government services: a citizen centric perspective. Presented at the *T-Government Workshop*.

Osman, I. H., Anouze, A. L., Hindi, N. M., Irani, Z., Lee, H., & Weerakkody, V. (2014). I-meet framework for the evaluation e-government services from engaging stakeholders' perspectives. European Scientific Journal, 10(10), 1-17.

Osman, I. H., Anouze, A. L., Irani, Z., Al-Ayoubi, B., Lee, H., Balcı, A., ... Weerakkody, V. (2014). COBRA framework to evaluate e-government services: A citizen-centric perspective. *Government Information Quarterly*, *31*(2), 243–256. doi:10.1016/j.giq.2013.10.009

Parasuraman, A., Zeithaml, V. A., & Berry, L. L. (1985). A Conceptual Model of Service Quality and Its Implications for Future Research. *Journal of Marketing*, *49*(4), 41–50. doi:10.2307/1251430

Parasuraman, A., Zeithaml, V. A., & Malhotra, A. (2005). E-S-QUAL A Multiple-Item Scale for Assessing Electronic Service Quality. *Journal of Service Research*, *7*(3), 213–233. doi:10.1177/1094670504271156

Rana, N. P., Dwivedi, Y. K., Williams, M. D., & Weerakkody, V. (2015). Investigating success of an e-government initiative: Validation of an integrated IS success model. *Information Systems Frontiers*, *17*(1), 127–142. doi:10.100710796-014-9504-7

Rogers, E. (2003). Diffusion of Innovations (5th ed.). New York: The Free Press.

Saxena, S., & Sharma, S.K. (2016). Integrating Big Data in "e-Oman": Opportunities and challenges. *Info, 18*(5), 79-97.

Schreiber, J. B., Nora, A., Stage, F. K., Barlow, E. A., & King, J. (2006). Reporting structural equation modeling and confirmatory factor analysis results: A review. *The Journal of Educational Research*, *99*(6), 323–338. doi:10.3200/JOER.99.6.323-338

Seng, W. M. (2013). E-Government Evaluation: An Assessment Approach Using ROI vs. ROR Matrix. *International Journal of Electronic Government Research*, *9*(1), 82–96. doi:10.4018/jegr.2013010105

Sharma, S. K., Al-Shihi, H., & Govindaluri, S. M. (2013). Exploring quality of e-Government services in Oman. *Education, Business and Society*, *6*(2), 87–100. doi:10.1108/EBS-12-2012-0055

Shostack, G. L. (1982). How to Design a Service. *European Journal of Marketing*, *16*(1), 49–63. doi:10.1108/EUM0000000004799

Tarhini, A., Teo, T., & Tarhini, T. (2015). A cross-cultural validity of the E-learning Acceptance Measure (ElAM) in Lebanon and England: A Confirmatory Factor Analysis. *Education and Information Technologies*, 1–14.

Tat-Kei Ho, A. (2002). Reinventing Local Governments and the E-Government Initiative. *Public Administration Review*, *62*(4), 434–444. doi:10.1111/0033-3352.00197

Tucker, C. (2017). Network Stability, Network Externalities, and Technology Adoption. In Entrepreneurship, Innovation, and Platforms (pp. 151-175). Emerald Publishing Limited. doi:10.1108/S0742-332220170000037006

Ullman, J. B. (2001). Structural equation modeling. In B. G. Tabachnick & L. S. Fidell (Eds.), *Using multivariate statistics* (4th ed.). Needham Heights, MA: Allyn & Bacon.

Van Dijk, J. A. G. M., Peters, O., & Ebbers, W. (2008). Explaining the acceptance and use of government Internet services: A multivariate analysis of 2006 survey data in the Netherlands. *Government Information Quarterly*, *25*(3), 379–399. doi:10.1016/j.giq.2007.09.006

Venkatesh, V., Morris, M. G., Davis, G. B., & Davis, F. D. (2003). User Acceptance of Information Technology: Toward a Unified View. *Management Information Systems Quarterly*, *27*(3), 425–478. doi:10.2307/30036540

Venkatesh, V., Thong, J. Y., Chan, F. K., & Hu, P. J. (2016). Managing Citizens' Uncertainty in E-Government Services: The Mediating and Moderating Roles of Transparency and Trust. *Information Systems Research*, *27*(1), 87–111. doi:10.1287/isre.2015.0612

Verdegem, P., & Verleye, G. (2009). User-centered E-Government in practice: A comprehensive model for measuring user satisfaction. *Government Information Quarterly*, *26*(3), 487–497. doi:10.1016/j.giq.2009.03.005

Webb, H. W., & Webb, L. A. (2004). SiteQual: An integrated measure of Web site quality. *Journal of Enterprise Information Management*, *17*(6), 430–440. doi:10.1108/17410390410566724

Weerakkody, V., El-Haddadeh, R., & Al-Shafi, S. (2011). Exploring the complexities of e-government implementation and diffusion in a developing country: Some lessons from the State of Qatar. *Journal of Enterprise Information Management*, *24*(2), 172–196. doi:10.1108/17410391111106293

Weerakkody, V., El-Haddadeh, R., Al-Sobhi, F., Shareef, M. A., & Dwivedi, Y. K. (2013). Examining the influence of intermediaries in facilitating e-government adoption: An empirical investigation. *International Journal of Information Management*, *33*(5), 716–725. doi:10.1016/j.ijinfomgt.2013.05.001

Weerakkody, V., Irani, Z., Kapoor, K., Sivarajah, U., & Dwivedi, Y. K. (2016). Open data and its usability: An empirical view from the Citizen's perspective. *Information Systems Frontiers*, 1–16.

Weerakkody, V., Irani, Z., Lee, H., Osman, I., & Hindi, N. (2013). E-government implementation: A bird's eye view of issues relating to costs, opportunities, benefits and risks. *Information Systems Frontiers*, 1–27.

Wirtz, B. W., & Kurtz, O. T. (2016). Determinants of Citizen Usage Intentions in e-Government: An Empirical Analysis. *Public Organization Review*, 1–20.

Wolfinbarger, M., & Gilly, M. C. (2003). eTailQ: dimensionalizing, measuring and predicting etail quality. *Journal of Retailing, 79*(3), 183–198.

Wu, Y. (2014). Protecting personal data in e-government: A cross-country study. *Government Information Quarterly, 31*(1), 150–159. doi:10.1016/j.giq.2013.07.003

# Compilation of References

911. Dispatch. (2014). *Required emergency information*. Retrieved September 27, 2014, from http://www.911dispatch.com/info/calltaking/calltaker.html

911. gov. (2014). *Current 911 data collection*. Retrieved September 27, 2014, from http://www.911. gov/pdf/Current911DataCollection-072613.pdf

Abanumy, A., Al-Badi, A., & Mayhew, P. (2005). e-Government Website accessibility: In-depth evaluation of Saudi Arabia and Oman. The Electronic. *Journal of E-Government*, *3*(3), 99–106.

Abu-Shanab, E. A., & Abu-Baker, A. N. (2011). Evaluating Jordan's e-government website: a case study. *Electronic Government, an International Journal, 8*(4), 271-289.

Abu-Shanab, E. A. (2014). Antecedents of trust in e-government services: an empirical test in Jordan. Transforming Government: People. *Process and Policy*, *8*(4), 480–499.

Abu-Shanab, E. A. (2015). Reengineering the open government concept: An empirical support for a proposed model. *Government Information Quarterly*, *32*(4), 453–463. doi:10.1016/j. giq.2015.07.002

Abu-Shanab, E. A. (2017). E-government contribution to better performance by public sector. *International Journal of Electronic Government Research*, *13*(2), 81–96. doi:10.4018/ IJEGR.2017040105

Abu-Shanab, E. A. (2017). E-government familiarity influence on Jordanians' perceptions. *Telematics and Informatics*, *34*(1), 103–113. doi:10.1016/j.tele.2016.05.001

Abu-Shanab, E. A., & Haidar, S. (2015). Major factors influencing the adoption of m-government in Jordan. Electronic Government. *International Journal (Toronto, Ont.)*, *11*(4), 223–240.

Abu-Shanab, E., & Al-Azzam, A. (2012). Trust dimensions and the adoption of e-government in Jordan. *International Journal of Information Communication Technologies and Human Development*, *4*(1), 39–51. doi:10.4018/jicthd.2012010103

Ahmed, K. M., & Campbell, J. (2015). Citizen Perceptions of E-Government in the Kurdistan Region of Iraq. *AJIS. Australasian Journal of Information Systems*, 19.

Ajzen, I. (1985). *From Intentions to Actions: A Theory of Planned Behavior.* In P. D. J. Kuhl & D. J. Beckmann (Eds.), *Action Control* (pp. 11–39). Springer Berlin Heidelberg.

Akyildiz, I. F., Su, W., Sankarasubramaniam, Y., & Cayirci, E. (2002). A survey on sensor networks. *IEEE Communications Magazine, 40*(8), 102–114. doi:10.1109/MCOM.2002.1024422

Al-Aama, A. Y. (2014). Technology knowledge management (TKM) taxonomy: using technology to manage knowledge in a Saudi municipality. *VINE: The Journal of Information and Knowledge Management Systems, 44*(1), 2-21.

Alateyah, S. A., Crowder, R. M., & Wills, G. B. (2013). Factors affecting the citizen's intention to adopt e-government in Saudi Arabia. *World Academy of Science Engineering and Technology International Journal of Social Science and Engineering, 7*(9), 2559–2564.

AlAwadhi, S., & Morris, A. (2009). Factors Influencing the Adoption of E-government Services. *Journal of Software, 4*(6), 584–590. doi:10.4304/jsw.4.6.584-590

Alcaide–Muñoz, L., Rodríguez–Bolívar, M. P., Cobo, M. J., & Herrera–Viedma, E. (2017). Analysing the scientific evolution of e-government using a science mapping approach. *Government Information Quarterly, 34*(3), 545–555. doi:10.1016/j.giq.2017.05.002

Alenezi, H., Tarhini, A., & Sharma, S. K. (2015). Development of quantitative model to investigate the strategic relationship between information quality and e-government benefits. Transforming Government: People. *Process and Policy, 9*(3), 324–351.

Alhabash, S., & Ma, M. (2017). A Tale of Four Platforms: Motivations and Uses of Facebook, Twitter, Instagram, and Snapchat Among College Students? Social Media + Society, 3(1).

Al-Jamal, M., & Abu-Shanab, E. (2015). Privacy Policy Of E-Government Websites: An Itemized Checklist Proposed And Tested. *Management Research and Practice, 7*(3), 80.

Al-Jamal, M., & Abu-Shanab, E. (2016). The influence of open government on e-government website: The case of Jordan. *International Journal of Electronic Governance, 8*(2), 159–179. doi:10.1504/IJEG.2016.078131

Aljazzaf, Z. M., Perry, M., & Capretz, M. A. (2010). Online trust: Definition and principles. In *Proceedings of the Fifth International Multi-conference on Computing in the Global Information Technology (ICCGI)* (pp. 163-168). Los Alamitos, CA: IEEE Computer Society Conference Publishing Services.

Allen, C. (2004). *Tracing the evolution of Social Software.* Retrieved from http://www.lifewithalacrity.com/2004/10/tracing_the_evo.html

Allen, D. K., Karanasios, S., & Norman, A. (2013). Information sharing and interoperability: The case of major incident management. *European Journal of Information Systems.*

Alomari, M. K., Sandhu, K., & Woods, P. (2014). "Exploring citizen perceptions of barriers to e-government adoption in a developing country," Transforming Government: People. *Process and Policy, 8*(1), 131–150.

Alomari, M., Woods, P., & Sandhu, K. (2012). Predictors for e-government adoption in Jordan: Deployment of an empirical evaluation based on a citizen-centric approach. *Information Technology & People*, *25*(2), 207–234. doi:10.1108/09593841211232712

Alonso, A. I., & Barbeito, R. L. (2016). Does e-participation Influence and Improve Political Decision Making Processes? Evidence From a Local Government. *Lex Localis-Journal of Local Self-Government*, *14*(4), 873–891.

Alraja, M. N., Hammami, S., Chikhi, B., & Fekir, S. (2016). The Influence of Effort and Performance Expectancy on Employees to adopt e-Government: Evidence from Oman. *International Review of Management and Marketing*, *6*(4), 930–934.

Alryalat, M., Rana, N., Sahu, G., Dwivedi, Y., & Tajvidi, M. (2017). Use of Social Media in Citizen-Centric Electronic Government Services: A Literature Analysis. *International Journal of Electronic Government Research*, *13*(3), 55–79. doi:10.4018/IJEGR.2017070104

Alsaghier, H., Ford, M., Nguyen, A., & Hexel, R. (2009). Conceptualising citizen's trust in e-government: Application of Q methodology. *Journal of E-Government*, *7*(4), 295–310.

Al-Sebie, M., & Irani, Z. (2005). Technical and organisational challenges facing transactional e-government systems: an empirical study. *Electronic Government, an International Journal*, *2*(3), 247-276.

Al-Shafi, S., & Weerakkody, V. (2007). Implementing and managing e-government in the State of Qatar: a citizens' perspective. *Electronic Government, an International Journal*, *4*(4), 436–450.

Al-Shafi, S., & Weerakkody, V. (2010). *Factors affecting e-government adoption in the state of Qatar*. Presented at the European and Mediterranean Conference on Information Systems (EMCIS) 2010, Abu Dhabi, UAE.

Al-Shafi, S., & Weerakkody, V. (2008). The Use of Wireless Internet Parks to Facilitate Adoption and Diffusion of E-Government Services: An Empirical Study in Qatar. Presented at the *14th Americas Conference on Information Systems*, Toronto, Canada.

Al-Shaqsi, S. (2010). Models of International Emergency Medical Service (EMS) Systems. *Oman Medical Journal*, *25*(4), 320–323. doi:10.5001/omj.2010.92 PMID:22043368

Al-Sobhi, F., & Weerakkody, V. 2010. The role of intermediaries in facilitating e-government diffusion in Saudi Arabia. In *Online Proceedings of the European, Mediterranean & Middle Eastern Conference on Information Systems (EMCIS)*. Retrieved from http://emcis.eu/Emcis_archive/EMCIS/EMCIS2010/Proceedings/Accepted%20Refereed%20Papers/C97.pdf

Al-Sobhi, F., Weerakkody, V., & Kamal, M. M. (2010). An exploratory study on the role of intermediaries in delivering public services in Madinah City: Case of Saudi Arabia. *Transforming Government: People, Process and Policy*, *4*(1), 14–36.

Alter, S. (2003). The IS Core -- XI Sorting Out Issues About The Core, Scope, And Identity Of The IS Field. *Communications of AIS*, *2003*(12), 607-628.

Alter, S. (2002). Sidestepping The IT Artifact, Scrapping The IS Solo, And Laying Claim To "Systems In Organizations". *Communications of AIS, 2003*(12), 494–526.

Al-Yafi, K., Osman, I. H., & Hindi, N. M. (2014). *Exploring user satisfaction of the public e-services in the State of Qatar: case of traffic violations e-service provided by the Ministry of Interior.* Presented at the *20th Americas Conference on Information Systems (AMCIS' 14)*, Savannah, GA.

Amadi-Obi, A., Gilligan, P., Owens, N., & O'Donnell, C. (2014). Telemedicine in pre-hospital care: A review of telemedicine applications in the pre-hospital environment. *International Journal of Emergency Medicine, 7*(1), 29. doi:10.118612245-014-0029-0 PMID:25635190

Amenta, E., & Ramsey, K. M. (2010). Institutional Theory. In K. T. Leicht & J. C. Jenkins (Eds.), Handbook of Politics: State and Society in Global Perspective, Handbooks of Sociology and Social Research (pp. 15–40). Springer Science+Business Media. doi:10.1007/978-0-387-68930-2_2

Ammenwerth, E., Buchauer, A., Bludau, B., & Haux, R. (2000). Mobile information and communication tools in the hospital. *International Journal of Medical Informatics, 57*(1), 21–40. doi:10.1016/S1386-5056(99)00056-8 PMID:10708253

Ammenwerth, E., Hackl, W. O., Binzer, K., Christoffersen, T. E., Jensen, S., Lawton, K., ... Nohr, C. (2012). Simulation studies for the evaluation of health information technologies: Experiences and results. *The HIM Journal, 41*(2), 14–21. doi:10.1177/183335831204100202 PMID:22700558

Anagreh, L. F., & Abu-Shanab, E. A. (2017). Voter's intention to use electronic voting systems. *International Journal of E-Business Research, 13*(3), 67–85. doi:10.4018/IJEBR.2017070105

Anand, L. K., Singh, M., & Kapoor, D. (2013). Prehospital trauma care services in developing countries. *Anaesthesia, Pain & Intensive Care, 17*(1), 65.

Andersen, K., Henriksen, H., & Medaglia, R. (2012). Beyond the Layne & Lee Legacy. Public Administration in the Information Age: Revisited, 205-220.

Andersen, K., Medaglia, R., & Henriksen, H. (2011). Frequency and costs of communication with citizens in local government. *International Conference on Electronic Government and the Information Systems Perspective* (LNCS 6866, pp. 15-25). Toulouse, France: Springer. 10.1007/978-3-642-22961-9_2

Andersen, K. N., Medaglia, R., & Henriksen, H. Z. (2012). Social Media in Public Health Care: Impact Domain Propositions. *Government Information Quarterly, 29*(4), 462–469.

Anderson, J., Donnellan, B., & Hevner, A. (2011). Exploring the relationship between design science research and innovation: A case study of innovation at Chevron. *Communications in Computer and Information Science,* (286): 116–131.

Andriopoulos, C., & Lewis, M. W. (2009). Exploitation-Exploration Tensions and Organizational Ambidexterity: Managing Paradoxes of Innovation. *Organization Science, 20*(4), 696–717. doi:10.1287/orsc.1080.0406

Anson, S., Watson, H., Wadhwa, K., & Metz, K. (2017). Analysing social media data for disaster preparedness: Understanding the opportunities and barriers faced by humanitarian actors. *International Journal of Disaster Risk Reduction, 21*, 131–139. doi:10.1016/j.ijdrr.2016.11.014

Aral, S., Dellarocas, C., & Godes, D. (2013). Social Media and Business Transformation: A Framework for Research. *Information Systems Research, 24*(1), 3–13. doi:10.1287/isre.1120.0470

Araujo, R. M., Borges, M. R. S., & Dias, M. S. (1997). A Framework for the Classification of Computer Supported Collaborative Design Approaches. *III CYTED-RITOS International Workshop on Groupware.*

Araujo, R., & Taher, Y. (2014). Refining IT Requirements for Government-Citizen Co-participation Support in Public Service Design and Delivery. *Conference for E-Democracy and Open Government, 1*, 61–72.

Arbuckle, J. (2009). *Amos 18 User's Guide.* Armonk, NY: SPSS Incorporated.

Archer, M. S. (1995). *Realist social theory: the morphogenetic approach.* Cambridge, UK: Cambridge University Press. doi:10.1017/CBO9780511557675

Armstrong, S., Bostrom, N., & Shulman, C. (2016). Racing to the precipice: A model of artificial intelligence development. *AI & Society, 31*(2), 201–206. doi:10.100700146-015-0590-y

Arnold, M. (2003). On the phenomenology of technology: The "Janus-faces" of mobile phones. *Information and Organization, 13*(4), 231–256. doi:10.1016/S1471-7727(03)00013-7

Arnstein, S. (1969). A ladder of citizen participation. *Journal of the American Institute of Planners, 35*(4), 216–224. doi:10.1080/01944366908977225

Arunachalam, R., & Sarkar, S. (2013). The New Eye of Government: Citizen Sentiment Analysis in Social Media. *Sixth International Joint Conference on Natural Language Processing.*

Ashrafi, R., & Murtaza, M. (2010). ICT adoption in SME in an Arab GCC Country Oman. E-strategies for Resource Management Systems: Planning and Implementation, 371-376.

Athmay, A. L., Al, A. A., Fantazy, K., & Kumar, V. (2016). E-government adoption and user's satisfaction: An empirical investigation. *EuroMed Journal of Business, 11*(1), 57–83. doi:10.1108/EMJB-05-2014-0016

Avgerou, C., Ciborra, C., Cordella, A., Kallinikos, J., & Smith, M. L. (2006, May). *E-government and trust in the state: lessons from electronic tax systems in Chile and Brazil* (London School of Economics and Political Science Department of Information Systems Working Paper Series No. 146). Retrieved from http://is2.lse.ac.uk/wp/pdf/WP146.PDF

Aziz, K., Haque, M. M., Rahman, A., Shamseldin, A. Y., & Shoaib, M. (2017). Flood estimation in ungauged catchments: Application of artificial intelligence based methods for Eastern Australia. *Stochastic Environmental Research and Risk Assessment, 31*(6), 1499–1514. doi:10.100700477-016-1272-0

Bachmann, D. J., Jamison, N. K., Martin, A., Delgado, J., & Kman, N. E. (2015). Emergency preparedness and disaster response: There's an app for that. *Prehospital and Disaster Medicine*, *30*(5), 486–490. doi:10.1017/S1049023X15005099 PMID:26369629

Baller, S., Dutta, S., & Lanvin, B. (2016). The global information technology report 2016 – Innovating in the Digital Economy. *World Economic Forum*.

Bannister, F., & Connolly, R. (2011). Trust and transformational government: A proposed framework for research. *Government Information Quarterly*, *28*(2), 137–147. doi:10.1016/j.giq.2010.06.010

Bannister, F., & Connolly, R. (2014). ICT, public values and transformative government : A framework and programme for research. *Government Information Quarterly*, *31*(1), 119–128. doi:10.1016/j.giq.2013.06.002

Bannister, F., & Connolly, R. (2015). The great theory hunt : Does e-government really have a problem? *Government Information Quarterly*, *32*(1), 1–11. doi:10.1016/j.giq.2014.10.003

Baran, P. (1964). On Distributed Communications Networks. *Communications Systems. IEEE Transactions on*, *12*(1), 1–9. doi:10.1109/TCOM.1964.1088883

Barley, S. R., & Tolbert, P. S. (1997). Institutionalization and Structuration: Studying the Links between Action and Institution. *Organization Studies*, *18*(1), 93–117. doi:10.1177/017084069701800106

Barnard, C. I. (1948). *The Functions of the Executive*. Boston: Harvard University Press.

Ba, S., & Pavlou, P. A. (2002). Evidence of the effect of trust building technology in electronic markets: Price premiums and buyer behavior. *Management Information Systems Quarterly*, *26*(3), 243–268. doi:10.2307/4132332

Bashshur, R. L. (2002). Chapter 1: Telemedicine and health care. *Telemedicine Journal and e-Health*, *8*(1), 5–12. doi:10.1089/15305620252933365 PMID:12020402

Bauman, E. B. (2013). *Game-based Teaching and Simulation in Nursing and Healthcare*. Springer Publishing Company.

Baytiyeh, H. The use of mobile technologies in the aftermath of terrorist attacks among low socioeconomic populations. *International Journal of Disaster Risk Reduction*. doi:10.1016/j.ijdrr.2018.02.001

Bean, C. (2015). Changing citizen confidence: Orientations towards political and social institutions in Australia, 1983-2010. *The Open Political Science Journal*, *8*(1), 1–9. doi:10.2174/1874949601508010001

Becker, J., Hündorf, H-P., Kill, C., & Lipp, R. (2006). *Lexikon Rettungsdienst*. Stumpf + Kossendey Verlag.

Bélanger, F., & Carter, L. (2008). Trust and risk in e-government adoption. *The Journal of Strategic Information Systems*, *17*(2), 165–176. doi:10.1016/j.jsis.2007.12.002

Bellavista, P., Cardone, G., Corradi, A., Foschini, L., & Ianniello, R. (2015). Crowdsensing in Smart Cities: Technical Challenges, Open Issues. Handbook of Research on Social, Economic, and Environmental Sustainability in the Development of Smart Cities, 316.

Benbasat, I., & Zmud, R. W. (2003). The identity crisis within the IS discipline: Defining and communication the discipline's core properties. *Management Information Systems Quarterly*, *27*(2), 183–194. doi:10.2307/30036527

Bener, A., & Bhugra, D. (2013). Lifestyle and depressive risk factors associated with problematic internet use in adolescents in an Arabian Gulf culture. *Journal of Addiction Medicine*, *7*(4), 236–242. doi:10.1097/ADM.0b013e3182926b1f PMID:23666321

Benson, J. K. (1977). Organizations: A Dialectical View. *Administrative Science Quarterly*, *22*(1), 1–21. doi:10.2307/2391741

Berlinger, L. R., Sitkin, S. B., Quinn, R. E., & Cameron, K. S. (1990). Paradox and Transformation: Toward a Theory of Change in Organization and Management. *Administrative Science Quarterly*, *35*(4), 740–744. doi:10.2307/2393523

Berntzen, L. (2013). Citizen-centric eGovernment Services: Use of indicators to measure degree of user involvement in eGovernment service development. *International Conference on Advances in Human-oriented and Personalized Mechanisms, Technologies and Services*, 132-136.

Bertot, J. C., & Jaeger, P. T. (2008). The E-Government paradox: Better customer service doesn't necessarily cost less. *Government Information Quarterly*, *25*(2), 149–154. doi:10.1016/j.giq.2007.10.002

Bertot, J., Jaeger, P., Munson, S., & Glaisyer, T. (2010). Engaging the public in open government: Social media technology and policy for government transparency. *Computer*, *43*(11), 53–59. doi:10.1109/MC.2010.325

Bider, I., Johannesson, P., & Perjons, E. (2013). Using empirical knowledge and studies in the frame of design science research. *Proceedings of the 8th International Conference on Design Science at the Intersection of Physical and Virtual Design*, 463-470. 10.1007/978-3-642-38827-9_38

Billig, M. (2015). Kurt Lewin's Leadership Studies and His Legacy to Social Psychology: Is There Nothing as Practical as a Good Theory? *Journal for the Theory of Social Behaviour*, *45*(4), 440–460. doi:10.1111/jtsb.12074

Binder, G. (1993). *Hilfsfrist. In Rechtsbegriffe in der Notfallmedizin* (pp. 38–38). Springer Berlin Heidelberg. doi:10.1007/978-3-642-52350-2_38

Bjerknes, G. (1991). Dialectical Reflection in Information Systems Development. *Scandinavian Journal of Information Systems*, *3*, 55–77.

Bleiler, R. (2003). SPU Technology Project Post-Implementation Review: Water Operations Mobile Computing. Seattle, WA: Academic Press.

Bloch, C., & Bugge, M. M. (2013). Public Sector Innovation—From Theory to Measurement. *Structural Change and Economic Dynamics*, *27*(0), 133–145. doi:10.1016/j.strueco.2013.06.008

Bollen, K. (1989). *Structural equations with latent variables*. New York: Wiley. doi:10.1002/9781118619179

Bonsón, E., Torres, L., Royo, S., & Floresc, F. (2012). Local e-government 2.0: Social media and corporate transparency in municipalities. *Government Information Quarterly*, *29*(2), 123–132. doi:10.1016/j.giq.2011.10.001

Boonstra, A., Broekhuis, M., Offenbeek, M. V., & Wortmann, H. (2011). Strategic alternatives in telecare design: Developing a value-configuration-based alignment framework. *The Journal of Strategic Information Systems*, *20*(2), 198–214. doi:10.1016/j.jsis.2010.12.001

Bostrom, R. P., Gupta, S., & Thomas, D. (2009). A Meta-Theory for Understanding Information Systems Within Sociotechnical Systems. *Journal of Management Information Systems*, *26*(1), 17–47. doi:10.2753/MIS0742-1222260102

Bounie, D., François, A., & Van Hove, L. (2017). Consumer payment preferences, network externalities, and merchant card acceptance: An empirical investigation. *Review of Industrial Organization*, *51*(3), 257–290. doi:10.100711151-016-9543-y

Boyatzis, R. E. (1998). *Transforming qualitative information: Thematic analysis and code development* (Vol. xvi). Thousand Oaks, CA: Sage Publications, Inc.

Brasil. (2009). *Lei complementar n° 131 – Disponibilização em tempo real de informações* (Supplementary Law no. 131 – Real-time provision of information). Retrieved from https://www.planalto.gov.br/ccivil_03/Leis/LCP/Lcp131.htm

Brasil. (2011). *Lei n° 12.527 – Lei de acesso à informação* (Law no. 12,527 – Law on information access). Retrieved from http://www.planalto.gov.br/ccivil_03/_ato2011-2014/2011/lei/l12527.htm

Bretschneider, S., & Parker, M. (2016). Organization formalization, sector and social media : Does increased standardization of policy broaden and deepen social media use in organizations? *Government Information Quarterly*, *33*(4), 614–628. doi:10.1016/j.giq.2016.09.005

Bronk, C., & Smith, T. (2010). Diplopedia Imagined: Building State's Diplomacy Wiki. In *Collaborative Technologies and Systems (CTS), 2010 International Symposium on*. IEEE.

Brooks, L. (1997). Structuration theory and new technology: Analysing organizationally situated computer-aided design (CAD). *Information Systems Journal*, *7*(2), 133–151. doi:10.1046/j.1365-2575.1997.00011.x

Brovelli, M. A., & Cannata, M. (2004). Digital Terrain model reconstruction in urban areas from airborne laser scanning data: The method and an example for Pavia (Northern Italy). *Computers & Geosciences*, *30*(4), 325–331. doi:10.1016/j.cageo.2003.07.004

Bryant, T. (2006). Social Software in Academia. *Educate Quarterly*, *6*, 61-64.

Bryant, C. G. A., & Jary, D. (1991). Introduction: Coming to terms with Anthony Giddens. In C. G. A. Bryant & D. Jary (Eds.), *Giddens' theory of structuration: a critical appreciation* (pp. 1–31). London: Routledge. doi:10.1007/978-1-4613-9714-4_1

Bui, D. T., Pradhan, B., Nampak, H., Bui, Q. T., Tran, Q. A., & Nguyen, Q. P. (2016). Hybrid artificial intelligence approach based on neural fuzzy inference model and metaheuristic optimization for flood susceptibilitgy modeling in a high-frequency tropical cyclone area using GIS. *Journal of Hydrology (Amsterdam), 540*, 317–330. doi:10.1016/j.jhydrol.2016.06.027

Bundesärztekammer. (2011). *Übersicht Notarztqualifikation in Deutschland.* Retrieved from www.bundesaerztekammer.de

Bwalya, K. J. (2009). Factors affecting adoption of e-government in Zambia. *The Electronic Journal on Information Systems in Developing Countries, 38*(4), 1–13. doi:10.1002/j.1681-4835.2009.tb00267.x

Callese, T. E., Richards, C. T., Shaw, P., Schuetz, S. J., Issa, N., Paladino, L., & Swaroop, M. (2014). Layperson trauma training in low- and middle-income countries: A review. *The Journal of Surgical Research, 190*(1), 104–110. doi:10.1016/j.jss.2014.03.029 PMID:24746252

Callese, T. E., Richards, C. T., Shaw, P., Schuetz, S. J., Paladino, L., Issa, N., & Swaroop, M. (2015). Trauma system development in low- and middle-income countries: A review. *The Journal of Surgical Research, 193*(1), 300–307. doi:10.1016/j.jss.2014.09.040 PMID:25450600

Campbell, D. A., Lambright, K. T., & Wells, C. J. (2014). *Looking for Friends, Fans, and Followers? Social Media Use in Public and Nonprofit Human Services.* Academic Press.

Cannata, M., Marzochhi, R., & Molinari, M. (2012). Modeling of landslide-generated tsunamis with GRASS. *Transactions in GIS, 16*(2), 191–214. doi:10.1111/j.1467-9671.2012.01315.x

Cannon-Diehl, M. R. (2009). Simulation in healthcare and nursing: State of the science. *Critical Care Nursing Quarterly, 32*(2), 128–136. doi:10.1097/CNQ.0b013e3181a27e0f PMID:19300077

Cappelli, C., Oliveira, A., & Leite, J. C. (2007). Exploring Business Process Transparency Concepts. *IEEE International Requirements Engineering Conference,* 389-390. 10.1109/RE.2007.35

Carlo, J. L., Lyytinen, K., & Boland, J. R. J. (2012). Dialectics of Collective Minding: Contradictory Appropriations of Information Technology in a High-Risk Project. *Management Information Systems Quarterly, 36*(4), 1081–A3.

Carter, L., & Bélanger, F. (2005). The utilization of e-government services: Citizen trust, innovation and acceptance factors. *Information Systems Journal, 15*(1), 5–25. doi:10.1111/j.1365-2575.2005.00183.x

Carter, L., Weerakkody, V., Phillips, B., & Dwivedi, Y. K. (2016). Citizen Adoption of E-Government Services: Exploring Citizen Perceptions of Online Services in the United States and United Kingdom. *Information Systems Management, 33*(2), 124–140. doi:10.1080/105805 30.2016.1155948

Carvalho, L. P., Santoro, F., & Cappelli, C. (2016). Using a Citizen Language in Public Process Models: The Case Study of a Brazilian University. *LNCS*, *9831*, 123–134.

Case, D. O. (2007). *Looking for information: a survey of research on information seeking, needs, and behavior* (2nd ed.). Amsterdam: Elsevier/Academic Press.

Castello, I., Etter, M., & Morsing, M. (2012). Why Stakeholder Engagement will not be Tweeted: Logic and the Conditions of Authority Corset. In Academy of Management 2012, Boston, MA.

Castells, M. (2000). *A sociedade em rede*. Paz e Terra São Paulo.

CCA. (2014). *About CCA*. Retrieved September 27, 2014, from https://competitivecarriers.org/about/about-rca-2/914473

Cegarra-Navarro, J.-G., Pachón, J. R. C., & Cegarra, J. L. M. (2012). E-government and Citizen's Engagement with Local Affairs through E-websites: The Case of Spanish Municipalities. *International Journal of Information Management*, *32*(5), 469–478. doi:10.1016/j.ijinfomgt.2012.02.008

CGCP-UNIRIO. (2012). *Coordenadoria de Gestão Corporativa de Processos da UNIRIO* (Coordination of Corporate Process Management). Retrieved from http://www2.unirio.br/unirio/cgcp/projetos/internos/proap-1/produtos

CGI.br. (2010). *TIC Governo Eletrônico*. Retrieved from http://www.cetic.br/tic/egov/2010/index.htm

Charalabidis, Y., & Loukis, E. (2012). Participative Public Policy Making Through Multiple Social Media Platforms Utilization. *International Journal of Electronic Government Research*, *8*(3), 78–97. doi:10.4018/jegr.2012070105

Charbaji, A., & Mikdashi, T. (2003). A path analytic study of the attitude toward e-government in Lebanon. *Corporate Governance*, *3*(1), 76–82. doi:10.1108/14720700310459872

Chen, R., Sharman, R., Rao, H. R., & Upadhyaya, S. J. (2013). Data model development for fire related extreme events: An activity theory approach. *Management Information Systems Quarterly*, *37*(1), 125–147. doi:10.25300/MISQ/2013/37.1.06

Cheong, F., & Cheong, C. (2011). Social Media Data Mining: A Social Network Analysis of Tweets During The 2010-2011 Australian Floods. *PACIS*, *11*, 46–46.

Chochliouros, I., Stephanakis, I., Spiliopoulou, A., Sfakianakis, E., & Ladid, L. (2012). Developing Innovative Live Video-to-Video Communications for Smarter European Cities. In L. Iliadis, I. Maglogiannis, H. Papadopoulos, K. Karatzas, & S. Sioutas (Eds.), *Artificial Intelligence Applications and Innovations* (Vol. 382, pp. 279–289). Springer Berlin Heidelberg. doi:10.1007/978-3-642-33412-2_29

Choi, S. J., Oh, M. Y., Kim, N. R., Jung, Y. J., Ro, Y. S., & Shin, S. D. (2017). Comparison of trauma care systems in Asian countries: A systematic literature review. *Emergency Medicine Australasia*, *29*(6), 697–711. doi:10.1111/1742-6723.12840 PMID:28782875

Chokotho, L., Mulwafu, W., Singini, I., Njalale, Y., Maliwichi-Senganimalunje, L., & Jacobsen, K. H. (2017). First Responders and Prehospital Care for Road Traffic Injuries in Malawi. *Prehospital and Disaster Medicine*, *32*(1), 14–19. doi:10.1017/S1049023X16001175 PMID:27923422

Cho, S., Mathiassen, L., & Robey, D. (2007). Dialectics of resilience: A multi-level analysis of a telehealth innovation. *Journal of Information Technology*, *22*(1), 24–35. doi:10.1057/palgrave.jit.2000088

Chua, A. Y. K., Goh, D. H., & Ang, R. P. (2012). Web 2.0 applications in government web sites: Prevalence, use and correlations with perceived web site quality. *Online Information Review*, *36*(2), 175–195. doi:10.1108/14684521211229020

Chu, C., & Smithson, S. (2007). E-business and organizational change: A structurational approach. *Information Systems Journal*, *17*(4), 369–389. doi:10.1111/j.1365-2575.2007.00258.x

Chun, S. A., & Cho, J. (2012). E-participation and transparent policy decision making. *Information Polity*, *17*(2), 129–145.

Churchman, C. W. (1979). *The Systems Approach*. Dell.

CitizenScape. (n.d.). Retrieved from http://www.citizenscape.net

Clark, B. Y., & Guzman, T. S. (2016). Does Technologically Enabled Citizen Participation Lead to Budget Adjustments? An Investigation of Boston, MA, and San Francisco, CA. *American Review of Public Administration*.

Classe, T., Araujo, R., & Xexéo, G. (2017). *Desaparecidos RJ – Um Jogo Digital para o Entendimento de Processos de Prestação de Serviços Públicos [Disappeared RJ – A Digital Game for Understanding the Public Service Provision Processes]*. Curitiba: Simpósio Brasileiro de Jogos e Entretenimento Digital.

Clawson, J. J., Gardett, I., Scott, G., Fivaz, C., Barron, T., Broadbent, M., & Olola, C. (2017). Hospital-Confirmed Acute Myocardial Infarction: Prehospital Identification Using the Medical Priority Dispatch System. *Prehospital and Disaster Medicine*, 1–7. doi:10.10171049023x1700704x PMID:29223194

Coad, A., Jack, L., & Kholeif, A. O. R. (2015). Structuration theory: Reflections on its further potential for management accounting research. *Qualitative Research in Accounting & Management*, *12*(2), 153–171. doi:10.1108/QRAM-01-2015-0013

Cockburn, P. (2017). Arbaeen: Millions of Shia Muslims take part in world's greatest pilgrimage as Isis is finally defeated. *The Independent*. Retrieved March 13, 2018 from: http://www.independent.co.uk/news/world/middle-east/arbaeen-pilgrimage-kerbala-shia-isis-defeat-muslims-thousands-killed-middle-east-iraq-najaf-a8046621.html

Cohen, I. J. (1989). *Structuration theory: Anthony Giddens and the constitution of social life.* New York: St. Martin's Press. doi:10.1007/978-1-349-20255-3

Colesca, S. E. (2009). Understanding trust in e-government. *Inzinerine Ekonomika -. The Engineering Economist*, *3*, 7–15.

Color Psychology. (2014). Retrieved September 27, 2014, from http://psychology.about.com/od/sensationandperception/a/colorpsych.htm

Conklin, E. (1997). *Designing Organizational Memory: Preserving Intellectual Assets in a Knowledge Economy*. Retrieved from http://cognexus.org/dom.pdf

CTIA. (2014). *Wireless quick facts*. Retrieved September 27, 2014, from http://www.ctia.org/your-wireless-life/how-wireless-works/wireless-quick-facts

Cullen, R., & Reilly, P. (2007). Information privacy and trust in government: A citizen-based perspective from New Zealand. In *Proceedings of the 40th Hawaii International Conference on System Sciences* (pp. 109-114). Los Alamitos, CA: IEEE Computer Society Conference Publishing Services. 10.1109/HICSS.2007.271

Cumbie, B. A., & Kar, B. (2015). The Role of Social Media in U.S. County Governments: The Strategic Value of Operational Aimlessness. *International Journal of Electronic Government Research*, *11*(1), 1–20. doi:10.4018/IJEGR.2015010101

Cummings, M. L. (2006). Can CWA inform the design of networked intelligent systems. *Proceedings of the 1st Moving Autonomy Forward Conference (MAF 2006)*, 1-6.

Czaplik, M., Bergrath, S., Rossaint, R., Thelen, S., Brodziak, T., Valentin, B., ... Brokmann, J. C. (2014). Employment of telemedicine in emergency medicine. Clinical requirement analysis, system development and first test results. *Methods of Information in Medicine*, *53*(2), 99–107. doi:10.3414/ME13-01-0022 PMID:24477815

Czarniawska, B. (2009). Emerging Institutions: Pyramids or Anthills? *Organization Studies*, *30*(4), 423–441. doi:10.1177/0170840609102282

Das, A., Singh, H., & Joseph, D. (2017). A longitudinal study of e-government maturity. *Information & Management*, *54*(4), 415–426. doi:10.1016/j.im.2016.09.006

Davis, D. P., Graydon, C., Stein, R., Wilson, S., Buesch, B., Berthiaume, S., ... Leahy, D. R. (2007). The positive predictive value of paramedic versus emergency physician interpretation of the prehospital 12-lead electrocardiogram. *Prehospital Emergency Care*, *11*(4), 399–402. doi:10.1080/10903120701536784 PMID:17907023

Davis, F. D. (1989). Perceived Usefulness, Perceived Ease of Use, and User Acceptance of Information Technology. *Management Information Systems Quarterly*, *13*(3), 319–340. doi:10.2307/249008

Davis, F. D., Bagozzi, R. P., & Warshaw, P. R. (1989). User Acceptance of Computer Technology: A Comparison of Two Theoretical Models. *Management Science*, *35*(8), 982–1003. doi:10.1287/mnsc.35.8.982

Debenham, S., Fuller, M., Stewart, M., & Price, R. R. (2017). Where There is No EMS: Lay Providers in Emergency Medical Services Care - EMS as a Public Health Priority. *Prehospital and Disaster Medicine, 32*(6), 593–595. doi:10.1017/S1049023X17006811 PMID:28797317

Dedrick, J., & West, J. (2003). Why firms adopt open source platforms: a grounded theory of innovation and standards adoption. *Proceedings of the workshop on standard making: A critical research frontier for information systems*, 236-257.

DeLone, W.H., & McLean, E.R. (2016). Information Systems Success Measurement. *Foundations and Trends® in Information Systems, 2*(1), 1-116.

Denhardt, J. V., & Denhardt, R. B. (2015). The New Public Service Revisited. *Public Administration Review, 75*(5), 664–672. doi:10.1111/puar.12347

DeSanctis, G., & Poole, M. S. (1994). Capturing the complexity in advanced technology use: Adaptive structuration theory. *Organization Science, 5*(2), 121–147. doi:10.1287/orsc.5.2.121

DETRAN-RJ. (n.d.). Retrieved from http://www.detran.rj.gov.br

DeutscherBundestag17.Wahlperiode. (2010). *Bericht über Maßnahmen auf dem Gebiet der Unfallverhütung im Straßenverkehr 2008 und 2009 (Unfallverhütungsbericht Straßenverkehr 2008/2009)*. Author.

Dib, J. E., Naderi, S., Sheridan, I. A., & Alagappan, K. (2006). Analysis and applicability of the Dutch EMS system into countries developing EMS systems. *The Journal of Emergency Medicine, 30*(1), 111–115. doi:10.1016/j.jemermed.2005.05.014 PMID:16434351

Dick, W. F. (2003). Anglo-American vs. Franco-German emergency medical services system. *Prehosp Disaster Med, 18*(1), 29-35.

Diirr, B., Araujo, R., & Cappelli, C. (2011). Propostas para aproximação entre Sociedade e Governo por meio de discussões apoiadas por TICs [Proposals for closer ties between society and government through discussions supported by ICTs]. *DIA-UNIRIO Technical Report (RelaTe-DIA)*. Retrieved from http://www.seer.unirio.br/index.php/monografiasppgi/article/view/1730

Diirr, B., Araujo, R., & Cappelli, C. (2009). An Approach for Defining Digital Democracy Support based on ICT. *International Conference on Computer Supported Cooperative Work in Design*, 203-208. 10.1109/CSCWD.2009.4968059

Downey, E. (2012). *Public Service, Governance and Web 2.0 Technologies: Future Trends in Social Media: Future Trends in Social Media*. Information Science Reference. doi:10.4018/978-1-4666-0071-3

DRING13. (n.d.). Retrieved from http://www.dring13.org

Dubé, L., & Robey, D. (2009). Surviving the Paradoxes of Virtual Teamwork. *Information Systems Journal, 19*(1), 3–30. doi:10.1111/j.1365-2575.2008.00313.x

Dünnebeil, S., Sunyaev, A., Blohm, I., Leimeister, J. M., & Krcmar, H. (2012). Determinants of physicians' technology acceptance for e-health in ambulatory care. *International Journal of Medical Informatics*, *81*(11), 746–760. doi:10.1016/j.ijmedinf.2012.02.002 PMID:22397989

Dwivedi, Y. K., Rana, N. P., Janssen, M., Lal, B., Williams, M. D., & Clement, M. (2017). An empirical validation of a unified model of electronic government adoption (UMEGA). *Government Information Quarterly*, *34*(2), 211–230. doi:10.1016/j.giq.2017.03.001

Ebrahim, Z., & Irani, Z. (2005). E-government adoption: Architecture and barriers. *Business Process Management Journal*, *11*(5), 589–611. doi:10.1108/14637150510619902

Economic and Social Committee, Section for Transport, Energy, Infrastructure and the Information Society. (2008). Opinion of the European Economic and Social Committee on the Communication from the Commission to the European Parliament, the Council, the European Economic and Social Committee and the Committee of the Regions on telemedicine for the benefit of patients, healthcare systems and society COM(2008) 689 final. Brussels: Author.

Edwards, M. (2015, April 8). *The trust deficit - concepts and causes of low public trust in governments*. Retrieved from http://workspace.unpan.org/sites/Internet/Documents/UNPAN94464.pdf

Eggers, W. D. (2007). *Government 2.0: Using Technology to Improve Education, Cut Red Tape, Reduce Gridlock, and Enhance Democracy*. Rowman & Littlefield.

Eisenhardt, K. M. (2000). Paradox, Spirals, Ambivalence: The New Language of Change and Pluralism. *Academy of Management Review*, *25*(4), 703–705. doi:10.5465/AMR.2000.3707694

Elbasha, T., & Wright, A. (2017). Reconciling structure and agency in strategy-as-practice research: Towards a strong-structuration theory approach. *M@n@gement, 20*(2), 107-128.

El-Haddadeh, R., Weerakkody, V., Al-Shafi, S., & Ali, M. (2010). E-Government implementation Challenges: A Case study. Presented at the *16th Americas Conference on Information Systems*.

Ellinger, K. (2011). *Kursbuch Notfallmedizin: orientiert am bundeseinheitlichen Curriculum Zusatzbezeichnung Notfallmedizin*. Dt. Ärzte-Verlag.

Ellis, D. Y., & Sorene, E. (2008). Magen David Adom—The EMS in Israel. *Resuscitation*, *76*(1), 5–10. doi:10.1016/j.resuscitation.2007.07.014 PMID:17767990

eMarketer. (2013). *Smartphone adoption tips past 50%*. Retrieved from http://www.emarketer.com/Article/Smartphone-Adoption-Tips-Past-50-Major-Markets-Worldwide/1009923

Engelbrecht, J., & Booysen, M. J., Van Rooyen, G-J., & Bruwer, F. J. (2015). Survey of smartphone-based sensing in vehicles for intelligent transportation system applications. *IET Intelligent Transport Systems*. doi:10.1049/iet-its.2014.0248

Engiel, P., Araujo, R., & Cappelli, C. (2014). Designing Public Service Process Models for Understandability. Electronic. *Journal of E-Government*, *12*, 95–111.

Eriksson, H., & Penker, M. (2000). *Business Modeling with UML: Business Patterns at Work.* New York: Wiley Publishers.

Erskine, M. A., & Pepper, W. (2016). Enhancing Emergency Response Management using Emergency Description Information Technology (EDIT): A Design Science Approach. In E-Health and Telemedicine: Concepts, Methodologies, Tools, and Applications (pp. 1264-1278). IGI Global.

Erskine, M. A., & Gregg, D. G. (2012). Utilizing volunteered geographic information to develop a real-time disaster mapping tool: a prototype and research framework. *Proceedings of the Conference on Information Resource Management.*

Erskine, M. A., Sibona, C., & Kalantar, H. (2013). Aggregating, analyzing and diffusing natural disaster information: a research framework. *Proceedings of the Nineteenth Americas Conference on Information Systems.*

Evans, D., & Yen, D. C. (2006). E-government: Evolving relationship of citizens and government, domestic, and international development. *Government Information Quarterly, 23*(2), 207–235. doi:10.1016/j.giq.2005.11.004

Faisal, M. N., & Talib, F. (2015). E-government to m-government: A study in a developing economy. *International Journal of Mobile Communications, 14*(6), 568–592. doi:10.1504/IJMC.2016.079301

Fawcett, J., & Downs, F. (1986). Types of Theory and Research. *The Relationship Between Theory and Research,* 4–7. Retrieved from http://www.indiana.edu/~educy520/readings/fawcett86.pdf

FCC. (2014a). Retrieved March 13, 2018, from https://www.fcc.gov/files/text-911-master-psap-registryxlsx

FCC. (2014b). Retrieved September 27, 2014, from http://www.fcc.gov/guides/wireless-911-Services

Feeney, O., & Pierce, B. (2016). Strong structuration theory and accounting information: An empirical study. *Accounting, Auditing & Accountability Journal, 29*(7), 1152–1176. doi:10.1108/AAAJ-07-2015-2130

Felzen, M., Brokmann, J. C., Beckers, S. K., Czaplik, M., Hirsch, F., Tamm, M., ... Bergrath, S. (2016). Improved technical performance of a multifunctional prehospital telemedicine system between the research phase and the routine use phase - an observational study. *Journal of Telemedicine and Telecare.* doi:10.1177/1357633x16644115 PMID:27080747

Femers, S., & Wiedemann, P. (1993). Public participation in waste management decision making: Analysis and management of conflicts. *Journal of Hazardous Materials, 33*(3), 355–368. doi:10.1016/0304-3894(93)85085-S

Ferneley, E., & Light, B. (2006). Secondary user relations in emerging mobile computing environments. *European Journal of Information Systems, 15*(3), 301–306.

Ferro, E., Loukis, E. N., Charalabidis, Y., & Osella, M. (2013). Policy making 2. 0 : From theory to practice. *Government Information Quarterly*, *30*(4), 359–368. doi:10.1016/j.giq.2013.05.018

Feuilherarde, P. (2013, October 8). Winning the hearts and minds of GCC public transport users. *MENA Rail News*.

Fidel, R., & Pejtersen, A. M. (2002). *Cognitive Work Analysis*. The Information School. Retrieved from http://projects.ischool.washington.edu/fidelr/RayaPubs/CWA-bookchapter.pdf

Fidel, R., Scholl, H. J., Liu, S., & Unsworth, K. (2007). *Mobile Government Fieldwork: Technological, organizational, and social challenges*. Paper presented at the 8th Annual International Conference on Digital Government Research (DG.O 2007), Philadelphia, PA.

Fidel, R., & Pejtersen, A. M. (2004). From information behaviour research to the design of information systems: The Cognitive Work Analysis framework. *Information Research*, *10*(1), 1–15.

Finnell, J. T., & Overhage, J. M. (2010). Emergency medical services: the frontier in health information exchange. *American Medical Informatics Association Annual Symposium Proceedings*, 222.

Fitzgerald, G., & Russo, N. L. (2005). The turnaround of the London ambulance service computer-aided dispatch system (LASCAD). *European Journal of Information Systems*, *14*(3), 244–257.

Fonseca, J. R. (2014). e-banking culture: A comparison of EU 27 countries and Portuguese case in the EU 27 retail banking context. *Journal of Retailing and Consumer Services*, *21*(5), 708–716. doi:10.1016/j.jretconser.2014.05.006

Fritz, P. Z., Gray, T., & Flanagan, B. (2008). Review of mannequin-based high-fidelity simulation in emergency medicine. *Emergency Medicine Australasia*, *20*(1), 1–9. doi:10.1111/j.1742-6723.2007.01022.x PMID:17999685

Fruhling, A., & Vreede, G. J. D. (2006). Field experiences with eXtreme programming: Developing an emergency response system. *Journal of Management Information Systems*, *22*(4), 39–68. doi:10.2753/MIS0742-1222220403

Fung, B. (2014a, April 27). Cellphone calls to 911 prove hard to trace. *Washington Post*.

Fung, B. (2014b, August 9). FCC is requiring broad support of text-to-911. *Washington Post*.

Gao, H., Barbier, G., & Goolsby, R. (2011). Harnessing the crowdsourcing power of social media for disaster relief. *IEEE Intelligent Systems*, *26*(3), 10–14. doi:10.1109/MIS.2011.52

Garcia, A. C., & Parmer, P. A. (1999). Misplaced mistrust: The collaborative construction of doubt in 911 emergency calls. *Symbolic Interaction*, *22*(4), 297–324. doi:10.1525i.1999.22.4.297

Gatian, A. W. (1994). Is User Satisfaction a Valid Measure of System Effectiveness? *Information & Management*, *26*(3), 119–131. doi:10.1016/0378-7206(94)90036-1

Giddens, A. (1982). A reply to my critics. *Theory, Culture & Society*, *1*(2), 107–113. doi:10.1177/026327648200100212

Giddens, A. (1984). *The constitution of society: outline of the theory of structuration.* Berkeley, CA: University of California Press.

Giddens, A. (1989). A reply to my critics. In D. Held & J. B. Thompson (Eds.), *Social theory of modern societies: Anthony Giddens and his critics* (pp. 249–305). Cambridge, MA: Cambridge University Press. doi:10.1017/CBO9780511557699.013

Giddens, A. (1991). Structuration Theory: Past, present and future. In C. G. A. Bryant & D. Jary (Eds.), *Giddens' theory of structuration: a critical appreciation* (pp. 201–221). London: Routledge.

Gil-Garcia, J. R. (2012). Towards a smart state? Inter-agency collaboration, information integration, and beyond. *Information Polity, 17*(3-4), 269–280.

Gil-Garcia, J. R., & Hassan, S. (2007). Structuration Theory and IT-Based Organizational Change. In G. D. Garson & M. Khosrow-Pour (Eds.), *Handbook of Research on Public Information Technology* (pp. 371–375). Hershey, PA: Information Science.

Gil-Garcia, J. R., Helbig, N., & Ojo, A. (2014). Being smart: Emerging technologies and innovation in the public sector. *Government Information Quarterly, 31*, I1–I8. doi:10.1016/j.giq.2014.09.001

Gil-Garcia, J. R., Zhang, J., & Puron-Cid, G. (2016). Conceptualizing smartness in government: An integrative and multi-dimensional view. *Government Information Quarterly, 33*(3), 524–534. doi:10.1016/j.giq.2016.03.002

Gill, A., Alam, S., & Eustace, J. (2014). *Using Social Architecture to Analyzing Online Social Network Use in Emergency Management.* Academic Press.

Gilmour, P., Coffey, B., & O'Toole, K. (2015). Trust and knowledge exchange in coastal settings. *Australian Journal of Maritime and Ocean Affairs, 7*(1), 66–74. doi:10.1080/18366503.2015.1014013

Golden-biddle, K., & Locke, K. (1993). Appealing Work: An Investigation of How Ethnographic Texts Convince. *Organization Science, 4*(4), 595–617. doi:10.1287/orsc.4.4.595

Goldsmith, S., & Eggers, W. D. (2005). *Governing by Network: The New Shape of the Public Sector.* Brookings Institution Press.

Gomes, W. (2004). *Transformações da política na era da comunicação de massa [Politics transformation in the mass communication era].* São Paulo: Paulus.

Goncalves, J., Cordeiro, L., Batista, P., & Monteiro, E. (2012). LiveCity: A Secure Live Video-to-Video Interactive City Infrastructure. In L. Iliadis, I. Maglogiannis, H. Papadopoulos, K. Karatzas, & S. Sioutas (Eds.), *Artificial Intelligence Applications and Innovations* (Vol. 382, pp. 260–267). Springer Berlin Heidelberg. doi:10.1007/978-3-642-33412-2_27

Gopal, A., Bostrom, R. P., & Chin, W. W. (1993). Applying Adaptive Structuration Theory to Investigate the Process of Group Support Systems Use. *Journal of Management Information Systems, 9*(3), 45–70. doi:10.1080/07421222.1992.11517967

Gorlenko, L., & Merrick, R. (2003). No wires attached: Usability challenges in the connected mobile world. *IBM Systems Journal*, *42*(4), 639–651. doi:10.1147j.424.0639

Gorman, G. E., Clayton, P., Rice-Lively, M. L., & Gorman, L. (1997). *Qualitative research for the information professional: a practical handbook*. London: Library Association Publishing.

Gregg, D. G., Kulkarni, U. R., & Vinzé, A. S. (2001). Understanding the philosophical underpinnings of software engineering research in information systems. *Information Systems Frontiers*, *3*(2), 169–183. doi:10.1023/A:1011491322406

Gregor, S., & Baskerville, R. (2012). The fusion of design science and social science research. *Information Systems Foundation Workshop*, Canberra, Australia.

Gremm, J., Barth, J., Fietkiewicz, K. J., & Stock, W. G. (2017). *Transitioning Towards a Knowledge Society: Qatar as a Case Study*. Springer.

Gries, A., Zink, W., Bernhard, M., Messelken, M., & Schlechtriemen, T. (2006). Realistic assessment of the physican-staffed emergency services in Germany. *Der Anaesthesist*, *55*(10), 1080–1086. doi:10.100700101-006-1051-2 PMID:16791544

Grimsley, M., & Meehan, A. (2007). e-Government information systems: Evaluation-led design for public value and client trust. *European Journal of Information Systems*, *16*(2), 134–148. doi:10.1057/palgrave.ejis.3000674

Grönlund, A. (2009). ICT is not Participation is not Democracy – eParticipation Development Models Revisited. *International Conference on eParticipation*, 12-23. 10.1007/978-3-642-03781-8_2

Grönroos, C. (1984). A Service Quality Model and its Marketing Implications. *European Journal of Marketing*, *18*(4), 36–44. doi:10.1108/EUM0000000004784

Groos, H. (2011). *Du musst die Menschen lieben: Als Ärztin im Rettungswagen, auf der Intensivstation und im Krieg*. Fischer E-Books.

Gruenerbl, A., Pirkl, G., Monger, E., Gobbi, M., & Lukowicz, P. (2015, September). Smart-watch life saver: smart-watch interactive-feedback system for improving bystander CPR. In *Proceedings of the 2015 ACM International Symposium on Wearable Computers* (pp. 19-26). ACM. 10.1145/2802083.2802086

Gupta, M. P., & Jana, D. (2003). E-government evaluation: A framework and case study. *Government Information Quarterly*, *20*(4), 365–387. doi:10.1016/j.giq.2003.08.002

Haahr, L. (2014b). Wrestling with Social Media on Information Systems' Home Ground. In *Nordic Contributions in IS Research. 5th Scandinavian Conference on Information Systems, SCIS 2014, Ringsted, Denmark, 10-13 August, 2014. Proceedings*. Springer.

Haahr, L. (2014a). Wrestling with Contradictions in Government Social Media Practices. *International Journal of Electronic Government Research*, *10*(1), 35–45. doi:10.4018/ijegr.2014010103

Hague, B. (1999). *Digital Democracy: Discourse and Decision Making in the Information Age* (1st ed.). London: Routledge.

Harding, U., Lechleuthner, A., Ritter, M. A., Schilling, M., Kros, M., Ohms, M., & Bohn, A. (2013). „Schlaganfall immer mit Notarzt?" – „Pro". *Medizinische Klinik, Intensivmedizin und Notfallmedizin, 108*(5), 408–411. doi:10.100700063-012-0137-7 PMID:23010854

Harri, O.-K., Kalle, L., & Youngjin, Y. (2010). Social Networks and Information Systems: Ongoing and Future Research Streams. *Journal of the Association for Information Systems, 11*(2), 61–68. doi:10.17705/1jais.00222

Harris, C. S., & Winter, J. S. (2013). An Exploratory Study of Social Networking Services as a Potential Vehicle for E-Participation in the City and County of Honolulu. *International Journal of Electronic Government Research, 9*(2), 63–84. doi:10.4018/jegr.2013040104

Hedberg, B. (1981). How organizations learn and unlearn. In P. Nystrom & W. Starbuck (Eds.), *Handbook of Organizational Design* (pp. 3–27). New York: Oxford University Press.

Heeks, R., & Bailur, S. (2007). Analyzing e-government research: Perspectives, philosophies, theories, methods, and practice. *Government Information Quarterly, 24*(2), 243–265. doi:10.1016/j.giq.2006.06.005

Hempel, C. G. (1958). The Theoretician's Dilemma: A Study in the Logic of Theory Construction. In Concepts, Theories, and the Mind-Body Problem (pp. 37–98). Academic Press.

Henriksen, F. L., Schorling, P., Hansen, B., Schakow, H., & Larsen, M. L. (2016). FirstAED emergency dispatch, global positioning of community first responders with distinct roles - a solution to reduce the response times and ensuring an AED to early defibrillation in the rural area Langeland. *International Journal of Networking and Virtual Organisations, 16*(1), 86. doi:10.1504/IJNVO.2016.075131

Henrique, G., Oliveira, M., & Welch, E. W. (2013). Social media use in local government : Linkage of technology, task, and organizational context Technology Task Organizational context. *Government Information Quarterly, 30*(4), 397–405. doi:10.1016/j.giq.2013.05.019

Heredero, C., Berzosa, D., & Santos, R. (2010). The implementation of free software in firms: An empirical analysis. *The International Journal of Digital Accounting Research, 10*, 113–130.

Heugens, P. P. M. A. R., & Lander, M. W. (2016). *Structure! Agency! (And Other Quarrels): A Meta-Analysis of Institutional Theories of Organization.* Academy of Management. Retrieved from http://www.jstor.org/stable/40390276

Hevner, A. R., & Chaterjee, S. (2010). *Design Research in Information Systems.* New York: Springer. doi:10.1007/978-1-4419-5653-8

Hevner, A. R., March, S. T., Park, J., & Ram, S. (2004). Design science in information systems research. *Management Information Systems Quarterly, 28*(1), 75–105. doi:10.2307/25148625

Hiller, J. S., & Bélanger, F. (2001, January). *Privacy strategies for electronic government.* Retrieved from http://www.businessofgovernment.org/sites/default/files/PrivacyStrategies.pdf

Hills, S. (2013). World's biggest religious festival comes to an end after 120 million pilgrims cleansed their sins during two month celebration. *The Daily Mail.* Retrieved March 13, 2018 from: http://www.dailymail.co.uk/news/article-2291379/Kumbh-Mela-Worlds-biggest-religious-festival-comes-end-120-million-pilgrims-cleansed-sins-month-celebration.html

Hirschman, A. O. (1970). *Exit, voice, and loyalty: Responses to decline in firms, organizations, and states.* Cambridge, MA: Harvard University Press.

Holl, K., Nass, C., Villela, K., & Vieira, V. (2016). Towards a lightweight approach for on-site interaction evaluation of safety-critical mobile systems. *Procedia Computer Science, 94,* 41–48. 10.1016/j.procs.2016.08.010

Holzner, B., & Holzner, L. (2006). *Transparency in global change: The vanguard of the open society.* Pittsburgh, PA: University of Pittsburgh Press.

Horita, F. E. A., Degrossi, L. C., de Assis, L. F. G., Zipf, A., & de Albuquerque, J. P. (2013). The use of volunteered geographic information (VGI) and crowdsourcing in disaster management: a systematic literature review. *Proceedings of the Nineteenth Americas Conference on Information Systems.*

Horita, F. E., & de Albuquerque, J. P. (2013). An approach to support decision-making in disaster management based on volunteer geographic information (VGI) and spatial decision support systems (SDSS). *Proceedings of the 10th International Conference on Information Systems for Crisis Response and Management,* 12-15.

Horita, F. E., de Albuquerque, J. P., Degrossi, L. C., Mendiondo, E. M., & Ueyama, J. (2015). Development of a spatial decision support system for flood risk management in Brazil that combines volunteered geographic information with wireless sensor networks. *Computers & Geosciences, 80,* 84–94. doi:10.1016/j.cageo.2015.04.001

Howie, C. (2008). What to do after a car accident. *CNN.* Retrieved September 27, 2014, from http://www.cnn.com/2008/LIVING/wayoflife/05/09/car.accident/

Hsia, R., Razzak, J., Tsai, A. C., & Hirshon, J. M. (2010). Placing emergency care on the global agenda. *Annals of Emergency Medicine, 56*(2), 142–149. doi:10.1016/j.annemergmed.2010.01.013 PMID:20138398

Huiyi, T. (2007). *A Study on Prehospital Emergency Medical Service System Status in Guangzhou.* Hong Kong: University of Hong Kong.

Hussain, Z. I., & Cornelius, N. (2009). The use of domination and legitimation in information systems implementation. *Information Systems Journal, 19*(2), 197–224. doi:10.1111/j.1365-2575.2008.00322.x

Hwang, J., & Manandhar, S. (2009). Cost-benefit analysis of OPEN system: A case study for Kathmandu Metropolitan City, *International Conference on Computer Sciences and Convergence Information Technology*, 1425-1430. 10.1109/ICCIT.2009.252

Iakovidis, I., Maglavera, S., & Trakatellis, A. (2000). *User Acceptance of Health Telematics Applications: Education and Training in Health Telematics*. IOS Press.

Iglesias, C. (2014). *Promovendo o entendimento de cartas de serviços ao cidadão* [Promoting the understanding of service letters to citizens] (Dissertation). Federal University of the State of Rio de Janeiro.

Imran, M., Castillo, C., Lucas, J., Meier, P., & Vieweg, S. (2014, April). AIDR: Artificial intelligence for disaster response. In *Proceedings of the 23rd International Conference on World Wide Web* (pp. 159-162). ACM.

Irani, Z., Weerakkody, V., Kamal, M., Hindi, N. M., Osman, I. H., Anouze, A. L., ... Al-Ayoubi, B. (2012). An analysis of methodologies utilised in e-government research: A user satisfaction perspective. *Journal of Enterprise Information Management, 25*(3), 298–313. doi:10.1108/17410391211224417

Izvercianu, M., Şeran, S. A., & Branea, A.-M. (2014). Prosumer-oriented Value Co-creation Strategies for Tomorrow's Urban Management. *Procedia: Social and Behavioral Sciences, 124*(0), 149–156. doi:10.1016/j.sbspro.2014.02.471

Jack, L. (2017). Strong structuration theory and management accounting research. *Advances in Scientific and Applied Accounting, 10*(2), 211–223. doi:10.14392/asaa.2017100205

Jack, L., & Kholeif, A. (2008). Enterprise Resource Planning and a contest to limit the role of management accountants: A strong structuration perspective. *Accounting Forum, 32*(1), 30–45. doi:10.1016/j.accfor.2007.11.003

Jackson, S. (2011). *Research Methods and Statistics: A Critical Thinking Approach*. Cengage Learning.

Jaeger, P. T., & Bertot, J. C. (2010). Designing, Implementing, and Evaluating User-centered and Citizen-centered E-government. *International Journal of Electronic Government Research, 6*(2), 1–17. doi:10.4018/jegr.2010040101

Janowski, T., Pardo, T. A., & Davies, J. (2012). Government Information Networks-Mapping Electronic Governance cases through Public Administration concepts. *Government Information Quarterly, 29*, S1-S10.

Janowski, T., Pardo, T. A., & Davies, J. (2012). Government Information Networks-Mapping Electronic Governance cases through Public Administration concepts. *Government Information Quarterly, 29*, S1–S10. doi:10.1016/j.giq.2011.11.003

Janssen, M., & Estevez, E. (2013). Lean government and platform-based governance—Doing more with less. *Government Information Quarterly, 30*, S1–S8. doi:10.1016/j.giq.2012.11.003

Jarvenpaa, S. L., & Lang, K. R. (2005). Managing the Paradoxes of Mobile Technology. *Information Systems Management, 22*(4), 7–23. doi:10.1201/1078.10580530/45520.22.4.20050901/90026.2

Jern, M., Brezzi, M., & Lundblad, P. (2010). Geovisual analytics tools for communicating emergency and early warning. In *Geographic Information and Cartography for Risk and Crisis Management* (pp. 379–394). Berlin: Springer. doi:10.1007/978-3-642-03442-8_26

Jiménez, C. E., Falcone, F., Solanas, A., Puyosa, H., Zoughbi, S., & González, F. (2014). Smart government: Opportunities and challenges in smart cities development. In Ć. Dolićanin, E. Kajan, D. Randjelović, & B. Stojanović (Eds.), *Handbook of research on democratic strategies and citizen-centered e government services* (pp. 1–19). Hershey, PA: IGI Global.

Johannessen, M. R., Sæbø, Ø., & Flak, L. S. (2016). Social media as public sphere : a stakeholder perspective. *Transforming Government: People. Process and Policy, 10*(2), 212–238.

Johannsson, H., Ayida, G., & Sadler, C. (2005). Faking it? Simulation in the training of obstetricians and gynaecologists. *Current Opinion in Obstetrics & Gynecology, 17*(6), 557–561. doi:10.1097/01.gco.0000188726.45998.97 PMID:16258334

John, P. (2001). Policy Networks. *The Blackwell Companion to Political Sociology,* 139-148.

Jones, M. R., & Karsten, H. (2008). Giddens's structuration theory and information systems research. *Management Information Systems Quarterly, 32*(1), 127–157. doi:10.2307/25148831

Jones, M. R., & Karsten, H. (2009). Divided by a common language? A response to Marshall Scott Poole. *Management Information Systems Quarterly, 33*(3), 589–595. doi:10.2307/20650311

Junglas, I. A., & Watson, R. T. (2008). Location-based services. *Communications of the ACM, 51*(3), 65–69. doi:10.1145/1325555.1325568

Kamal, M. M., & Alsudairi, M. (2009). Investigating the importance of factors influencing integration technologies adoption in local government authorities. *Transforming Government: People, Process and Policy, 3*(3), 302–331.

Karavasilis, I., Zafiropoulos, K., & Vrana, V. (2010). Factors affecting the adoption of eGovernance by teachers in Greece. In *Proceedings of the 10th European Conference on e-Government* (pp. 221-229). Reading, UK: Academic Publishing Limited.

Kasper, N., Nabecker, S., Twerenbold, G. A., Gurtner, S., & Greif, R. (2017). Keeping laypersons as first responders engaged: A qualitative, focus group interview study. *Resuscitation, 118,* e10. doi:10.1016/j.resuscitation.2017.08.037

Katzenmeier, C., & Schrag-Slavu, S. (2010). *Einführung. In Rechtsfragen des Einsatzes der Telemedizin im Rettungsdienst* (Vol. 2, pp. 1–22). Springer Berlin Heidelberg. doi:10.1007/978-3-540-85132-5_1

Kazley, A. S., McLeod, A. C., & Wager, K. A. (2012). Telemedicine in an international context: Definition, use, and future. *Advances in Health Care Management, 12,* 143–169. doi:10.1108/S1474-8231(2012)0000012011 PMID:22894049

Khan, A. (2016, February). *Central bank governance and the role of nonfinancial risk management* (International Monetary Fund Working Paper No. 16/34). Retrieved from https://www.imf.org/external/pubs/ft/wp/2016/wp1634.pdf

Khan, G. F., Swar, B., & Lee, S. K. (2014). Social Media Risks and Benefits : A Public Sector Perspective. *Social Science Computer Review*, *32*(5), 606–627. doi:10.1177/0894439314524701

Khatri, S. (2013, December 9). Official: Qatar's population could grow another 15 percent by 2015. *Doha News*.

Khosrowjerdi, M. (2016). Trust in People, Organizations, and Government: A Generic Model. *International Journal of Electronic Government Research*, *12*(3), 55–70. doi:10.4018/IJEGR.2016070104

Klein, H. K., & Myers, M. D. (1999). A Set of Principles for Conducting and Evaluating Interpretive Field Studies in Information Systems. *Management Information Systems Quarterly*, *23*(1), 67–93. doi:10.2307/249410

Klesel, M., Mokosch, G., & Niehaves, B. (2015). Maturing, Flagshipping and Piggybacking: On the Use of Structuration Theory in Information Systems Research. In *Proceedings of the 21st Americas Conference on Information Systems (AMCIS 2015)* (pp. 1-11). Fajardo, Puerto Rico: Association for Information Systems (AIS).

Kowitlawakul, Y. (2011). The technology acceptance model: Predicting nurses' intention to use telemedicine technology (eICU). *Computers, Informatics, Nursing*, *29*(7), 411–418. doi:10.1097/NCN.0b013e3181f9dd4a PMID:20975536

Krafft, T., Garcia Castrillo-Riesgo, L., Edwards, S., Fischer, M., Overton, J., Robertson-Steel, I., & Konig, A. (2003). European Emergency Data Project (EED Project): EMS data-based health surveillance system. *European Journal of Public Health*, *13*(3Suppl), 85–90. doi:10.1093/eurpub/13.suppl_1.85 PMID:14533755

Kryvasheyeu, Y., Chen, H., Moro, E., Van Hentenryck, P., & Cebrian, M. (2015). Performance of social network sensors during Hurricane Sandy. *PLoS One*, *10*(2), e0117288. doi:10.1371/journal.pone.0117288 PMID:25692690

Kupari, P., Skrifvars, M., & Kuisma, M. (2017). External validation of the ROSC after cardiac arrest (RACA) score in a physician staffed emergency medical service system. *Scandinavian Journal of Trauma, Resuscitation and Emergency Medicine*, *25*(1), 34. doi:10.118613049-017-0380-2 PMID:28356134

Kurfalı, M., Arifoğlu, A., Tokdemir, G., & Paçin, Y. (2017). Adoption of e-government services in Turkey. *Computers in Human Behavior*, *66*, 168–178. doi:10.1016/j.chb.2016.09.041

Kvale, S. (1996). *Interviews: an introduction to qualitative research interviewing*. Thousand Oaks, CA: Sage.

Kwan, J., & Ng, Y. Y. (2017). Asking the right questions. *Resuscitation*, *116*, A9–A10. doi:10.1016/j.resuscitation.2017.05.013 PMID:28506864

Kyle, R., & Murray, W. B. (2010). *Clinical Simulation*. Elsevier Science.

Lateef, F. (2006). The emergency medical services in Singapore. *Resuscitation, 68*(3), 323–328. doi:10.1016/j.resuscitation.2005.12.007 PMID:16503277

Latour, B. (2001). *A Esperança de Pandora: ensaios sobre a realidade dos estudos científicos*. Bauro: Edusc.

Latour, B. (2005). *Reassembling the Social: An Introduction to Actor-Network-Theory*. Oxford University Press.

Latour, B., & Woolgar, S. (1986). *Laboratory Life: The Construction of Scientific Facts*. Princeton University Press.

Lean, O. K., Zailani, S., Ramayah, T., & Fernando, Y. (2009). Factors influencing intention to use e-government services among citizens in Malaysia. *International Journal of Information Management, 29*(6), 458–475. doi:10.1016/j.ijinfomgt.2009.03.012

Lee, G., Kwak, Y. H., Gwanhoo, L., & Young Hoon, K. (2012). An Open Government Maturity Model for Social Media-Based Public Engagement. *Government Information Quarterly, 29*(4), 492–503. doi:10.1016/j.giq.2012.06.001

Lee, J., Kim, H. J., & Ahn, M. J. (2011). The willingness of e-Government service adoption by business users: The role of offline service quality and trust in technology. *Government Information Quarterly, 28*(2), 222–230. doi:10.1016/j.giq.2010.07.007

Lee-Kelley, L., & Kolsaker, A. (2004). E-government: the 'fit' between supply assumptions and usage drivers. *Electronic Government, an International Journal, 1*(2), 130–140.

Leidner, D. E., & Kayworth, T. (2006). Review: a review of culture in information systems research: toward a theory of information technology culture conflict. *Management Information Systems Quarterly, 30*(2), 357–399. doi:10.2307/25148735

Leidner, D. E., Pan, G., & Pan, S. L. (2009). The role of IT in crisis response: Lessons from the SARS and Asian Tsunami disasters. *The Journal of Strategic Information Systems, 18*(2), 80–99. doi:10.1016/j.jsis.2009.05.001

Levine, A. I., DeMaria, S., Schwartz, A. D., & Sim, A. J. (2013). *The Comprehensive Textbook of Healthcare Simulation*. Springer. doi:10.1007/978-1-4614-5993-4

Linders, D. (2012). From E-Government to We-Government: Defining a Typology for Citizen Coproduction in the Age of Social Media. *Government Information Quarterly, 29*(4), 446–454. doi:10.1016/j.giq.2012.06.003

Lindsey, B. (2011). Social media and disasters: Current uses, future options, and policy considerations. *Congressional Research Service, 7*(5700), 1–10.

Liu, S., Unsworth, K., Fidel, R., & Scholl, H. J. (2007). Fully mobile wirelessly connected technology applications: Organizational communication, social, and information challenges. *Proceedings of the American Society for Information Science and Technology*. 10.1002/meet.1450440237

Loiacono, E., Watson, R., & Goodhue, D. (2007). WebQual: An Instrument for Consumer Evaluation of Web Sites. *International Journal of Electronic Commerce, 11*(3), 51–87. doi:10.2753/JEC1086-4415110302

Lorincz, K., Malan, D. J., Fulford-Jones, T. R., Nawoj, A., Clavel, A., Shnayder, V., ... Moulton, S. (2004). Sensor networks for emergency response: Challenges and opportunities. *IEEE Pervasive Computing, 3*(4), 16–23. doi:10.1109/MPRV.2004.18

Loukis, E., Xenakis, A., & Tseperli, N. (2009). Using argument visualization to enhance e-participation in the legislation formation process. *International Conference on eParticipation*, 125-138. 10.1007/978-3-642-03781-8_12

Luiz, T., Dittrich, S., Pollach, G., & Madler, C. (2017). Kenntnisstand der Bevölkerung über Leitsymptome kardiovaskulärer Notfälle und Zuständigkeit und Erreichbarkeit von Notrufeinrichtungen. *Der Anaesthesist, 66*(11), 840–849. doi:10.100700101-017-0367-4 PMID:29046934

Luna-Reyes, L. F., Gil-Garcia, J. R., & Romero, G. (2012). Towards a multidimensional model for evaluating electronic government: Proposing a more comprehensive and integrative perspective. *Government Information Quarterly, 29*(3), 324–334. doi:10.1016/j.giq.2012.03.001

Lüscher, L. S., & Lewis, M. W. (2008). Organizational Change and Managerial Sensemaking: Working Through Paradox. *Academy of Management Journal, 2*(2), 221–240. doi:10.5465/AMJ.2008.31767217

Luscher, L. S., Lewis, M., & Ingram, A. (2006). The Social Construction of Organizational Change Paradoxes. *Journal of Organizational Change Management, 19*(4), 491–502. doi:10.1108/09534810610676680

Mahmood, M. (2016). Enhancing Citizens' Trust and Confidence in Government through Digital Transformation. *International Journal of Electronic Government Research, 12*(1), 99–110. doi:10.4018/IJEGR.2016010105

Manoj, B. S., & Baker, A. H. (2007). Communication challenges in emergency response. *Communications of the ACM, 50*(3), 51–53. doi:10.1145/1226736.1226765

Mansour, A. M. (2012). E-Government in the Gulf Cooperation Council Countries: A Comparative Study. *Journal of the Social Sciences, 40*(1), 2102.

March, J. G. (1991). Exploration and exploitation in organizational learning. *Organization Science, 2*(1), 71–87. doi:10.1287/orsc.2.1.71

March, S. T., & Smith, G. F. (1995). Design and natural science research on information technology. *Decision Support Systems, 15*(4), 251–266. doi:10.1016/0167-9236(94)00041-2

Markus, M. L., Majchrzak, A., & Gasser, L. (2002). A design theory for systems that support emergent knowledge processes. *Management Information Systems Quarterly, 26*(3), 179–212.

Martins, L. (2015). *Ambiente de discussões sobre normas jurídicas nos processos de negócio da administração pública* [Environment for discussions about legal norms in business processes of public administration] (Dissertation). Federal University of the State of Rio de Janeiro.

Masterson, S., Wright, P., O'Donnell, C., Vellinga, A., Murphy, A. W., Hennelly, D., ... Deasy, C. (2015). Urban and rural differences in out-of-hospital cardiac arrest in Ireland. *Resuscitation, 91*, 42–47. doi:10.1016/j.resuscitation.2015.03.012 PMID:25818707

McGovern, A., Elmore, K. L., Gagne, D. J. II, Haupt, S. E., Karstens, C. D., Lagerquist, R., ... Williams, J. K. (2017). Using Artificial Intelligence to Improve Real-Time Decision-Making for High-Impact Weather. *Bulletin of the American Meteorological Society, 98*(10), 2073–2090. doi:10.1175/BAMS-D-16-0123.1

McKelvey, B. (2009). Organisation Studies: Discipline or Field. In R. Westwood & S. Clegg (Eds.), Debating Organization: Point Counter-point in Organisation Studies (pp. 47–66). Blackwell Publishing Ltd.

McNeal, R., Hale, K., & Dotterweich, L. (2008). Citizen–government interaction and the Internet: Expectations and accomplishments in contact, quality, and trust. *Journal of Information Technology & Politics, 5*(2), 213–229. doi:10.1080/19331680802298298

Medaglia, R., & Zheng, L. (2017). Mapping government social media research and moving it forward : A framework and a research agenda. *Government Information Quarterly, 34*(3), 496–510. doi:10.1016/j.giq.2017.06.001

Medina, C., & Rufin, R. (2015). Social Media Use and Perception of Transparency in the Generation of Trust in Public Services. *Hawaii International Conference on System Sciences.* 10.1109/HICSS.2015.290

Meijer, A. J., & Torenvlied, R. (2016). Social Media and the New Organization of Government Communications : An Empirical Analysis of Twitter Usage by the Dutch Police. *American Review of Public Administration, 46*(2), 143–161. doi:10.1177/0275074014551381

Meijer, A., & Bekkers, V. (2015). A metatheory of e-government : Creating some order in a fragmented research fi eld. *Government Information Quarterly, 32*(3), 237–245. doi:10.1016/j.giq.2015.04.006

Mergel, I. (2016). Social media institutionalization in the U. S. federal government. *Government Information Quarterly, 33*(1), 142–148. doi:10.1016/j.giq.2015.09.002

Metelmann, B., & Metelmann, C. (2016). M-Health in Prehospital Emergency Medicine: Experiences from the EU funded Project LiveCity. In M. Anastasius (Ed.), *M-Health Innovations for Patient-Centered Care* (pp. 197–212). Hershey, PA: IGI Global. doi:10.4018/978-1-4666-9861-1.ch010

Miah, S., Gammack, J., & Greenfield, G. (2009). An infrastructure for implementing e-participation services in developing countries. *IEEE International Conference on Digital Ecosystems and Technologies*, 407-411. 10.1109/DEST.2009.5276686

Mishler, W., & Rose, R. (2005). What are the political consequences of trust? A test of cultural and institutional theories in Russia. *Comparative Political Studies*, *38*(9), 1050–1078. doi:10.1177/0010414005278419

Mohammed, F., Ibrahim, O., & Ithnin, N. (2016). Factors influencing cloud computing adoption for e-government implementation in developing countries: Instrument development. *Journal of Systems and Information Technology*, *18*(3), 297–327. doi:10.1108/JSIT-01-2016-0001

Molnar, A., Janssen, M., & Weerakkody, V. (2015, May). E-government theories and challenges: findings from a plenary expert panel. In *Proceedings of the 16th Annual International Conference on Digital Government Research* (pp. 160-166). ACM. 10.1145/2757401.2757419

Moody, D., Iacob, M., & Amrit, C. (2010). In Search of Paradigms: Identifying the Theoretical Foundations of the IS Field. *Ecis*, (2010), 15. Retrieved from http://aisel.aisnet.org/ecis2010/43/

Moon, M. J. (2003). Can IT help government to restore public trust? Declining public trust and potential prospects of IT in the public sector. *Proceedings of the 36th Hawaii International Conference on System Sciences*. 10.1109/HICSS.2003.1174303

Moreno, A., Garrison, P., & Bhat, K. (2017). WhatsApp for monitoring and response during critical events: Aggie in the Ghana 2016 election. *Proceedings of the 14th ISCRAM Conference*.

Morgeson, F. V. III, VanAmburg, D., & Mithas, S. (2011). Misplaced trust? Exploring the structure of the e-government-citizen trust relationship. *Journal of Public Administration: Research and Theory*, *21*(2), 257–283. doi:10.1093/jopart/muq006

Mossberger, K. (2013). Connecting Citizens and Local governments? Social Media and Interactivity in Major U.S. Cities. *Government Information Quarterly*.

Mossberger, K., Wu, Y., & Crawford, J. (2013). Connecting citizens and local governments? Social media and interactivity in major U. S. cities ☆. *Government Information Quarterly*, *30*(4), 351–358. doi:10.1016/j.giq.2013.05.016

Moss, G., Kennedy, H., Moshonas, S., & Birchall, C. (2015). Knowing your publics : The use of social media analytics in local government. *Information Policy*, *20*(4), 287–298. doi:10.3233/IP-150376

Mungiu-Pippidi, A., Dadašov, R., Fazekas, M., Tóth, I. J., Kocsis, G., Jancsis, D., Kortas, A.-M., … Skolkay, A. (2015, January 1). *Public Integrity and Trust in Europe*. Retrieved from https://www.government.nl/documents/reports/2016/01/18/public-integrity-and-trust-in-europe

Myers, M. (1997). *Qualitative research in information systems*. MIS Quarterly Discovery.

Myers, M. (2009). Qualitative Research in Business and Management. *Sage (Atlanta, Ga.)*.

Myers, M. D., & Newman, M. (2007). The qualitative interview in IS research: Examining the craft. *Information and Organization, 17*(1), 2–26.

Naikar, N. (2017). Cognitive work analysis: An influential legacy extending beyond human factors and engineering. *Applied Ergonomics, 59*(Part B), 528-540. doi:10.1016/j.apergo.2016.06.001

Naikar, N., & Elix, B. (2016). Reflections on Cognitive Work Analysis and Its Capacity to Support Designing for Adaptation. *Journal of Cognitive Engineering and Decision Making, 10*(2), 123–125. doi:10.1177/1555343416654846

Nam, T. (2012). Citizens' attitudes toward Open Government and Government 2.0. *International Review of Administrative Sciences, 78*(2), 346–368. doi:10.1177/0020852312438783

Naor, M., & Bernardes, E. S., & Coman, A. (2012). Theory of constraints: is it a theory and a good one? *International Journal of Production Research, 51*, 1–13. doi:10.1080/00207543.2011.654137

Nehme, Z., Andrew, E., Bernard, S., & Smith, K. (2014). The impact of partial resuscitation attempts on the reported outcomes of out-of-hospital cardiac arrest in Victoria, Australia: Implications for Utstein-style outcome reports. *Resuscitation, 85*(9), 1185–1191. doi:10.1016/j.resuscitation.2014.05.032 PMID:24914831

NENA. (2014). *911 Statistics*. Retrieved September 27, 2014, from https://www.nena.org/?page=911Statistics

Neuman, W. L. (2006). *Social Research Methods. Qualitative and Quantitative Approaches.* Pearson.

Newcombe, T. (2002, November). Mobile mapping, Report. *Government Technology*. Retrieved from http://www.govtech.net/magazine/sup_story.php?id=29377&story_pg=3

Niehaves, B., & Malsch, R. (2009). Democratizing Process Innovation? On Citizen Involvement in Public Sector BPM. *IFIP Conference on Electronic Government* (LNCS 5693, pp. 245-256). Springer-Verlag Berlin Heidelberg.

Nielsen, K., Mock, C., Joshipura, M., Rubiano, A. M., Zakariah, A., & Rivara, F. (2012). Assessment of the Status of Prehospital Care in 13 Low- and Middle-Income Countries. *Prehospital Emergency Care, 16*(3), 381–389. doi:10.3109/10903127.2012.664245 PMID:22490009

Nilsen, J. E. (2012). *Improving quality of care in the Emergency Medical Communication Centres (EMCC).* Paper presented at the Konferanse for medisinsk nødmeldetjeneste, Sola, Norway.

Niskanen, T. (2017). Implementation of a novel taxonomy based on cognitive work analysis in the assessment of safety performance. *International Journal of Occupational Safety and Ergonomics*. (accepted)

Noveck, B. S. (2009). *Wiki Government: How Technology Can Make Government Better, Democracy Stronger, and Citizens More Powerful.* Brookings Institution Press.

Nunes, A. A., Galvão, T., & Cunha, J. F. e. (2014). Urban Public Transport Service Co-creation: Leveraging Passenger's Knowledge to Enhance Travel Experience. *Procedia: Social and Behavioral Sciences*, *111*(0), 577–585. doi:10.1016/j.sbspro.2014.01.091

O'Neill, R. (2009). The transformative impact of e-government on public governance in New Zealand. *Public Management Review*, *11*(6), 751–770. doi:10.1080/14719030903318939

O'Reilly, T. (2009). *What is Web 2.0: Design Patterns and Business Models for the Next Generation of Software. Communications & Strategies, (1), 17* .

Oates, B. (2011). Evidence-based information systems: A decade later. *ECIS 2011 Proceedings*. Retrieved from http://aisel.aisnet.org/ecis2011/222

Oates, S. (2008). *Introduction to media and politics*. London: Sage Publications.

OECD. (2001). *Citizens as partners, Handbook on information, consultation and public participation in policy-making*. Paris: OECD Publications.

OECD. (2001). *Engaging Citizens in Policy-making: Information*. Consultation and Public Participation.

Office for National Statistics. (2012). *London 2012 Olympic & Paralympic Games attracted 680,000 overseas visitors*. Retrieved September 27, 2014, from http://www.ons.gov.uk/ons/dcp29904_287477.pdf

Okoli, C., & Schabram, K. (2010). A guide to conducting a systematic literature review of information systems research. *Sprouts: Working Papers on Information Systems, 10*(26). Retrieved from http://sprouts.aisnet.org/10-26

Oktoberfest. (2013). *The Oktoberfest 2013 roundup*. Retrieved September 27, 2014, from http://www.oktoberfest.de/en/article/About+the+Oktoberfest/About+the+Oktoberfest/The+Oktoberfest+2013+roundup/3734/

Oliveira, A. C., Araujo, R. M., & Borges, M. R. S. (2007) Telling Stories about System Use: Capturing Collective Tacit Knowledge for System Maintenance. *International Conference on Software Engineering and Knowledge Engineering*, 337-342.

Omar, A., Weerakkody, V., & El-Haddadeh, R. (2014). The Institutional And Structuration Dimensions Of Ict Enabled Public Sector Transformation: A Systematic Literature Review. *European, Mediterranean & Middle Eastern Conference on Information Systems*.

Omar, A., & El-Haddadeh, R. (2016). Structuring Institutionalization of Digitally-Enabled Service Transformation in Public Sector : Does Actor or Structure Matters? Full paper. *Twenty-second Americas Conference on Information Systems*, 1–7.

Omar, A., El-Haddadeh, R., & Weerakkody, V. (2016). Exploring Digitally Enabled Service Transformation in the Public Sector. *Would Institutional and Structuration Theory Concepts Keep the Research Talking*, *12*(4), 1–18. doi:10.4018/IJEGR.2016100101

Omar, A., & Osmani, M. (2015a). Digitally Enabled Service Transformations in Public Sector. *International Journal of Electronic Government Research*, *11*(3), 76–94. doi:10.4018/IJEGR.2015070105

Omar, A., Weerakkody, V., & Sivarajah, U. (2017). Digitally enabled service transformation in UK public sector: A case analysis of universal credit. *International Journal of Information Management*, *37*(4), 350–356. doi:10.1016/j.ijinfomgt.2017.04.001

OMG. (2011). *Object Management Group Business Process Model Notation*. Retrieved from http://www.bpmn.org

Orlikowski, W. (1991). Integrated Information Environment or Matrix of Control? The Contradictory Implications of Information technology. *Accounting Management and Information Technologies*.

Orlikowski, W. J. (1992). The duality of technology: Rethinking the concept of technology in organizations. *Organization Science*, *3*(3), 398–427. doi:10.1287/orsc.3.3.398

Orlikowski, W. J., & Robey, D. (1991). Information technology and the structuring of organizations. *Information Systems Research*, *2*(2), 143–169. doi:10.1287/isre.2.2.143

Osher, C. N. (2013). Operator error: how emergency calls are managed by dispatchers can be problematic. *The Denver Post*. Retrieved September 27, 2014, from http://www.denverpost.com/ci_22500950/denvers-911-call-performance-audits-reveal-problems

Osman, I. H., Anouze, A. L., Hindi, N. M., Irani, Z., Lee, H., & Weerakkody, V. (2014). I-meet framework for the evaluation e-government services from engaging stakeholders' perspectives. European Scientific Journal, 10(10), 1-17.

Osman, I. H., Anouze, A. L., Irani, Z., Al-Ayoubi, B., Lee, H., Balcı, A., ... Weerakkody, V. (2014). COBRA framework to evaluate e-government services: A citizen-centric perspective. *Government Information Quarterly*, *31*(2), 243–256. doi:10.1016/j.giq.2013.10.009

Osman, I., Anouze, A., Irani, Z., Lee, H., Balcı, A., Medeni, T., & Weerakkody, V. (2011). A new COBRAS framework to evaluate e-government services: a citizen centric perspective. Presented at the *T-Government Workshop*.

Outhwaite, W. (1987). *New Philosophies of Social Science: Realism, Hermeneutics, and Critical Theory* (A. Giddens, Ed.). Macmillan Education Ltd. doi:10.1007/978-1-349-18946-5

Palace of the City. (n.d.). *Prefeitura Do Rio De Janeiro*. Retrieved from http://www.rio.rj.gov.br/web/relacoesinternacionais/contato

Palma, D., Goncalves, J., Cordeiro, L., Simoes, P., Monteiro, E., Magdalinos, P., & Chochliouros, I. (2013). Tutamen: An Integrated Personal Mobile and Adaptable Video Platform for Health and Protection. In H. Papadopoulos, A. Andreou, L. Iliadis, & I. Maglogiannis (Eds.), *Artificial Intelligence Applications and Innovations* (Vol. 412, pp. 442–451). Springer Berlin Heidelberg. doi:10.1007/978-3-642-41142-7_45

Palumbo, L., Kubincanek, J., Emerman, C., Jouriles, N., Cydulka, R., & Shade, B. (1996). Performance of a system to determine EMS dispatch priorities. *The American Journal of Emergency Medicine*, *14*(4), 388–390. doi:10.1016/S0735-6757(96)90056-X PMID:8768162

Paramewaran, M., & Whinston, A. (2007). Research issues in social computing. *Journal of the Association for Information Systems*, *8*(6), 336–350. doi:10.17705/1jais.00132

Parasuraman, A., Zeithaml, V. A., & Berry, L. L. (1985). A Conceptual Model of Service Quality and Its Implications for Future Research. *Journal of Marketing*, *49*(4), 41–50. doi:10.2307/1251430

Parasuraman, A., Zeithaml, V. A., & Malhotra, A. (2005). E-S-QUAL A Multiple-Item Scale for Assessing Electronic Service Quality. *Journal of Service Research*, *7*(3), 213–233. doi:10.1177/1094670504271156

Parker, J. (2006). Structuration's Future? From 'All and Every'to 'Who Did What, Where, When, How and Why?'. *Journal of Critical Realism*, *5*(1), 122–138.

Pepper, W., Aiken, M., & Garner, B. (2011). Usefulness and usability of a multilingual electronic meeting system. *Global Journal of Computer Science and Technology*, *11*(5), 34–40.

Pew Research Center. (2018). *Mobile Fact Sheet*. Retrieved March 13, 2018 from: http://www.pewinternet.org/fact-sheet/mobile/

Pflanz, N., Classe, T., Araujo, R., & Vossen, G. (2016). Designing Serious Games for Citizen Engagement in Public Service Processes. *Workshop on Social and Human Aspects of Business Process Management*.

Pina, V., Torres, L., & Royo, S. (2009). E-government evolution in EU local governments: A comparative perspective. *Online Information Review*, *33*(6), 1137–1168. doi:10.1108/14684520911011052

Polanyi, M. (1966). The tacit dimension (1st ed.). Garden City, NY: Doubleday.

Polanyi, M., & Grene, M. G. (1969). *Knowing and being; essays*. University of Chicago Press.

Poole, M. S. (2009). Response to Jones and Karsten, "Giddens's Structuration Theory and Information Systems Research. *Management Information Systems Quarterly*, *33*(3), 583–587. doi:10.2307/20650310

Poole, M. S., & van de Ven, A. H. (1989). Using Paradox to Build Management and Organization Theories. *Academy of Management Review*, *14*(4), 562–578.

Portal 1746. (n.d.). *Ligue 1746*. Retrieved from http://www.1746.rio.gov.br

Portal e-Cidadania. (n.d.). *ecidadania*. Retrieved from https://www12.senado.leg.br/ecidadania

Portal e-Democracia. (n.d.). *Camera dos Deputados*. Retrieved from http://edemocracia.camara.gov.br

Portal of Transparency. (n.d.). *Portal da Transparencia*. Retrieved from http://www. portaltransparencia.gov.br

Porwol, L., Ojo, A., & Breslin, J. G. (2016). An ontology for next generation e-Participation initiatives. *Government Information Quarterly, 33*(3), 583–594. doi:10.1016/j.giq.2016.01.007

Pozzebon, M., & Pinsonneault, A. (2005). Challenges in conducting empirical work using structuration theory: Learning from IT research. *Organization Studies, 26*(9), 1353–1376. doi:10.1177/0170840605054621

Prusty, A. R., & Mohanty, A. (2018). Prospect of Low Power Sensor Network Technology in Disaster Management for Sustainable Future. In *Handbook of Research on Environmental Policies for Emergency Management and Public Safety* (pp. 123–145). IGI Global. doi:10.4018/978-1-5225-3194-4.ch007

Puron-Cid, G. (2013). Interdisciplinary application of structuration theory for e-government: A case study of an IT-enabled budget reform. *Government Information Quarterly, 30*(Supplement 1), S46–S58. doi:10.1016/j.giq.2012.07.010

Qaisar, N., & Khan, H. (2010). E-government challenges in public sector: A case study of Pakistan. *International Journal of Computer Science Issues, 7*(5), 310–317. Retrieved from http://www. ijcsi.org/papers/7-5-310-317.pdf

Quinn, R. E., & Cameron, K. S. (1988). *Paradox transformation: Toward a theory of change in organization and management*. Cambridge: Ballinger.

Rana, N. P., Dwivedi, Y. K., Williams, M. D., & Weerakkody, V. (2015). Investigating success of an e-government initiative: Validation of an integrated IS success model. *Information Systems Frontiers, 17*(1), 127–142. doi:10.100710796-014-9504-7

Rasmussen, J., Pejtersen, A. M., & Schmidt, K. (1990). *Taxonomy for Cognitive Work Analysis*. Retrieved from http://www.itu.dk/~schmidt/papers/taxonomy.pdf

Rasmussen, J. (1986). *Information processing and human-machine interaction: an approach to cognitive engineering*. New York: North-Holland.

Rasmussen, J., Pejtersen, A. M., & Goodstein, L. P. (1994). *Cognitive systems engineering*. New York: Wiley.

Razzak, J. A., & Kellermann, A. L. (2002). Emergency medical care in developing countries: Is it worthwhile? *Bulletin of the World Health Organization, 80*(11), 900–905. PMID:12481213

Read, G. J. M., Salmon, P. M., & Lenné, M. G. (2012). From work analysis to work design: A review of cognitive work analysis design applications In *Proceedings of the human factors and ergonomics society annual meeting* (1st ed.; Vol. 56, pp. 368-372). Los Angeles, CA: SAGE Publications. 10.1177/1071181312561084

Read, G. J. M., Salmon, P. M., Lenné, M. G., & Stanton, N. A. (2015). Designing sociotechnical systems with cognitive work analysis: Putting theory back into practice. *Ergonomics*, *58*(5), 822–851. doi:10.1080/00140139.2014.980335 PMID:25407778

Reeves, S., Albert, M., Kuper, A., & Hodges, B. D. (2008). Why use theories in qualitative research? *BMJ (Clinical Research Ed.)*, *337*(September), a949. doi:10.1136/bmj.a949 PMID:18687730

Reuter, C., Ludwig, T., Kaufhold, M. A., & Hupertz, J. (2017). Social Media Resilience during Infrastructure Breakdowns using Mobile Ad-Hoc Networks. Advances and New Trends in Environmental Informatics, 75-88. doi:10.1007/978-3-319-44711-7_7

Reuver, M., Stein, S., Hampe, F., & Bouwman, H. (2010). Towards a service platform and business model for mobile participation. *International Conference on Mobile Business*, 305-311. 10.1109/ICMB-GMR.2010.57

Rhodes, R. A. (1986). *European Policy-Making, Implementation and Subcentral Governments: A Survey*. European Institute of Public Administration Maastricht.

Rho, M. J., Choi, I. Y., & Lee, J. (2014). Predictive factors of telemedicine service acceptance and behavioral intention of physicians. *International Journal of Medical Informatics*, *83*(8), 559–571. doi:10.1016/j.ijmedinf.2014.05.005 PMID:24961820

Richardson, H., & Robinson, B. (2007). The mysterious case of the missing paradigm: A review of critical information systems research 1991-2001. *Information Systems Journal*, *17*(3), 251–270. doi:10.1111/j.1365-2575.2007.00230.x

Rio, I. T. S. (n.d.). *Plataforma Brasil*. Retrieved from http://plataformabrasil.org.br/?/

Ritchie, J., Lewis, J., & Gillian, E. (2003). Designing and selecting samples. In J. Ritchie & J. Lewis (Eds.), *Qualitative research practice: a guide for social science students and researchers* (pp. 77–108). London: Sage Publications.

Robey, D., & Abdalla Mikhaeil, C. (2016). Déjà Vu or Art Nouveau? A comment on Demetis and Lee's "Crafting theory to satisfy the requirements of systems science". *Information and Organization*, *26*(4), 127–130. doi:10.1016/j.infoandorg.2016.10.001

Robey, D., & Boudreau, M.-C. (1999). Accounting for the Contradictory Organizational Consequences of Information Technology: Theoretical Directions and Methodological Implications. *Information Systems Research*, *10*(2), 167–185. doi:10.1287/isre.10.2.167

Rød, E. G., & Weidmann, N. B. (2015). Empowering activists or autocrats? The Internet in authoritarian regimes. *Journal of Peace Research*, *52*(3), 338–351. doi:10.1177/0022343314555782

Roessler, M., & Zuzan, O. (2006). EMS systems in Germany. *Resuscitation*, *68*(1), 45–49. doi:10.1016/j.resuscitation.2005.08.004 PMID:16401522

Rogers, E. (2003). Diffusion of Innovations (5th ed.). New York: The Free Press.

Rogers, H., Madathil, K. C., Agnisarman, S., Narasimha, S., Ashok, A., Nair, A., ... McElligott, J. T. (2017). A Systematic Review of the Implementation Challenges of Telemedicine Systems in Ambulances. *Telemedicine Journal and e-Health, 23*(9), 707–717. doi:10.1089/tmj.2016.0248 PMID:28294704

Rogers-Hayden, T., & Pidgeon, N. (2008). Developments in nanotechnology public engagement in the UK: 'upstream' towards sustainability? *Journal of Cleaner Production, 16*(8–9), 1010–1013. doi:10.1016/j.jclepro.2007.04.013

Roman, A., & Miller, H. (2013). New Questions for E-Government: Efficiency but not (yet?) Democracy. *International Journal of Electronic Government Research, 9*(1), 65–81. doi:10.4018/jegr.2013010104

Roudsari, B., Nathens, A., Cameron, P., Civil, I., Gruen, R., Koepsell, T., ... Rivara, F. (2007). International comparison of prehospital trauma care systems. *Injury, 38*(9), 993–1000. doi:10.1016/j.injury.2007.03.028 PMID:17640641

Rousseau, L. (2008). The essential principles of graphic design. In Color (pp. 14-16). F+W Publications.

Sabnis, D., & Glick, R. L. (2012). Innovative community-based crisis and emergency services. In *Handbook of Community Psychiatry* (pp. 379–387). Springer New York. doi:10.1007/978-1-4614-3149-7_31

Sajjad, F., Lee, H., Kamal, M., & Irani, Z. (2011). Workflow technology as an e-participation tool to support policy-making processes. *Journal of Enterprise Information Management, 2*(24), 197–212. doi:10.1108/17410391111106301

Santos, H. R. (2015). E-democracy and sociopolitical digital interactions: analysing co-creation in public sector innovation (Mestrado em Administração Pública). Universidade Federal de Lavras, Brazil.

Santos, H.R., Tonelli, D.F., & Bermejo, P.H. (2014) Sociopolitical digital interactions' maturity: analyzing the brazilian states. *Int. J. Electr. Gov. Res., 10*(4), 76–93. doi:10.4018/ijegr.2014100104

Sarshar, P., Nunavath, V., & Radianti, J. (2015). On the Usability of Smartphone Apps in Emergencies. An HCI Analysis of GDACSmobile and SmartRescue Apps. In M. Kurosu (Ed.), Human-Computer Interaction, Part II (LNCS 9170, pp. 765–774). Springer. doi:10.1007/978-3-319-20916-6_70

Sasser, S., Varghese, M., Kellermann, A., & Lormand, J. D. (2005). *Prehospital trauma care systems.* Geneva: World Health Organization.

Saxena, S., & Sharma, S.K. (2016). Integrating Big Data in "e-Oman": Opportunities and challenges. *Info, 18*(5), 79-97.

Sayed, A. H., Tarighat, A., & Khajehnouri, N. (2005). Network-based wireless location: Challenges faced in developing techniques for accurate wireless location information. *IEEE Signal Processing Magazine, 22*(4), 24–40. doi:10.1109/MSP.2005.1458275

Schleicher, R., Westermann, T., & Reichmuth, R. (2014). *Mobile Human Computer–Interaction Quality of Experience*. Heidelberg, Germany: Springer.

Schmiedel, R., & Behrendt, H. (2011). *Leistungen des Rettungsdienstes 2008/09*. Bonn: Dr. Schmiedel GmbH.

Scholl, H. J., Fidel, R., Liu, S., Paulsmeyer, M., & Unsworth, K. (2007). E-Gov Field Force Automation: Promises, Challenges, and Stakeholders. In M. Wimmer, H. J. Scholl, & A. Groenlund (Eds.), *Electronic Government: Sixth International Conference, EGOV 2007* (Vol. 4656, pp. 127-142). Regensburg, Germany: Springer Verlag.

Scholl, H. J., Liu, S., Fidel, R., & Unsworth, K. (2007). *Choices and Challenges in e-Government Field Force Automation Projects: Insights from Case Studies*. Paper presented at the ICEGOV, Macao, China. 10.1145/1328057.1328142

Scholl, H. J. (2005a). E-government-induced business process change (BPC): An empirical study of current practices. *International Journal of Electronic Government Research, 1*(2), 25–47. doi:10.4018/jegr.2005040102

Scholl, H. J. (2005b). Motives, strategic approach, objectives & focal areas in e-Gov-induced change. *International Journal of Electronic Government Research, 1*(1), 58–77. doi:10.4018/jegr.2005010104

Scholl, H. J. J., & Dwivedi, Y. K. (2014). Forums for electronic government scholars: Insights from a 2012/2013 study. *Government Information Quarterly, 31*(2), 229–242. doi:10.1016/j.giq.2013.10.008

Scholl, H. J., Fidel, R., Mai, J.-E., & Unsworth, K. (2006). Seattle's Mobile City Project. *Proceedings of Euro mGov 2006: The Second European Conference on Mobile Government*.

Schreiber, J. B., Nora, A., Stage, F. K., Barlow, E. A., & King, J. (2006). Reporting structural equation modeling and confirmatory factor analysis results: A review. *The Journal of Educational Research, 99*(6), 323–338. doi:10.3200/JOER.99.6.323-338

Schroeder, B. L., Whitmer, D. E., & Sims, V. K. (2017). Toward a User-Centered Approach for Emergency Warning Distribution. *Ergonomics in Design, 25*(1), 4–10. doi:10.1177/1064804616662420

Schwamm, L. H., Holloway, R. G., Amarenco, P., Audebert, H. J., Bakas, T., Chumbler, N. R., ... Wechsler, L. R. (2009). A review of the evidence for the use of telemedicine within stroke systems of care: A scientific statement from the American Heart Association/American Stroke Association. *Stroke, 40*(7), 2616–2634. doi:10.1161/STROKEAHA.109.192360 PMID:19423852

Scott, R. L. (2000). Evaluation of a mobile crisis program: Effectiveness, efficiency, and consumer satisfaction. *Psychiatric Services (Washington, D.C.), 51*(9), 1153–1156. doi:10.1176/appi.ps.51.9.1153 PMID:10970919

Sebillo, M., Vitiello, G., Paolino, L., & Ginige, A. (2016). Training emergency responders through augmented reality mobile interfaces. *Multimedia Tools and Applications, 75*(16), 9609–9622. doi:10.100711042-015-2955-0

Sell, M. (2016). *Regra clara: Uma proposta de design de artefato para compreensão de regras de negócios em processos de prestação de serviços públicos* [Regra Clara: An artifact design proposal for understanding business rules in public services] (Dissertation). Federal University of the State of Rio de Janeiro.

Selvi, M. S. (2016). Attitudes of University Students Voters Towards Political Messages in Social Media. *International Journal of Electronic Government Research, 12*(4), 67–89. doi:10.4018/IJEGR.2016100105

Seng, W. M. (2013). E-Government Evaluation: An Assessment Approach Using ROI vs. ROR Matrix. *International Journal of Electronic Government Research, 9*(1), 82–96. doi:10.4018/jegr.2013010105

Shah, S., Bao, F., Lu, C. T., & Chen, I. R. (2011). Crowdsafe: crowd sourcing of crime incidents and safe routing on mobile devices. In *Proceedings of the 19th ACM SIGSPATIAL International Conference on Advances in Geographic Information Systems* (pp. 521-524). ACM. 10.1145/2093973.2094064

Sharma, S. K., Al-Shihi, H., & Govindaluri, S. M. (2013). Exploring quality of e-Government services in Oman. *Education, Business and Society, 6*(2), 87–100. doi:10.1108/EBS-12-2012-0055

Sharma, S., & Gupta, J. (2003). Building blocks of an e-government: A framework. *Journal of Electronic Commerce in Organizations, 1*(4), 34–48. doi:10.4018/jeco.2003100103

Shirky, C. (2008). *Here comes everybody: The power of organizing without organization.* The Penguin Press.

Shostack, G. L. (1982). How to Design a Service. *European Journal of Marketing, 16*(1), 49–63. doi:10.1108/EUM0000000004799

Silva, L. (2007). Epistemological and theoretical challenges for studying power and politics in information systems. *Information Systems Journal, 17*(2), 165–183. doi:10.1111/j.1365-2575.2007.00232.x

Singapore. Government. (2013). *e-Gov2015 Masterplan (2011-2015). Vision & Strategic.* Available: http://www.egov.gov.sg/egov-masterplans-introduction;jsessionid=542A47297AB7144B00189EF45E04FA67

Sivarajah, U., Irani, Z., & Weerakkody, V. (2015). Evaluating the use and impact of Web 2.0 technologies in local government. *Government Information Quarterly, 32*(4), 473–487. doi:10.1016/j.giq.2015.06.004

Smith, L. (2017). Hajj 2017: Two million Muslim pilgrims from all over the world head to Mecca. *The Independent.* Retrieved March 13, 2018 from: http://www.independent.co.uk/news/world/middle-east/hajj-2017-muslim-pilgrimage-mecca-islam-pilgrims-saudi-arabia-a7917851.html

Smith, W. K., & Lewis, M. W. (2011). Toward a Theory of Paradox: A Dynamic Equilibrium Model of Organizing. *Academy of Management Review, 36*(2), 381–403.

Snooks, H., Williams, S., Crouch, R., Foster, T., Hartley-Sharpe, C., & Dale, J. (2002). NHS emergency response to 999 calls: Alternatives for cases that are neither life threatening nor serious, *BMJ. British Medical Journal, 325*(7359), 330–333. doi:10.1136/bmj.325.7359.330 PMID:12169513

Sood, S., Mbarika, V., Jugoo, S., Dookhy, R., Doarn, C. R., Prakash, N., & Merrell, R. C. (2007). What is telemedicine? A collection of 104 peer-reviewed perspectives and theoretical underpinnings. *Telemedicine Journal and e-Health, 13*(5), 573–590. doi:10.1089/tmj.2006.0073 PMID:17999619

Soroka, S. N. (2007). Canadian perceptions of the health care system. Toronto: Academic Press.

Stones, R. (2005). *Structuration theory*. Wiley Online Library. doi:10.1007/978-0-230-21364-7

Strauss, A. L., & Corbin, J. M. (1998). *Basics of qualitative research: techniques and procedures for developing grounded theory* (2nd ed.). Thousand Oaks, CA: Sage Publications.

Sundaramurthy, C., & Lewis, M. (2003). Control and Collaboration: Paradoxes of Governance. *Academy of Management Review, 28*(3), 397–415.

Sunstein, C. (2006). *Infotopia: How Many Minds Produce Knowledge*. New York: Oxford University Press.

Suri, M., & Hofierka, J. (2004). A new GIS-based solar radiation model and its application to photovoltaic assessments. *Transactions in GIS, 8*(2), 175–190. doi:10.1111/j.1467-9671.2004.00174.x

Suryanto, P., Plummer, V., & Boyle, M. (2017). EMS Systems in Lower-Middle Income Countries: A Literature Review. *Prehospital and Disaster Medicine, 32*(1), 64–70. doi:10.1017/S1049023X1600114X PMID:27938449

Sutton, J., Palen, L., & Shklovski, I. (2008). Backchannels on the front lines: emergent uses of social media in the 2007 southern California wildfires. *Proceedings of the 5th International ISCRAM Conference*, 624-632.

Szkuta, K., Pizzicannella, R., & Osimo, D. (2014). Collaborative approaches to public sector innovation: A scoping study. *Telecommunications Policy, 38*(5–6), 558–567. doi:10.1016/j.telpol.2014.04.002

Tapia, A. H., Giacobe, N. A., Soule, P. J., & LaLone, N. J. (2016). Scaling 911 texting for large-scale disasters: Developing practical technical innocations for emergency management at public universities. *International Journal of Public Administration in the Digital Age, 3*(3), 73–85. doi:10.4018/IJPADA.2016070105

Tarhini, A., Teo, T., & Tarhini, T. (2015). A cross-cultural validity of the E-learning Acceptance Measure (ElAM) in Lebanon and England: A Confirmatory Factor Analysis. *Education and Information Technologies*, 1–14.

Tashakkori, H., Rajabifard, A., & Kalantari, M. (2015). A new 3D indoor/outdoor spatial model for indoor emergency response facilitation. *Building and Environment*, *89*, 170–182. doi:10.1016/j.buildenv.2015.02.036

Tat-Kei Ho, A. (2002). Reinventing Local Governments and the E-Government Initiative. *Public Administration Review*, *62*(4), 434–444. doi:10.1111/0033-3352.00197

Tavares, A., Soares, D., & Estevez, E. (2016). Electronic Governance for Context-Specific Public Service Delivery: A Survey of the Literature. *International Conference on Theory and Practice of Electronic Governance*, 135-138. 10.1145/2910019.2910110

Teo, T. S., Srivastava, S. C., & Jiang, L. (2008). Trust and electronic government success: An empirical study. *Journal of Management Information Systems*, *25*(3), 99–132. doi:10.2753/MIS0742-1222250303

Thompson, J. D. (2017). *Organizations in Action: Social Science Bases of Administrative Theory*. Taylor & Francis.

Thompson, S., Altay, N., Green, W. G. III, & Lapetina, J. (2006). Improving disaster response efforts with decision support systems. *International Journal of Emergency Management*, *3*(4), 250–263. doi:10.1504/IJEM.2006.011295

Thrift, N. (1985). Bear and Mouse or Bear and Tree? Anthony Giddenss Reconstitution of Social Theory. *Sociology*, *19*(4), 609–623. doi:10.1177/0038038585019004009

Thygerson, S. M., West, J. H., Rassbach, A. R., & Thygerson, A. L. (2012). iPhone apps for first aid: A content analysis. *Journal of Consumer Health on the Internet*, *16*(2), 213–225. doi:10.1080/15398285.2012.673465

Tilson, D., Lyytinen, K., & Sørensen, C. (2010). Digital Infrastructures: The Missing IS Research Agenda. *Information Systems Research*, *21*(4), 748–759. doi:10.1287/isre.1100.0318

Timerman, S., Gonzalez, M. M. C., Zaroni, A. C., & Ramires, J. A. F. (2006). Emergency medical services: Brazil. *Resuscitation*, *70*(3), 356–359. doi:10.1016/j.resuscitation.2006.05.010 PMID:16901612

Tolbert, C. J., & Mossberger, K. (2006). The effects of e-government on trust and confidence in government. *Public Administration Review*, *66*(3), 354–369. doi:10.1111/j.1540-6210.2006.00594.x

Tonelli, D. F., de Brito, M. J., & Zambalde, A. L. (2011). Empreendedorismo na Ótica da Teoria Ator-Rede: Explorando Alternativa às Perspectivas Subjetivista e Objetivista. *Cadernos EBAPE. BR*, 9.

Tracy, K., & Tracy, S. J. (1998). Rudeness at 911 reconceptualizing face and face attack. *Human Communication Research*, 25(2), 225–251. doi:10.1111/j.1468-2958.1998.tb00444.x

Tregear, R., & Jenkins, T. (2007). Government Process Management: a review of key differences between the public and private sectors and their influence on the achievement of public sector process management. *BPTrends*. Retrieved from www.bptrends.com

Tucker, C. (2017). Network Stability, Network Externalities, and Technology Adoption. In Entrepreneurship, Innovation, and Platforms (pp. 151-175). Emerald Publishing Limited. doi:10.1108/S0742-332220170000037006

Ulbig, S. (2002). Policies, procedures, and people: Sources of support for government? *Social Science Quarterly*, 83(3), 789–809. doi:10.1111/1540-6237.00115

Ullman, J. B. (2001). Structural equation modeling. In B. G. Tabachnick & L. S. Fidell (Eds.), *Using multivariate statistics* (4th ed.). Needham Heights, MA: Allyn & Bacon.

Vaitkaitis, D. (2008). EMS systems in Lithuania. *Resuscitation*, 76(3), 329–332. doi:10.1016/j.resuscitation.2007.07.028 PMID:17822828

Van De Ven, A. H., & Poole, M. S. (1995). Explaining Development and Change in Organizations. *Academy of Management Review*, 20(3), 510–540. doi:10.2307/258786

Van Dijk, J. A. G. M., Peters, O., & Ebbers, W. (2008). Explaining the acceptance and use of government Internet services: A multivariate analysis of 2006 survey data in the Netherlands. *Government Information Quarterly*, 25(3), 379–399. doi:10.1016/j.giq.2007.09.006

Van Veenstra, A. F., Janssen, M., & Tan, Y. H. (2010). Towards an understanding of e-government induced change-drawing on organization and structuration theories. Lecture Notes in Computer Science, 6228, 1–12. doi:10.1007/978-3-642-14799-9_1

van Veenstra, A. F., Melin, U., & Axelsson, K. (2014). Theoretical and Practical Implications From the Use of Structuration Theory in Public Sector Is Research. *Twenty Second European Conference on Information Systems*, 1–12.

Veenstra, A. F. v., Melin, U., & Axelsson, K. (2014). Theoretical and practical implications from the use of structuration theory in public sector information systems research. *Proceedings of the 22nd European Conference on Information Systems (ECIS 2014)*, 1-12.

Venable, J., Pries-Heje, J., & Baskerville, R. (2014). FEDS: A framework for evaluation in design science research. *European Journal of Information Systems*, 1–13.

Venkatesh, V. (2013). *Rankings based on AIS Senior Scholar's Basket Of Journals*, Retrieved September 27, 2014, from http://www.vvenkatesh.com/isranking/

Venkatesh, V., Morris, M. G., Davis, G. B., & Davis, F. D. (2003). User Acceptance of Information Technology: Toward a Unified View. *Management Information Systems Quarterly*, 27(3), 425–478. doi:10.2307/30036540

Venkatesh, V., Thong, J. Y., Chan, F. K., & Hu, P. J. (2016). Managing Citizens' Uncertainty in E-Government Services: The Mediating and Moderating Roles of Transparency and Trust. *Information Systems Research*, *27*(1), 87–111. doi:10.1287/isre.2015.0612

Verdegem, P., & Verleye, G. (2009). User-centered E-Government in practice: A comprehensive model for measuring user satisfaction. *Government Information Quarterly*, *26*(3), 487–497. doi:10.1016/j.giq.2009.03.005

Vicente, K. J. (1999). *Cognitive work analysis: toward safe, productive, and healthy computer-based work*. Mahwah, NJ: Lawrence Erlbaum Associates.

VoteWatch. (2018). *Vote Watch Europe*. Retrieved from http://www.votewatch.eu

Wacker, J. G. (1998). A definition of theory research guidelines for different-theory building research methods in operations management. *Journal of Operations Management*, *16*(4), 361–385. doi:10.1016/S0272-6963(98)00019-9

Wacker, J. G. (2008). A conceptual understanding of requirements for theory-building research: Guidelines for scientific theory building. *The Journal of Supply Chain Management*, *44*(3), 5–15. doi:10.1111/j.1745-493X.2008.00062.x

Wade, V. A., Eliott, J. A., & Hiller, J. E. (2014). Clinician Acceptance is the Key Factor for Sustainable Telehealth Services. *Qualitative Health Research*, *24*(5), 682–694. doi:10.1177/1049732314528809 PMID:24685708

Waller, P., & Weerakkody, V. (2016, June). *Digital government: Overcoming the systemic failure of transformation* (Brunel University London Working Paper No. 2). Retrieved from http://bura.brunel.ac.uk/handle/2438/12732

Walls, J. G., Widmeyer, G. R., & El Sawy, O. A. (1992). Building an information system design theory for vigilant EIS. *Information Systems Research*, *3*(1), 36–59. doi:10.1287/isre.3.1.36

Walsham, G. (1995). Interpretive case studies in IS research: Nature and method. *Organization Science*, (1973).

Walsham, G. (1995). Interpretive case studies in IS research: Nature and method. *European Journal of Information Systems*, *4*(2), 74–81. doi:10.1057/ejis.1995.9

Walsham, G. (2005). Learning about being critical. *Information Systems Journal*, *15*(2), 111–117. doi:10.1111/j.1365-2575.2004.00189.x

Walsham, G., & Han, C. K. (1991). Structuration theory and information systems research. *Journal of Applied Systems Analysis*, *15*(1), 77–85.

Wandling, M. W., Nathens, A. B., Shapiro, M. B., & Haut, E. R. (2016). Police transport versus ground EMS: A trauma system-level evaluation of prehospital care policies and their effect on clinical outcomes. *The Journal of Trauma and Acute Care Surgery*, *81*(5), 931–935. doi:10.1097/TA.0000000000001228 PMID:27537514

Wang, W., & Benbasat, I. (2005). Trust in and adoption of online recommendation agents. *Journal of the Association for Information Systems*, *6*(3), 72–101. doi:10.17705/1jais.00065

Wang, Y., Hu, W., Wu, Y., & Cao, G. (2014). SmartPhoto: A Resource-Aware Crowdsourcing Approach for Image Sensing with Smartphones. *IEEE Transactions on Mobile Computing*, *15*. doi:10.1145/2632951.2632979

Webb, H. W., & Webb, L. A. (2004). SiteQual: An integrated measure of Web site quality. *Journal of Enterprise Information Management*, *17*(6), 430–440. doi:10.1108/17410390410566724

Weber, R. (2003). Editor's Comments: Theoretically Speaking. *Management Information Systems Quarterly*, *27*(3), 3–12. doi:10.2307/30036536

Weerakkody, V., El-Haddadeh, R., & Al-Shafi, S. (2011). Exploring the complexities of e-government implementation and diffusion in a developing country: Some lessons from the State of Qatar. *Journal of Enterprise Information Management*, *24*(2), 172–196. doi:10.1108/17410391111106293

Weerakkody, V., El-Haddadeh, R., Al-Sobhi, F., Shareef, M. A., & Dwivedi, Y. K. (2013). Examining the influence of intermediaries in facilitating e-government adoption: An empirical investigation. *International Journal of Information Management*, *33*(5), 716–725. doi:10.1016/j.ijinfomgt.2013.05.001

Weerakkody, V., El-Haddadeh, R., Chochliouros, I., & Morris, D. (2012). Utilizing a High Definition Live Video Platform to Facilitate Public Service Delivery. In L. Iliadis, I. Maglogiannis, H. Papadopoulos, K. Karatzas, & S. Sioutas (Eds.), *Artificial Intelligence Applications and Innovations* (Vol. 382, pp. 290–299). Springer Berlin Heidelberg. doi:10.1007/978-3-642-33412-2_30

Weerakkody, V., Irani, Z., Kapoor, K., Sivarajah, U., & Dwivedi, Y. K. (2016). Open data and its usability: An empirical view from the Citizen's perspective. *Information Systems Frontiers*, 1–16.

Weerakkody, V., Irani, Z., Lee, H., Osman, I., & Hindi, N. (2013). E-government implementation: A bird's eye view of issues relating to costs, opportunities, benefits and risks. *Information Systems Frontiers*, 1–27.

Weerakkody, V., Janssen, M., & Dwivedi, Y. (2011). Transformational change and business process reengineering (BPR): Lessons from the British and Dutch public sector. *Government Information Quarterly*, *28*(3), 320–328. doi:10.1016/j.giq.2010.07.010

Weerakkody, V., Omar, A., El-Haddadeh, R., & Al-Busaidy, M. (2016). Digitally-enabled service transformation in the public sector: The lure of institutional pressure and strategic response towards change. *Government Information Quarterly*, *11*. doi:10.1016/j.giq.2016.06.006

Weick, K. E. (1979). *The Social Psychology of Organizing* (2nd ed.). Reading, MA: Addison-Wesley.

Welch, E. W., & Feeney, M. K. (2014). Technology in government : How organizational culture mediates information and communication technology outcomes. *Government Information Quarterly*, *31*(4), 506–512. doi:10.1016/j.giq.2014.07.006

Welch, E. W., Hinnant, C. C., & Moon, M. J. (2005). Linking citizen satisfaction with e-government and trust in government. *Journal of Public Administration: Research and Theory, 15*(3), 371–391. doi:10.1093/jopart/mui021

Whalen, J., & Zimmerman, D. H. (1998). Observations on the display and management of emotion in naturally occurring activities: The case of hysteria in calls to 9-1-1. *Social Psychology Quarterly, 61*(2), 141–159. doi:10.2307/2787066

Whittington, R. (1992). Putting Giddens into action: Social systems and managerial agency. *Journal of Management Studies, 29*(6), 693–712. doi:10.1111/j.1467-6486.1992.tb00685.x

WHO. (1996). Report: Investing in health research and development; WHO reference number: TDR/Gen/96.1. Geneva: World Health Organization: Ad Hoc Committee on Health Research Relating to Future Intervention Options.

WHO. (2010). *Injuries and violence: the facts.* Geneva: WHO.

WHO. (2011). *Telemedicine – Opportunities and developments in Member States: report on the second global survey on eHealth 2009. In Global Observatory for eHealth series* (Vol. 2). World Health Oragnization.

Winroither, E., & Kocina, E. (2014). *Donauinselfest will Gäste aus dem Ausland.* Retrieved September 27, 2014, from http://diepresse.com/home/kultur/popco/Festivals/donauinselfest/3827487/Donauinselfest-will-Gaeste-aus-dem-Ausland

Winters, M., Karim, A., & Martawardaya, B. (2014). Public Service Provision under Conditions of Insufficient Citizen Demand: Insights from the Urban Sanitation Sector in Indonesia. *World Development, 60*, 31–42. doi:10.1016/j.worlddev.2014.03.017

Wirtz, B. W., & Kurtz, O. T. (2016). Determinants of Citizen Usage Intentions in e-Government: An Empirical Analysis. *Public Organization Review*, 1–20.

Wolak, J., & Palus, C. K. (2010). The dynamics of public confidence in U.S. state and local government. *State Politics & Policy Quarterly, 10*(4), 421–445. doi:10.1177/153244001001000407

Wolfinbarger, M., & Gilly, M. C. (2003). eTailQ: dimensionalizing, measuring and predicting etail quality. *Journal of Retailing, 79*(3), 183–198.

Wood County 911. (2013). Retrieved September 27, 2014, from http://www.woodcounty911.com/calling.htm

Wu, Y. (2014). Protecting personal data in e-government: A cross-country study. *Government Information Quarterly, 31*(1), 150–159. doi:10.1016/j.giq.2013.07.003

Xu, H., Teo, H. H., Tan, B. C., & Agarwal, R. (2009). The role of push-pull technology in privacy calculus: The case of location-based services. *Journal of Management Information Systems, 26*(3), 135–174. doi:10.2753/MIS0742-1222260305

Yang, L., Su, G., & Yuan, H. (2012). Design principles of integrated information platform for emergency responses: The case of 2008 Beijing Olympic games. *Information Systems Research*, *23*(3), 761–786. doi:10.1287/isre.1110.0387

Yeongtak, Jaehoon, & Youngjoon. (2015). Feedback algorithm for high-quality CPR based on smartphone. *Telemedicine & eHealth, 21*(1).

Yuan, Y., Archer, N., Connelly, C. E., & Zheng, W. (2010). Identifying the ideal fit between mobile work and mobile work support. *Information & Management*, *47*(3), 125–137. doi:10.1016/j. im.2009.12.004

Yuan, Y., & Zhang, J. (2003). Towards an appropriate business model for m-commerce. *International Journal of Mobile Communications*, *1*(1/2), 35–56. doi:10.1504/IJMC.2003.002459

Zailani, S., Gilani, M. S., Nikbin, D., & Iranmanesh, M. (2014). Determinants of Telemedicine Acceptance in Selected Public Hospitals in Malaysia: Clinical Perspective. *Journal of Medical Systems*, *38*(9), 1–12. doi:10.100710916-014-0111-4 PMID:25038891

Zapletal, B., Greif, R., Stumpf, D., Nierscher, F. J., Frantal, S., Haugk, M., ... Fischer, H. (2014). Comparing three CPR feedback devices and standard BLS in a single rescuer scenario: A randomised simulation study. *Resuscitation*, *85*(4), 560–566. doi:10.1016/j.resuscitation.2013.10.028 PMID:24215730

Zhang, N., Zhao, X., Zhang, Z., Meng, Q., & Tan, H. (2017). What factors drive open innovation in China's public sector? A case study of of fi cial document exchange via microblogging (ODEM) in Haining. *Government Information Quarterly*, *34*(1), 126–133. doi:10.1016/j.giq.2016.11.002

Zheng, L. (2013). Social media in Chinese government : Drivers, challenges and capabilities. *Government Information Quarterly*, *30*(4), 369–376. doi:10.1016/j.giq.2013.05.017

Zheng, L., & Zheng, T. (2014). Innovation through social media in the public sector : Information and interactions. *Government Information Quarterly*, *31*, S106–S117. doi:10.1016/j.giq.2014.01.011

Zuurmond, A. (1998). From bureaucracy to infocracy: Are democratic institutions lagging behind. In I. T. M. Snellen & W. van de Donk (Eds.), *Public administration in an information age; A handbook* (pp. 259–272). Amsterdam: IOS Press.

# Related References

To continue our tradition of advancing information science and technology research, we have compiled a list of recommended IGI Global readings. These references will provide additional information and guidance to further enrich your knowledge and assist you with your own research and future publications.

Abdel-Hameid, S. O., & Wilson, E. (2018). Gender, Organization, and Change in Sudan. In N. Mahtab, T. Haque, I. Khan, M. Islam, & I. Wahid (Eds.), *Handbook of Research on Women's Issues and Rights in the Developing World* (pp. 107–120). Hershey, PA: IGI Global. doi:10.4018/978-1-5225-3018-3.ch007

Abdulazeez, N. J. (2016). Reconciliation of Identity Groups in Iraq: Conflict Analysis and Political Means of Ethnic Accommodation. In F. Cante & H. Quehl (Eds.), *Handbook of Research on Transitional Justice and Peace Building in Turbulent Regions* (pp. 278–297). Hershey, PA: IGI Global. doi:10.4018/978-1-4666-9675-4.ch014

Abdullahi, R. B. (2018). Volunteerism in Urban Development the Case of Non-Cash, Non-Digital Crowdfunding Growth in Nigeria. In U. Benna & A. Benna (Eds.), *Crowdfunding and Sustainable Urban Development in Emerging Economies* (pp. 188–210). Hershey, PA: IGI Global. doi:10.4018/978-1-5225-3952-0.ch010

Abioye, T. O., Oyesomi, K., Ajiboye, E., Omidiora, S., & Oyero, O. (2017). Education, Gender, and Child-Rights: Salient Issues in SDGS Years in ADO-ODO/OTA Local Government Area of Ogun State, Nigeria. In O. Nelson, B. Ojebuyi, & A. Salawu (Eds.), *Impacts of the Media on African Socio-Economic Development* (pp. 141–154). Hershey, PA: IGI Global. doi:10.4018/978-1-5225-1859-4.ch009

Acuña, Y. G. (2016). From the Studies of Violences to Memories: The Construction of Victims and its Articulations with the State. In F. Cante & H. Quehl (Eds.), *Handbook of Research on Transitional Justice and Peace Building in Turbulent Regions* (pp. 332–355). Hershey, PA: IGI Global. doi:10.4018/978-1-4666-9675-4.ch017

Adhikary, M., & Khatun, M. (2016). Issues of Convergence: Some Evidences of SAARC Countries. In R. Das (Ed.), *Handbook of Research on Global Indicators of Economic and Political Convergence* (pp. 119–143). Hershey, PA: IGI Global. doi:10.4018/978-1-5225-0215-9.ch006

Adisa, W. B. (2018). Land Use Policy and Urban Sprawl in Nigeria: Land Use and the Emergence of Urban Sprawl. In A. Eneanya (Ed.), *Handbook of Research on Environmental Policies for Emergency Management and Public Safety* (pp. 256–274). Hershey, PA: IGI Global. doi:10.4018/978-1-5225-3194-4.ch014

Afolabi, O. S., Amao-Kolawole, T. G., Shittu, A. K., & Oguntokun, O. O. (2018). Rule of Law, Governance, and Sustainable Development: The Nigerian Perspective. In K. Teshager Alemu & M. Abebe Alebachew (Eds.), *Handbook of Research on Sustainable Development and Governance Strategies for Economic Growth in Africa* (pp. 273–290). Hershey, PA: IGI Global. doi:10.4018/978-1-5225-3247-7.ch015

Agyei-Mensah, B. K. (2016). Impact of Adopting IFRS in Ghana: Empirical Evidence. In E. Uchenna, M. Nnadi, S. Tanna, & F. Iyoha (Eds.), *Economics and Political Implications of International Financial Reporting Standards* (pp. 191–230). Hershey, PA: IGI Global. doi:10.4018/978-1-4666-9876-5.ch010

Agyemang, O. S. (2018). Institutional Structures and the Prevalence of Foreign Ownership of Firms: Empirical Evidence From Africa. In K. Teshager Alemu & M. Abebe Alebachew (Eds.), *Handbook of Research on Sustainable Development and Governance Strategies for Economic Growth in Africa* (pp. 455–479). Hershey, PA: IGI Global. doi:10.4018/978-1-5225-3247-7.ch024

Aham-Anyanwu, N. M., & Li, H. (2017). E-State: Realistic or Utopian? *International Journal of Public Administration in the Digital Age*, 4(2), 56–76. doi:10.4018/IJPADA.2017040105

Ahmad, M. B., Pride, C., & Corsy, A. K. (2016). Free Speech, Press Freedom, and Democracy in Ghana: A Conceptual and Historical Overview. In L. Mukhongo & J. Macharia (Eds.), *Political Influence of the Media in Developing Countries* (pp. 59–73). Hershey, PA: IGI Global. doi:10.4018/978-1-4666-9613-6.ch005

Al-Jamal, M., & Abu-Shanab, E. (2018). Open Government: The Line between Privacy and Transparency. *International Journal of Public Administration in the Digital Age*, 5(2), 64–75. doi:10.4018/IJPADA.2018040106

Alsaç, U. (2017). EKAP: Turkey's Centralized E-Procurement System. In R. Shakya (Ed.), *Digital Governance and E-Government Principles Applied to Public Procurement* (pp. 126–150). Hershey, PA: IGI Global. doi:10.4018/978-1-5225-2203-4.ch006

Amadi, L. A., & Igwe, P. (2018). Open Government and Bureaucratic Secrecy in the Developing Democracies: Africa in Perspective. In A. Kok (Ed.), *Proliferation of Open Government Initiatives and Systems* (pp. 1–28). Hershey, PA: IGI Global. doi:10.4018/978-1-5225-4987-1.ch001

Anthopoulos, L., Janssen, M., & Weerakkody, V. (2016). A Unified Smart City Model (USCM) for Smart City Conceptualization and Benchmarking. *International Journal of Electronic Government Research, 12*(2), 77–93. doi:10.4018/IJEGR.2016040105

Ayeni, A. O. (2018). Environmental Policies for Emergency Management and Public Safety: Implementing Green Policy and Community Participation. In A. Eneanya (Ed.), *Handbook of Research on Environmental Policies for Emergency Management and Public Safety* (pp. 40–59). Hershey, PA: IGI Global. doi:10.4018/978-1-5225-3194-4.ch003

Ayodele, J. O. (2017). The Influence of Migration and Crime on Development in Lagos, Nigeria. In G. Afolayan & A. Akinwale (Eds.), *Global Perspectives on Development Administration and Cultural Change* (pp. 192–230). Hershey, PA: IGI Global. doi:10.4018/978-1-5225-0629-4.ch009

Baarda, R. (2017). Digital Democracy in Authoritarian Russia: Opportunity for Participation, or Site of Kremlin Control? In R. Luppicini & R. Baarda (Eds.), *Digital Media Integration for Participatory Democracy* (pp. 87–100). Hershey, PA: IGI Global. doi:10.4018/978-1-5225-2463-2.ch005

Bagwell, T. C., & Jackson, S. L. (2016). The Mode of Information – Due Process of Law and Student Loans: Bills of Attainder Enter the Digital Age. In R. Cropf & T. Bagwell (Eds.), *Ethical Issues and Citizen Rights in the Era of Digital Government Surveillance* (pp. 16–34). Hershey, PA: IGI Global. doi:10.4018/978-1-4666-9905-2.ch002

Balakrishnan, K. (2017). The Rationale for Offsets in Defence Acquisition from a Theoretical Perspective. In K. Burgess & P. Antill (Eds.), *Emerging Strategies in Defense Acquisitions and Military Procurement* (pp. 263–276). Hershey, PA: IGI Global. doi:10.4018/978-1-5225-0599-0.ch015

Banerjee, S. (2017). Globalization and Human Rights: How Globalization Can Be a Tool to Protect the Human Rights. In C. Akrivopoulou (Ed.), *Defending Human Rights and Democracy in the Era of Globalization* (pp. 1–16). Hershey, PA: IGI Global. doi:10.4018/978-1-5225-0723-9.ch001

Batırel, Ö. F. (2016). The Distributional Effects of Tax Policy: Tax Expenditures in Turkey. In M. Erdoğdu & B. Christiansen (Eds.), *Handbook of Research on Public Finance in Europe and the MENA Region* (pp. 391–428). Hershey, PA: IGI Global. doi:10.4018/978-1-5225-0053-7.ch018

Batrancea, L., Nichita, A., Batrancea, I., & Kirchler, E. (2016). Tax Compliance Behavior: An Upshot of Trust in and Power of Authorities across Europe and MENA. In M. Erdoğdu & B. Christiansen (Eds.), *Handbook of Research on Public Finance in Europe and the MENA Region* (pp. 248–267). Hershey, PA: IGI Global. doi:10.4018/978-1-5225-0053-7.ch012

Bessant, J. (2017). Digital Humour, Gag Laws, and the Liberal Security State. In R. Luppicini & R. Baarda (Eds.), *Digital Media Integration for Participatory Democracy* (pp. 204–221). Hershey, PA: IGI Global. doi:10.4018/978-1-5225-2463-2.ch010

Boachie, C. (2016). The Effect of International Financial Reporting Standards Adoption on Foreign Direct Investment and the Economy. In E. Uchenna, M. Nnadi, S. Tanna, & F. Iyoha (Eds.), *Economics and Political Implications of International Financial Reporting Standards* (pp. 342–361). Hershey, PA: IGI Global. doi:10.4018/978-1-4666-9876-5.ch017

Boachie, C. (2017). Public Financial Management and Systems of Accountability in Sub-National Governance in Developing Economies. In E. Schoburgh & R. Ryan (Eds.), *Handbook of Research on Sub-National Governance and Development* (pp. 193–217). Hershey, PA: IGI Global. doi:10.4018/978-1-5225-1645-3.ch009

Boachie, C., & Adu-Darko, E. (2018). Socio-Economic Impact of Foreign Direct Investment in Developing Countries. In V. Malepati & C. Gowri (Eds.), *Foreign Direct Investments (FDIs) and Opportunities for Developing Economies in the World Market* (pp. 66–81). Hershey, PA: IGI Global. doi:10.4018/978-1-5225-3026-8.ch004

Bolgherini, S., & Lippi, A. (2016). Italy: Remapping Local Government from Re-Allocation and Re-Shaping to Re-Scaling. In U. Sadioglu & K. Dede (Eds.), *Theoretical Foundations and Discussions on the Reformation Process in Local Governments* (pp. 265–287). Hershey, PA: IGI Global. doi:10.4018/978-1-5225-0317-0.ch011

Borràs, S. (2017). Rights of Nature to Protect Human Rights in Times of Environmental Crisis. In C. Akrivopoulou (Ed.), *Defending Human Rights and Democracy in the Era of Globalization* (pp. 225–261). Hershey, PA: IGI Global. doi:10.4018/978-1-5225-0723-9.ch010

Brusca, I., Olmo, J., & Labrador, M. (2018). Characterizing the Risk Factors for Financial Sustainability in Spanish Local Governments. In M. Rodríguez Bolívar & M. López Subires (Eds.), *Financial Sustainability and Intergenerational Equity in Local Governments* (pp. 206–223). Hershey, PA: IGI Global. doi:10.4018/978-1-5225-3713-7.ch009

Caccioppoli, L. (2016). Bridging the Gaps with Nonprofits: The Intersection of Institutions, Interests, and the Health Policy Process. In R. Gholipour & K. Rouzbehani (Eds.), *Social, Economic, and Political Perspectives on Public Health Policy-Making* (pp. 233–256). Hershey, PA: IGI Global. doi:10.4018/978-1-4666-9944-1.ch011

Callanan, M. (2016). Institutionalizing the Politics-Administration Dichotomy in Local Government: Reforming the Council-Manager System in Ireland. In U. Sadioglu & K. Dede (Eds.), *Theoretical Foundations and Discussions on the Reformation Process in Local Governments* (pp. 153–178). Hershey, PA: IGI Global. doi:10.4018/978-1-5225-0317-0.ch007

Campbell, A. (2016). "Imperialism" and "Federalism": The Ambiguity of State and City in Russia. In U. Sadioglu & K. Dede (Eds.), *Theoretical Foundations and Discussions on the Reformation Process in Local Governments* (pp. 353–372). Hershey, PA: IGI Global. doi:10.4018/978-1-5225-0317-0.ch015

Carini, C., & Teodori, C. (2016). Potential Uses and Usefulness of Italian Local Government Consolidated Financial Reporting: The Case of the Town Council of Brescia. In A. Ferreira, G. Azevedo, J. Oliveira, & R. Marques (Eds.), *Global Perspectives on Risk Management and Accounting in the Public Sector* (pp. 68–89). Hershey, PA: IGI Global. doi:10.4018/978-1-4666-9803-1.ch004

Carter, S. D. (2016). Increased Workforce Diversity by Race, Gender, and Age and Equal Employment Opportunity Laws: Implications for Human Resource Development. In J. Prescott (Ed.), *Handbook of Research on Race, Gender, and the Fight for Equality* (pp. 398–423). Hershey, PA: IGI Global. doi:10.4018/978-1-5225-0047-6.ch018

Cebeci, K., & Zülfüoğlu, Ö. (2016). Financial Market Regulations in a Globalized World: Some Remarks for the MENA Region. In M. Erdoğdu & B. Christiansen (Eds.), *Comparative Political and Economic Perspectives on the MENA Region* (pp. 180–198). Hershey, PA: IGI Global. doi:10.4018/978-1-4666-9601-3.ch008

Chen, M., & Su, F. (2017). Global Civic Engagement as an Empowering Device for Cross-Ethnic and Cross-Cultural Understanding in Taiwan. In R. Shin (Ed.), *Convergence of Contemporary Art, Visual Culture, and Global Civic Engagement* (pp. 24–45). Hershey, PA: IGI Global. doi:10.4018/978-1-5225-1665-1.ch002

Cheng, J. Y. (2016). Local Governments in China. In U. Sadioglu & K. Dede (Eds.), *Comparative Studies and Regionally-Focused Cases Examining Local Governments* (pp. 207–227). Hershey, PA: IGI Global. doi:10.4018/978-1-5225-0320-0.ch010

Cheong, D. D. (2016). Countering Online Violent Extremism: State Action as Strategic Communication. In M. Khader, L. Neo, G. Ong, E. Mingyi, & J. Chin (Eds.), *Combating Violent Extremism and Radicalization in the Digital Era* (pp. 283–306). Hershey, PA: IGI Global. doi:10.4018/978-1-5225-0156-5.ch014

Chigwata, T. C. (2017). Fiscal Decentralization: Constraints to Revenue-Raising by Local Government in Zimbabwe. In E. Schoburgh & R. Ryan (Eds.), *Handbook of Research on Sub-National Governance and Development* (pp. 218–240). Hershey, PA: IGI Global. doi:10.4018/978-1-5225-1645-3.ch010

Chowdhury, M. A. (2017). The Nexus Between Institutional Quality and Foreign Direct Investments (FDI) in South Asia: Dynamic Heterogeneous Panel Approach. In T. Dorożyński & A. Kuna-Marszałek (Eds.), *Outward Foreign Direct Investment (FDI) in Emerging Market Economies* (pp. 293–310). Hershey, PA: IGI Global. doi:10.4018/978-1-5225-2345-1.ch015

Christopher, M. E., & Tsushima, V. G. (2017). Police Interactions with Persons-in-Crisis: Emergency Psychological Services and Jail Diversion. In C. Mitchell & E. Dorian (Eds.), *Police Psychology and Its Growing Impact on Modern Law Enforcement* (pp. 274–294). Hershey, PA: IGI Global. doi:10.4018/978-1-5225-0813-7.ch014

Citro, F., Lucianelli, G., & Santis, S. (2018). Financial Conditions, Financial Sustainability, and Intergenerational Equity in Local Governments: A Literature Review. In M. Rodríguez Bolívar & M. López Subires (Eds.), *Financial Sustainability and Intergenerational Equity in Local Governments* (pp. 101–124). Hershey, PA: IGI Global. doi:10.4018/978-1-5225-3713-7.ch005

Covell, C. E. (2018). Theoretical Application of Public Sector Planning and Budgeting. In M. Rodríguez Bolívar & M. López Subires (Eds.), *Financial Sustainability and Intergenerational Equity in Local Governments* (pp. 248–279). Hershey, PA: IGI Global. doi:10.4018/978-1-5225-3713-7.ch011

Cuadrado-Ballesteros, B., García-Sánchez, I. M., & Martínez-Ferrero, J. (2016). Commercialization of Local Public Services. In A. Ferreira, G. Azevedo, J. Oliveira, & R. Marques (Eds.), *Global Perspectives on Risk Management and Accounting in the Public Sector* (pp. 132–150). Hershey, PA: IGI Global. doi:10.4018/978-1-4666-9803-1.ch007

Cunha, A., Ferreira, A. D., & Fernandes, M. J. (2016). The Influence of Accounting Information in the Re-Election of the Mayors in Portugal. In A. Ferreira, G. Azevedo, J. Oliveira, & R. Marques (Eds.), *Global Perspectives on Risk Management and Accounting in the Public Sector* (pp. 108–131). Hershey, PA: IGI Global. doi:10.4018/978-1-4666-9803-1.ch006

Cunha, A. M., Ferreira, A. D., & Fernandes, M. J. (2018). The Impact of Accounting Information and Socioeconomic Factors in the Re-Election of Portuguese Mayors. In G. Azevedo, J. da Silva Oliveira, R. Marques, & A. Ferreira (Eds.), *Handbook of Research on Modernization and Accountability in Public Sector Management* (pp. 406–432). Hershey, PA: IGI Global. doi:10.4018/978-1-5225-3731-1.ch019

da Rosa, I., & de Almeida, J. (2017). Digital Transformation in the Public Sector: Electronic Procurement in Portugal. In R. Shakya (Ed.), *Digital Governance and E-Government Principles Applied to Public Procurement* (pp. 99–125). Hershey, PA: IGI Global. doi:10.4018/978-1-5225-2203-4.ch005

Daramola, O. (2018). Revisiting the Legal Framework of Urban Planning in the Global South: An Explanatory Example of Nigeria. In K. Teshager Alemu & M. Abebe Alebachew (Eds.), *Handbook of Research on Sustainable Development and Governance Strategies for Economic Growth in Africa* (pp. 258–271). Hershey, PA: IGI Global. doi:10.4018/978-1-5225-3247-7.ch014

Dau, L. A., Moore, E. M., Soto, M. A., & LeBlanc, C. R. (2017). How Globalization Sparked Entrepreneurship in the Developing World: The Impact of Formal Economic and Political Linkages. In B. Christiansen & F. Kasarcı (Eds.), *Corporate Espionage, Geopolitics, and Diplomacy Issues in International Business* (pp. 72–91). Hershey, PA: IGI Global. doi:10.4018/978-1-5225-1031-4.ch005

Dean, G. (2016). Framing the Challenges of Online Violent Extremism: "Policing-Public-Policies-Politics" Framework. In M. Khader, L. Neo, G. Ong, E. Mingyi, & J. Chin (Eds.), *Combating Violent Extremism and Radicalization in the Digital Era* (pp. 226–259). Hershey, PA: IGI Global. doi:10.4018/978-1-5225-0156-5.ch012

Drenner, K. (2017). Introduction to Faith in State Legislatures: Land of the Brave and the Home of the Free – The Star-Spangled Banner. In *Impacts of Faith-Based Decision Making on the Individual-Level Legislative Process: Emerging Research and Opportunities* (pp. 1–25). Hershey, PA: IGI Global. doi:10.4018/978-1-5225-2388-8.ch001

Drenner, K. (2017). The Holy Wars of Marriage. In *Impacts of Faith-Based Decision Making on the Individual-Level Legislative Process: Emerging Research and Opportunities* (pp. 92–116). Hershey, PA: IGI Global. doi:10.4018/978-1-5225-2388-8.ch004

Drenner, K. (2017). The Implications of Religious Liberty. In *Impacts of Faith-Based Decision Making on the Individual-Level Legislative Process: Emerging Research and Opportunities* (pp. 143–162). Hershey, PA: IGI Global. doi:10.4018/978-1-5225-2388-8.ch006

Edwards, S. B. III. (2016). The Right to Privacy Is Dying: Technology Is Killing It and We Are Letting It Happen. In R. Cropf & T. Bagwell (Eds.), *Ethical Issues and Citizen Rights in the Era of Digital Government Surveillance* (pp. 103–126). Hershey, PA: IGI Global. doi:10.4018/978-1-4666-9905-2.ch006

Elena, S., & van Schalkwyk, F. (2017). Open Data for Open Justice in Seven Latin American Countries. In C. Jiménez-Gómez & M. Gascó-Hernández (Eds.), *Achieving Open Justice through Citizen Participation and Transparency* (pp. 210–231). Hershey, PA: IGI Global. doi:10.4018/978-1-5225-0717-8.ch011

Eneanya, A. N. (2016). Health Policy Implementation and Its Barriers: The Case Study of US Health System. In R. Gholipour & K. Rouzbehani (Eds.), *Social, Economic, and Political Perspectives on Public Health Policy-Making* (pp. 42–63). Hershey, PA: IGI Global. doi:10.4018/978-1-4666-9944-1.ch003

Eneanya, A. N. (2018). Integrating Ecosystem Management and Environmental Media for Public Policy on Public Health and Safety. In A. Eneanya (Ed.), *Handbook of Research on Environmental Policies for Emergency Management and Public Safety* (pp. 321–338). Hershey, PA: IGI Global. doi:10.4018/978-1-5225-3194-4.ch017

Erdoğdu, M. M., Yılmaz, B. E., Aydın, M., & User, İ. (2016). Political Economy of Tax Evasion and Tax Loss in the Real Estate Sector: A Property Tax Reform Proposal for Turkey. In M. Erdoğdu & B. Christiansen (Eds.), *Handbook of Research on Public Finance in Europe and the MENA Region* (pp. 268–298). Hershey, PA: IGI Global. doi:10.4018/978-1-5225-0053-7.ch013

Essien, E. D. (2018). Strengthening Performance of Civil Society Through Dialogue and Critical Thinking in Nigeria: Its Ethical Implications. In S. Chhabra (Ed.), *Handbook of Research on Civic Engagement and Social Change in Contemporary Society* (pp. 82–102). Hershey, PA: IGI Global. doi:10.4018/978-1-5225-4197-4.ch005

Fanaian, T. (2017). The Theocratic Deception Trap: Khomeini's Persuasion Techniques and Communication Patterns in His Books, Guardianship of the Jurist 1979 and Testament 1989. In E. Lewin, E. Bick, & D. Naor (Eds.), *Comparative Perspectives on Civil Religion, Nationalism, and Political Influence* (pp. 62–105). Hershey, PA: IGI Global. doi:10.4018/978-1-5225-0516-7.ch003

Farrag, N. A., & Ezzat, A. M. (2016). The Impact of Corruption on Economic Growth: A Comparative Analysis between Europe and MENA Countries. In M. Erdoğdu & B. Christiansen (Eds.), *Handbook of Research on Comparative Economic Development Perspectives on Europe and the MENA Region* (pp. 74–97). Hershey, PA: IGI Global. doi:10.4018/978-1-4666-9548-1.ch005

Farzanegan, M. R. (2016). Demographic Transition, Oil, and Institutions: Lessons from the Global Experience for Iran. In M. Erdoğdu & B. Christiansen (Eds.), *Comparative Political and Economic Perspectives on the MENA Region* (pp. 261–291). Hershey, PA: IGI Global. doi:10.4018/978-1-4666-9601-3.ch012

Feickert, H. (2016). Enforcing Central Authority: Nuri al-Maliki and the Tradition of Iraq's Authoritarian State. In F. Cante & H. Quehl (Eds.), *Handbook of Research on Transitional Justice and Peace Building in Turbulent Regions* (pp. 233–252). Hershey, PA: IGI Global. doi:10.4018/978-1-4666-9675-4.ch012

Fidanoski, F., Sergi, B. S., Simeonovski, K., Naumovski, V., & Sazdovski, I. (2018). Effects of Foreign Capital Entry on the Macedonian Banking Industry: Two-Edged Sword. In B. Sergi, F. Fidanoski, M. Ziolo, & V. Naumovski (Eds.), *Regaining Global Stability After the Financial Crisis* (pp. 308–338). Hershey, PA: IGI Global. doi:10.4018/978-1-5225-4026-7.ch015

Fiske, R. R. (2016). The Borders of Corruption: Living in the State of Exception. In R. Cropf & T. Bagwell (Eds.), *Ethical Issues and Citizen Rights in the Era of Digital Government Surveillance* (pp. 1–15). Hershey, PA: IGI Global. doi:10.4018/978-1-4666-9905-2.ch001

Franconi, A. I. (2018). Economic Variations and Their Impact on Labor Legislation Throughout History in Argentina. In S. Amine (Ed.), *Employment Protection Legislation in Emerging Economies* (pp. 77–98). Hershey, PA: IGI Global. doi:10.4018/978-1-5225-4134-9.ch004

Franzke, J. (2016). Structure of the Local Tiers in Germany: Trends and Challenges in Local Governance and Autonomy. In U. Sadioglu & K. Dede (Eds.), *Comparative Studies and Regionally-Focused Cases Examining Local Governments* (pp. 51–70). Hershey, PA: IGI Global. doi:10.4018/978-1-5225-0320-0.ch003

Friedrich, P., & Chebotareva, M. (2017). Options for Applying Functional Overlapping Competing Jurisdictions (FOCJs) for Municipal Cooperation in Russia. In M. Lewandowski & B. Kożuch (Eds.), *Public Sector Entrepreneurship and the Integration of Innovative Business Models* (pp. 73–107). Hershey, PA: IGI Global. doi:10.4018/978-1-5225-2215-7.ch004

Gałuszka, J. (2016). Decentralization and Sub-National Government in Poland: Territorial Governance, Competencies, Fiscal Autonomy of Local Governments. In U. Sadioglu & K. Dede (Eds.), *Comparative Studies and Regionally-Focused Cases Examining Local Governments* (pp. 91–112). Hershey, PA: IGI Global. doi:10.4018/978-1-5225-0320-0.ch005

Game, C. (2016). Decentralisation and Devolution in the United Kingdom. In U. Sadioglu & K. Dede (Eds.), *Comparative Studies and Regionally-Focused Cases Examining Local Governments* (pp. 1–34). Hershey, PA: IGI Global. doi:10.4018/978-1-5225-0320-0.ch001

García, M. J., & Sancino, A. (2016). Directly Elected Mayors vs. Council Appointed Mayors – Which Effects on Local Government Systems?: A Comparison between Italy and Spain. In U. Sadioglu & K. Dede (Eds.), *Theoretical Foundations and Discussions on the Reformation Process in Local Governments* (pp. 288–303). Hershey, PA: IGI Global. doi:10.4018/978-1-5225-0317-0.ch012

Garita, M. (2018). The Negotiation and Effects of Fiscal Privileges in Guatemala. In M. Garita & C. Bregni (Eds.), *Economic Growth in Latin America and the Impact of the Global Financial Crisis* (pp. 119–137). Hershey, PA: IGI Global. doi:10.4018/978-1-5225-4981-9.ch008

Gascó-Hernández, M. (2017). Digitalizing Police Requirements: Opening up Justice through Collaborative Initiatives. In C. Jiménez-Gómez & M. Gascó-Hernández (Eds.), *Achieving Open Justice through Citizen Participation and Transparency* (pp. 157–172). Hershey, PA: IGI Global. doi:10.4018/978-1-5225-0717-8.ch008

Gáspár-Szilágyi, S. (2017). Human Rights Conditionality in the EU's Newly Concluded Association Agreements with the Eastern Partners. In C. Akrivopoulou (Ed.), *Defending Human Rights and Democracy in the Era of Globalization* (pp. 50–79). Hershey, PA: IGI Global. doi:10.4018/978-1-5225-0723-9.ch003

Gavrielides, T. (2017). Reconciling Restorative Justice with the Law for Violence Against Women in Europe: A Scheme of Structured and Unstructured Models. In D. Halder & K. Jaishankar (Eds.), *Therapeutic Jurisprudence and Overcoming Violence Against Women* (pp. 106–120). Hershey, PA: IGI Global. doi:10.4018/978-1-5225-2472-4.ch007

Gechlik, M., Dai, D., & Beck, J. C. (2017). Open Judiciary in a Closed Society: A Paradox in China? In C. Jiménez-Gómez & M. Gascó-Hernández (Eds.), *Achieving Open Justice through Citizen Participation and Transparency* (pp. 56–92). Hershey, PA: IGI Global. doi:10.4018/978-1-5225-0717-8.ch004

Gerst, M., & Gao, X. (2016). IP and Electric Vehicles Standards: Local Policies vs. Global Standards? Standardization Management in a Multi-Stakeholder Environment in China. In K. Jakobs (Ed.), *Effective Standardization Management in Corporate Settings* (pp. 236–264). Hershey, PA: IGI Global. doi:10.4018/978-1-4666-9737-9.ch011

Gessler, H. A. (2016). Reformulating Government-Citizen Relations in a Digitally Connected World: The Twitter Ban Phenomenon in Turkey. In T. Deželan & I. Vobič (Eds.), *R)evolutionizing Political Communication through Social Media* (pp. 75–93). Hershey, PA: IGI Global. doi:10.4018/978-1-4666-9879-6.ch005

Gholipour, R. (2016). Policy Making: A New Method to Manage Public Issues. In R. Gholipour & K. Rouzbehani (Eds.), *Social, Economic, and Political Perspectives on Public Health Policy-Making* (pp. 1–19). Hershey, PA: IGI Global. doi:10.4018/978-1-4666-9944-1.ch001

Gillath, N. (2017). Avoiding Conscription in Israel: Were Women Pawns in the Political Game? In E. Lewin, E. Bick, & D. Naor (Eds.), *Comparative Perspectives on Civil Religion, Nationalism, and Political Influence* (pp. 226–256). Hershey, PA: IGI Global. doi:10.4018/978-1-5225-0516-7.ch009

Giousmpasoglou, C., Marinakou, E., & Paliktzoglou, V. (2016). Economic Crisis and Higher Education in Greece. In P. Ordóñez de Pablos & R. Tennyson (Eds.), *Impact of Economic Crisis on Education and the Next-Generation Workforce* (pp. 120–148). Hershey, PA: IGI Global. doi:10.4018/978-1-4666-9455-2.ch006

Gomes, P., Camões, S. M., & Carvalho, J. (2016). Determinants of the Design and Use of PMS in Portuguese Government Agencies: A Complementary Theoretical Approach. In A. Ferreira, G. Azevedo, J. Oliveira, & R. Marques (Eds.), *Global Perspectives on Risk Management and Accounting in the Public Sector* (pp. 320–345). Hershey, PA: IGI Global. doi:10.4018/978-1-4666-9803-1.ch016

Gonçalves, T. A., & Rosendo, D. (2016). New Communication Technologies: Women's Rights Violations, Limits on Freedom of Expression, and Alternative ways to Promote Human Rights. In J. Wilson & N. Gapsiso (Eds.), *Overcoming Gender Inequalities through Technology Integration* (pp. 144–162). Hershey, PA: IGI Global. doi:10.4018/978-1-4666-9773-7.ch007

Grant, B., Woods, R., & Tan, S. F. (2017). Subnational Finance in Australia and China: The Case for Municipal Bond Banks. In E. Schoburgh & R. Ryan (Eds.), *Handbook of Research on Sub-National Governance and Development* (pp. 150–166). Hershey, PA: IGI Global. doi:10.4018/978-1-5225-1645-3.ch007

Grecco, M. C., & Geron, C. M. (2016). The Brazilian Case of IFRS Adoption: The Impacts and the New Perspectives. In E. Uchenna, M. Nnadi, S. Tanna, & F. Iyoha (Eds.), *Economics and Political Implications of International Financial Reporting Standards* (pp. 303–318). Hershey, PA: IGI Global. doi:10.4018/978-1-4666-9876-5.ch015

Gül, H., Kamalak, İ., & Kiriş, H. M. (2016). Local and Urban Administrations, Politics, and Elections in Turkey. In U. Sadioglu & K. Dede (Eds.), *Comparative Studies and Regionally-Focused Cases Examining Local Governments* (pp. 182–206). Hershey, PA: IGI Global. doi:10.4018/978-1-5225-0320-0.ch009

Guner, A., & Keles, R. (2016). A Comparative Study of Local Governments in the Constitutions of Selected EU Countries and Turkey. In U. Sadioglu & K. Dede (Eds.), *Comparative Studies and Regionally-Focused Cases Examining Local Governments* (pp. 349–363). Hershey, PA: IGI Global. doi:10.4018/978-1-5225-0320-0.ch016

Gür, B. (2016). Economic and Political Factors Affecting Foreign Direct Investment in the MENA Region. In M. Erdoğdu & B. Christiansen (Eds.), *Comparative Political and Economic Perspectives on the MENA Region* (pp. 221–245). Hershey, PA: IGI Global. doi:10.4018/978-1-4666-9601-3.ch010

Gurpinar, B. (2018). Supporter, Activist, Rebel, Terrorist: Children in Syria. In C. Akrivopoulou (Ed.), *Global Perspectives on Human Migration, Asylum, and Security* (pp. 97–114). Hershey, PA: IGI Global. doi:10.4018/978-1-5225-2817-3.ch005

Gussen, B. F. (2018). The United States. In *Ranking Economic Performance and Efficiency in the Global Market: Emerging Research and Opportunities* (pp. 109–136). Hershey, PA: IGI Global. doi:10.4018/978-1-5225-2756-5.ch005

Hadji-Janev, M. (2016). International Legal Aspects of Protecting Civilians and Their Property in the Future Cyber Conflict. In M. Hadji-Janev & M. Bogdanoski (Eds.), *Handbook of Research on Civil Society and National Security in the Era of Cyber Warfare* (pp. 423–449). Hershey, PA: IGI Global. doi:10.4018/978-1-4666-8793-6.ch019

Hankel, G. (2016). Gacaca Courts in Rwanda: Experience and Perspectives. In F. Cante & H. Quehl (Eds.), *Handbook of Research on Transitional Justice and Peace Building in Turbulent Regions* (pp. 218–231). Hershey, PA: IGI Global. doi:10.4018/978-1-4666-9675-4.ch011

Haque, T. (2018). Women-Friendly Working Environment in Bangladesh: Critical Analysis. In N. Mahtab, T. Haque, I. Khan, M. Islam, & I. Wahid (Eds.), *Handbook of Research on Women's Issues and Rights in the Developing World* (pp. 52–68). Hershey, PA: IGI Global. doi:10.4018/978-1-5225-3018-3.ch004

Hartzel, K. S., & Gerde, V. W. (2016). Using Duality Theory to Reframe E-Government Challenges. In R. Cropf & T. Bagwell (Eds.), *Ethical Issues and Citizen Rights in the Era of Digital Government Surveillance* (pp. 35–56). Hershey, PA: IGI Global. doi:10.4018/978-1-4666-9905-2.ch003

Heilmann, D. (2016). Post-Conflict Justice in Cambodia: The Legacy of the Khmer Rouge Tribunal. In F. Cante & H. Quehl (Eds.), *Handbook of Research on Transitional Justice and Peace Building in Turbulent Regions* (pp. 201–217). Hershey, PA: IGI Global. doi:10.4018/978-1-4666-9675-4.ch010

Heuva, W. E. (2017). Deferring Citizens' "Right to Know" in an Information Age: The Information Deficit in Namibia. In N. Mhiripiri & T. Chari (Eds.), *Media Law, Ethics, and Policy in the Digital Age* (pp. 245–267). Hershey, PA: IGI Global. doi:10.4018/978-1-5225-2095-5.ch014

Idris, S. (2016). Challenge of Democracy and Local Governance in Pakistan. In U. Sadioglu & K. Dede (Eds.), *Comparative Studies and Regionally-Focused Cases Examining Local Governments* (pp. 259–279). Hershey, PA: IGI Global. doi:10.4018/978-1-5225-0320-0.ch012

Islam, M. R. (2018). Abuse Among Child Domestic Workers in Bangladesh. In I. Tshabangu (Ed.), *Global Ideologies Surrounding Children's Rights and Social Justice* (pp. 1–21). Hershey, PA: IGI Global. doi:10.4018/978-1-5225-2578-3.ch001

Jankovic-Milic, V., & Džunić, M. (2017). Measuring Governance: The Application of Grey Relational Analysis on World Governance Indicators. In J. Stanković, P. Delias, S. Marinković, & S. Rochhia (Eds.), *Tools and Techniques for Economic Decision Analysis* (pp. 104–128). Hershey, PA: IGI Global. doi:10.4018/978-1-5225-0959-2.ch005

Jenne, C. (2016). Increase of Transportation Efficiencies and Emission Reduction within a City. In G. Hua (Ed.), *Smart Cities as a Solution for Reducing Urban Waste and Pollution* (pp. 91–125). Hershey, PA: IGI Global. doi:10.4018/978-1-5225-0302-6.ch004

Jiménez-Gómez, C. E. (2017). Open Judiciary Worldwide: Best Practices and Lessons Learnt. In C. Jiménez-Gómez & M. Gascó-Hernández (Eds.), *Achieving Open Justice through Citizen Participation and Transparency* (pp. 1–15). Hershey, PA: IGI Global. doi:10.4018/978-1-5225-0717-8.ch001

Kabullah, M. I., & Wahab, S. (2016). The Curbing of Corruption by Formal and Informal Accountability at the Indonesian Local Governments: Learning from Yogyakarta City. In U. Sadioglu & K. Dede (Eds.), *Theoretical Foundations and Discussions on the Reformation Process in Local Governments* (pp. 441–461). Hershey, PA: IGI Global. doi:10.4018/978-1-5225-0317-0.ch018

Karatzimas, S., & Miquela, C. G. (2018). Two Approaches on Local Governments' Financial Sustainability: Law vs. Practice in Catalan Municipalities. In M. Rodríguez Bolívar & M. López Subires (Eds.), *Financial Sustainability and Intergenerational Equity in Local Governments* (pp. 58–81). Hershey, PA: IGI Global. doi:10.4018/978-1-5225-3713-7.ch003

Kerasidou, X., Buscher, M., Liegl, M., & Oliphant, R. (2016). Emergency Ethics, Law, Policy & IT Innovation in Crises. *International Journal of Information Systems for Crisis Response and Management*, 8(1), 1–24. doi:10.4018/IJISCRAM.2016010101

Khanh, N. T., Danh, M. T., & Gim, G. (2016). E-Government in Vietnam: Situation, Prospects, Trends, and Challenges. In I. Sodhi (Ed.), *Trends, Prospects, and Challenges in Asian E-Governance* (pp. 256–280). Hershey, PA: IGI Global. doi:10.4018/978-1-4666-9536-8.ch013

Kiran, M. (2016). Legal Issues Surrounding Connected Government Services: A Closer Look at G-Clouds. In Z. Mahmood (Ed.), *Cloud Computing Technologies for Connected Government* (pp. 322–344). Hershey, PA: IGI Global. doi:10.4018/978-1-4666-8629-8.ch013

Kita, Y. (2017). An Analysis of a Lay Adjudication System and Open Judiciary: The New Japanese Lay Adjudication System. In C. Jiménez-Gómez & M. Gascó-Hernández (Eds.), *Achieving Open Justice through Citizen Participation and Transparency* (pp. 93–109). Hershey, PA: IGI Global. doi:10.4018/978-1-5225-0717-8.ch005

Klimczuk, A., & Klimczuk-Kochańska, M. (2016). Changes in the Local Government System and Regional Policy in Poland: The Impact of Membership in the European Union. In U. Sadioglu & K. Dede (Eds.), *Theoretical Foundations and Discussions on the Reformation Process in Local Governments* (pp. 328–352). Hershey, PA: IGI Global. doi:10.4018/978-1-5225-0317-0.ch014

Klimovský, D. (2016). Experience with Managerial and Political Reform Measures at the Local Level in Slovakia: Intended and Unintended Outcomes. In U. Sadioglu & K. Dede (Eds.), *Comparative Studies and Regionally-Focused Cases Examining Local Governments* (pp. 135–160). Hershey, PA: IGI Global. doi:10.4018/978-1-5225-0320-0.ch007

Küçükali, U. F. (2016). Ecological Influences on the Evolving Planning System in Turkey. In U. Benna & S. Garba (Eds.), *Population Growth and Rapid Urbanization in the Developing World* (pp. 298–312). Hershey, PA: IGI Global. doi:10.4018/978-1-5225-0187-9.ch015

Kumari, S., Patil, Y., & Rao, P. (2017). An Approach to Sustainable Watershed Management: Case Studies on Enhancing Sustainability with Challenges of Water in Western Maharashtra. In P. Rao & Y. Patil (Eds.), *Reconsidering the Impact of Climate Change on Global Water Supply, Use, and Management* (pp. 252–271). Hershey, PA: IGI Global. doi:10.4018/978-1-5225-1046-8.ch014

Kumburu, N. P., & Pande, V. S. (2018). Decentralization and Local Governance in Tanzania: Theories and Practice on Sustainable Development. In K. Teshager Alemu & M. Abebe Alebachew (Eds.), *Handbook of Research on Sustainable Development and Governance Strategies for Economic Growth in Africa* (pp. 131–148). Hershey, PA: IGI Global. doi:10.4018/978-1-5225-3247-7.ch007

Kunock, A. I. (2017). Boko Haram Insurgency in Cameroon: Role of Mass Media in Conflict Management. In N. Mhiripiri & T. Chari (Eds.), *Media Law, Ethics, and Policy in the Digital Age* (pp. 226–244). Hershey, PA: IGI Global. doi:10.4018/978-1-5225-2095-5.ch013

Laha, A. (2016). Association between Governance and Human Development in South Asia: A Cross Country Analysis. In R. Das (Ed.), *Handbook of Research on Global Indicators of Economic and Political Convergence* (pp. 254–273). Hershey, PA: IGI Global. doi:10.4018/978-1-5225-0215-9.ch012

Lawrie, A. (2017). The Subnational Region: A Utopia? The Challenge of Governing Through Soft Power. In E. Schoburgh & R. Ryan (Eds.), *Handbook of Research on Sub-National Governance and Development* (pp. 96–115). Hershey, PA: IGI Global. doi:10.4018/978-1-5225-1645-3.ch005

Lewin, E., & Bick, E. (2017). Introduction: Civil Religion and Nationalism on a Godly-Civil Continuum. In E. Lewin, E. Bick, & D. Naor (Eds.), *Comparative Perspectives on Civil Religion, Nationalism, and Political Influence* (pp. 1–31). Hershey, PA: IGI Global. doi:10.4018/978-1-5225-0516-7.ch001

Lisney, T., & Kiefer, A. (2016). Cooperation between Local Authorities in Europe as a Force for Strengthening Local Democracy. In U. Sadioglu & K. Dede (Eds.), *Theoretical Foundations and Discussions on the Reformation Process in Local Governments* (pp. 85–109). Hershey, PA: IGI Global. doi:10.4018/978-1-5225-0317-0.ch004

Lobina, M., & Bottone, M. (2016). Building Trust in Politics: Causes of Widespread Disillusionment in Latin American Countries. In M. Garita & J. Godinez (Eds.), *Business Development Opportunities and Market Entry Challenges in Latin America* (pp. 127–157). Hershey, PA: IGI Global. doi:10.4018/978-1-4666-8820-9.ch007

Lourenço, R. P. (2016). Evidence of an Open Government Data Portal Impact on the Public Sphere. *International Journal of Electronic Government Research*, *12*(3), 21–36. doi:10.4018/IJEGR.2016070102

Luyombya, D. (2018). Management of Records and Archives in Uganda's Public Sector. In P. Ngulube (Ed.), *Handbook of Research on Heritage Management and Preservation* (pp. 275–297). Hershey, PA: IGI Global. doi:10.4018/978-1-5225-3137-1.ch014

Mabe, M., & Ashley, E. A. (2017). The Local Command Structure and How the Library Fits. In *In The Developing Role of Public Libraries in Emergency Management: Emerging Research and Opportunities* (pp. 44–60). Hershey, PA: IGI Global. doi:10.4018/978-1-5225-2196-9.ch004

Magalhães, F. R., & Santos, C. (2016). Online Financial Transparency: Local Governments of the MERCOSUR Member Countries. In A. Ferreira, G. Azevedo, J. Oliveira, & R. Marques (Eds.), *Global Perspectives on Risk Management and Accounting in the Public Sector* (pp. 252–273). Hershey, PA: IGI Global. doi:10.4018/978-1-4666-9803-1.ch013

Maher, C. (2016). Public Policies Impact on Third Sector Social Enterprises in UK Regions. In L. Carvalho (Ed.), *Handbook of Research on Entrepreneurial Success and its Impact on Regional Development* (pp. 246–266). Hershey, PA: IGI Global. doi:10.4018/978-1-4666-9567-2.ch012

Maher, C. (2018). Legal Framework, Funding, and Procurement Polices to Accelerate the Growth of the Social Enterprise Ecosystem. In *Influence of Public Policy on Small Social Enterprises: Emerging Research and Opportunities* (pp. 52–83). Hershey, PA: IGI Global. doi:10.4018/978-1-5225-2770-1.ch003

Malik, I., Putera, V. S., & Putra, I. E. (2018). Traditional Leaders in the Reconciliation of Muslim-Christian Conflicts in Moluccas. In A. Campbell (Ed.), *Global Leadership Initiatives for Conflict Resolution and Peacebuilding* (pp. 235–248). Hershey, PA: IGI Global. doi:10.4018/978-1-5225-4993-2.ch011

Manzoor, A. (2016). Cloud Computing Applications in the Public Sector. In Z. Mahmood (Ed.), *Cloud Computing Technologies for Connected Government* (pp. 215–246). Hershey, PA: IGI Global. doi:10.4018/978-1-4666-8629-8.ch009

Marinescu, V. (2016). The Crisis of Public Health as a Media Event: Between Media Frames and Public Assessments. In A. Fox (Ed.), *Global Perspectives on Media Events in Contemporary Society* (pp. 78–89). Hershey, PA: IGI Global. doi:10.4018/978-1-4666-9967-0.ch006

Martin, S. M. (2017). Transnational Crime and the American Policing System. In M. Dawson, D. Kisku, P. Gupta, J. Sing, & W. Li (Eds.), Developing Next-Generation Countermeasures for Homeland Security Threat Prevention (pp. 72-92). Hershey, PA: IGI Global. doi:10.4018/978-1-5225-0703-1.ch004

Marwah, G. S., & Ladhani, V. (2016). Financial Sector in Afghanistan: Regulatory Challenges in Financial Sector of Afghanistan. In A. Kashyap & A. Tomar (Eds.), *Financial Market Regulations and Legal Challenges in South Asia* (pp. 224–262). Hershey, PA: IGI Global. doi:10.4018/978-1-5225-0004-9.ch011

Masrom, M. (2016). E-Government, E-Surveillance, and Ethical Issues from Malaysian Perspective. In R. Cropf & T. Bagwell (Eds.), *Ethical Issues and Citizen Rights in the Era of Digital Government Surveillance* (pp. 249–263). Hershey, PA: IGI Global. doi:10.4018/978-1-4666-9905-2.ch013

*Related References*

McNeal, R. S., Schmeida, M., & Holmes, J. (2016). The E-Government Surveillance in the United States: Public Opinion on Government Wiretapping Powers. In R. Cropf & T. Bagwell (Eds.), *Ethical Issues and Citizen Rights in the Era of Digital Government Surveillance* (pp. 208–230). Hershey, PA: IGI Global. doi:10.4018/978-1-4666-9905-2.ch011

Mhiripiri, N. A., & Chikakano, J. (2017). Criminal Defamation, the Criminalisation of Expression, Media and Information Dissemination in the Digital Age: A Legal and Ethical Perspective. In N. Mhiripiri & T. Chari (Eds.), *Media Law, Ethics, and Policy in the Digital Age* (pp. 1–24). Hershey, PA: IGI Global. doi:10.4018/978-1-5225-2095-5.ch001

Mishaal, D. A., & Abu-Shanab, E. A. (2017). Utilizing Facebook by the Arab World Governments: The Communication Success Factor. *International Journal of Public Administration in the Digital Age, 4*(3), 53–78. doi:10.4018/IJPADA.2017070105

Morim, A. C., Inácio, H., & Vieira, E. (2018). Internal Control in a Public Hospital: The Case of Financial Services Expenditure Department. In G. Azevedo, J. da Silva Oliveira, R. Marques, & A. Ferreira (Eds.), *Handbook of Research on Modernization and Accountability in Public Sector Management* (pp. 77–102). Hershey, PA: IGI Global. doi:10.4018/978-1-5225-3731-1.ch005

Mupepi, M. G. (2017). Developing Democratic Paradigms to Effectively Manage Business, Government, and Civil Society: The African Spring. In E. Schoburgh & R. Ryan (Eds.), *Handbook of Research on Sub-National Governance and Development* (pp. 432–462). Hershey, PA: IGI Global. doi:10.4018/978-1-5225-1645-3.ch020

Nam, T. (2016). Citizen Attitudes about Open Government and Government 2.0: A Path Analysis. *International Journal of Electronic Government Research, 12*(4), 46–66. doi:10.4018/IJEGR.2016100104

Navaratnam, R., & Lee, I. Y. (2017). Globalization as a New Framework for Human Rights Protection. In C. Akrivopoulou (Ed.), *Defending Human Rights and Democracy in the Era of Globalization* (pp. 17–49). Hershey, PA: IGI Global. doi:10.4018/978-1-5225-0723-9.ch002

Naz, R. (2016). Challenges En-Route towards E-Governance in Small Developing Island Nations of the South Pacific: The Case of Papua New Guinea. In I. Sodhi (Ed.), *Trends, Prospects, and Challenges in Asian E-Governance* (pp. 1–34). Hershey, PA: IGI Global. doi:10.4018/978-1-4666-9536-8.ch001

Nemec, J., Meričková, B. M., Svidroňová, M. M., & Klimovský, D. (2017). Co-Creation as a Social Innovation in Delivery of Public Services at Local Government Level: The Slovak Experience. In E. Schoburgh & R. Ryan (Eds.), *Handbook of Research on Sub-National Governance and Development* (pp. 281–303). Hershey, PA: IGI Global. doi:10.4018/978-1-5225-1645-3.ch013

Nemec, J., Soukopova, J., & Merickova, B. M. (2016). Local Public Service Delivery Arrangements in the Czech Republic and Slovakia. In U. Sadioglu & K. Dede (Eds.), *Comparative Studies and Regionally-Focused Cases Examining Local Governments* (pp. 405–423). Hershey, PA: IGI Global. doi:10.4018/978-1-5225-0320-0.ch019

Neupane, A., Soar, J., Vaidya, K., & Aryal, S. (2017). Application of E-Government Principles in Anti-Corruption Framework. In R. Shakya (Ed.), *Digital Governance and E-Government Principles Applied to Public Procurement* (pp. 56–74). Hershey, PA: IGI Global. doi:10.4018/978-1-5225-2203-4.ch003

Nurdin, N., Stockdale, R., & Scheepers, H. (2016). Influence of Organizational Factors in the Sustainability of E-Government: A Case Study of Local E-Government in Indonesia. In I. Sodhi (Ed.), *Trends, Prospects, and Challenges in Asian E-Governance* (pp. 281–323). Hershey, PA: IGI Global. doi:10.4018/978-1-4666-9536-8.ch014

Ogunde, O. (2017). Democracy and Child Rights Protection: The Problem of the Nigerian Constitution. In C. Akrivopoulou (Ed.), *Defending Human Rights and Democracy in the Era of Globalization* (pp. 123–144). Hershey, PA: IGI Global. doi:10.4018/978-1-5225-0723-9.ch006

Ohsugi, S. (2016). Changing Local Government System in Japan: "Unfinished" Decentralization Reform and Local Revitalization. In U. Sadioglu & K. Dede (Eds.), *Theoretical Foundations and Discussions on the Reformation Process in Local Governments* (pp. 373–399). Hershey, PA: IGI Global. doi:10.4018/978-1-5225-0317-0.ch016

Ojedokun, U. A. (2017). Crime Witnesses' Non-Cooperation in Police Investigations: Causes and Consequences in Nigeria. In S. Egharevba (Ed.), *Police Brutality, Racial Profiling, and Discrimination in the Criminal Justice System* (pp. 89–99). Hershey, PA: IGI Global. doi:10.4018/978-1-5225-1088-8.ch005

Okeke, G. S. (2018). The Politics of Environmental Pollution in Nigeria: Emerging Trends, Issues, and Challenges. In A. Eneanya (Ed.), *Handbook of Research on Environmental Policies for Emergency Management and Public Safety* (pp. 300–320). Hershey, PA: IGI Global. doi:10.4018/978-1-5225-3194-4.ch016

Ökten, S., Akman, E., & Akman, Ç. (2018). Modernization and Accountability in Public-Sector Administration: Turkey Example. In G. Azevedo, J. da Silva Oliveira, R. Marques, & A. Ferreira (Eds.), *Handbook of Research on Modernization and Accountability in Public Sector Management* (pp. 18–39). Hershey, PA: IGI Global. doi:10.4018/978-1-5225-3731-1.ch002

Oladapo, O. A., & Ojebuyi, B. R. (2017). Nature and Outcome of Nigeria's #NoToSocialMediaBill Twitter Protest against the Frivolous Petitions Bill 2015. In O. Nelson, B. Ojebuyi, & A. Salawu (Eds.), *Impacts of the Media on African Socio-Economic Development* (pp. 106–124). Hershey, PA: IGI Global. doi:10.4018/978-1-5225-1859-4.ch007

Olukolu, Y. R. (2017). Harmful Traditional Practices, Laws, and Reproductive Rights of Women in Nigeria: A Therapeutic Jurisprudence Approach. In D. Halder & K. Jaishankar (Eds.), *Therapeutic Jurisprudence and Overcoming Violence Against Women* (pp. 1–14). Hershey, PA: IGI Global. doi:10.4018/978-1-5225-2472-4.ch001

Omwoha, J. (2016). The Political Significance and Influence of Talk Radio Debates in Kenya. In L. Mukhongo & J. Macharia (Eds.), *Political Influence of the Media in Developing Countries* (pp. 75–96). Hershey, PA: IGI Global. doi:10.4018/978-1-4666-9613-6.ch006

Onyebadi, U., & Mbunyuza-Memani, L. (2017). Women and South Africa's Anti-Apartheid Struggle: Evaluating the Political Messages in the Music of Miriam Makeba. In U. Onyebadi (Ed.), *Music as a Platform for Political Communication* (pp. 31–51). Hershey, PA: IGI Global. doi:10.4018/978-1-5225-1986-7.ch002

Osmani, A. R. (2017). Tipaimukh Multipurpose Hydroelectric Project: A Policy Perspective – Indo-Bangla Priorities, Indigenous Peoples' Rights, and Environmental Concerns. In P. Rao & Y. Patil (Eds.), *Reconsidering the Impact of Climate Change on Global Water Supply, Use, and Management* (pp. 227–251). Hershey, PA: IGI Global. doi:10.4018/978-1-5225-1046-8.ch013

Owolabi, T. O. (2018). Free Media and Bank Reforms in West Africa: Implications for Sustainable Development. In A. Salawu & T. Owolabi (Eds.), *Exploring Journalism Practice and Perception in Developing Countries* (pp. 18–39). Hershey, PA: IGI Global. doi:10.4018/978-1-5225-3376-4.ch002

Oz, S. (2016). Diffusion of Technology via FDI and Convergence of Per Capita Incomes: Comparative Analysis on Europe and the MENA Region. In M. Erdoğdu & B. Christiansen (Eds.), *Handbook of Research on Comparative Economic Development Perspectives on Europe and the MENA Region* (pp. 236–264). Hershey, PA: IGI Global. doi:10.4018/978-1-4666-9548-1.ch012

Paez, G. R. (2016). Retaliation in Transitional Justice Scenarios: The Experiences of Argentina and Colombia. In F. Cante & H. Quehl (Eds.), *Handbook of Research on Transitional Justice and Peace Building in Turbulent Regions* (pp. 315–331). Hershey, PA: IGI Global. doi:10.4018/978-1-4666-9675-4.ch016

Panara, C. (2016). Concept and Role of Local Self-Government in the Contemporary State. In U. Sadioglu & K. Dede (Eds.), *Theoretical Foundations and Discussions on the Reformation Process in Local Governments* (pp. 42–84). Hershey, PA: IGI Global. doi:10.4018/978-1-5225-0317-0.ch003

Panda, P., & Sahu, G. P. (2017). Public Procurement Framework in India: An Overview. In R. Shakya (Ed.), *Digital Governance and E-Government Principles Applied to Public Procurement* (pp. 229–248). Hershey, PA: IGI Global. doi:10.4018/978-1-5225-2203-4.ch010

Pande, V. S., & Kumburu, N. P. (2018). An Overview of Population Growth and Sustainable Development in Sub-Saharan Africa. In K. Teshager Alemu & M. Abebe Alebachew (Eds.), *Handbook of Research on Sustainable Development and Governance Strategies for Economic Growth in Africa* (pp. 480–499). Hershey, PA: IGI Global. doi:10.4018/978-1-5225-3247-7.ch025

Paulin, A. A. (2017). Informating Public Governance: Towards a Basis for a Digital Ecosystem. *International Journal of Public Administration in the Digital Age, 4*(2), 14–32. doi:10.4018/IJPADA.2017040102

Pečarič, M. (2016). The Awareness of Mentality in Public Administration as the Key for the Management of Its Complexity. In A. Ferreira, G. Azevedo, J. Oliveira, & R. Marques (Eds.), *Global Perspectives on Risk Management and Accounting in the Public Sector* (pp. 1–24). Hershey, PA: IGI Global. doi:10.4018/978-1-4666-9803-1.ch001

Perelló-Sobrepere, M. (2017). Building a New State from Outrage: The Case of Catalonia. In M. Adria & Y. Mao (Eds.), *Handbook of Research on Citizen Engagement and Public Participation in the Era of New Media* (pp. 344–359). Hershey, PA: IGI Global. doi:10.4018/978-1-5225-1081-9.ch019

Pohl, G. M. (2017). The Role of Social Media in Enforcing Environmental Justice around the World. In K. Demirhan & D. Çakır-Demirhan (Eds.), *Political Scandal, Corruption, and Legitimacy in the Age of Social Media* (pp. 123–156). Hershey, PA: IGI Global. doi:10.4018/978-1-5225-2019-1.ch006

Popoola, I. S. (2016). The Press and the Emergent Political Class in Nigeria: Media, Elections, and Democracy. In L. Mukhongo & J. Macharia (Eds.), *Political Influence of the Media in Developing Countries* (pp. 45–58). Hershey, PA: IGI Global. doi:10.4018/978-1-4666-9613-6.ch004

Popoola, T. (2017). Ethical and Legal Challenges of Election Reporting in Nigeria: A Study of Four General Elections, 1999-2011. In N. Mhiripiri & T. Chari (Eds.), *Media Law, Ethics, and Policy in the Digital Age* (pp. 78–100). Hershey, PA: IGI Global. doi:10.4018/978-1-5225-2095-5.ch005

Porras-Sanchez, F. J. (2016). Local Government and Governance in Mexico. In U. Sadioglu & K. Dede (Eds.), *Comparative Studies and Regionally-Focused Cases Examining Local Governments* (pp. 323–348). Hershey, PA: IGI Global. doi:10.4018/978-1-5225-0320-0.ch015

Rahman, K. F. (2016). Human Rights Education for Peace and Conflict Resolution. In K. Pandey & P. Upadhyay (Eds.), *Promoting Global Peace and Civic Engagement through Education* (pp. 89–105). Hershey, PA: IGI Global. doi:10.4018/978-1-5225-0078-0.ch006

Rahman, M. S. (2017). Politics-Administration Relations and the Effect on Local Governance and Development: The Case of Bangladesh. In E. Schoburgh & R. Ryan (Eds.), *Handbook of Research on Sub-National Governance and Development* (pp. 256–279). Hershey, PA: IGI Global. doi:10.4018/978-1-5225-1645-3.ch012

Reddy, P. S. (2017). Political-Administrative Interface at the Local Sphere of Government with Particular Reference to South Africa. In E. Schoburgh & R. Ryan (Eds.), *Handbook of Research on Sub-National Governance and Development* (pp. 242–255). Hershey, PA: IGI Global. doi:10.4018/978-1-5225-1645-3.ch011

Reid, M. (2016). Contemporary Local Government Reform in New Zealand: Efficiency or Democracy. In U. Sadioglu & K. Dede (Eds.), *Theoretical Foundations and Discussions on the Reformation Process in Local Governments* (pp. 205–236). Hershey, PA: IGI Global. doi:10.4018/978-1-5225-0317-0.ch009

Rombo, D. O., & Lutomia, A. N. (2018). Tracing the Rights of Domestic and International Kenyan House Helps: Profiles, Policy, and Consequences. In N. Mahtab, T. Haque, I. Khan, M. Islam, & I. Wahid (Eds.), *Handbook of Research on Women's Issues and Rights in the Developing World* (pp. 1–18). Hershey, PA: IGI Global. doi:10.4018/978-1-5225-3018-3.ch001

Rouzbehani, K. (2017). Health Policy Implementation: Moving Beyond Its Barriers in United States. In N. Wickramasinghe (Ed.), *Handbook of Research on Healthcare Administration and Management* (pp. 541–552). Hershey, PA: IGI Global. doi:10.4018/978-1-5225-0920-2.ch032

Ruano, J. M., & Álvarez, J. M. (2016). Local Structure and Municipal Associations in Spain: Facts, Trends and Problems. In U. Sadioglu & K. Dede (Eds.), *Comparative Studies and Regionally-Focused Cases Examining Local Governments* (pp. 71–90). Hershey, PA: IGI Global. doi:10.4018/978-1-5225-0320-0.ch004

Ruffin, F., & Martins, W. K. (2016). Legal Empowerment as Social Entrepreneurship: The KwaZulu-Natal Cases of Bulwer and New Hanover. In Z. Fields (Ed.), *Incorporating Business Models and Strategies into Social Entrepreneurship* (pp. 267–291). Hershey, PA: IGI Global. doi:10.4018/978-1-4666-8748-6.ch015

Ryan, R., & Woods, R. (2017). Decentralization and Subnational Governance: Theory and Praxis. In E. Schoburgh & R. Ryan (Eds.), *Handbook of Research on Sub-National Governance and Development* (pp. 1–33). Hershey, PA: IGI Global. doi:10.4018/978-1-5225-1645-3.ch001

Sabao, C., & Chingwaramusee, V. R. (2017). Citizen Journalism on Facebook and the Challenges of Media Regulation in Zimbabwe: Baba Jukwa. In N. Mhiripiri & T. Chari (Eds.), *Media Law, Ethics, and Policy in the Digital Age* (pp. 193–206). Hershey, PA: IGI Global. doi:10.4018/978-1-5225-2095-5.ch011

Sadioglu, U., & Dede, K. (2016). Current Discussions on the Question: Remarks of Local Government's Reform through Comparative Perspective. In U. Sadioglu & K. Dede (Eds.), *Theoretical Foundations and Discussions on the Reformation Process in Local Governments* (pp. 1–23). Hershey, PA: IGI Global. doi:10.4018/978-1-5225-0317-0.ch001

Sadioglu, U., Dede, K., & Yüceyılmaz, A. A. (2016). The Significance of The 2014 Local Elections in Turkey for Decentralisation and Local Autonomy. In U. Sadioglu & K. Dede (Eds.), *Comparative Studies and Regionally-Focused Cases Examining Local Governments* (pp. 364–389). Hershey, PA: IGI Global. doi:10.4018/978-1-5225-0320-0.ch017

Sanchez-Barrios, L. J., Gomez-Araujo, E., Gomez-Nuñez, L., & Rodriguez, S. (2016). Opportunities and Challenges for Entrepreneurial Activity and Non-Entrepreneurial Engagement in Colombia. In M. Garita & J. Godinez (Eds.), *Business Development Opportunities and Market Entry Challenges in Latin America* (pp. 170–198). Hershey, PA: IGI Global. doi:10.4018/978-1-4666-8820-9.ch009

Santoro, L., & Capasso, S. (2016). Public Spending and Governance Performance: Evidence from Europe and the MENA Region. In M. Erdoğdu & B. Christiansen (Eds.), *Handbook of Research on Public Finance in Europe and the MENA Region* (pp. 136–155). Hershey, PA: IGI Global. doi:10.4018/978-1-5225-0053-7.ch007

Scherr, K. M. (2016). Of Justice, Accountability, and Reconciliation: Preliminary Stocktaking on Transitional Justice Efforts in South Sudan. In F. Cante & H. Quehl (Eds.), *Handbook of Research on Transitional Justice and Peace Building in Turbulent Regions* (pp. 181–200). Hershey, PA: IGI Global. doi:10.4018/978-1-4666-9675-4.ch009

Schmeida, M., & McNeal, R. S. (2016). U.S. Public Support to Climate Change Initiatives?: Setting Stricter Carbon Dioxide Emission Limits on Power Plants. In M. Erdoğdu, T. Arun, & I. Ahmad (Eds.), *Handbook of Research on Green Economic Development Initiatives and Strategies* (pp. 605–624). Hershey, PA: IGI Global. doi:10.4018/978-1-5225-0440-5.ch026

Shahsavandi, E., Mayah, G., & Rahbari, H. (2016). Impact of E-Government on Transparency and Corruption in Iran. In I. Sodhi (Ed.), *Trends, Prospects, and Challenges in Asian E-Governance* (pp. 75–94). Hershey, PA: IGI Global. doi:10.4018/978-1-4666-9536-8.ch004

Shakya, R. K., & Schapper, P. R. (2017). Digital Governance and E-Government Principles: E-Procurement as Transformative. In R. Shakya (Ed.), *Digital Governance and E-Government Principles Applied to Public Procurement* (pp. 1–28). Hershey, PA: IGI Global. doi:10.4018/978-1-5225-2203-4.ch001

Siphambe, H., Kolobe, M., & Oageng, I. P. (2018). Employment Protection Legislation and Unemployment in Botswana. In S. Amine (Ed.), *Employment Protection Legislation in Emerging Economies* (pp. 157–191). Hershey, PA: IGI Global. doi:10.4018/978-1-5225-4134-9.ch008

Slaveski, S., & Popovska, B. (2016). Access to Information in the Republic of Macedonia: Between Transparency and Secrecy. In M. Hadji-Janev & M. Bogdanoski (Eds.), *Handbook of Research on Civil Society and National Security in the Era of Cyber Warfare* (pp. 162–179). Hershey, PA: IGI Global. doi:10.4018/978-1-4666-8793-6.ch008

Snauwaert, D. T. (2016). Securing a Human Right to Peace: A Peace Education Imperative. In K. Pandey & P. Upadhyay (Eds.), *Promoting Global Peace and Civic Engagement through Education* (pp. 19–35). Hershey, PA: IGI Global. doi:10.4018/978-1-5225-0078-0.ch002

Sodhi, I. S. (2016). E-Government in China: Status, Challenges, and Progress. In I. Sodhi (Ed.), *Trends, Prospects, and Challenges in Asian E-Governance* (pp. 36–54). Hershey, PA: IGI Global. doi:10.4018/978-1-4666-9536-8.ch002

Song, M. Y., & Abelson, J. (2017). Public Engagement and Policy Entrepreneurship on Social Media in the Time of Anti-Vaccination Movements. In M. Adria & Y. Mao (Eds.), *Handbook of Research on Citizen Engagement and Public Participation in the Era of New Media* (pp. 38–56). Hershey, PA: IGI Global. doi:10.4018/978-1-5225-1081-9.ch003

Sonmez, Y. (2016). Latest Developments on the Way to EU Accession: Turkish Case. In V. Erokhin (Ed.), *Global Perspectives on Trade Integration and Economies in Transition* (pp. 166–184). Hershey, PA: IGI Global. doi:10.4018/978-1-5225-0451-1.ch009

Stacey, E. (2018). Networked Protests: A Review of Social Movement Literature and the Hong Kong Umbrella Movement (2017). In S. Chhabra (Ed.), *Handbook of Research on Civic Engagement and Social Change in Contemporary Society* (pp. 347–363). Hershey, PA: IGI Global. doi:10.4018/978-1-5225-4197-4.ch020

Stamatakis, N. (2017). Authority and Legitimacy: A Quantitative Study of Youth's Perceptions on the Brazilian Police. In S. Egharevba (Ed.), *Police Brutality, Racial Profiling, and Discrimination in the Criminal Justice System* (pp. 151–213). Hershey, PA: IGI Global. doi:10.4018/978-1-5225-1088-8.ch009

Sugars, J. M. (2017). Refoulement and Refugees. In C. Akrivopoulou (Ed.), *Defending Human Rights and Democracy in the Era of Globalization* (pp. 181–197). Hershey, PA: IGI Global. doi:10.4018/978-1-5225-0723-9.ch008

Tabansky, L. (2016). Israel's Cyber Security Policy: Local Response to the Global Cybersecurity Risk. In M. Hadji-Janev & M. Bogdanoski (Eds.), *Handbook of Research on Civil Society and National Security in the Era of Cyber Warfare* (pp. 475–494). Hershey, PA: IGI Global. doi:10.4018/978-1-4666-8793-6.ch021

Tan, S. F. (2017). Local Representation in Australia: Preliminary Findings of a National Survey. In E. Schoburgh & R. Ryan (Eds.), *Handbook of Research on Sub-National Governance and Development* (pp. 368–384). Hershey, PA: IGI Global. doi:10.4018/978-1-5225-1645-3.ch017

Tavares, M. D., & Rodrigues, L. L. (2018). Strategic Responses of Public Sector Entities to GRI Sustainability Reports. In G. Azevedo, J. da Silva Oliveira, R. Marques, & A. Ferreira (Eds.), *Handbook of Research on Modernization and Accountability in Public Sector Management* (pp. 159–188). Hershey, PA: IGI Global. doi:10.4018/978-1-5225-3731-1.ch008

Thakre, A. G. (2017). Sexual Harassment of Women in Workplace in India: An Assessment of Implementation of Preventive Laws and Practicing of Therapeutic Jurisprudence in New Delhi. In D. Halder & K. Jaishankar (Eds.), *Therapeutic Jurisprudence and Overcoming Violence Against Women* (pp. 135–146). Hershey, PA: IGI Global. doi:10.4018/978-1-5225-2472-4.ch009

Tiwary, A. (2017). Key Elements of CEAF. In *Driving Efficiency in Local Government Using a Collaborative Enterprise Architecture Framework: Emerging Research and Opportunities* (pp. 25–61). Hershey, PA: IGI Global. doi:10.4018/978-1-5225-2407-6.ch002

Toscano, J. P. (2017). Social Media and Public Participation: Opportunities, Barriers, and a New Framework. In M. Adria & Y. Mao (Eds.), *Handbook of Research on Citizen Engagement and Public Participation in the Era of New Media* (pp. 73–89). Hershey, PA: IGI Global. doi:10.4018/978-1-5225-1081-9.ch005

Tosun, M. S., Uz, D., & Yılmaz, S. (2016). Fiscal Decentralization and Local Borrowing in Turkish Provinces. In M. Erdoğdu & B. Christiansen (Eds.), *Handbook of Research on Public Finance in Europe and the MENA Region* (pp. 505–519). Hershey, PA: IGI Global. doi:10.4018/978-1-5225-0053-7.ch022

Treiber, M. (2016). Informality and Informalization among Eritrean Refugees: Why Migration Does Not Provide a Lesson in Democracy. In F. Cante & H. Quehl (Eds.), *Handbook of Research on Transitional Justice and Peace Building in Turbulent Regions* (pp. 158–180). Hershey, PA: IGI Global. doi:10.4018/978-1-4666-9675-4.ch008

Tshishonga, N. (2017). Operation Sukuma-Sakhe: A New Social Contract for Decentralized Service Delivery and Responsive Governance in KwaZulu-Natal. In E. Schoburgh & R. Ryan (Eds.), *Handbook of Research on Sub-National Governance and Development* (pp. 304–323). Hershey, PA: IGI Global. doi:10.4018/978-1-5225-1645-3.ch014

Tsygankov, S., & Gasanova, E. (2017). Electronification of the Public Procurement System: A Comparative Analysis of the Experience of the Russian Federation and Ukraine. In R. Shakya (Ed.), *Digital Governance and E-Government Principles Applied to Public Procurement* (pp. 267–277). Hershey, PA: IGI Global. doi:10.4018/978-1-5225-2203-4.ch013

Tüzünkan, D. (2018). The International Migration Movements and Immigrant Policies From the Ottoman Empire 1299 to Republican Turkey 2016. In Ş. Erçetin (Ed.), *Social Considerations of Migration Movements and Immigration Policies* (pp. 13–45). Hershey, PA: IGI Global. doi:10.4018/978-1-5225-3322-1.ch002

Uchenna, E., & Iyoha, F. (2016). IFRS, Foreign Investment, and Prevailing Institutional Structure in Africa. In E. Uchenna, M. Nnadi, S. Tanna, & F. Iyoha (Eds.), *Economics and Political Implications of International Financial Reporting Standards* (pp. 83–104). Hershey, PA: IGI Global. doi:10.4018/978-1-4666-9876-5.ch005

Ugangu, W. (2016). Kenya's Difficult Political Transitions Ethnicity and the Role of Media. In L. Mukhongo & J. Macharia (Eds.), *Political Influence of the Media in Developing Countries* (pp. 12–24). Hershey, PA: IGI Global. doi:10.4018/978-1-4666-9613-6.ch002

Vaillancourt, F., & Bird, R. M. (2016). Decentralization in European and MENA Countries: Glue or Solvent? In M. Erdoğdu & B. Christiansen (Eds.), *Comparative Political and Economic Perspectives on the MENA Region* (pp. 1–27). Hershey, PA: IGI Global. doi:10.4018/978-1-4666-9601-3.ch001

Vakkala, H., & Leinonen, J. (2016). Current Features and Developments of Local Governance in Finland: The Changing Roles of Citizens and Municipalities. In U. Sadioglu & K. Dede (Eds.), *Theoretical Foundations and Discussions on the Reformation Process in Local Governments* (pp. 304–327). Hershey, PA: IGI Global. doi:10.4018/978-1-5225-0317-0.ch013

Valenzuela, R., & Ochoa, A. (2018). Open Mexico Network in the Implementation of National Open Data Policy. In A. Kok (Ed.), *Proliferation of Open Government Initiatives and Systems* (pp. 50–67). Hershey, PA: IGI Global. doi:10.4018/978-1-5225-4987-1.ch003

Vaquero, M. G., & Saiz-Alvarez, J. M. (2016). Smart Cities in Spain – Policy, Sustainability, and the National Plan: New Political Measures, Agents, and Sustainability. In A. Goswami & A. Mishra (Eds.), *Economic Modeling, Analysis, and Policy for Sustainability* (pp. 266–283). Hershey, PA: IGI Global. doi:10.4018/978-1-5225-0094-0.ch014

Waller, P. (2017). Co-Production and Co-Creation in Public Services: Resolving Confusion and Contradictions. *International Journal of Electronic Government Research*, *13*(2), 1–17. doi:10.4018/IJEGR.2017040101

Washington, A. L. (2016). The Interoperability of US Federal Government Information: Interoperability. In A. Aggarwal (Ed.), *Managing Big Data Integration in the Public Sector* (pp. 1–19). Hershey, PA: IGI Global. doi:10.4018/978-1-4666-9649-5.ch001

Whyte, D. (2016). The Neo-Colonial State of Exception in Occupied Iraq. In F. Cante & H. Quehl (Eds.), *Handbook of Research on Transitional Justice and Peace Building in Turbulent Regions* (pp. 298–313). Hershey, PA: IGI Global. doi:10.4018/978-1-4666-9675-4.ch015

Williams, K. Y. (2016). The Need for a National Data Breach Notification Law. In E. de Silva (Ed.), *National Security and Counterintelligence in the Era of Cyber Espionage* (pp. 190–202). Hershey, PA: IGI Global. doi:10.4018/978-1-4666-9661-7.ch011

Wodecka-Hyjek, A. (2017). Co-Operation between the Public Administration and Non-Profit Organisations as a Condition of the Development of Public Entrepreneurship: On the Example of the Selected World Solutions. In V. Potocan, M. Üngan, & Z. Nedelko (Eds.), *Handbook of Research on Managerial Solutions in Non-Profit Organizations* (pp. 253–275). Hershey, PA: IGI Global. doi:10.4018/978-1-5225-0731-4.ch012

Yang, J. G. (2016). The Principle of Nexus in E-Commerce Tax. In I. Lee (Ed.), *Encyclopedia of E-Commerce Development, Implementation, and Management* (pp. 329–341). Hershey, PA: IGI Global. doi:10.4018/978-1-4666-9787-4.ch025

Yang, J. G. (2016). What Is New York's Amazon Tax on Internet Commerce? In I. Lee (Ed.), *Encyclopedia of E-Commerce Development, Implementation, and Management* (pp. 397–409). Hershey, PA: IGI Global. doi:10.4018/978-1-4666-9787-4.ch029

Yang, J. G., Lohrey, P. L., & Lauricella, L. J. (2016). Current Developing Trend of Sales Tax on E-Business. In I. Lee (Ed.), *Encyclopedia of E-Commerce Development, Implementation, and Management* (pp. 1045–1057). Hershey, PA: IGI Global. doi:10.4018/978-1-4666-9787-4.ch074

Yang, K. C., & Kang, Y. (2017). Social Media, Political Mobilization, and Citizen Engagement: A Case Study of the March 18, 2014, Sunflower Student Movement in Taiwan. In M. Adria & Y. Mao (Eds.), *Handbook of Research on Citizen Engagement and Public Participation in the Era of New Media* (pp. 360–388). Hershey, PA: IGI Global. doi:10.4018/978-1-5225-1081-9.ch020

Yeo, S., Birch, A. S., & Bengtsson, H. I. (2016). The Role of State Actors in Cybersecurity: Can State Actors Find Their Role in Cyberspace? In E. de Silva (Ed.), *National Security and Counterintelligence in the Era of Cyber Espionage* (pp. 217–246). Hershey, PA: IGI Global. doi:10.4018/978-1-4666-9661-7.ch013

Zhao, B. (2018). A Privacy Perspective of Open Government: Sex, Wealth, and Transparency in China. In A. Kok (Ed.), *Proliferation of Open Government Initiatives and Systems* (pp. 29–48). Hershey, PA: IGI Global. doi:10.4018/978-1-5225-4987-1.ch002

Zhi-Wei, T., Fei, D., & Ping, J. (2016). An Empirical Study on Temporal Evolution Rule of Network Clustering Behavior. *International Journal of Information Systems for Crisis Response and Management*, 8(4), 56–70. doi:10.4018/IJISCRAM.2016100104

# About the Contributors

**Karim Al-Yafi** is an assistant professor of management information system at the College of Business and Economics at Qatar University. With a software engineering and business analysis background, he obtained his PhD in Management science and Information Systems from Brunel Business School, Brunel University London. The main research interests of Dr. Al-Yafi include the evolution and evaluation of e-Government solutions and the role of ICT in policymaking and public sector strategic management. His research interests extend to cover also the use of multi-agent systems to evaluate the use of mobile and ubiquitous technologies to optimize enterprises' functional performance and underlying information systems infrastructure. In this context, he co-authored and participated in several research project proposals submitted to European Commission, EPSRC UK, and the Qatar National Research Fund (QNRF). Other technical fields in which Dr. Al-Yafi is interested are Web 2.0 programming, open source software, e-Learning and business intelligence & data mining. Dr. Al-Yafi has presented his research through multiple research papers and international conferences and workshops, notably at the IEEE international workshop on Enabling Technologies.

**Renata Araujo** obtained her D.Sc. in Computer Science from the Federal University of Rio de Janeiro (UFRJ) in 2000. She is an Associate Professor at UNIRIO (Federal University of the State of Rio de Janeiro), Brazil. She has been member of the Information Systems Special Committee in the Brazilian Computer Society since its establishment (2010). Her research interests are: Information Systems, Digital Governance and Democracy, Business Process Management. She coordinates the Research and Innovation Group in CiberDemocracy (https://sites.google.com/site/ciberdem/). Her current research focuses on how to turn organizations more democratic by the use of business process management, collaborative support and social tools.

**Claudia Cappelli** obtained her D.Sc. degree in Computer Science at PUC-RJ in 2009. She is Assistant Professor at UNIRIO (Federal University of the State of Rio de Janeiro). She is author of some publications in national and international congresses. She also coordinates consulting projects at companies and develops works in the field of Business Process Modeling, Enterprise Architecture, Information Systems, Digital Governance and Democracy and Organizational Transparency. She worked as Project Manager, Chief Architect and Technology Director in some big companies. She coordinates the Research Group in Organizational Transparency (http://uniriotec.br/~transparencia/). Her current research focuses on how to turn organizations more transparent by the use of business process management and Enterprise Architecture.

**Bruna Diirr** obtained her D.Sc. in Informatics from the Federal University of Rio de Janeiro (UFRJ) in 2016. She is a Substitute Professor at Fluminense Federal University (UFF) and a Postdoctoral scholar at Federal University of the State of Rio de Janeiro (UNIRIO). Her experience and research work focus on Information Systems, e-Democracy, Collaboration, Process Management, Knowledge Management, Emergency Management and Improvisation. Her current research focuses on how to manage interorganizational relationships by the use of business process management and collaborative support.

**Michael A. Erskine** is an Assistant Professor at the Jones College of Business at Middle Tennessee State University. Previously, he served as the Director of the Educational Technology Center at Metropolitan State University of Denver. Michael received his Ph.D. in Computer Science and Information Systems from the University of Colorado Denver. His research interests include disaster management, IT governance, educational technology, and spatial decision support systems. He has published in Information Systems Frontiers, the International Journal of Human-Computer Interaction, the Journal of Computer Information Systems, and the International Journal of Electronic Government Research. He is a member of the Association for Information Systems, the Project Management Institute, and the Decision Sciences Institute.

**Lars Haahr** is Assistant Professor at Department of Management at Aarhus BSS, Aarhus University in Denmark. Haahr's research focuses on how organisations manage digital transformation. Before his starting his research career, Haahr had several years of managerial and consultancy experience with digital transformation.

**Craig Johnson** is a Senior Lecturer at the Faculty of Management and Law at University of Bradford. He has almost 20 years of experience of working in both the public and private sectors. He started his career as a software engineer, working on training simulators for the fire service and the Institute of Chemical Engineers. He went on to become operations manager for the national fire service computer, the Fire Information National Data Service (FINDS). He then returned to programming, acting as software consultant to implement the command and control systems for Dublin Fire and Ambulance Service and a second system for the Munster region of Ireland. His PhD was entitled "Standing on the Toes of Giants: Social Movement Theory and the Case of the Learning Organisation". This involved an assessment of how management theory is developed in general (social movements), the phenomenon known as management gurus (the giants) and how this related to theories of the learning organisation. A structural equation model was derived from survey responses by Chief Executives and Human Resource Director of FTSE- and AIM-Listed companies. The model demonstrated a high level of convergent validity of what constitutes successful management in a large, commercial organisation.

**Mohamed Mahmood** is a leading innovator in the regulation and management of telecommunications and related information technology. He received a Bachelor's Degree in Computer Science from the University of Bahrain, a Masters Degree in Internet Technology from Aston University, and, in 2017, a Ph.D. from Brunel University Business School. He previously served as an executive at the Telecommunications Regulatory Authority (TRA) of Bahrain and is now an independent consultant in the areas of strategic planning, ICT, excellence and quality specializing in wide-scale management of projects, resources and personnel. As part of this work, he implemented Ahlia University's first strategic plan along with the management structure to successfully meet wide-scale KPIs. Mr. Mahmood was also a member of the jury for the 2017 eGovernment Excellence Award. Mr. Mahmood's research interests includes issues related to the governance of e-government regimes, digital transformation of government and public administration.

**Bibiana Metelmann**, M.D., was born 1987, graduated from medical school at Greifswald University, Germany in December 2012 and started working as a resident physician at the Department of Anesthesiology and Intensive Care Medicine at Greifswald University. Besides working as an emergency physician, at the intensive care unit and in the operating theatre, she was a researcher in the FP7-EU-funded LiveCity Project (Live Video-to-Video Supporting Interactive City Infrastructure). Her main research area is telemedicine in emergency medicine, which is also the focus of her current research project Land|Rettung.

**Camilla Metelmann**, M.D., was born 1987 and attended medical school in Greifswald, Germany and joined the Department of Anesthesiology and Intensive Care Medicine, Greifswald University Medicine as a resident physician in 2013. In addition to clinical rotations in the operating theatre, the intensive care unit and working as an emergency physician, she got involved in an FP7-EU-funded collaborative project dealing with telemedicine aspects of emergency medicine, which has evolved into a successful contribution to the LiveCity consortium. She is currently pursuing an integrated physician-scientist career pathway and works in the research project Land|Rettung.

**Amizan Omar** is a Ph.D Researcher in Digital Governance at Brunel University. She is also a Research Assistant for several R&D projects funded by the European Commission. Her primary research interests are in the areas of Digitally Enabled Service Transformation, Organisational Transformation and Strategic Management in Public and Private sectors. Her works were published in journals and conference proceedings (e.g. Government Information Quarterly, Americas Conference on Information Systems, and International Conference on Theory and Practice of Electronic Governance). She is also invited member of editorial advisory board of Journal of Information Technology (JIT) and Journal of Electronic Government Research (IJEGR). Amizan is at present a member of British Academy of Management (BAM) and also an Associate Member of Chartered Institute of Professional Development, CIPD UK.

**Will Pepper** received his PhD in Management Information Systems from the University of Mississippi and based his research around the usefulness and usability of free software for business. He speaks and consults with businesses and organizations that want to improve their marketing efforts, get the most out of their technology, and improve their overall leadership through manageable steps, not broad jumps. He frequently is called upon to create content for one the top 5 online MBA universities in the world in the subjects of Leadership, IT Management, Risk Management, and Marketing.

**Herman Resende Santos** received his MS in Public Administration from the Federal University of Lavras-Brazil in 2015. In 2003 he founded his first company and continually undertakes, also investing in technological innovation and startups. Through his research efforts, he conciliates academic approaches with practical visions of manager, in order to generate actionable knowledge that advance theoretical understanding and at the same time be useful to governments' administration and business. He writes and presents on issues of sociopolitical digital interactions, co-creation, smart government, entrepreneurship and strategic management.

**Hans J. Scholl** serves as a Full Professor at the University of Washington's Information School. He is Past President of the Digital Government Society, and Past Chair of the IFIP WG 8.5. He co-chairs the influential E-Government Track at HICSS.

**Dany Flávio Tonelli** received his Doctorate in Administration from the Federal University of Lavras in 2011. In 2009 he was hired as assistant professor of public management at Federal University of Alfenas. In 2011 he assumed the position of adjunct professor of public administration in the Department of Administration and Economy of the Federal University of Lavras – Brazil. He currently teaches public administration and is vice dean of outreach and culture, where is responsible for the Coordinating of Technological and Social Development. His publications approach the thematic of public policies of science, technology, innovation under the theories of collaborative governance, co-creation and Actor-Network Theory.

**Vishanth Weerakkody** is a Professor in Management Information Systems and Governance at the Faculty of Management and Law at University of Bradford. His research expertise lies in the area of electronic service delivery, technology adoption, diffusion and evaluation in public sector context. He has published over 150 peer reviewed articles and guest-edited special issues of leading journals and books on these themes. He is currently an investigator in several European Commission Framework-7 and Horizon 2020 Programmes on ICT and Social Sciences covering themes such as smart cities, social innovation, participatory budgeting and policy-making and life- long learning. He is also the Editor-in-Chief of the International Journal of Electronic Government Research. A Chartered IT professional and a Fellow of the UK Higher Education Academy, Professor Weerakkody combines over 25 years of practical industry-based knowhow with academic and teaching experience.

# Index

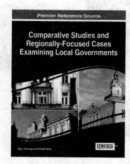

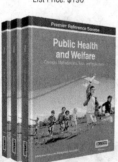

Stay Current on the Latest Emerging Research Developments

# Become an IGI Global Reviewer for Authored Book Projects

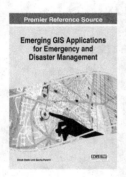

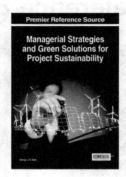

## The overall success of an authored book project is dependent on quality and timely reviews.

In this competitive age of scholarly publishing, constructive and timely feedback significantly decreases the turnaround time of manuscripts from submission to acceptance, allowing the publication and discovery of progressive research at a much more expeditious rate. Several IGI Global authored book projects are currently seeking highly qualified experts in the field to fill vacancies on their respective editorial review boards:

## Applications may be sent to:
### development@igi-global.com

Applicants must have a doctorate (or an equivalent degree) as well as publishing and reviewing experience. Reviewers are asked to write reviews in a timely, collegial, and constructive manner. All reviewers will begin their role on an ad-hoc basis for a period of one year, and upon successful completion of this term can be considered for full editorial review board status, with the potential for a subsequent promotion to Associate Editor.

If you have a colleague that may be interested in this opportunity,
we encourage you to share this information with them.

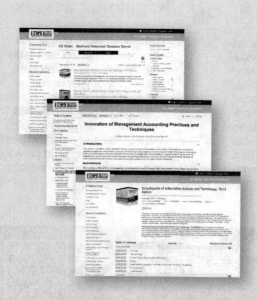